MW00856098

3,000 YEARS OF WAR AND PEACE IN THE MAYA LOWLANDS

3,000 Years of War and Peace in the Maya Lowlands presents the cutting-edge research of 25 authors in the fields of archaeology, biological anthropology, art history, ethnohistory, and epigraphy. Together, they explore issues central to ancient Maya identity, political history, and warfare.

The Maya lowlands of Guatemala, Belize, and southeast Mexico have witnessed human occupation for at least 11,000 years, and settled life reliant on agriculture began some 3,100 years ago. From the earliest times, Maya communities expressed their shifting identities through pottery, architecture, stone tools, and other items of material culture. Although it is tempting to think of the Maya as a single unified culture, they were anything but homogeneous, and differences in identity could be expressed through violence. *3,000 Years of War and Peace in the Maya Lowlands* explores the formation of identity, its relationship to politics, and its manifestation in warfare from the earliest pottery-making villages through the late colonial period by studying the material remains and written texts of the Maya.

This volume is an invaluable reference for students and scholars of the ancient Maya, including archaeologists, art historians, and anthropologists.

Geoffrey E. Braswell is Professor of Anthropology at the University of California, San Diego. Among his numerous works are *The Maya and Teotihuacan*, *The Ancient Maya of Mexico*, and *The Maya and Their Central American Neighbors*.

Routledge Archaeology of the Ancient Americas

Series Editor: Geoffrey E. Braswell

For more information about this series, please visit: www.routledge.com/
Routledge-Archaeology-of-the-Ancient-Americas/book-series/RAAA

3,000 YEARS OF WAR AND PEACE IN THE MAYA LOWLANDS

Identity, Politics, and Violence

Edited by Geoffrey E. Braswell

Routledge
Taylor & Francis Group

LONDON AND NEW YORK

Cover image: © Geoffrey E. Braswell

First published 2022
by Routledge
2 Park Square, Milton Park, Abingdon, Oxon OX14 4RN

and by Routledge
605 Third Avenue, New York, NY 10158

Routledge is an imprint of the Taylor & Francis Group, an informa business

© 2022 selection and editorial matter, Geoffrey E. Braswell; individual
chapters, the contributors

The right of Geoffrey E. Braswell to be identified as the author of the
editorial material, and of the authors for their individual chapters, has
been asserted in accordance with sections 77 and 78 of the Copyright,
Designs and Patents Act 1988.

All rights reserved. No part of this book may be reprinted or reproduced
or utilised in any form or by any electronic, mechanical, or other
means, now known or hereafter invented, including photocopying and
recording, or in any information storage or retrieval system, without
permission in writing from the publishers.

Trademark notice: Product or corporate names may be trademarks
or registered trademarks, and are used only for identification and
explanation without intent to infringe.

British Library Cataloguing-in-Publication Data
A catalogue record for this book is available from the British Library

Library of Congress Cataloging-in-Publication Data
A catalog record for this book has been requested

ISBN: 978-1-138-57704-6 (hbk)
ISBN: 978-1-138-57705-3 (pbk)
ISBN: 978-1-351-26800-4 (ebk)

DOI: 10.4324/9781351268004

Typeset in Bembo
by Apex CoVantage, LLC

To Ritamarie,

Who encouraged my first tentative journeys into the Maya world and has been wondering why ever since.

CONTENTS

FIGURES

TABLES

CONTRIBUTORS

Jaime J. Awe, Department of Anthropology, Northern Arizona University

Tomás Barrientos Q., Departamento de Arqueología, Universidad del Valle de Guatemala

Brooke Bonorden, Pape-Dawson Engineers, Inc., Tomball, Texas

Geoffrey E. Braswell, Department of Anthropology, University of California, San Diego

Oswaldo Chinchilla Mazariegos, Department of Anthropology, Yale University

Claire E. Ebert, Department of Anthropology, University of Pittsburgh

Keith Eppich, Department of History, Geography, and Anthropology, TJC-The College of East Texas

Carolyn Freiwald, Department of Sociology and Anthropology, University of Mississippi

Kirsten Green Mink, Department of Anthropology, University of Montana

Annabeth Headrick, School of Art and Art History, University of Denver

Christophe Helmke, Institute of Cross-cultural and Regional Studies, University of Copenhagen

Bernard Hermes, Nakum Archaeological Project, Flores, Guatemala

Julie A. Hoggarth, Department of Anthropology, Baylor University

John W. Hoopes, Department of Anthropology, University of Kansas

Brett A. Houk, Department of Sociology, Anthropology, and Social Work, Texas Tech University

Mary Kate Kelly, Department of Anthropology, Tulane University

Damien Marken, Department of Anthropology, Bloomsburg University of Pennsylvania

Ashley H. McKeown, Department of Anthropology, Texas State University

Olivia C. Navarro-Farr, Department of Sociology and Anthropology, The College of Wooster

Iken Paap, Ibero-American Institute, Prussian Cultural Heritage Foundation, Berlin

Nancy Peniche May, Universidad Modelo, Mérida, Mexico

Juan Carlos Pérez, Proyecto Arqueológico Waka', Guatemala City

Griselda Pérez Robles, Proyecto Arqueológico Waka', Guatemala City

Patricia Powless, Department of Anthropology, Ashford University

Jarosław Źrałka, Institute of Archeology, Jagiellonian University, Kraków

1

IDENTITY, POLITICS, AND VIOLENCE

An introduction to *3,000 Years of War and Peace in the Maya Lowlands*

Geoffrey E. Braswell

As an archaeologist whose research is in southeastern Mexico and Central America, I often am asked: "What is it like to work in South America?" Some 35 years into my career, the follow-up question is still even more exasperating: "Why did the Maya disappear?" When I try to explain that the people I live among and work with each year are not extinct, have not gone anywhere, and would be surprised to learn that they have disappeared, I am usually met with either incomprehension or a sly smile that implies, "You know what I mean and are avoiding my question." Sadly, I *do not* have a definitive explanation for the Classic Maya Collapse and I *do* understand the misconceptions behind the interchange. I also know that for very many of the indigenous people I have worked with over the years, "Maya" would not be the first word that springs to mind when choosing a label for their own identity.

This confusion underscores several basic questions. Who were and are the Maya? Who gets to define what "Maya" means? What are the different characteristics that are salient to the definition? For most Americans and Europeans, "Maya" principally refers to the builders of the ancient stone pyramids of Yucatan and northern Central America (together all too often misidentified as "South America"), who carved complicated monuments with enigmatic hieroglyphic texts, and who were eventually overwhelmed by noxious jungle foliage that grows faster than kudzu in Alabama. The more enlightened realize that the ancient Maya were indigenous Americans, while the more prejudiced and hidebound cannot possibly believe that Indians were capable of such achievements on their own without the assistance of lost tribes or really lost ancient aliens. When an archaeologist self-identifies as a "Mayanist," we reify all these notions and corporealize Indiana Jones. Some of us willingly embrace this incarnation and apotheosis, wear silly outfits, and appear frequently on the Discovery Channel or even more questionable media. Others sheepishly

DOI: 10.4324/9781351268004-1

and rather ineffectively explain how this is not who we are or what we do. Such apologia acknowledge that the Maya are a living people and that we are not the ones who should be defining them, in a way parallel to our colleagues who have long rejected the culture concept yet somehow cling to the brand of cultural anthropology. Most of us just try to keep our heads down and avoid the distraction.

Nonetheless, the formation of identity – our own, the artifacts we analyze, the people we indirectly study through their material remains, and living indigenous people – is central to all we do as archaeologists. The expressed purpose of the culture history period in archaeology was to classify artifacts and define archaeological cultures from them. These archaeological cultures were seen as the material representations of what were once living cultures and could be traced using the direct historical approach to ethnographic cultures viewed as their descendants. Put another way, archaeologists assigned identity to artifacts, assumed this identity mapped with that of an ancient people, and sought to understand those people through analogies with the living, themselves often classified into identity groups by cultural anthropologists, linguists, or even physical anthropologists. Today, we recognize and acknowledge the many problems with this paradigm and endeavor to consider material culture not as equivalent to identity, but as one of myriad ways it may be materialized and expressed.

The archaeological ways of recognizing the ancient identities we have created often still boil down to the appearance of certain types or artifact classes. Were there Maya before the pyramids, stelae, hieroglyphic texts, and polychrome vessels of the Classic period? Of course. For a ceramicist, the first identifiably Maya artifacts have long been pottery assigned to the Mamom complex. This is so ingrained that even collections from sites that largely lack Mamom pottery have been assigned to the Mamom sphere (Chapter 3), and earlier Maya pottery – whether or not it is related to and directly followed by Mamom material – is called "pre-Mamom." Many lithicists working in northern Belize are confident identifying preceramic sites of the terminal Archaic as "Maya" if they find constricted unifaces made of chert, and as a specialist in obsidian, I do not hesitate to label prismatic blades found in the lowlands from the Middle Preclassic onwards as "Maya." Similarly, many epigraphers are not troubled calling the earliest hieroglyphic texts from the lowlands or Kaminaljuyu "Mayan," even though many cannot be read and the spoken languages they reflect are not definitively known. In these ways we continue the old practice of assigning identity to artifacts and people, often without sufficient reflection.

Our book takes a new look at identity from different perspectives and at various scales. My contention is that group identity is strongly local, that all conscious and many unconscious expressions of it are programmatic, that these local identities and programs are often tied to political goals and their resultant structures, and that violence – warfare, if you will – is a common expression of contested, challenged, and competitive identities.

Local identities, local Maya

Many years ago, while working for the first time in the highlands of Guatemala, I had a conversation with four men from *aldea* Choatalum about research we were conducting there. When I naively archaeosplained that their ancestors built the nearby site known as Mixco Viejo, they laughed. "You mean our grandmothers, our grandfathers were *Jicaques*?" I was confused by their use of this ethnonym, which I thought referred to non-Mayan speakers from Caribbean Honduras. Instead, they used the term to refer to an extinct race of decidedly unintelligent giants. These Jicaques feature in many local stories and fables, while the word "Maya" does not. At that time, it was still largely a foreign rather than a local concept.

The word "Maya," therefore, was not widely used until recently by the indigenous people of southeastern Mexico, Guatemala, or Belize to describe themselves as a single and unified identity group. In fact, its earlier usages by indigenous people are still quite common and most often refer to the language of Yucatan or to the people and language of the related Mopan Maya of southern Belize and southeast Peten. In contrast, both popular and scholarly uses of "Maya" and "Mayan" as ethnonyms for living people are drawn not from these specific indigenous concepts but from linguistic anthropology and the common but mistaken assumption that language – in this case, language family – determines ethnicity. Such linguistic definitions of identity lump and divide people into groups that may or may not be meaningful to the millions who are thereby essentialized. The imposition of ethnicity through linguistic classification is obviously colonialist and problematical. Elsewhere, I have argued that ethnicity is most often imposed by established power structures rather than by the subaltern people so described and cannot exist without the state (Braswell 2016). This example of the use of the word "Maya" is no different. When we distinguish "the Maya" from other modern-day people of Mexico, Belize, and Guatemala, we may unintentionally reify existing inequalities and power structures. It is important, too, to remember that in Guatemala, "the Maya" are a majority, not a minority, and that many power structures are maintained to prevent their enfranchisement and limit democracy.

A second problem with linguistic definitions of "the Maya" are that the distinctions among etically defined languages do not always carry emic meaning. It is true that Mopan and Q'eqchi' speakers living in two villages in southern Belize may not be able to speak with each other in their own languages and that this communication gap may emphasize existing differences in identity. But in the central highlands of Guatemala, speakers of Kaqchikel, K'iche', Tzutujil, Sakapulteko, Sipakapeño, and Uspanteko – languages on an overlapping continuum with fewer clear boundaries – may not ascribe central or primary importance to language as an essential classificatory factor in determining their identity. Once visiting the K'iche' *municipio* of Nahuala, I spoke to a woman in Kaqchikel because I did not know K'iche'. She laughed with delight, clapped her hands, and said, "You speak *our* language, but like people from Solola," a nearby Kaqchikel-speaking town. Key here is that she identified my speech with a town, not a language. Of course, contemporary linguists recognize that divisions between languages are not clear-cut and within their field challenge boundaries of all sorts (e.g., Neumann et al. 2017). Nonetheless, once lines have been drawn on a map they are difficult to erase.

In Guatemala, many people still identify by the *municipio*, or political township, where they were born (for persistence of this identity, see Tax 1937). As another anecdotal example, while living in San Martín Jilotepeque from 1990 to 1993, I never heard people refer to themselves as "Kaqchikel," let alone "Maya." Instead, they were "Martinecos," distinct from the "Xoyas" of the K'iche'-speaking *municipio* Joyabaj just to the north. For centuries, traditional dress has been an important reflection of local political identity, and distinct woven patterns and color schemes typify different *municipios* in an emblematic fashion akin to sports jerseys. This practice may have its origin in colonial desires to control movement and has largely faded among men but still is followed by many women. Thus, clothing and language are visual and aural clues to the different corporate identities of the people of these two adjacent *municipios*, but they are not essential; many indigenous people in both townships speak Spanish and wear western clothes. Instead, it is local place, history, and related rights to resources that are much more important in determining group identity. Speech and clothing are merely emblematic elements of the language of rights to tangible and intangible property. Group identity at the *municipio* level, therefore, is a program identity as defined by Castells (1997). Following Roseberry (1996) I see all conscious identities as programmatic in nature. Numerous community *títulos*, maps, and histories of the colonial period demonstrate that this kind of collective community identity has been linked to the program of maintaining and increasing property rights for at least 600 years. As you read this book, you should ask if the colonial and modern political identity of the *municipio* reflects earlier concerns and program identities of the small kingdoms of the Postclassic and Classic Maya as much as it does Spanish principles of political organization.

On a larger scale beyond a particular *municipio*, individuals in the highlands might say that they are *"chapines"* (Guatemalans), and in the recent past often would say *"somos todos indios pobres."* This last identity may map reasonably well in Guatemala and Chiapas with "Maya," but the implication is one of race and class; it is not an identity that primarily reflects a particular language, let alone rights to property. I have never heard it uttered in Kaqchikel, emphasizing in a distressing manner how power differences and the imposition of poverty and otherness create helplessness. To me, this statement better than any other reflects the enforcement of ethnic categorization and concomitant subaltern status imposed within the state.

Nonetheless, this identity is now being claimed and retooled. Over the last 35 years, a new transnational identity as "Maya" and "Indian" has formed and flourished over much of southeastern Mexico and northern Central America. In

Guatemala, two of many realms of expression for this identity have been language revitalization (manifested in school programs, the writing and publishing of new literature, and an interest in ancient hieroglyphs), and a selective embrace of past religious practices and beliefs that is now expressed beyond the home community at many archaeological sites. Archaeologists understand and welcome this as the reclamation of physical space where rites communicate rights to tangible and intangible property. When I witness the practice of *costumbre* at Kaminaljuyu or Tikal, I envision early colonial maps that mark places of ritual practice in establishing a corporate claim to the landscape. In Belize, the most obvious expression of political identity has been the legal cases brought by the Maya Leaders Alliance and the Toledo Alcaldes Association concerning customary title, usufruct, and occupancy rights as understood through ancestral land-tenure practices. In contrast, Mexico has witnessed the Zapatista movement for political enfranchisement in a struggle that, although most of the participants have been Maya, is best viewed more in terms of universal indigeneity and human rights that go far beyond the group of speakers of a single language family.

These different facets of a pan-Maya and global indigenous identity are each unique yet share much in common. At their heart, they are manifestations of a program identity that seeks to change the lived reality of native peoples by achieving goals that are cultural, economic, social, spiritual, educational, and political in nature. The expression of this program identity has resulted in violence, usually instigated by those who are challenged by or seek to undermine the political aspects of the program. In Chiapas, the Mexican army was deployed against the Zapatistas, and throughout the Maya area, individuals active in the revitalization movement have been assassinated in political rather than personal acts. There has been less physical violence in Belize than elsewhere, and the drama there has been one fought primarily in the media and courtrooms. In such courts, the political use of delay tactics has been central to resisting reform. Politics and warfare are two sides of the same coin: "it can therefore be said that politics is war without bloodshed, while war is politics with bloodshed" (Mao 1938:153).

I raise the topic of contemporary identities, their changing scales, the expression of their programmatic nature, and conflict for several reasons. The first is to emphasize perseverance of the people we call the Maya and who now are increasingly co-opting that word to describe their own identity. The imaginary boundary of the conquest is often a convenient hindrance to understanding the past and the present, and it divorces us as scholars from the people who still are all around us today. Our book, in fact, considers Maya identity on both sides of that boundary, as well as others that archaeologists use to divide the long centuries of the past 3,000 years into more digestible chunks and special foci of research.

Second, our work considers many of the same classes of material culture and theoretical issues that are important today. For example, I have described how dress plays an emblematic role in the expression of identity in the highlands of Guatemala. Although Maya archaeologists have limited ability to study that particular aspect of material culture, we have long struggled with pottery, recognizing that ceramics can tell us much about conscious and unconscious identity, as well as how ancient individuals perceived the world around them and reacted to it. At the same time, we acknowledge that woven *huipiles* and ceramics are merely expressions of identity, that is, neither *po'ots* nor pots are people. Most importantly, although race was not a concept before European colonization and ethnicity did not exist without the pluralistic state, the themes of our book – the relationship of identity, politics, and systemic violence – are universal and continue.

Thus, group identity may be signaled emblematically through material culture, tangible and intangible property rights are key to the program identity of groups, struggles over corporate property may be acted out through systemic violence, and when directed by rulers these conflicts may be considered political warfare or warlike politics.

Contents of the volume

Issues of identity and its expression are both central to and unavoidable in archaeological inquiry. Political structure and systemic violence, which I define here to mean conducted with the sanction of political structure, are two more common themes. The chapters of our work all address one or more of these topics, often through the study of pottery and architecture as emblems of identity and sometimes as targets of destruction. Chapter 2, by Bernard Hermes and Jarosław Źrałka, provides a complete synthesis of what we know about Preclassic occupation of Yaxha and Nakum, two of the most important ancient sites of eastern Peten (Figure 1.1). Permanent occupation of these sites began in the early Middle Preclassic period (ca. 1100/1150–700 BC), albeit only in the last 200 years of that time period. The first agricultural villages of the Maya lowlands were settled quite late compared to the Pacific Coast of Guatemala and Chiapas, the Olmec and Zapotec regions, the Basin of Mexico, and other areas of Mesoamerica. Although some scholars prefer to call the first permanent villages in the Maya lowlands Early Preclassic, the earliest secure calibrated radiocarbon dates fall within the twelfth century BC, about or slightly after the uncalibrated date of 1850 BP. This is equivalent to uncalibrated 900 bc, the traditional date used by archaeologists for the onset of the Middle Preclassic/Formative period in Mesoamerica. For this reason, I prefer to label the earliest lowland villages of the Maya area Middle Preclassic. Whether characterized as late Early Preclassic or early Middle Preclassic, the villagers in the lowlands at that time used pottery that ceramicists call "pre-Mamom," meaning before the first universally agreed-upon material culture viewed as unambiguously Maya. This opens up two questions: who were the first villagers in the lowlands? and should we call them "Maya"?

Hermes and Źrałka stress that there were at least five spatially distinct ceramic spheres in the Maya lowlands at the beginning of the first millennium BC. In

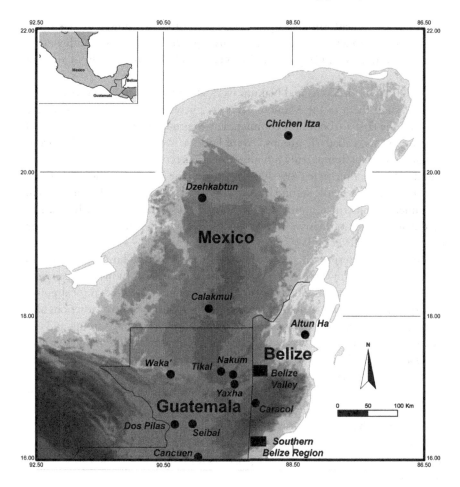

FIGURE 1.1   The Maya lowlands showing the sites and regions discussed throughout
this work.

Source: Adapted from Figure 10.1 by Iken Paap.

particular, they note similarity between the earliest pottery of Nakum and Yaxha –
not surprising given their proximity – and argue that both are related to pre-
Mamom complexes defined for central and southwestern Peten. For this reason,
they posit that the earliest inhabitants of Nakum and Yaxha came from the west
or, especially, the southwest. In contrast, they see significant differences between
the earliest pottery of their sites in eastern Peten and slightly earlier ceramics
assigned to the Cunil/Kanocha sphere of nearby western Belize. Although pots
are not people, we must wonder if early settlers in these two adjoining regions
of the Maya lowlands maintained distinct identities during the early first millennium BC and utilized pottery as expressions of these identities. Importantly,
Nakum is one of the few sites where pre-Mamom architecture has been found,

including a low platform and a probable steam bath, providing data for future comparisons with architecture at Seibal (also spelled "Ceibal") in southwestern Peten, as well as with Cahal Pech (Chapter 3) and Blackman Eddy in western Belize.

By 700 BC, both Yaxha and Nakum were sites whose pottery allows ceramicists to assign them to the Mamom ceramic sphere. Both grew to considerable size, and the first astronomical commemorative groups that tracked solstice and equinox events, called "E-groups," were built, as well as the first ballcourt at Nakum. Construction of truly monumental architecture began at Yaxha during the later Middle Preclassic (700–300 BC). During the Late Preclassic (300 BC–AD 1) that site grew to be the second largest in what today is Guatemala, surpassed in monumental construction only by El Mirador. This period is especially marked by the appearance of massive triadic complexes, which at many sites were the largest structures ever built by the Maya.

How do we interpret the earliest monumental structures built by Maya who used Mamom and, in the Late Preclassic, Chicanel pottery? In marking agricultural cycles, Hermes and Źrałka argue that E-groups also served as focal points of corporate ritual and, therefore, identity. Such monumental constructions also symbolized the founding of permanent ceremonial centers. In E-groups and triadic structures, therefore, we see a transition from agricultural villages, which may have shifted location every generation or two as they now do among the Q'eqchi' of southern Belize, to permanent political territories. The Late Preclassic also saw the appearance of carved monuments and hieroglyphic texts celebrating ritual acts of the first *ajawob*, or "speakers," of the Maya. Nonetheless, evidence that these Preclassic *ajawob* were divine kings who ruled states is ambiguous. We have yet to identify in the Maya lowlands any burial indicative of royal status or any administrative palace consistent with a complex state-level bureaucracy.

Chapter 3, by Nancy Peniche May, Jaime J. Awe, and Claire E. Ebert, tackles head-on the questions of Preclassic identity and systemic inter-group conflict. The Maya site of Cahal Pech, located on a hilltop within the modern town of San Ignacio Cayo, Belize, is small but has proven to be one of the most important in understanding developments in western Belize and, more generally, the southern Maya lowlands. This is due to its remarkably long occupation, lasting a full 2,000 years. Cunil/Kanocha pottery, argued to be the oldest yet known in the Maya lowlands, has been found there in contexts dating to 1100 BC. The material foci of this chapter, however, are the pottery and architecture of a later Middle Preclassic phase that is divided into two facets: early Kanluk (750–650 BC) and late Kanluk (650–350 BC). As the authors explain, a key point is that Kanluk (as well as neighboring Jenney Creek) ceramics are *not* Mamom. Very small quantities of Mamom pottery were imported to the Belize Valley – perhaps from sites such as Nakum and Yaxha – by the end of the early Kanluk/Jenney Creek facet, but even during the late facet such materials made up no more than a small fraction of the ceramic inventory of the region. That is, western Belize decidedly was *not* part of the widespread Mamom sphere of the late Middle Preclassic Maya. This raises a point and a question. First, given that Cunil/Kanocha pottery of western Belize did not develop into and was not followed by a complex dominated by Mamom pottery, it should not be called "pre-Mamom." Instead, it is properly depicted as "pre-Kanluk/Jenney Creek." Second, given that Mamom pottery is the earliest material that archaeologists have universally recognized as Maya, it is logical to ask: who, then, were the people living in the Belize Valley before the Late Preclassic?

It is precisely this question that Peniche and colleagues answer. Earlier work by Joseph Ball and Jennifer Taschek (2003) reasonably hypothesized that the initial Cunil/Kanocha pottery of ca. 1000 BC might have been made by Mixe-Zoquean speakers because of the incised motifs found on some vessels, which also are known from Olmec pottery. But of course, these designs too were incorporated by non-Olmec people into their own pottery, raising a second possibility that the earliest settlers of western Belize could have been Maya. Early Kanluk/Jenney Creek pottery, it is agreed, represents a continuation of Cunil/Kanocha traditions with adaptations and change. To Ball and Taschek, a critical transformation occurred when Mamom pottery began to enter the Belize Valley in greater amounts, and a novel kind of pottery representing a fusion of Mamom and local traditions began to be produced. This implied to them that around 700 BC, a new group of Maya migrated to the Belize Valley – either from eastern Peten or northern Belize – and interacted with the previously established local population. They posit that this interaction was not always peaceful and that competition in various forms – think of warfare and competitive emulation in Renfrew and Cherry's (1986) peer-polity interaction model – stimulated the emergence of social and political complexity. Evidence of destruction and the co-appearance of Mamom pottery at Blackman Eddy have been seen as support of inter-group conflict at this time (Brown and Garber 2003). Thus, Ball and Taschek provided a testable hypothesis involving material expressions of corporate identity, violence, and the emergence of political institutions.

But migration, trade, and emulation are not always easy to tease apart. Peniche and her colleagues examine this model at Cahal Pech and find no convincing evidence for migration, let alone conflict or warfare. They do this by systematically and carefully surveying the development of both ceramics and architecture at the site. In so doing, they note remarkable continuity and only gradual change in both, a pattern that they also see for the Belize Valley as a whole. That Mamom-related pottery never constituted more than a few percent of Middle Preclassic ceramics anywhere in the Belize Valley also does not support the arrival of a significant group of settlers who competed with the occupants of existing sites. Demonstrating migration is a complex matter, and the authors argue for approaches that rely on more than just one or two kinds of material evidence. In sum, they consider the Middle Preclassic inhabitants of the Belize Valley to be Maya and the ancestors of the Late Preclassic and Classic people of the region, even though Mamom pottery was never of central importance to the ceramic inventory. I argue that identity was almost certainly local and that the Middle Preclassic Maya of the Belize Valley and elsewhere viewed themselves primarily as inhabitants of particular sites with rights to local territory and resources, while recognizing that certain cultural practices distinguished them from communities outside of the valley. I can imagine that the inhabitants of Cahal Pech occasionally visited much grander sites like Nakum and Yaxha, engaged in small-scale trade for Mamom vessels and other goods, and enjoyed watching as outsiders the identity-confirming festivals conducted at the E-groups of those places. In much the same way, my Martineco friends and I once piled into a borrowed Land Cruiser to cross the Motagua and "go look at some Xoyas" whirl from a pole in front of a church on the feast day of the Assumption. For such Middle Preclassic and modern travelers, identity may be marked and expressed by pottery, dress, language, and ritual, but it is local place and history that define who they are.

Chapters 4, 5, and 6 were originally planned as a single work that I divided because of its excessive length. In these chapters, I seek to characterize and describe the long history of occupation of inland southern Toledo District, Belize, an archaeological area commonly called the Southern Belize Region (SBR). In so doing, I begin by noting material similarities – what archaeologists of the culture history period called "cultural traits" – that Richard Leventhal (1990) used to define the SBR as a region but also note the significant differences among the four principal sites, three of which I have excavated. Thus, like the Belize Valley, the SBR shares commonalities, yet each site exhibits distinct local identities. Ultimately, I find these differences in local identities, and not what is shared, to be central in understanding the historical trajectory of the SBR.

In Chapter 4, I review quite fascinating and very recent work conducted by my friends Keith Prufer, Douglas Kennett, and their colleagues concerning the earliest evidence of a human presence in the SBR. From the perspective of artifacts, this boils down to a single Paleoindian projectile point and a few Archaic bifacially worked and hafted tools called Lowe points. What makes the work so important is that the latter were recovered from excavated stratigraphic contexts in a rockshelter. To date, most such finds have come from surface, shallow, or mixed contexts in northern Belize and have been assigned to the late Archaic. Prufer and colleagues (2019) have re-dated Lowe points to the end of the Paleoindian or early Archaic period, thousands of years earlier than previously thought. Also recovered from the rockshelters are a series of direct-dated human burials that stretch back to the Paleoindian period. Genetic studies of these remains imply waves of migrations through the narrow hourglass of Central America and that the earliest people were not direct ancestors of the contemporary Maya: a conclusion with politically charged implications for the present. If this is sustained and the early dates for Lowe points are upheld, the latter cannot be considered as indicators of an identity that could be linked to what archaeologists call "Maya." Finally, and most controversially, isotopic analyses of remains and their radiocarbon dates imply that the transition to a maize-based diet began during the third millennium BC and that reliance on that crop as a dietary staple developed no later than 2000 BC (Kennett et al. 2020). The conundrum posed by this conclusion is that there is as yet no evidence for settled village life or the production of ceramics at such an early date anywhere else within the Maya lowlands. It has been asserted that pottery accompanied burials in the rockshelters dating to the second millennium, but these vessels have yet to be presented or described. If there truly is pottery this ancient – or even contemporary with the pre-Mamom materials discussed in Chapters 2 and 3 – it will be a very important discovery. As of 2021, the oldest pottery from anywhere in the SBR that has been presented to scholars is a Mamom vessel dating to the second half of the Middle Preclassic period. There are no known villages that old in the region, so for the moment we must assume that this pot was brought to the rockshelter from somewhere else, probably southeastern Peten.

Chapters 5 and 6 summarize what we know about the period of permanent occupation within the SBR, which began at the dawn of the Early Classic period (AD 150/250–600). The first two settled communities were Nim li Punit and Uxbenka. At the beginning, their pottery was very similar, indicating that settlers came from the same region or site or that the two new communities regularly interacted in trade. But by AD 400, the ceramics of the two communities began to diverge. There is no reason to think that they were sites within the same kingdom, that one had hierarchical control above the other (the rulers of both erected multiple carved stelae), that they were allied, or even that there was much trade or interaction between them. Instead, they seem to have been two petty polities that controlled their own resources and had distinct rather than overlapping economies. After AD 400, Uxbenka seems to have turned increasingly inwards, while the rulers of Nim li Punit sought trade and political interaction with more distant partners. This is evidenced in hieroglyphic texts, pottery, and other classes of artifacts. Late Classic (AD 600–790) texts at Nim li Punit seem to document interaction with Cahal Pech, Caracol, Altun Ha, Quirigua or another allied site, and just possibly Copan. Nonetheless, it is important to note that no SBR site, including Nim li Punit, is mentioned in texts found in other parts of the Maya world.

The largest site in the SBR and the only one that merits being called a city was Pusilha. It was settled shortly before AD 600, and political fragmentation occurred just 200 years later. The pottery of Pusilha is quite different from that used at the other sites, and the closest ceramic connections seem to be with southwest Peten, especially the Pasion zone. During its short history, and in contrast to the other SBR sites including Nim li Punit, the rulers of Pusilha geysered hieroglyphic texts discussing their history. That history seems to have been characterized by dynastic succession issues and warfare. Monuments at the site document at least eight military conflicts, including a cataclysmic attack by the rulers of a place that probably was Altun Ha. Isotopic evidence implies that two individuals interred in the royal acropolis came from Copan, while others came from the northern Maya lowlands and the highlands of Guatemala. This is in stark contrast to Uxbenka, where very little evidence for in-migration has been documented. Lubaantun was the last of the four well-studied sites of the SBR to be settled sometime in the middle of the eighth century. The rather impoverished ceramic inventory of the site is identical to that of contemporary Uxbenka, and the closest parallels in architecture are also found at that site. Jillian Jordan, my colleague from Uxbenka, and I agree that Lubaantun was a satellite or daughter site that budded off Uxbenka and quickly eclipsed it as the latter contracted towards the end of the eighth century AD.

For most of its existence, the SBR was largely cut off from the political machinations of central Peten and the lowlands of Maya Mexico. Moreover, the identities of each site were expressed in different ways. Nim li Punit is the only site that sought to celebrate its foreign connections on nearly all its carved monuments. At Lubaantun, there are no significant texts and no stelae at all. Pusilha celebrated victories over small, unidentified, and presumably nearby enemies, as well as a stunning defeat at the hand of a more distant kingdom. But other than this, the rulers of that city commemorated or commiserated over no external events or interactions with powerful sites. Moreover, the pottery of the SBR – again with the exception of Nim li Punit – exhibits very little evidence of trade within the region, let alone with more distant Maya sites, before the Terminal Classic period (AD 790–900). Common pottery pieces, like unslipped red jars, have necks that are decorated one way at Pusilha, another at Nim li Punit, and a third way at Lubaantun. The overall picture that has emerged from my full *k'atun* of research and ten years of a parallel project at Uxbenka is that the inland SBR was divided into three petty kingdoms centered at Nim li Punit, Pusilha, and Uxbenka, with Lubaantun emerging as a new capital that replaced Uxbenka. Identity and politics – at least as far as expressed on monuments and in ceramics – were local more than regional.

In Chapter 7, Olivia C. Navarro-Farr and her colleagues consider identity at three scales: the individual, the community, and the multi-kingdom alliance. Their fascinating work especially addresses the conscious manipulation of identity by two women to achieve personal programmatic goals of political power and the resulting persistence of social memory within their adopted community. The authors also consider inter-site alliances as reinforced through royal marriage. Navarro-Farr and colleagues assert that although female hypogamy, the practice of royal women marrying an inferior from a less-powerful kingdom, is now widely recognized as an important strategy for cementing the allegiance of lesser lords and even incorporating smaller polities into greater ones (Marcus 1993), seldom have the women involved been considered as conscious actors with programmatic goals of their own. The authors consider the case of Waka', an important second-tier polity within the hegemony of Kaanul (the Snakehead Kingdom), which was based at Calakmul during the Late Classic period. In particular, two queens of Waka', Early Classic Ix Ikoom and Late Classic Lady K'abel, were princesses of Kaanul who married into and invigorated the Waka' dynasty. Much more is known about Lady K'abel, buried in an important structure with a long history. Still later versions of this platform were decorated with stelae fragments that evoked the function of the structure as a *wiinte' naah*, or origin house/fire shrine. Their excavations reveal that the structure was indeed used as a fire shrine before being ritually sealed early in the Terminal Classic period. As an *ix kaloomte'*, Lady K'abel was not merely an overlord but also the founder or rejuvenator of a dynastic line. Many other sites, including Pusilha (Chapter 6), refer to lineage founders with this title, and some, like K'inich Yax K'uk' Mo' of Copan, conducted rituals at an origin house before ascending to power. Still to be tested through excavation is the hypothesis that the structure in which Lady K'abel was buried contains within it an earlier origin house/fire shrine that a retrospective monument claims was visited by Siyaj K'ak' in AD 378 before his "arrival" at Tikal. If so, her burial in a later version of the platform was explicitly designed to reference her rejuvenation of Waka' and tie her to an important event in the distant past, while the later incorporation of monument fragments that mention Ix Ikoom, an earlier queen from Kaanul, was a conscious evocation of the enduring importance of the relationship that Lady K'abel fostered through her marriage and actions as a great leader of Waka'. Given what has so far been discovered in this platform that is attached to a much larger pyramid, we can only wonder what lies within the greater structure.

Tomás Barrientos Q. describes the growth of a large Maya administrative, ritual, and residential structure during the decades leading up to the famous Classic Collapse. His analysis of the Cancuen palace, presented in Chapter 8, focuses on understanding changes to political organization that occurred at this pivotal time. As he points out, the largest palaces ever built in the southern Maya lowlands date to the second half of the eighth century AD, a time of momentous change. Although lowland polities still focused on the figure of the *k'uhul ajaw*, or holy lord/speaker, the nature of governance had changed. Specifically, power was shared with elite groups within the kingdom, including a merchant class that brought prosperity to the realm and secondary lords. Barrientos argues that this important change is reflected in the growth and structure of palaces, which were not restricted but contained many "passage palaces," each with multiple doorways providing access and chambers in which groups could confer. In all, the huge palace of Cancuen – a rather small Maya kingdom that gained independence for little more than a single generation – contained an estimated 130 vaulted chambers and could hold as many as 650 people in its roofed space and dozen patios. This was not merely a residence, but a place where the complex administration of a polity with decentralized rulership and multiple stakeholders could be conducted. The development of new and redefinition of old identities would have been central to the political transformation of the kingdom.

As Barrientos describes, such decentralized and less hierarchical governmental forms developed as satellite polities broke away from greater centers such as Calakmul and Tikal, but similar changes can also be seen at major capitals. Giant palaces were built or expanded at those two cities during the eighth century, as was the palace compound of Yax Pasaj Chan Yopaat and his predecessor, the last two important kings of Copan (Harrison and Andrews 2004). This Copan palace was constructed during a time of demonstrated and well-documented power sharing, supporting Barrientos' argument.

In the southern Maya lowlands, political transformation – materialized in the construction of great administrative palaces designed for sharing power – ended only a few decades after it began, yet this process continued in the northern lowlands through the fifteenth century AD. The great palaces of the Rio Bec, Puuc, and Chenes regions (Chapter 10) reflect such political restructuring, as do the great colonnaded halls of Chichen Itza and Mayapan.

While Chapter 3 considers the early centuries of permanent occupation within the Belize Valley, Julie A. Hoggarth and her colleagues provide in Chapter 9 a synthesis of demographic growth and the complex web of political relations during the Classic period, and they investigate in greater detail the Classic Maya Collapse and Postclassic occupation of the same region. The importance of the broad scope of Chapter 9 is its use of hieroglyphic texts to understand political relations and a conjunctive approach combining ceramic data, the study of burial patterns, and strontium isotope assays used to determine if individuals were local – and therefore may have shared a local identity – or came from somewhere else. Anchoring these studies is an extensive AMS direct-dating program.

The authors appeal to settlement studies to argue that most sites in the Belize Valley reached peak populations around AD 750–850 and that population declined rapidly and dramatically thereafter. Radiocarbon dates from burials also support a rapid decline, contrasting with ceramic models that suggest a more gradual transition from Classic to Postclassic occurred at some sites. The western Belize burial pattern – extended, prone, with head to the south – was established by Late Preclassic times and continued throughout the Classic, demonstrating remarkable continuity of mortuary practice, the ideology underlying it, and the maintenance of a local identity. This was true even though isotopic analyses demonstrate that a substantial percent of Late Classic inhabitants moved to the Belize Valley communities from other places, albeit ones that were not too distant. Burial patterns began to change significantly during the Collapse period as populations declined. Although it is tempting to argue that this was caused by in-migration of people with new identities and practices, it very well may be that changing conditions within the valley itself led to changing practices and perhaps changing views of the self and community.

After the dramatic demographic collapse of the ninth century AD, population levels remained quite low. Although some Early Postclassic pottery is found at sites like Baking Pot and Barton Ramie on the Belize River itself, it is not clear if their populations were significant until the Late Postclassic. At that time, isotopic evidence suggests the majority of the people came from elsewhere and migrated to the valley, bringing new burial practices with them.

Chapter 10 picks up where Chapter 8 leaves off by considering events at Dzehkabtun, a site in the Chenes region that flourished during the late eighth and ninth centuries AD, that is, at the same time and for at least 100 years after Cancuen. Moreover, as in Barrientos' contribution, Iken Paap focuses on a palace at that site. Like a fractal, the processes described by Barrientos for the entire southern lowlands can be viewed in the Terminal Classic Chenes and Rio Bec at a regional level and, indeed, seen within individual sites where range structures were added onto, often forming impressive and multiple palaces within a heterarchically structured polity. Building 269/425 Dzehkabtun is such a structure that seems to have been in the process of conversion into a two-floor palace, construction that was abruptly and violently interrupted when the building was deliberately destroyed.

Unfortunately, as Paap describes, archaeology of the Chenes region has lagged far behind other parts of the Maya area. In recent years, several of the greatest palaces of the largest Chenes site, Santa Rosa Xtampak, have been reconstructed without an accompanying program of scientific investigation. Most of what is known about that great city comes from survey (Jansen et al. 2019; Morales López and Folan 2005), architectural studies made prior to reconstruction (Andrews 1997; Hohmann 2017), and the study of stelae and painted lintels (Graña-Behrens 2004). The last are important because texts are otherwise extremely rare in the Chenes zone. The hieroglyphic dates of the stelae fall within the interval AD 646–911, and the lintels of the three-storey palace have dates that appear to span AD 791–948, supporting Paap's chronology for the development of the Dzehkabtun palace. I stress how little is known about the Chenes zone to emphasize the ground-breaking nature of Paap's research. While she may not yet have definitive answers to all the major questions concerning the development and collapse of the region, the Dzehkabtun project is collecting the data that will provide the foundation to address them. Among her conclusions, both tentative and more secure, are that the inhabitants of Dzehkabtun suffered increased environmental stress and became increasingly isolated from other sites and regions during the Terminal Classic period. This is manifested by offerings that emphasize water and aquatic animals, a possible increase in paleopathologies, and ever shrinking access to imported pottery. Finally, she asks: who destroyed Building 269/425, apparently killing someone or at least leaving a body on the floor? Paap indicates that the violent end of the building and, we may guess, the site as a whole was conducted without clear evidence of foreign involvement. It may be that a local faction destroyed Dzehbaktun sometime in the early tenth century AD.

Annabeth Headrick and John W. Hoopes open Chapter 11 by noting that discourse on Chichen Itza has long focused on issues of identity, especially during the "Toltec-Maya" period of the tenth and early eleventh centuries AD. Moreover, because of a lack of clear depictions of kings and the appearance of novel architectural features such as large, open, colonnaded halls surrounding patios, the nature of political structure and rulership at Chichen Itza during that same century has been hotly debated. What does seem clear is that processes of political decentralization and power sharing noted by Barrientos in Chapter 8 continued during the Early Postclassic. Rather than enter passionate arguments concerning a foreign invasion of Chichen Itza or engage in yet more conjecture about governance of the city, Headrick and Hoopes choose to focus on a single important facet of the Itza state: the military. They argue that the Itza military, like the later Aztec *pochteca*, was integrally involved in the economy, long-distance trade, and acts of war whose purpose was to seize booty. The art of Chichen Itza shows individuals in military garb wearing gold and other items of wealth obtained from distant realms. That these depictions are so very common reflects the central role played by the military in the economy of the great city and the resulting prestige and political power held by members of that institution.

The painted murals of Chichen Itza and the hammered gold discs found in the Sacred Cenote provide important clues as to which groups the Itza viewed as friends and which as foes. Put another way, such art labels in emblematic ways – including physical appearance, hairstyle, garb, and even watercraft – neighboring and very distant peoples with whom the Itza military interacted. These works not only show us emic categories and distinctions considered important by the Itza but also tell us how they classified people as enemies or allies. In much the same way, ancient Egyptian art presents each of the traditional enemies of that civilization through canonical representations that are easily "read" by viewers past and present. Unfortunately, we do not yet understand as well the referents in the art of Chichen Itza.

In their very important contribution considering politics, economy, violence, and identity – I think "ethnicity" might be appropriate here – Headrick and Hoopes make important steps towards identifying who was who in the greater worldview of Chichen Itza. Of great interest, they identify trading partners and defeated enemies in places far to the southeast in lower Central America and perhaps northern South America, rather than in central Mexico.

Chapter 12, by Oswaldo Chinchilla, continues the focus on warfare and systemic violence, but rather than consider these from an economic or a political viewpoint, he regards them from the perspective of religious ritual and myth. These myths date to the early colonial and Late Postclassic periods and come from highland Maya and central Mexican sources, but as Chinchilla points out, they are pan-Mesoamerican in nature and consistent with what can be ascertained concerning warfare from Classic Maya texts and painted vases. They tell us that humanity was created to worship and feed the gods through sacrifice and that warfare was the primary way to provide victims. The myths also tell us that it is the qualities of piety, strength, and humility – rather than sophistication, urbanity, wealth, and elegance – that triumph. But we may wonder if this distinction between the traits of Chichimecs and Toltecs was a late introduction; the characteristics of the former are certainly not what is on display at Chichen Itza. Finally, female goddesses or women appear in several of these stories as fearsome warriors who weaponize sexual aggression. This provides us a view of gender roles and identity in these societies and perhaps of the fears held by men.

These myths tell us, therefore, that warfare was not carried out only or even primarily for earthly gains but for the sacred purposes of assuring the fertility of the earth and the rise of the sun. Despite the obvious tie that E-groups provide for the link between fertility and solar worship and the prevalence of images of sun discs at Chichen Itza and Mayapan, there has not been enough scholarly focus on such beliefs and their relationship to Maya warfare.

The final chapter in our volume, by Brooke Bonorden and Brett A. Houk, examines relations among the Maya, white overseers, and black loggers during the nineteenth century. Within the context of the British empire, these relations were steeped with colonialist and Victorian-era ideas concerning race, ethnicity, and property. Rather than adopt a world-systems perspective that removes agency from and portrays as passive the native and indentured inhabitants of northwestern Belize, the authors of Chapter 13 consider Maya and black loggers as actors in a frontier zone where new forms of program identity (including but not limited to resistance) were forming in a way that evokes the work of Lightfoot and Martinez (1995). Fleeing the Caste War and following a battle with British forces, the San Pedro Maya were reduced to rent-paying tenancy on what they viewed as their own lands, yet subsistence farming provided no way for them to earn the money to pay rent to the logging company that held title. Selective participation at the margins of the cash economy, such as collecting *chicle* sap, became a way of life that provided funds allowing the persistence of traditional subsistence practices. It seems likely, too, that they traded food and the goods they produced to loggers for items from company stores that could be used in place of locally produced pottery and *manos* and *metates*. Similarly, the descendants of former slaves, indentured to the company through the implementation of the "advance" system, learned and adopted native Maya ways of construction in order to minimize the costs that kept them indebted to the company and supplemented their diets through trade with the Maya. Such activities undermined certain aspects of older identities, allowed others to continue, and forged new local ones on the fringes of a colonial empire.

The chapters in this volume paint pictures of identity, politics, and violence made visible through a wide range of artifact classes, practices, artistic expressions, mythology, and history. The research presented in our contributions illustrates progress in documenting the long arc of history in several regions and in tracing some of the many and changing ways that ancient people expressed their identities. It is unlikely that the Maya saw themselves as members of a large and unified ethnic group until quite recently; instead, they probably looked first to their local community, their local ruling lineage, or their *ajaw* and petty kingdom. When asked who the Maya were and what happened to them, perhaps we should respond: which ones do you mean?

References cited

Andrews, George F. 1997 Architecture of the Chenes Region. In *Pyramids and Palaces, Monsters and Masks: The Golden Age of Maya Architecture*, edited by George F. Andrews, Vol. 2, pp. 243–320. Labyrinthos, Culver City, CA.

Ball, Joseph, and Jennifer Taschek 2003 Reconsidering the Belize Valley Preclassic: A Case for Multiethnic Interactions in the Development of a Regional Culture Tradition. *Ancient Mesoamerica* 14:179–217.

Braswell, Geoffrey E. 2016 The Problem of Ethnicity and the Construction of K'iche'an Identity. In *Archaeology and Identity on the Pacific Coast and Southern Highlands of Mesoamerica*, edited by Claudia García-Des Lauriers and Michael W. Love, pp. 172–184. University of Utah Press, Salt Lake City.

Brown, M. Kathryn, and James F. Garber 2003 Evidence of Conflict during the Middle Formative in the Maya Lowlands: A View from Blackman Eddy, Belize. In *Ancient Maya Warfare*, edited by M. Kathryn Brown and Travis W. Stanton, pp. 91–108. Altamira Press, Walnut Creek, CA.

Castells, Manuel 1997 *The Power of Identity: The Information Age: Economy, Society, and Culture*, Vol. 2. Blackwell Publishing, Oxford.

Graña-Behrens, Daniel 2004 Santa Rosa Xtampak, Campeche, y sus inscripciones. *Estudios de cultura maya* 25:33–45.

Harrison, Peter D., and E. Wyllys Andrews 2004 Palaces of Tikal and Copán. In *Palaces of the Ancient New World*, edited by Susan T. Evans and Joanne Pillsbury, pp. 113–147. Dumbarton Oaks Research Library and Collection, Washington, DC.

Hohmann, Hasso 2017 *The Maya Temple-Palace of Santa Rosa Xtampak, Mexico: Documentation and Reconstruction of Form, Construction, and Function*. Verlag der Technischen Universität Graz, Austria.

Jansen, Philipp, Iken Paap, and Ivan Urdapilleta Caamal 2019 *Santa Rosa Xtampak, Campeche: 2018 Map Set*. Online Document. Ibero-Amerikanisches Institut, Berlin. http://publications.iai.spk-berlin.de/receive/reposis-iai_mods_00003049, accessed July 15, 2021.

Kennett, Douglas J., Keith M. Prufer, Brendan J. Culleton, et al. 2020 Early Isotopic Evidence for Maize as a Staple Grain in the Americas. *Science Advances* 5:eaba3245.

Leventhal, Richard M. 1990 Southern Belize: An Ancient Maya Region. In *Vision and Revision in Maya Studies*, edited by Flora S. Clancy and Peter D. Harrison, pp. 125–141. University of New Mexico Press, Albuquerque.

Lightfoot, Kent G., and Antoinette Martinez 1995 Frontiers and Boundaries in Archaeological Perspective. *Annual Review of Anthropology* 24:471–492.

Mao, Zedong 1938 On Protracted War. In *Selected Works*, Vol. 2, pp. 152–153. Peking Foreign Languages Press, Beijing.

Marcus, Joyce 1993 *Mesoamerican Writing Systems: Propaganda, Myth and History in Four Ancient Civilizations*. Princeton University Press, Princeton, NJ.

Morales López, and William J. Folan 2005 Santa Rosa Xtampak, Campeche: su patrón de asentamiento del Preclásico al Clásico. *Mayab* 18:5–16.

Neumann, Stella, Rebekah Wegener, Jennifer fest, Paula Niemietz, and Nicole Hützen (editors) 2017 *Challenging Boundaries in Linguistics: Systemic Functional Perspectives*. Peter Lang, Frankfurt.

Prufer, Keith M., Asia V. Alsgaard, Mark Robinson, Clayton R. Meredith, et al. 2019 Linking Late Paleoindian Stone Tool Technologies and Populations in North, Central and South America. *PLoS One* 14(7):e0219812.

Renfrew, Colin, and John F. Cherry (editors) 1986 *Peer Polity Interaction and Socio-Political Change*. Cambridge University Press, Cambridge.

Roseberry, William 1996 Hegemony, Power, and Languages of Contention. In *The Politics of Difference: Ethnic Premises in a World of Power*, edited by Edwin N. Wilmsen and Patrick McAllister, pp. 71–84. University of Chicago Press, Chicago.

Tax, Sol 1937 The Municipios of the Midwestern Highlands of Guatemala. *American Anthropologist* 39:423–444.

2

IDENTITY AND POWER OF THE EARLIEST MAYA

Preclassic architecture and cultural development of Nakum and Yaxha, Peten, Guatemala

Bernard Hermes and Jarosław Źrałka

Yaxha and Nakum are two important Maya centers where intensive investigations have been conducted during the last three decades. Both sites are situated in strategic locations that today are within the Triangle National Park of northeastern Guatemala (Figure 2.1). The ruins of Yaxha are spread along the northern shore of Lake Yaxha, and Nakum is situated on the banks of the Holmul River, which once was an important means of communication and trade in this part of the Maya lowlands. Recent research has been carried out at both sites by three different projects: the *Proyecto Desarrollo Sostenible de Peten* (PDS), the Triangle Project of the Guatemalan Institute of Anthropology and History (IDAEH), and the Nakum Archaeological Project (NAP) of the Jagiellonian University in Kraków, Poland. This work indicates that during the Preclassic period, Yaxha and Nakum rose to power and became important polities. Each had many examples of monumental architecture such as E–groups, triadic complexes, ballcourts, causeways, and other constructions. The scale of monumental architecture documented at Yaxha indicates that it was one of the largest Late Preclassic cities in the southern Maya lowlands and must have dominated other neighboring centers. Nakum, although smaller in size and scale of monumentality, has examples of various public constructions from the same epoch, some of which were embellished with beautifully rendered stucco friezes.

We aim to show the evolution of monumental architecture at both sites from its beginning in the early Middle Preclassic through the Terminal Preclassic or Protoclassic period, when many Maya centers collapsed. We address the subject of political organization and the rise of kingship and complex society at both centers during the Preclassic times. Our chapter constitutes a comprehensive synthesis of Preclassic occupation at Yaxha and Nakum, with an emphasis on the development of public architecture at both sites.

DOI: 10.4324/9781351268004-2

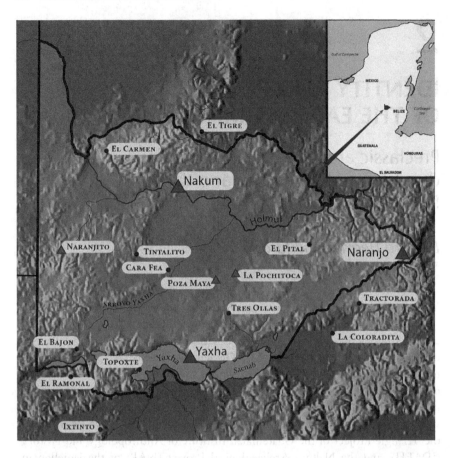

FIGURE 2.1 Nakum and Yaxha in the Triangle Park of northeastern Guatemala.
Source: Piotr Kołodziejczyk

Nakum at the dawn of the Middle Preclassic period

The first part of the Middle Preclassic, sometimes termed "pre-Mamom" because it predates the great spread of the Mamom ceramic sphere, is characterized by many important socio-cultural changes, but mainly by the spread of village life and pottery in the Maya lowlands. It seems that this area, especially the Peten, was largely uninhabited during previous epochs, although important evidence of preceramic or Archaic occupation is found at some sites (Lohse et al. 2006; Lohse 2010). It is still not clear if the appearance of ceramics and the spread of village life was the result of the migration of sedentary populations from other regions, or of the local evolution of preceramic communities documented at some sites, especially in Belize (Iceland 2005; Lohse 2010; Rosenswig 2015:141; see also Chapter 4 and Clark and Cheetham 2002).

The Middle Preclassic period is traditionally divided into two ceramic horizons: pre-Mamom and Mamom. The former is represented by the first documented settled villagers of much of the Maya lowlands. We divide pre-Mamom pottery into at least five major interaction and stylistic groups: (1) the Xe complex of the western Pasion area; (2) the central Peten group encompassing ceramic complexes including Eb at Tikal, Ah Pam in the Yaxha–Sacnab Lakes region, and Ox at Nakbe; (3) the Cunil complex of the Belize River Valley; (4) the Swasey/Bladen complex of northern Belize; and (5) the Ek complex of the northwest Yucatan (Andrews et al. 2008; Braswell 2012:6–7; Clark and Cheetham 2002; Estrada-Belli 2011:37, 2016:234). To this list, Francisco Estrada-Belli (2016:234) adds a sixth pre-Mamom group for Holmul, which in his opinion represents a distinct stylistic unit.

To date, few Maya sites with pre-Mamom pottery have been identified. Evidence of pre-Mamom occupation is usually found in elevated, sacred places that in subsequent periods were successively enlarged and which must have played an important role in the ceremonial life of the first lowland communities (Estrada-Belli 2011:39, 2016:236). Pre-Mamom ceramics are usually found in deeply buried contexts, sometimes directly on bedrock below large architectural complexes of a later date or in the lowest levels of plazas. In most cases, such pottery has not been found associated with contemporary architecture. Exceptions include Blackman Eddy (Garber et al. 2004:28–29), Cahal Pech (Healey et al. 2004), and Ceibal (also spelled 'Seibal'; Inomata et al. 2013, 2015), where pre-Mamom materials are associated with monumental architecture of substantial size (Chapter 3).

Nakum and Yaxha have evidence of pre-Mamom occupation. Both sites were settled by ceramic-using populations that spread through this part of the Maya lowlands, possibly along the rivers and lakes, during the period 900–700 BC. Other neighboring sites associated with rivers and different water features also have shown important evidence of pre-Mamom occupation, namely Holmul (Estrada-Belli 2011; Neivens de Estrada 2016), Buenavista-Nuevo San José (on Lake Peten Itza, Castellanos and Foias 2017), and Tikal (Culbert 1979).

The pre-Mamom phase was especially well studied at Nakum during the recent research of the NAP (Źrałka et al. 2021). Our investigations carried out in the Northern Sector (Figure 2.2) reveal important evidence of construction and other activities dating to pre-Mamom times. We have identified a new period in the development of Nakum named the Chämach phase (Figure 2.3). Our earliest Chämach ceramics reveal close links to the early ceramic assemblages of Tikal, Uaxactun, Altar de Sacrificios, and Ceibal. They differ significantly from the earliest ceramic collections known from Belize assigned to the Cunil and Swasey/Bladen complexes. Thus, we surmise that Nakum was settled by populations that came from the west or, more probably, the southwest. Nakum seems to have been occupied slightly later than Ceibal and Tikal. Chämach pottery shares similarities with the Real 2 and 3 complexes of Ceibal, and our radiocarbon assays date the Nakum materials to later pre-Mamom times: ca. 900/800–700 BC (Hermes 2019).

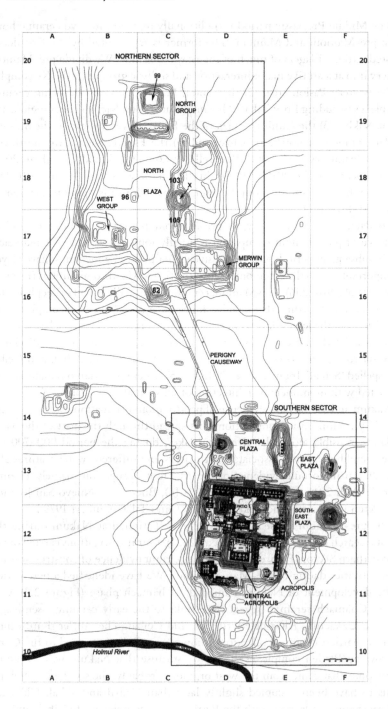

FIGURE 2.2 Nakum, Guatemala.

Source: After Quintana and Wurster 2002 with corrections made by Department of Conservation and Rescue of Prehispanic Archaeological Sites (DECORSIAP), Institute of Anthropology and History of Guatemala (IDAEH).

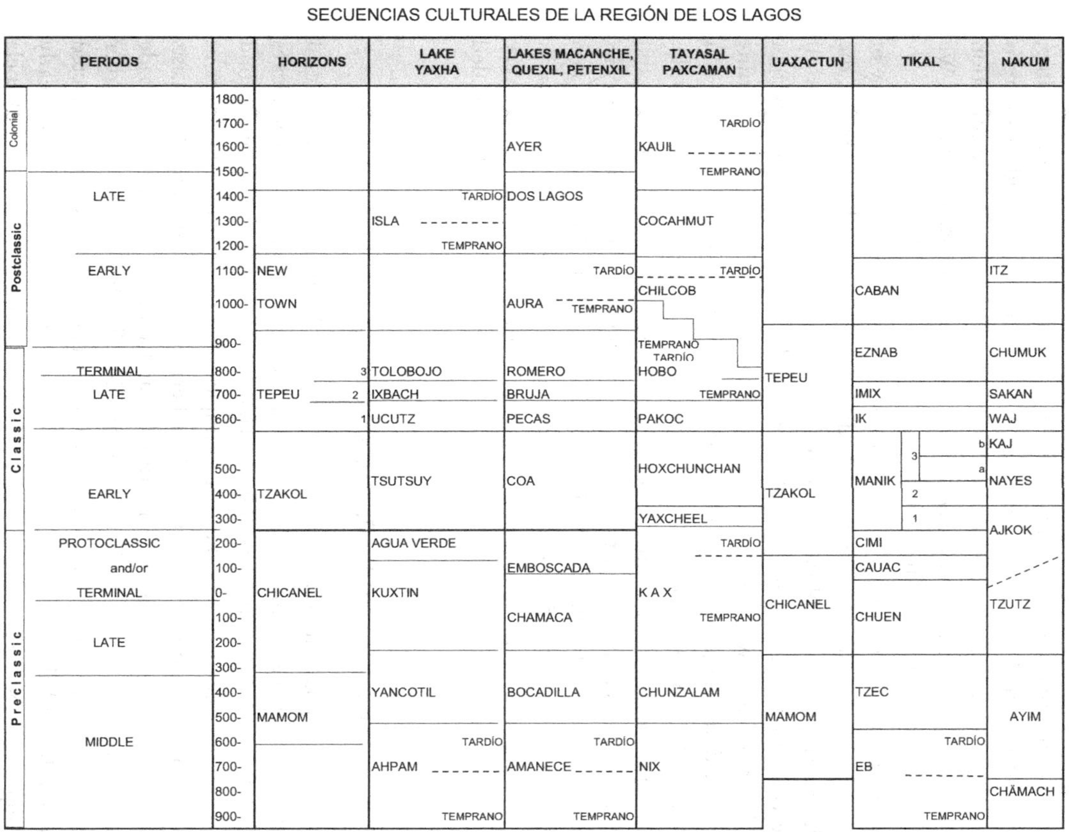

SECUENCIAS CULTURALES DE LA REGIÓN DE LOS LAGOS

PERIODS		HORIZONS		LAKE YAXHA	LAKES MACANCHE, QUEXIL, PETENXIL	TAYASAL PAXCAMAN	UAXACTUN	TIKAL	NAKUM
Colonial	LATE		1800- 1700- 1600- 1500-		AYER	KAUIL TARDIO / TEMPRANO			
Postclassic	LATE		1400- 1300-	TARDIO DOS LAGOS / ISLA / TEMPRANO	DOS LAGOS	COCAHMUT			
	EARLY	NEW TOWN	1200- 1100- 1000-		AURA TARDIO / TEMPRANO	CHILCOB TARDIO / TEMPRANO		CABAN	ITZ
Classic	TERMINAL		900-	TOLOBOJO (3)	ROMERO	TEMPRANO TARDIO HOBO	TEPEU	EZNAB	CHUMUK
	LATE	TEPEU	800- 700-	IXBACH (2)	BRUJA	TEMPRANO		IMIX	SAKAN
			600-	UCUTZ (1)	PECAS	PAKOC		IK	WAJ
	EARLY	TZAKOL	500-	TSUTSUY	COA	HOXCHUNCHAN	TZAKOL	MANIK (3,2,1)	b KAJ / a NAYES
			400- 300-			YAXCHEEL		CIMI	AJKOK
Preclassic	PROTOCLASSIC and/or TERMINAL	CHICANEL	200- 100- 0-	AGUA VERDE	EMBOSCADA	KAX	CHICANEL	CAUAC	TZUTZ
	LATE		100- 200- 300-	KUXTIN	CHAMACA			CHUEN	
			400-	YANCOTIL	BOCADILLA	CHUNZALAM		TZEC	AYIM
	MIDDLE	MAMOM	500- 600-				MAMOM		
			700- 800-	AHPAM TARDIO / TEMPRANO	AMANECE TARDIO / TEMPRANO	NIX		EB TARDIO / TEMPRANO	CHAMACH TEMPRANO
			900-						

FIGURE 2.3 Chronologies of Nakum, Yaxha, and other Peten sites.

Source: Chase 1984; Hermes et al. 1997; Rice 1987 and Willey et al. 1967

We documented vestiges of pre-Mamom architecture during field work at Nakum, especially below Structure 103, where we found modifications to bedrock and evidence of a low platform-like feature partly carved out of the bedrock and covered with a layer of stone slabs and dark mud (Phase 103–1 Sub). There also is a meter-deep chultun-like feature associated with this low platform (Figure 2.4a). These features may be related to an important early settlement or public building that once existed in this elevated part of the site. Later in time, the earliest platform was covered by a second platform 1.8 m high. Its core is made of pebbles and almost no mortar (Structure 103 Sub-1). This construction can be dated to the transition between the pre-Mamom and Mamom phases. We believe it had a ceremonial function (Źrałka et al. 2018, 2021).

Another important location that may be associated with the ritual activity of the earliest inhabitants of Nakum is a bedrock construction discovered in the southwestern part of the North Plaza. It has a very sophisticated, symmetrical shape consisting of a principal chamber (with a hearth at its northern end), a corridor, two stairs (which connect this space to the neighboring plaza), a tunnel, and a drain (Figure 2.4b). The whole construction functioned as a steam bath. It might also have been perceived as an artificial cave associated with the underworld, ancestors, and other supernatural beings. Associated materials and radiocarbon dates indicate that the steam bath dates to the Middle Preclassic. Its earliest version might have been built during the end of pre-Mamom times, and it was certainly remodeled during the succeeding Mamom and Chicanel periods. Our investigations indicate that the steam bath must have been used for a very long period, until the end of the Late Preclassic when it was buried and sealed beneath later constructions.

Nakum in the later Middle Preclassic period

The Chämach phase at Nakum is followed by the A'yim phase. It was a local manifestation of the Mamom horizon or of the Late Eb and Tzec complexes defined for Tikal (Figure 2.3). This period, and more precisely its second part, saw the construction of the first examples of monumental architecture at Nakum. An E-group was built in the Northern Sector at this time. It consists of a very low western platform (Structure 96) and a long eastern platform made up of Structures 103, 104, and 105 (Figure 2.5). This E-group covered earlier pre-Mamom architecture documented below Structure 103. It was connected in the south to a ballcourt dating to the same period. We stress that many early E-groups are associated with ballcourts (Aimers and Rice 2006:89–90; Drápela 2014). To the south of the ballcourt, another construction was built: the first version of the Merwin Group. At this early time, it was a platform measuring about 25–30 m long at its base and standing 2.2 m high. This construction was accessed by a ramp and stairway that encompassed its western side and the western ends of the northern and southern façades of the platform. The Merwin Group might have supported residential structures.

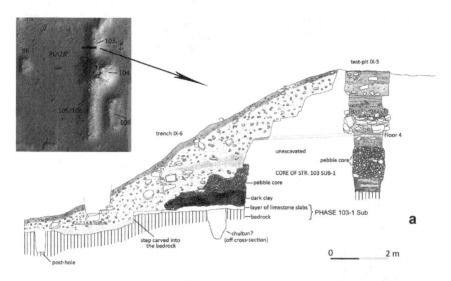

b

FIGURE 2.4   Middle Preclassic architecture at Nakum: (a) cross-section of Nakum Structure 103 showing the earliest architecture dated to pre-Mamom and Mamom phases; (b) reconstruction of a steam bath found in the southwestern corner of the Northern Sector of Nakum.

Source: Reconstruction by Piotr Kołodziejczyk

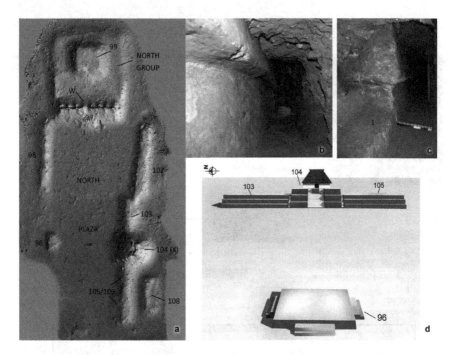

FIGURE 2.5 E-group in the Northern Sector of Nakum: (a) DEM plan featuring E-group; (b-c) view of the first and second terraces of the first version (stage X Sub-1) of Structure 104, the central building of the E-group; (d) reconstruction of E-group.

Source: DEM by Bolesław Zych, photos by Jarosław Źrałka, reconstruction by Breitner González.

Other A'yim buildings were discovered in the Southern Sector of Nakum in the lowest levels of the Acropolis. In its final architectural form (dated to the Terminal Classic), this complex consisted of more than 40 structures arranged around 16 courtyards and patios. Most of these structures had a residential function (Quintana 2014). Nonetheless, extensive excavations carried out by both IDAEH and NAP revealed features of the earliest structures of the Acropolis buried deep in the northern and central parts of this complex. The oldest and most important constructions were found below Patio 1 (the largest courtyard of the Acropolis) and under two Classic period buildings called Structures D and G, as well as beneath the immense complex of the Central Acropolis, which constitutes the highest and most inaccessible part of the Acropolis. The early structure found in the northern extreme of the Acropolis must have been the entrance to this complex. It dates to the end of the Middle or the beginning of the Late Preclassic period. This building was partly exposed during recent NAP investigations and was found about 1.4 m below the northeastern corner of Patio 1, partially buried by Structure D, a large Classic period palace (Figure 2.6a-b). To the south, we documented another early construction that is buried below both

FIGURE 2.6 Buried early architecture in the northern part of the Nakum Acropolis: (a-b) Middle Preclassic or early Late Preclassic building found below Patio 1 and Structure D; (c-d) Middle Preclassic Structure G Sub-1 discovered below Patio 1 and Building G. Note the inset stairway and sloping wall of the substructure.

Source: Wiesław Koszkul and Robert Słaboński

Patio 1 and Structure G. Labelled Structure G Sub-1, it is a platform 2.1 m high and about 40 m long (east-west). It has an inset stair 15 m long flanked by sloping walls (Figure 2.6c-d). This platform may not have supported a superstructure. Instead, it may have provided access to an important early complex now buried below the immense platform of the Central Acropolis.

IDAEH excavations supervised by Zoila Calderón indicate that the first version of the Central Acropolis dates to the final part of the Middle Preclassic. Subsequently, during the Late Preclassic, it was covered by a triadic group. The extent and shape of the earliest version of the Central Acropolis is not well-known because its lowest strata were only partly excavated. Nevertheless, two Middle Preclassic floors in the lowest layers of this complex indicate that construction began during Mamom times; whether the first triadic group or a plain basal platform was erected here at that time is unknown (Calderón et al. 2008).

Nakum during the Late Preclassic period

The most important Late Preclassic complex of Nakum is the Central Acropolis. It grew considerably during the Chicanel phase (Tzutz ceramic complex; see Figure 2.3). Intense research carried out by the *Proyecto Triángulo* revealed a basal platform comprised of two sloping terraces, each 2.25 m high. It dates to the early Late Preclassic period. The platform is surmounted by a triadic group with two additional constructions located to its north (Figure 2.7). The most thoroughly investigated building of the Central Acropolis is the western structure of the triadic complex, which is 13 m long (north-south) and 12.5 m wide (east-west). Its three terraces rise to a height of 4.0 m. Its major or eastern façade is embellished by two masks representing jaguar heads. The other two structures of the triadic group probably also were decorated with stucco masks. The southern, major structure of the triadic group was only partially excavated by means of tunneling. It has a stairway 3.25 m wide consisting of 13 steps. A beautiful stucco frieze was found on the upper terrace of the basal platform. It represents two snake heads flanking (or, alternatively, coming out of the mouth of) a centrally located crocodilian head (Calderón et al. 2008). Two such friezes flank the central stairway leading to the Central Acropolis from the north. The central masks evoke the sacred mountain or earthly realm symbolized by a crocodile, an animal strictly related in Maya iconography to the surface of the earth. Calderón's excavations indicate that there probably was an even earlier version of the triadic group. Its remains were only partly revealed, but it also seems to date to the Late Preclassic period (Calderón et al. 2008).

The Late Preclassic also saw several important architectural programs in the Northern Sector of Nakum. Recent investigations of the NAP indicate that one of the first versions of Structure 82 – a large platform at the southwestern corner of the Northern Sector – was erected during this period. It is a large platform that seems to lack a masonry superstructure. Its function in the Late Preclassic period is unknown, but during the Classic it may have supported a residential compound.

Much of the North Group also was constructed during the Late Preclassic Tzutz phase. At that time, a large basal platform was built. It was surmounted by several structures, among them a possible triadic group that now lies buried below Structure 99. Moreover, at this time the 256 m long Perigny causeway was built connecting the Southern and Northern Sectors of the site. Its construction may reflect important socio-political changes that led to the unification of two separate architectural groups. The oldest-known carved monument at Nakum, Stela 4, was erected at this time (Figure 2.8a). It was found in the center of the North Plaza, where it might have been transported from an original, unknown location during the Late or Terminal Classic period. Stela 4 depicts a single

FIGURE 2.7 Reconstruction of the Central Acropolis of Nakum: (a) view from the northeast featuring the last architectural version of the Central Acropolis dating to the Terminal Classic, below which the Late Preclassic triadic group (marked as 1–3) is shown; (b) Late Preclassic version of the Central Acropolis depicting triadic group (marked as 1, 2, and unmarked building in upper left), two additional structures (marked as 4 and 5), and the platform decorated with stucco friezes.

Source: Reconstructions by Breitner González and Telma Tobar, PROSIAPETEN

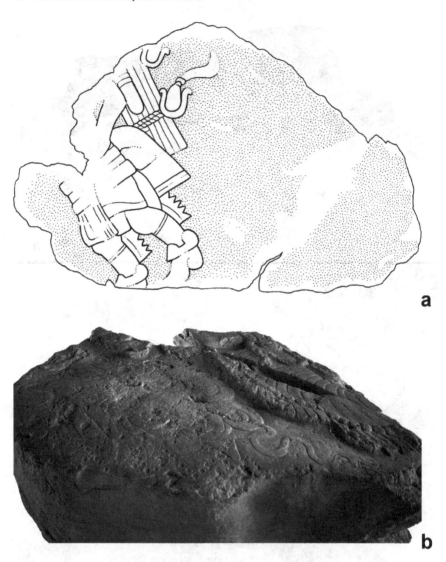

FIGURE 2.8 Late Preclassic stelae: (a) Nakum Stela 4; (b) Yaxha Stela 42.

Source: Drawing by Christophe Helmke, photo by Jarosław Źrałka

person, possibly a local lord, in a very dynamic position. He wears a possible ball-game belt around his waist. On his back the individual carries an element that may be interpreted as a set of reeds embellished with two oval elements. These may symbolically refer to *puh* ('reed') or, alternatively, may depict stylized maize cobs. Stela 4 is stylistically dated to the Late Preclassic period. The dynamic striding pose and several stylistic elements, such as pointed adornments worn on the ankles of the individual, make it very similar to early Maya monuments including Kaminaljuyu Stela 11, Takalik Ab'aj Stela 5, Nakbe Stela 1, Cival Stela 2, and Actuncan Stela 1 (Helmke et al. 2018).

Yaxha during the Middle Preclassic period

The Middle Preclassic occupation of nearby Yaxha is not as well-documented as that of Nakum. This may be because research carried out at Yaxha put major focus on the excavations of the final architectural phases with minimal tunneling or deep trenching of major pyramids or complexes.

The pre-Mamom pottery of Yaxha is assigned to the Early Ah Pam phase, identified by Prudence and Don Rice during their research in the central Peten Lakes region (Figure 2.3; Rice 1979:16–18, 1987:Figure 2.3). Recent research at Yaxha has yielded more ceramics of the Early Ah Pam phase in different parts of the site, but none came from sealed, undisturbed archaeological contexts. Moreover, Early Ah Pam sherds are not associated with architectural features. Their distribution at Yaxha indicates that there must have been some early pre-Mamom occupation in the western and north-central parts of the monumental core (Figure 2.9). There are very close typological and modal similarities between Early Ah Pam pottery from Yaxha and Chämach ceramics from nearby Nakum. This may indicate that the sites were settled by related groups of people. Alternatively, they could have adopted ceramics from the same source or traded with each other.

The Mamom sphere at Yaxha is represented by the Yancotil ceramic complex, which is contemporaneous with the Late Eb and Tzec phases from Tikal and the A'yim complex of Nakum (Figure 2.3). Evidence at Yaxha for construction dating to the second half of the Middle Preclassic is found at several locations in the form of clay fills and stucco pavements, both forming level surfaces above bedrock. Such activity was documented below the East Acropolis, in the lowest strata of Plazas F and G, in the North Acropolis, the West Group, the South Acropolis, and the Maler Group. Apart from revealing the levelling of the bedrock hill on which the East Acropolis was built in later times and the construction of a plaza floor from the Yancotil phase, IDAEH investigations in the East Acropolis also discovered a multiple burial dating to the same period. The interment, which contained one Juventud Red vessel, was found below this early floor (Hermes 2000:279).

Yancotil phase activity also was documented in the Maler Group, the northernmost complex of the epicenter of Yaxha (Figure 2.10a). An interesting and rare architectural model made of stucco forms part of the oldest paved floor in the Maler Group plaza and may date to this time (Figure 2.10b). The model consists of five pyramidal platforms, each about 20 cm high, built in three terraces and painted red (Morales 2001:131–132). The exact meaning of this feature is unknown. The models do not recall any known structures at Yaxha, especially at such an early period of time. They could represent different stages in the construction of pyramidal structures, that is, be a guide for architects and builders, because their forms indicate that they represent unfinished buildings.

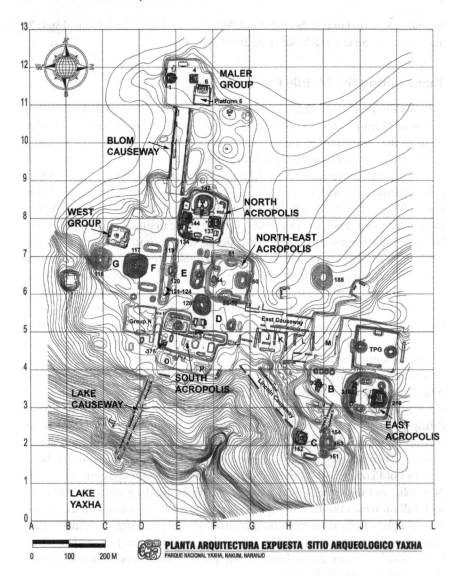

FIGURE 2.9 Yaxha, Guatemala.

Source: Jean Pierre Courau, Oscar Quintana, and Raul Noriega, after Quintana et al. 2000

The first version of the enormous North Acropolis was built during the late Middle Preclassic (García 2001:113–114; Hermes 2007). In its final form, this complex consisted of a large basal platform with rounded corners, measuring 100 × 120 m. It supported 10 structures, including an immense triadic complex (Figure 2.11a). A tunnel excavated at the western side of the base platform revealed several architectural stages, the first of which is about 2 m below the current plaza level and dates to the end of the Middle Preclassic period. This earliest platform is 4.5 m high and consists

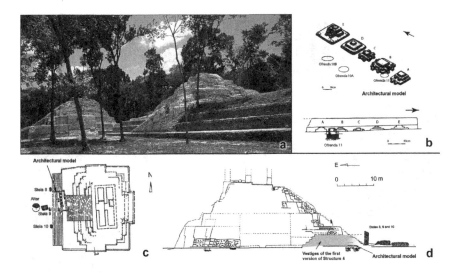

FIGURE 2.10   Maler Group, Yaxha: (a) Structures 4 and 6 and Platform 6 (left to right) viewed from the southwest; (b) general view and cross-section of architectural model found below Structure 4 (late Middle Preclassic); (c-d) plan and cross-section of Structure 4 showing locations of the architectural model and the first version of Structure 4.

Source: Photo by Jarosław Źrałka, drawings by Katarzyna Radnicka after Morales 2001:figures 2–4

of two or three sloping bodies. The early platform is T-shaped in plan and supports a triadic group consisting of the first versions of Structures 137, 142, and 144.

Minimal evidence of architectural activity dating to the transition between Mamom and Chicanel times was documented below the West Group in the north-central part of Yaxha. This compound was first investigated by Hellmuth (1993) and later by Hermes. In its last architectural phase, it consists of a small patio surrounded by several structures, most of which might have served as residences. Hermes' excavations in the lowest levels of this complex yielded evidence of leveling of the natural, uneven terrain and the construction of floors dating to the transition between the Middle and Late Preclassic (Yancotil and Kuxtin ceramic complexes). This construction could be related to the widespread leveling of terrain documented by the extensive test-pitting program in the western part of the Yaxha epicenter, especially in Plaza G. Finally, we emphasize that construction of the monumental E-group in Plaza F and the Northeast Acropolis may have begun in the Middle Preclassic period. However, these two complexes have not yet been excavated (cf. Hermes 2000:279).

Yaxha during the Late Preclassic period

Our excavations at Yaxha clearly demonstrate that the Late Preclassic (represented by the Kuxtin ceramic complex) was a period of unprecedented growth.

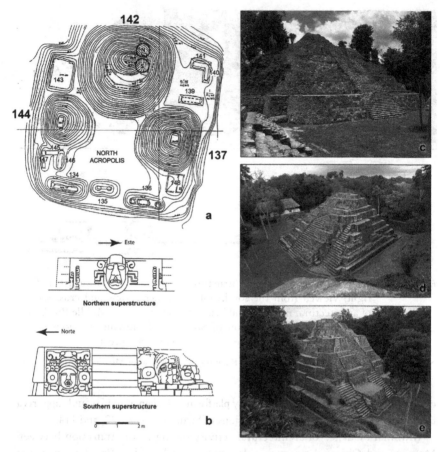

FIGURE 2.11 North Acropolis, Yaxha: (a) triadic group made of Structures 137, 142, and 144; (b) superstructures decorated with stucco masks located on top of the basal pyramid of Structure 142 (marked in [a] as N and S); (c) Structure 142; (d) Structure 144; (e) Structure 137.

Source: [a] modified from Quintana et al. 2000; [b] by Katarzyna Radnicka after García 2000:figure 6, [c-e] photos by Jarosław Źrałka and Robert Słaboński

The scale of architectural programs dating to this time only can be compared to what we know from the Mirador area (Hansen 2004, 2016). The immense monumentality of Late Preclassic Yaxha indicates that it must have been one of the most powerful centers in the Maya lowlands at that time and that it was much bigger than neighboring Tikal.

The North Acropolis

The greatest architectural program at Yaxha during the Late Preclassic was the construction of the immense triadic group of the North Acropolis (Figure

2.11). Our excavations of these platforms were largely superficial works aimed at exposing and restoring their last architectural phases, but short tunnels also were excavated in Structures 137 and 142 (García 2001). These reveal that all three pyramids are, fundamentally, the result of the Kuxtin phase construction activity. Only in Structure 144 did we expose the earliest late Middle Preclassic pyramid that once stood on the first basal platform of the North Acropolis. It is possible that the first stages of Structures 137 and 142 also were erected at that time, but this remains to be demonstrated.

Despite this tantalizing evidence, the North Acropolis dates mainly to the Late Preclassic period and underwent many remodeling programs at that time. We documented three major architectural stages of Structure 144 – the best-studied pyramid of the triadic complex – dating to the Kuxtin phase. Structures 137 and 142 each had five major Kuxtin/Chicanel architectural stages. The focal pyramid, Structure 142, consists of a large basal pyramid platform 18.1 m high surmounted by a smaller pyramid with sloping walls that rises to a total height of about 26.6 m (Figure 2.11c). To the east of this small summit pyramid are two other platforms embellished with stucco masks (Figure 2.11a). The southern superstructure is a platform 2.1 m high with a west-facing façade containing a central staircase flanked by two masks (Figure 2.11b lower). The northern mask on this superstructure is well-preserved, but the southern one was found in a deteriorated state (García 2001:115). Both masks measure about 4 m × 2 m. The second northern superstructure (Figure 2.11b upper) is only about 1.5 m high, and its façade is decorated by a single anthropomorphic mask with traces of red paint (García 2001:115).

The location of these two superstructures on top of the pyramidal platform of Structure 142, out of sight of people gathered on the plaza of the North Acropolis, indicates that they had a more private character than other buildings in this complex. They might have been used during rituals reserved for a limited group of people, perhaps members of elite families. The stucco masks that decorate both superstructures are different from contemporaneous examples in the Maler Group that feature deities. Instead, the Structure 142 masks may depict local lords or deified ancestors. It is also possible that the masks represent the Maize God, who is usually depicted with more anthropomorphic features; Late Preclassic masks of this deity are reported at Calakmul, among other sites (Estrada-Belli 2011:87).

The basal platform on which the triadic pattern complex stands is fairly well-understood, thanks to the excavation of a tunnel on its western side and a trench intersecting its major axis in the area of the principal stair (i.e., on the southern side of the platform). The trench revealed five stages of the stair (Figure 2.12a). The earliest three stages date to the late Middle Preclassic and Late Preclassic periods. Built in the latter period is a beautiful frieze flanking the eastern side of the stair (Figure 2.12b). It depicts a complex mythological scene that, sadly, is largely destroyed. A snake deity with a skeletal head, however, is still clearly visible. This snake most probably flanked a central mask of which only minute

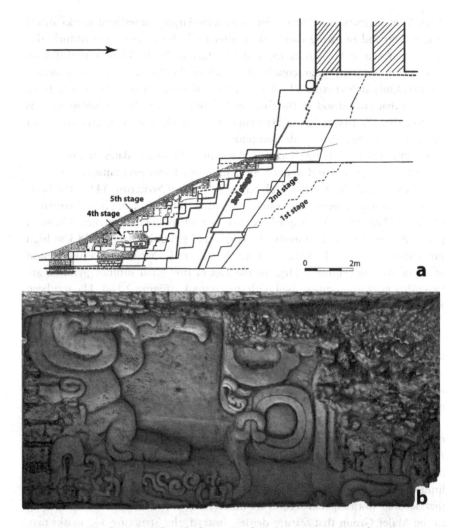

FIGURE 2.12 North Acropolis platform, Yaxha: (a) cross-section showing major architectural stages (Stage 1 is Middle Preclassic, Stages 2 and 3 are Late Preclassic, Stage 4 is Late Classic, and Stage 5 is Terminal Classic; note Stela 42 placed in the core of the Stage 4 stairway); (b) stucco frieze on Late Preclassic version of the base platform of the North Acropolis.

Source: Drawing by Carlos Rax Pacay, Proyecto Yaxha-PDS; photogrammetry by Piotr Kołodziejczyk and Jarosław Źrałka

traces survive, including an earflare worn by a supernatural being. This mask might have been flanked by another skeletal serpent that possibly once existed on the other side. The central mask might have depicted an animated, sacred mountain (a mythological location associated with creation as well as ancestors and deities) or another important supernatural being typically featured on the façades of Preclassic buildings, such as the Principal Bird Deity, embodying the sun and the sky. It seems that the narrative program of the façade of the North Acropolis platform at Yaxha is quite similar to monumental sculpture from Structure 3 of Group H at Uaxactun or Building B-1st at Holmul where central masks denoting sacred, mythical locations were flanked by snakes or skulls (Estrada-Belli 2011:93–95). Skeletal serpents also appear in the E-group of San Bartolo (Saturno et al. 2018:320–323; Doyle 2017:77). This Yaxha frieze was situated so that a large group of people could see it from the vast plaza stretching to the south of the North Acropolis.

We found four fragments of Stela 42 (Figure 2.8b) in the construction fill of the North Acropolis stairway that dates to the Late Classic period. Stela 42 can be dated stylistically to the final part of the Late Preclassic period and is the oldest carved monument known from Yaxha. It is very probable that it once stood within the North Acropolis or close to this complex. Several hundred years later it was sealed in the core of the new stairway leading to the monumental group.

In addition to the triadic group, the basal platform of the North Acropolis supports several other constructions. Structure 134 is located in the southwestern corner of the platform. This construction was the subject of very detailed excavations carried out by Hermes between 2002 and 2007 during the PDS. Investigations reveal that its earliest version, called Structure 134 Sub-1, was erected during the Late Preclassic period. Unfortunately, it was largely destroyed during the remodeling that took place in the Late Classic. Nevertheless, we found a beautifully rendered stucco frieze decorating the exterior part of its western façade. The frieze covers the lower terrace of the Structure 134 Sub-1 platform and once continued on its upper terrace, which was heavily mutilated during later remodeling. The frieze features two floating supernatural beings, each having a helmet-like headdress (Figure 2.13). The individual on the left carries a lance directed towards the right figure, who has a very characteristic element hiding the lower part of his face. The scene seems to take place in a mythical location and involves two mythical beings. The style of the frieze is very similar to other Chicanel phase decorations known from Uaxactun (Group H) and El Mirador (Hansen 2016:397, 400, Figure 8.35), as well as Late Preclassic carved monuments including Nakbe Stela 1 and Kaminaljuyu Stela 11. The exact function of

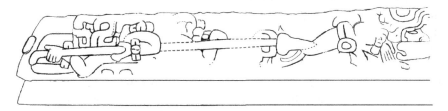

FIGURE 2.13   Mythological stucco frieze on Structure 134 Sub-1.

Source: Hiroshi Iwamoto, Proyecto Yaxha-PDS.

Structure 134 Sub-1 is not well-known because its superstructure was not excavated. Nonetheless, its location at the entrance to the triadic complex indicates
some ceremonial or public significance.

The Maler Group

The North Acropolis is connected by the Blom Causeway to the Maler Group
(Figure 2.9), another important construction of the Late Preclassic period. The
first version of the Blom Causeway was constructed during Chicanel times and
was about 300 m long by 10 m wide. The causeway has sloping walls and was
elevated about 50 cm above the surrounding *bajo* (Hermes and Ramos 2004).
Another road built in the same period is the Lake Causeway, which most probably formed a major entrance route for people entering Yaxha from the side of
the lake (Hermes et al. 1999:116).

IDAEH and PDS investigations in the Maler Group reveal that it saw extensive building programs during the Late Preclassic (Cabrera 2000; Morales 2001).
The first architectural stages of all the major buildings of this complex – the
pyramidal temples or platforms of Structures 1, 4, and 6 – were all built during the Late Preclassic. One of these buildings, Structure 4, was erected above
the stucco model representing five pyramids constructed during the late Middle
Preclassic (Figure 2.10b–d). Three offerings (Ofrendas 10A, 10B, and 11) were
placed in circular holes cut into the bedrock immediately next to the architectural model before the first version of Structure 4 was built (Figure 2.10b). They
included ceramic vessels, greenstone artifacts, and fragments of the upper jaw of
a child (Morales 2001:132).

Excavations of Structure 4 document up to four architectural stages dating to
the Kuxtin phase. In its final Late Preclassic version, Structure 4 consisted of a
platform composed of two superimposed terraces with a staircase on its principal,
western façade. A multiple burial was discovered in the core of the first terrace
(Morales 2001:132–133).

In the southeastern part of the Maler Group there is a vast platform measuring 47 × 42 m (Platform 6; Figures 2.9 and 2.10a), which was constructed in
several architectural stages during the Late Preclassic (Cabrera 2000; Morales
2001). Its first version was only 90 cm high and supported three superstructures
that Morales (2001:132–133) speculates had a "palatial" function. During the
succeeding stage, the platform was raised by more than 2 m and covered these
three superstructures. On its summit a pyramidal platform, Structure 6, was
erected. This construction is one of the most beautiful Late Preclassic buildings
at Yaxha. It is only 8 meters high and consists of four terraces topped by a temple
building with three rooms. The major façade of Structure 6 was embellished by
four masks flanking the major staircase located on its southern side. A fifth mask
decorated the rear or northern side of the building (Morales 2001:132–133). The
masks were not well-preserved when found, but what remains indicates that they
represented unknown supernatural beings.

E-groups or commemorative astronomical complexes

Other important Late Preclassic building projects at Yaxha include the construction of two E-groups located in Plazas F and C (Figure 2.9). The E-group in Plaza F is of special importance but remains largely unexcavated. We dug several test-pits in its plaza that revealed levels and floors dating to the Middle and Late Preclassic. It seems very likely that the first version of this E-group dates to the Middle Preclassic because of similarities in layout to the early E-group at Cival. At each site, a large pyramidal construction (Structure 116 at Yaxha, Structure 20 at Cival) stands to the west of the western pyramid of the E-group and on the major east-west axis of the complex. To the east of each E-group and on the same axis is a triadic group (see Estrada-Belli 2011:Figure 4.1). Similar planning appears at several other Maya sites where triadic groups follow the central east-west axis of early E-groups. At Cival, the E-group was constructed during the Middle Preclassic and the triadic group was added during the Late Preclassic to the east of it (Estrada-Belli 2011). It is very probable that the construction of the E-group and Structure 116 in Plaza F of Yaxha took place during the Middle Preclassic, establishing the symbolic center of the site, and its major east-west axis which was later extended to the east by the construction of the triadic group in the Northeast Acropolis.

The E-group in Plaza C of Yaxha consists of a western pyramid (Structure 152) and eastern platform (surmounted by Structures 151, 153 and 154). Pyramid 152 was excavated first by Nicholas Hellmuth (unfortunately no records are available) and later by Hermes as part of the PDS project (Figure 2.14a-b). Our research revealed eight Late Preclassic versions of Structure 152, indicating that the E-group was intensively remodeled during Chicanel times.

Other Late Preclassic constructions

Other neighboring complexes also witnessed extensive construction during the Late Preclassic. Among these is the Northeast Acropolis, another triadic complex, which was probably constructed during the Late Preclassic period.

In the East Acropolis, a large pyramid (Structure 216 Sub-1) was constructed. It consists of three terraces with sloping walls. Its major façade has three staircases interspersed with sloping walls, a style that is similar to contemporary buildings of the North Acropolis (Structures 137, 142, and 144; Hermes et al. 1997).

Just west of the East Acropolis, we found evidence of Late Preclassic construction in Plaza B. At the beginning of that period, the bedrock was levelled and later covered by a 28 m (north-south) × 8 m (east-west) platform with rounded corners. The platform (Structure 90 Sub-1) consists of three terraces and stands 3.5 m high. It did not support a stone superstructure.

In layout and function, the South Acropolis of Yaxha is similar to the famous Central Acropolis of Tikal. The former is built on a platform measuring 100 m x120 m. This supports six courtyards surrounded by structures that were, with

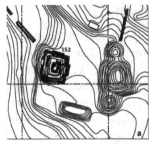

FIGURE 2.14 Late Preclassic architecture, Yaxha: (a-b) E-group in Plaza C; (b) Structure 152 after restoration by PDS project; (c) photo of the South Acropolis platform (north side), Stages 1 to 3 date to the final part of the Late Preclassic.

Source: (a) map by Jean Pierre Courau, Oscar Quintana and Raul Noriega, after Quintana et al. 2000; (b) photo by Jarosław Źrałka; (c) photo by Bernard Hermes.

one exception, residences of the apical elite (Structure 363 might have been a temple). Our archaeological investigations included the excavation of nine test-pits in the courtyards, a series of trenches on the northern side of the platform, and a tunnel in the southwestern corner of the complex. We discovered that this complex commenced in the final part of the Middle Preclassic or the beginning of the Late Preclassic (Hermes 2010). At least three architectural stages of the South Acropolis basal platform date to the Late Preclassic period (Figure 2.14c), and these may have supported residences. Structure 375, located at the south-western corner of the South Acropolis, is one of the best-studied buildings on the platform. Its earliest substructure is a masonry building dating to the Late Preclassic that stands on one of the first versions of the South Acropolis platform. We have not identified its function.

Discussion and conclusions

The area now defined as the Yaxha-Nakum-Naranjo Triangle Park was settled no later than the beginning of the first millennium BC. Early sedentary farmers

made and used pre-Mamom pottery. It is not clear from where these populations or their ceramic tradition originated. We have discovered no firm evidence of a preceramic occupation, although we have several radiocarbon dates
from Nakum that span the second millennium BC (Hermes 2019:Appendix
1; Źrałka et al. 2021). These early dates on their own do not demonstrate an
Archaic occupation because no artifacts or features from this period have been
discovered. Pre-Mamom occupants might have spread along rivers and lakes,
picking out elevated locations close to water for their settlements. In the case of
Nakum, the earliest settlement is on a karstic outcrop of the Northern Sector.
At Yaxha, early settlers chose hills, which were later buried beneath the East and
North Acropolises, spreading north of Lake Yaxha.

The late Middle Preclassic saw the construction of the first monumental architecture at Yaxha and Nakum. These include a ballcourt and the first
E-groups. These monumental constructions constituted the most important
civic-ceremonial architecture at both sites. E-groups might have been particularly important as the foci of ritual activities centered on the cult and observation
of the sun on the horizon. Such observations enabled the Maya to celebrate the
arrival of the rainy season. Thus, E-groups might have played a crucial role in
scheduling the most important solar and agricultural moments and rituals (Aylesworth 2004; Aveni et al. 2003; Estrada-Belli 2011:78–79). By emphasizing shared
ritual practice, such complexes might also have served as markers of cultural,
social, and political identity for the earliest inhabitants of the Maya lowlands.
Kin-based or unrelated groups might have formed communities centered around
the earliest E-groups. Thus E-groups may be interpreted as places where early
communities gathered during ceremonial events and political acts of belonging
to a respective place (Doyle 2017). The construction of E-groups at Nakum,
Yaxha, and other sites can be connected to the physical and symbolic founding of
a ceremonial center (Doyle 2017:38; Estrada-Belli 201:74). E-groups, therefore,
might have marked the earliest territorial or political units in the central Maya
lowlands (Laporte 1993:314; Doyle 2012:369). Nonetheless, the existence of large
complexes and the scale of Middle Preclassic monumentality should not be taken
as markers of political complexity because many early societies throughout the
world created large buildings using corporate labor without social stratification
or the authority of kings (cf. Doyle 2017:28; Inomata et al. 2015). For the Maya,
this changed during the Late Preclassic, the period that saw the rise of political
complexity and kingship.

The Late Preclassic was a period of intense growth at both sites but particularly at Yaxha, which evolved into an important regional power. At that site,
many new E-groups, triadic complexes, pyramidal temples, and possibly even
palaces (i.e., the South Acropolis and Maler Group) were built. An important
neighboring center that may have rivalled Yaxha in size and monumentality
was Naranjo, where the first versions of all triadic complexes, as well as of an
E-group and other public constructions, were built during the Late Preclassic
(Fialko 2005; Gamez 2005).

The widespread construction of Late Preclassic triadic groups throughout the Maya lowlands merits special attention. In most Maya centers they were the largest monuments ever constructed. Apart from their mythological and symbolic meaning, triadic groups are thought to reflect the political authority of the earliest Maya rulers. Such complexes were embellished with impressive stucco friezes, as seen at both Yaxha and Nakum. Triadic groups were important markers on the landscape that most probably evoked the concept of the axis mundi. They were sacred loci with which local people identified (Doyle 2017:102).

The Late Preclassic architecture at Nakum is of a much smaller scale than that of Yaxha, but a large triadic group decorated with sophisticated stucco masks and several other large complexes were built at that time. Moreover, Nakum underwent a Late Preclassic urban transformation that may reflect important political changes. Before ca. 300 BC, what we now define as the single archaeological site of Nakum consisted of two distinct settlements that evolved on top of two natural karstic hills. These two important units were centered around an E-group (in the Northern Sector) and a monumental complex now buried below the Acropolis (in the Southern Sector). We speculate that these might have been two independent social or political units that were connected by a causeway in the Late Preclassic, forming a single entity. The construction of the causeway might have been contemporaneous with other architectural changes. For example, the bedrock steam bath built during the Middle Preclassic was sealed, and the North Group was significantly expanded and rebuilt. We do not know if architectural unification reflects the actions of a single, powerful ruler or of a group of elites.

Stone monuments depicting local lords first appeared during the Late Preclassic at many sites across the Maya lowlands and highlands (Estrada-Belli 2011). The rise of kingship during the Late Preclassic is suggested by the discovery of Stela 4 at Nakum. It features a probable local lord wearing the trappings of power (Figure 2.8a). Yaxha Stela 42, the earliest example known at that site, also was carved during the Late Preclassic and was found at the North Acropolis, the largest architectural complex of that period. Although only a few fragments of this monument have been found, it displays a very complex scene and may depict a local lord (Figure 2.8b). Moreover, according to Nikolai Grube (2000:253), Yaxha Stelae 4, 6, and 10 are Late Preclassic monuments that were re-carved in an Early Classic style and set in the two E-group complexes located in Plazas C and F. These were built in the Preclassic and may indicate that a royal family was able to commission important architectural programs and commemorative monuments with their representations. Excavations suggest that residences of early rulers are buried beneath the South Acropolis and Maler Group.

The monumental scale of public works and iconographic programs at Yaxha and Nakum may indicate the emergence of centralized power and religion. Similar sculptural programs are seen adorning the architecture of most Late Preclassic central Maya lowland sites, demonstrating widespread, shared belief. At Yaxha and Nakum, we can trace evidence of monumental architecture, kingship, and complex public rituals, as well as the participation in long-distance trade as indicated by the appearance of jade, obsidian, and other imported materials. These demonstrate social and political complexity at both centers and imply that the two sites were independent political units ruled by elite families and headed by kings.

The politico-religious prerogatives of early lords are not well-known, but they might have differed from what we know for Classic period kings. The power of the earliest *ajaw* most probably focused more on mythology and ritual actions in gathering places than the "interaction between city-states that we know from the Classic Maya" (Doyle 2017:71). We have no royal burials that can be interpreted as the resting places of early lowland rulers that predate the first or second century AD (Estrada-Belli 2016:255–256). This may because such interments are hard to discover or because joint or theocratic rule at most Maya centers precluded the creation of such burials (Estrada-Belli 2011:55–56, 2016:251–252).

Important changes came at the end of the Preclassic, called either the Terminal Preclassic or Protoclassic period. Yaxha shared the fate of many other Maya centers during this period of crisis. Archaeological evidence at Yaxha pertaining to this period of transition and to the Early Classic is very meager, especially when compared to the dramatic growth of the site during the Late Preclassic. Almost no construction at Yaxha can be dated to the Protoclassic or Early Classic periods. In contrast, the nearby site of Poza Maya experienced significant growth during the Protoclassic and Early Classic periods, especially during Tzakol 2 times. This may indicate the movement of the royal dynasty from Yaxha to Poza Maya and the founding of a new important political center there.

Nakum, on the other hand, experienced stable growth if not a surge during the Preclassic to Classic transition. Many constructions and complexes in the Northern and Southern sectors were erected or rebuilt (Źrałka et al. 2018). These data indicate that Nakum might have been able to take advantage of the collapse and demise of other neighboring and more powerful polities, thus establishing new political and economic links and expanding its political role in the region.

Acknowledgments

Our data were collected during several research projects for which the authors worked. These include the Triangle Project of the Guatemalan Institute of Anthropology and History, the *Proyecto Desarrollo Sostenible de Peten* financed by Banco Interamericano de Desarrollo, and the Nakum Archaeological Project of the Jagiellonian University, Kraków, Poland. Recent investigations of the last have been financed by the National Science Center, Poland (under the agreement no. UMO-2014/14/E/HS3/00534).

References

Aimers, James, and Prudence Rice 2006 Astronomy, Ritual, and the Interpretation of Maya 'E-Group' Architectural Assemblages. *Ancient Mesoamerica* 17:79–96.

Andrews, E. Wyllys, V, George J. Bey III, and Christopher Gunn 2008 Rethinking the Early Ceramic History of the Northern Maya Lowlands: New Evidence and Interpretations. *Paper presented at the 73rd Annual Meeting of the Society for American Archaeology*, Vancouver.

Aveni, Anthony, Anne Dowd, and Benjamin Vining 2003 Maya Calendar Reform? Evidence from Orientations of Specialized Architectural Assemblages. *Latin American Antiquity* 14:159–178.

Aylesworth, Grant 2004 Astronomical Interpretations of Ancient Maya E-Group Architectural Complexes. *Archaeoastronomy* 18:34–66.

Braswell, Geoffrey E. 2012 The Ancient Maya of Mexico: Reinterpreting the Past of the Northern Maya Lowlands. In *The Ancient Maya of Mexico: Reinterpreting the Past of the Northern Maya Lowlands*, edited by Geoffrey E. Braswell, pp. 1–41. Routledge, London and New York.

Cabrera, Tania 2000 Resultados preliminares de las investigaciones realizadas en el Grupo Maler, Yaxha, Petén. In *XIII Simposio de Investigaciones Arqueológicas en Guatemala, 1999*, edited by Juan Pedro Laporte, Héctor Escobedo, Bárbara Arroyo, and Ana C. de Suasnávar, pp. 354–373. Museo Nacional de Arqueología y Etnología, Guatemala City.

Calderón, Zoila, Bernard Hermes, Breitner González, and Telma Tobar 2008 La acrópolis interior de Nakum. In *XXI Simposio de Investigaciones Arqueológicas en Guatemala, 2007*, edited by Juan Pedro Laporte, Bárbara Arroyo, and Héctor Mejía, pp. 349–356. Museo Nacional de Arqueología y Etnología, Guatemala City.

Castellanos, Jeanette, and Antonia Foias 2017 The Earliest Maya Farmers of Peten: New Evidence from Buenavista-Nuevo San José, Central Peten Lakes Region, Guatemala. *Journal of Anthropology* 2017:1–45.

Chase, Arlen 1984 The Ceramic Complexes of the Tayasal-Paxcaman Zone. *Ceramica de la Cultura Maya* 13:27–41.

Clark, John, and David Cheetham 2002 Mesoamerica's Tribal Foundations. In *The Archaeology of Tribal Societies*, edited by William Parkinson, pp. 278–339. International Monographs in Prehistory, University of Michigan, Ann Arbor.

Culbert, Patrick T. 1979 *The Ceramics of Tikal*. Tikal, Report 25B. Unpublished manuscript in the possession of the authors.

Doyle, James 2012 Regroup on 'E-Groups': Monumentality and Early Centers in the Middle Preclassic Maya Lowlands. *Latin American Antiquity* 23:355–379.

—— 2017 *Architecture and the Origins of Preclassic Maya Politics*. Cambridge University Press, Cambridge.

Drápela, Tomas 2014 Rethinking the Function of E-Group Assemblages of the Maya Southern Lowlands. *Axis Mundi* 9:91–101.

Ebert, Claire, Nancy Peniche May, Brendan Culleton, Jaime Awe, and Douglas Kennett 2017 Regional Response to Drought during the Formation and Decline of Preclassic Maya Societies. *Quaternary Science Reviews* 173:211–235.

Estrada-Belli, Francisco 2011 *The First Maya Civilization: Ritual and Power before the Classic Period*. Routledge, London.

—— 2016 Regional and Interregional Interactions and the Preclassic Maya. In *The Origins of Maya States*, edited by Loa Traxler and Robert Sharer, pp. 225–270. University of Pennsylvania Museum of Archaeology and Anthropology, Philadelphia.

Fialko, Vilma 2005 Proceso evolutivo del epicentro monumental de Naranjo, Peten. In *XVIII Simposio de Investigaciones Arqueologicas en Guatemala*, edited by Juan Pedro Laporte, Bárbara Arroyo, and Héctor Mejía, pp. 225–233. Museo Nacional de Arqueología y Etnologia, Guatemala City.

Gamez, Laura 2005 Investigaciones en los templos B-19 y B-24 de Naranjo: La evolucion del eje norte-sur de la Plaza Central. In *XVIII Simposio de Investigaciones Arqueológicas en Guatemala*, edited by Juan Pedro Laporte, Bárbara Arroyo, and Héctor Mejía, pp. 235–242. Museo Nacional de Arqueología y Etnologia, Guatemala City.

Garber, James, Kathryn Brown, Jaime Awe, and Christopher Hartman 2004 Middle Formative Prehistory of the Central Belize Valley: An Examination of Architecture, Material Culture, and Sociopolitical Change at Blackman Eddy. In *The Ancient Maya of the Belize Valley: Half a Century of Archaeological Research*, edited by James Garber, pp. 25–47. University Press of Florida, Gainesville.

García, Edgar Vinicio 2001 Investigaciones en la parte norte de Yaxha. In *XIV Simposio de Investigaciones Arqueológicas en Guatemala, 2000*, edited by Juan Pedro Laporte, Ana C. Suasnávar, and Bárbara Arroyo, pp. 113–130. Museo Nacional de Arqueología y Etnología, Guatemala City.

Grube, Nikolai 2000 Monumentos esculpidos e inscripciones jeroglíficas en el triangulo Yaxha-Nakum- Naranjo. In *El Sitio Maya de Topoxté: Investigaciones en una isla del lago Yaxhá, Petén, Guatemala*, edited by Wolfang W. Wurster, pp. 249–268. Materialien zur Allgemeinen und Vergleichenden Archäologie, Vol. 57. Kommission für Allgemeine und Vergleichende Archäologie, Verlag Philipp von Zabern, Mainz am Rhein.

Hansen, Richard 2004 El Mirador, Guatemala: el apogeo del Preclásico en el área maya. *Arqueología Mexicana* 66:28–33.

——— 2016 Cultural and Environmental Components of the First Maya States: A Perspective from the Central and Southern Maya Lowlands. In *The Origins of Maya States*, edited by Loa Traxler and Robert Sharer, pp. 329–416. University of Pennsylvania Museum of Archaeology and Anthropology, Philadelphia.

Healey, Paul, David Cheetham, Terry Powis, and Jaime Awe 2004 Cahal Pech: The Middle Formative Period. In *The Ancient Maya of the Belize Valley: Half a Century of Archaeological Research*, edited by James Garber, pp. 103–124. University Press of Florida, Gainesville.

Hellmuth, Nicholas 1993 *A Report for IDAEH on Research Accomplished at the Maya Ruins of Yaxha, Peten, Guatemala*. Unpublished report, Foundation for Latin American Anthropological Research, Guatemala City.

Helmke, Christophe, Simon Martin, Jarosław Źrałka, Bolesław Zych, Wiesław Koszkul, Magdalena Rusek, and Juan Luis Velásquez 2018 Los monumentos monolíticos de Nakum, Guatemala. In *XXXI Simposio de Investigaciones Arqueológicas en Guatemala, 2017*, edited by Bárbara Arroyo, Luis Méndez, and Gloria Ajú, pp. 851–866. Museo Nacional de Arqueología y Etnología, Guatemala City.

Hermes, Bernard 2000 El plano del sitio Maya de Yaxha, Petén, Guatemala. *Beiträge zur Allgemeinen und Vergleichenden Archäologie* 20:261–286.

——— 2007 *Informe final de los trabajos de investigación arqueológica efectuados durante la ampliación a la segunda fase del PDS – Yaxha (octubre 2005 – marzo 2007)*. Unpublished report submitted to Ministerio de Ambiente y Recursos Naturales, Guatemala City.

——— 2010 Investigación Arqueológica en Yaxha: la Acrópolis Sur. In *XXIII Simposio de Investigaciones Arqueológicas en Guatemala, 2009*, edited by Bárbara Arroyo, Adriana Linares, and Lorena Paiz, pp. 510–529. Museo Nacional de Arqueología y Etnología, Guatemala.

——— 2019 *La cerámica del sitio maya Nakum, Petén, Guatemala*. Jagiellonian University Press, Kraków.

Hermes, Bernard, Paulino Morales, and Sebastian Möllers 1999 Investigación arqueológica en Yaxha, Petén: La Calzada del Lago y la Vía 5. In *XII Simposio de Investigaciones*

Arqueológicas en Guatemala, 1998, edited by Juan Pedro Laporte, and Héctor Escobedo, pp. 110–138. Museo Nacional de Arqueología y Etnología, Guatemala City.

Hermes, Bernard, Raul Noriega, and Zoila Calderón 1997 Investigación arqueológica y trabajos de conservación en el Edificio 216 de Yaxha. *Beiträge zur Allgemeinen und Vergleichenden Archäologie* 17:257–309.

Hermes, Bernard, and Carmen Ramos 2004 Investigación arqueológica en la Calzada Blom, Yaxha, Petén. In *XVIII Simposio de Investigaciones Arqueológicas en Guatemala, 2003*, edited by Juan Pedro Laporte, Bárbara Arroyo, Héctor Escobedo, and Héctor Mejía, pp. 607–620. Museo Nacional de Arqueología y Etnología, Guatemala City.

Iceland, Harry B. 2005 The Preceramic to Early Middle Formative Transition in Northern Belize: Evidence for the Ethnic Identity of the Preceramic Inhabitants. In *New Perspectives on Formative Mesoamerican Cultures*, edited by Terry Powis, pp. 15–26. BAR International Series 1377, Archaeopress, Oxford.

Inomata, Takeshi, Jessica MacLellan, Daniela Triadan, Jessica Munson, Melissa Burham, Kazuo Aoyama, Hiroo Nasu, Flory Pinzon, and Hitoshi Yonenobu 2015 Development of Sedentary Communities in the Maya Lowlands: Coexisting Mobile Groups and Public Ceremonies at Ceibal, Guatemala. *PNAS* 112(14):4268–4273.

Inomata, Takeshi, Daniela Triadan, Kazuo Aoyama, Victor Castillo, and Hitoshi Yonenobu 2013 Early Ceremonial Constructions at Ceibal, Guatemala, and the Origins of Lowland Maya Civilization. *Science* 340:467–471.

Laporte, Juan Pedro 1993 Architecture and Social Change in Late Classic Maya Society: The Evidence from Mundo Perdido, Tikal. In *Lowland Maya Civilization in the Eighth Century A.D.*, edited by Jeremy A. Sabloff and John S. Henderson, pp. 299–320. Dumbarton Oaks, Washington, DC.

Lohse, Jon C. 2010 Archaic Origins of the Lowland Maya. *Latin American Antiquity* 21:312–352.

Lohse, Jon C., Jaime Awe, Cameron Griffith, Robert M. Rosenswig, and Fred Valdez, Jr. 2006 Preceramic Occupations in Belize: Updating the Paleoindian and Archaic Record. *Latin American Antiquity* 17:209–226.

Morales, Paulino 2001 Rasgos arquitectónicos y prácticas rituales en el Grupo Maler de Yaxha, Petén. In *XIV Simposio de Investigaciones Arqueológicas en Guatemala, 2000*, edited by Juan Pedro Laporte, Ana C. Suasnávar, and Bárbara Arroyo, pp. 131–150. Museo Nacional de Arqueología y Etnología, Guatemala City.

Neivens de Estrada, Nina 2016 The K'awil Complex. In *Ceramic Sequence of the Holmul Region, Guatemala*, edited by Michael Callaghan and Nina Neivens de Estrada, pp. 30–65. Anthropological Papers of the University of Arizona, No. 77. The University of Arizona Press, Tucson 2016.

Quintana, Oscar 2014 Nakum – Ciudad Maya, Petén, Guatemala. *Zeitschrift für Archäologie Außereuropäischer Kulturen* 6:145–246.

Quintana, Oscar, and Wolfgang Wurster 2002 Un nuevo plano del sitio Maya de Nakum, Peten, Guatemala. *Beiträge Zur Allgemeinen und Vergleichenden Archäologie* 22:243–275.

Quintana, Oscar, Wolfgang Wurster, Bernard Hermes, Jean Pierre Courau, and Hugo Galindo 2000 El plano del sitio Maya de Yaxha, Peten, Guatemala. *Beiträge zur Allgemeinen und Vergleichenden Archäologie* 20:261–286.

Rice, Prudence 1979 *Ceramic and Non-Ceramic Artifacts of Lakes Yaxha and Sacnab, El Peten, Guatemala. Part I. The Ceramics. Cerámica de Cultura Maya* 10:1–36.

——— 1987 *Macanche Island, El Peten: Guatemala: Excavations, Pottery, and Artifacts.* University Press of Florida, Gainesville.

Rosenswig, Robert 2015 A Mosaic of Adaptation: The Archaeological Record for Mesoamerica's Archaic Period. *Journal of Archaeological Research* 23:115–162.

Saturno, William, Franco Rossi, and Boris Beltran 2018 Changing Stages: Royal Legitimacy and the Architectural Development of the Pinturas Complex at San Bartolo, Guatemala. In *Path to Complexity: A View from the Maya Lowlands*, edited by Kathryn Brown and George Bey III, pp. 315–335. University Press of Florida, Gainesville.

Willey, Gordon R., Patrick T. Culbert, and Richard E. W. Adams 1967 Maya Lowland Ceramics: A Report from the 1965 Guatemala City Conference. *American Antiquity* 32:289–315.

Źrałka, Jarosław, Bernard Hermes, and Wiesław Koszkul 2018 The Maya "Protoclassic" from the Perspective of Recent Research at Nakum, Peten, Guatemala. *Journal of Field Archaeology* 43:236–256.

Źrałka, Jarosław, Wiesław Koszkul, Bernard Hermes, Juan Luis Velásquez, Ronald Bishop, and Michał Wasilewski 2021 In Search of the Oldest Ceramics and Architecture: Pre-Mamom Phase at Nakum, Petén, Guatemala, and Its Surroundings. In *Pre-Mamom Pottery Variation and the Preclassic Origins of the Lowland Maya*, edited by Debra Walker. University of Colorado Press, Boulder, in press.

3

MIGRATION AND CONFLICT, OR EMULATION AND INTERACTION?

The Belize Valley during the Middle Preclassic

Nancy Peniche May, Jaime J. Awe, and Claire E. Ebert

Research in the upper Belize River Valley has identified several of the earliest settlements in the Maya lowlands, as well as substantial evidence for Paleoindian and Archaic activity in western Belize (e.g., Stemp et al. 2016). The first permanent settlements in the Belize Valley were founded by the end of the Early Preclassic period, during the period 1200–1000 BC (Figure 3.1; Ebert and Awe 2020; Ebert et al. 2017). The populations that occupied these early villages practiced maize agriculture and engaged in long-distance interactions at an ever-increasing frequency (Chase and Chase 2012). They also built public and domestic architecture and began producing ceramics diagnostic of the Cunil and Kanocha complexes of western Belize (Sullivan and Awe 2013; Sullivan et al. 2018). By the start of the Middle Preclassic period ca. 900 BC, there is evidence for continued sociopolitical and economic changes. This meant an increase in regional and interregional exchange, the specialized production of luxury items, and the introduction of more diverse public architectural construction programs. It is also at this time that an emergent elite class began to manipulate economic resources and ideological concepts to legitimize power and control over their communities, which eventually resulted in the institutionalization of inequality and increasing social complexity in the Belize River Valley sub-region of the Maya lowlands (Awe 2021; Brown 2008; Powis 2009).

The Middle Preclassic period also was characterized by important changes in the local pottery tradition of the Belize Valley, reflecting increasing contact and interaction with other regions of the Maya lowlands. First defined by Gordon Willey and his colleagues (1965) as the Jenney Creek phase at Barton Ramie, Middle Preclassic pottery from that site was initially considered to be affiliated with coeval ceramics from the Mamom horizon in the Peten region of Guatemala (Gifford 1976). To Gifford and Willey, classifying the Jenney Creek ceramic complex as a regional manifestation of the Mamom horizon seemed

DOI: 10.4324/9781351268004-3

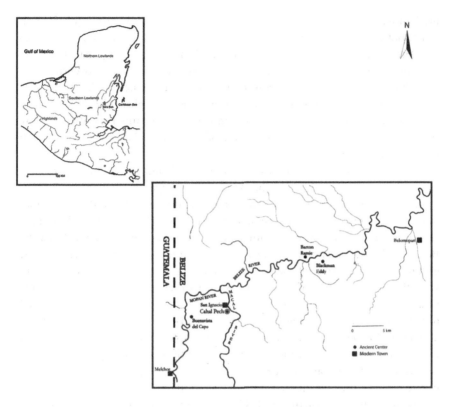

FIGURE 3.1 The Valley of Belize showing the location of sites mentioned in the text.

quite logical and reasonable, particularly given the presence of Mamom types (e.g., Joventud, Chunhinta, Pital, and Muxanal groups) in the Middle Preclassic ceramic assemblage of Barton Ramie. Unfortunately, because few sites had been excavated in the 1950s, and because of their effort to identify regional connections with limited comparative data, both Gifford (1976) and Willey et al. (1965) failed to realize that there were actually greater regional variations in the paste, slip, temper, and forms of early Mamom horizon pottery than there were similarities.

With the advantage of time, and with access to a much larger data base than was available to Gifford in the 1960s, today we recognize that the early ceramic traditions of the Belize Valley differ substantially from those of the Peten. Research at Cahal Pech, Blackman Eddy, and Xunantunich, for example, have confirmed that Middle Preclassic Kanluk pottery, which is the equivalent of Jenney Creek pottery at Barton Ramie, developed directly from the earlier Cunil/ Kanocha ceramic complexes at Cahal Pech and Blackman Eddy (Sullivan and Awe 2013; Sullivan et al. 2018). More recent studies have also confirmed that Middle Preclassic ceramic complexes in the Belize Valley are characterized by the predominance of Mars Orange ware and the Jocote ceramic group (Ebert et al. 2019), both of which are present in the Mamom inventories of Peten and northern Belize but only in limited frequencies (Ball and Taschek 2003). Furthermore, it is now evident that Mamom horizon diagnostic types, such as Joventud Red, Chunhinta Black, and Pital Cream, remain relatively limited in the Belize Valley until almost the end of the early facet of the Kanluk phase (750–650 BC) and that even then the frequency of Mamom ceramics remained significantly low (less than 10%) in the pottery assemblage of the region (Ball and Taschek 2003; Garber et al. 2007:17).

Ball and Taschek (2003; see also Andrews 1990) suggest that in the late facet of the Kanluk phase, potters in the Belize Valley began to produce vessels that represent a mixture of the local Mars Orange tradition with the Peten Mamom tradition, designated as Yesoso Orange Paste pottery. Based on these data, these researchers proposed that two ethnic and linguistic groups likely inhabited the Belize Valley at the end of the early facet of Kanluk. They claim that the first group were descendants of the Cunil/Kanocha and Jenney Creek potters, who were the earliest settlers of the region, and that they had a Mixe-Zoquean cultural and linguistic affiliation. The second were a Maya group that immigrated to the Belize Valley from the Peten or northern Belize after 700 BC. In Ball and Taschek's (2003) model, these two groups of people came into conflict, and this competition stimulated an increase in sociopolitical complexity in the region. According to Brown and Garber (2003:91–92), this hypothesis might be supported by what they interpreted as the desecration of the principal public temple at Blackman Eddy (Structure B-1/4A). They note that shattered vessels were placed inside the structure, then it was set ablaze and intentionally destroyed in a ritual termination event that occurred in ca. 650 BC, contemporaneous with the appearance of "unequivocally Maya pottery" at Blackman Eddy (Brown and Garber 2003:102). Following Ball and Taschek (2003), Brown and Garber suggested that the destruction could have been the result of tension between the original inhabitants of the Belize Valley and the newly arrived Maya group.

Our aim in this chapter is to evaluate these hypothetical migrations and their associated conflicts in the Belize Valley during the transition from the early to late Kanluk phases of the Middle Preclassic period. Our conclusions are that ceramic and architectural evidence from the nearby site of Cahal Pech do not support a model of ethnic conflict. Alternatively, we suggest that the introduction of new ceramic types into the Belize Valley during the Middle Preclassic can be better explained as a result of regional interaction and emulation rather than as a consequence of migrations from the Peten or northern Belize.

Conflict and migration: explaining material culture

War and other forms of conflict play central roles in theories that explain the development of sociopolitical complexity (Carneiro 1981; Webster 2011), in part because they achieve political and ideological objectives (Brown and Garber

2003:91). The study of ancient warfare can be a difficult undertaking, however, because warfare likely included many forms of organized inter-group conflict ranging from two-person contests to large-scale combat. Furthermore, some facets of war may not leave tangible remains in the archaeological record (Tuerenhout 2001:143). In order to overcome their limited data, archaeologists continue to develop interpretations of the role and nature of warfare and other forms of conflict using information derived from various lines of diachronic evidence (Brown and Garber 2003).

Perhaps the most fruitful sources of information for studying warfare in the Maya lowlands have been artistic images and hieroglyphic texts found in various Classic period media including murals, carved monuments, and portable objects. There are abundant iconographic representations of war scenes, weapons, and military clothing, as well as images of warriors and war captives in the archaeological record (Kettunen 2014:97–99; Miller 1986; Tuerenhout 2001). Through the epigraphic study of texts, it also has been possible to reconstruct warfare events that occurred in the southern lowlands during the Early and Late Classic periods and to identify some of the actors involved in these martial activities (Freidel et al. 2003; Helmke and Awe 2016a, 2016b; Kettunen 2014; Martin 2020:196–232; Tuerenhout 2001). Simon Martin (2020), for example, has identified glyphs in the epigraphic record that refer to distinct forms of warfare, which are transcribed as follows: *chuk* (to seize, tie up), *ch'ak* (to damage, attack), *jub* (to take, knock down), *pul* (to burn), and the famous "star war." These artistic and textual sources of information, however, are not available for earlier times, making it challenging to identify military engagements during the Middle Preclassic period. Brown and Garber (2003; see also Webster 2011), however, argue that it is in this period that warfare began, especially in areas with great demographic potential and perhaps due to competition for resources (Carneiro 1981). Given the lack of written records and art depicting warfare, interpretations of these early times must therefore be based on information derived from the archaeological record (Alcover Firpi and Golden 2020).

Archaeologists have used settlement pattern data to infer the practice of ancient Maya warfare as well as to investigate strategies and tactics (Webster 1993:420–422). Thus, warlike behaviors have been inferred based on the presence of defensive features in and around settlements, such as walls, palisades, and moats; the location of sites in strategic defensive places; and the existence of a "no-man's land" between political entities (Sheets 2003:294). Scholars have also reported fortification- and barricade-type walls around part or all of a settlement at Late Preclassic sites in the Petexbatun area (Demarest et al. 1997; Inomata 1997), the Tikal region (Puleston and Callender 1967), the Rio Bec zone (Webster 1976), the northern Maya lowlands (Ringle et al. 2004; Dahlin 2000; Suhler et al. 2004), the Lake Peten Itza region, and possibly the Belize Valley region (Ford 2016), among others (Alcover Firpi and Golden 2020:481–482). Although the presence of walls has been used by some researchers to infer conflicts, there also is considerable evidence that some of these features were constructed for purposes other than defense (Awe and Morton n.d.). Indeed, walls throughout the Maya area are known to have been used to delimit social spaces, to manage water flow, to direct traffic into and out of sites, and to limit access into locations of ritual significance (Awe and Morton n.d.; Dahlin 2000). Moreover, their functions may have changed over time. At Chichen Itza, for example, it has been suggested that the wall surrounding the Great Platform was initially built to define the monumental nucleus as a sacred or elite space, and in later times was modified to become a barricade and served to defend the city epicenter (Hahn and Braswell 2012:277).

The identification of profaning or violent termination rituals also has been used by some researchers as evidence for warfare (Brown and Garber 2003; Freidel et al. 2003). Archaeological indicators of these rituals include the burning and desecration of architecture, the deposition of *sascab* (i.e., decomposed limestone breccia or marl), the breaking of pottery, and the destruction of monuments or burials (Pagliaro et al. 2003). The practice of these ritual activities has been reported throughout the Maya lowlands and was a long-lived tradition that began no later than the Middle Preclassic (Brown and Garber 2003; Freidel and Schele 1989:239; Peniche May 2012:77; Stanton and Ardren 2005:113). It is important to note that these activities were not limited to violent termination events, acts of desecration, and warfare-related destruction. All these features were very much a part of ritual activities conducted during pilgrimages to sacred places and as part of peaceful termination and renewal ceremonies (Awe et al. 2020a, 2020b; Burke et al. 2020; Hoggarth et al. 2020; Palka 2014). We should be careful, therefore, not to readily assume that these practices were associated only with violence and martial activities.

Changes in the production and distribution of goods, including pottery, also have been used as data to identify and interpret ancient warfare (Bey 2003:19). Specifically, "the appearance of new types in the ceramic record of a site or region are considered by some as evidence of conquest or conflict" (Bey 2003:27). Such conflict may be either internal or external (Ball 1993; Foias and Bishop 1997). Suhler and colleagues (1998), for example, have argued that the addition of domestic pottery types from Coba to the ceramic inventory of Yaxuna reflect the conquest of the latter by the former. Those scholars recovered Arena Rojo vessels – a ceramic type abundant at Coba, its coastal ports, and along the Coba-Yaxuna causeway – from four burials at Yaxuna. Significantly, however, only half of the ceramic types used at Coba at that time were recorded at Yaxuna. In spite of that limited distribution, Bey (2003:22) points out that these data argue that pottery served as a crucial element of conquest, subjugation, and identity for Coba. Nonetheless, Foias and Bishop (1997), in their study of ceramic distribution in southern Peten, argue that the elite of the Petexbatun region did not control the production and distribution of domestic ceramics even in times of conflict. Through their careful analysis of domestic pottery, they note that communities continued to use local utilitarian ceramic vessels before, during, and after recorded conflicts. Moreover, although there were changes in pottery during the collapse period, those changes were minor.

Ceramics also have been an important element in modeling population movements in the Maya. Models of migration, invasion, or political influence are often based on the assumption that ceramic styles contain emblematic information that can be used to identify ethnic or political affiliations (Stanton and Ardren 2005:213). This is equivalent to the controversial assumption that "pots are people," which grossly simplifies past sociopolitical interaction without considering other mechanisms that could explain the presence of new types or attributes, including emulation or the exchange of ideas. Moreover, such models do not consider the agency of potters and consumers. Finally, ceramic style and technology may have other unidentified uses for a social group. In the words of Stanton and Ardren (2005:216): "people consume style [and technology] in diverse ways and with varied meanings." Pottery, therefore, does not necessarily denote ethnic affiliation, and the appearance of new styles and technology does not necessarily imply migration or conflict. These can, and often do, reflect interaction, emulation, and the consumption of exotic items by elite members of a society who appropriate these objects in an effort to reflect their affluence and build status. To make an analogy, the presence in a modern home of a set of imported fine china used only for special occasions has nothing to do with invasion, warfare, or conquest.

The use of the concept of ethnicity when considering Middle Preclassic Maya migrations also is problematic. Many reconstructions assume that ethnicity is equivalent to biological groups, cultural characteristics, or linguistic affiliation (cf. Andrews 1990). In reality, this is a false assumption (Barth 1969:10). What, in fact, is an ethnic group? Ethnicity is a mental construct built through a dynamic process of identification and differentiation. Actors themselves proclaim ascription and identification with certain people, and, at the same time, others outside the group accept the identification or attribute of another (Barth 1969:10; Emberling 1997:299). Members of an ethnic group tend to share language, cultural heritage, and symbolic systems because membership often is proclaimed based on a shared real or mythical ancestor (Emberling 1997:302,304). Of utmost importance is the fact that, by definition, ethnic groups exist in relation to state-level. In pre-state societies, the expression of this social identity has not been observed at the ethnographic level (Emberling 1997:304) and, according to Braswell (2016:175), cannot exist. Given the limited nature of our data, the identification of different ethnic groups in pre-state societies, especially those of the Middle Preclassic central Maya lowlands, not only is difficult but also can be fraught with error.

Even when ethnicity existed in the ancient past, the identification of particular groups in the archaeological record can be difficult because the correlation between ethnicity and material culture is complex (Barth 1969; Carr and Neitzel 1995; Emberling 1997:307, 310; Manahan 2008:174). Problems in identification arise in three general areas. First, individual ethnic identity can be situational according to the political or social contexts in which it is expressed. Second, members of different groups may choose to mark their ethnicity using different

sets of material or immaterial cultural traits, and these markers may have varying levels of preservation in the archaeological record (Emberling 1997). Third,
there is not always a straightforward correlation between the boundaries of material culture styles and those of ethnic groups or other social identities (Masson
1997:299). Therefore, the identification of ethnic groups in a territory must be
demonstrated by multiple lines of evidence that include, but are not limited to,
domestic material culture, settlement patterns, ritual practices, burial practices,
iconography, and cuisine (e.g., Brown and Garber 2003; Joyce 2003; Masson
1997).

The identification of ethnic enclaves within a large site is often an easier task
because there generally is a stylistic redundancy in various media to mark differences between groups (Santley et al. 1987). For example, the locally produced
domestic ceramic inventory of two "neighborhoods" in Matacapan, Veracruz,
exhibited similarities to that of Teotihuacan. Additionally, public architecture
and burial practices at the two Matacapan sites were similar to those of Teotihuacan. This evidence allowed Santley to propose that the two neighborhoods of
Matacapan were enclaves of Teotihuacano merchants. Nevertheless, the appearance in the archaeological record of artifacts that differ in style from those that
predominate in a territory should not be interpreted directly as the presence
of a foreign ethnic group. The proposed Putun invasion of the Pasion Basin,
for example, was discredited along these very lines by Willey (1990). Changes
in material culture also can be due to local processes. For example, during
the Terminal Classic to Postclassic transition, various sites in northern Belize
witnessed transformations in architecture and pottery and began to resemble
northern Yucatan sites in those expressions of material culture. These changes
were not caused by a migration to the southeast. Instead, they were the result of
emulation. Although material culture assumed new appearances, it continued
to function in ways that reproduced past local behavior (Masson 1997:294, 299).

To reiterate, the use of ceramics or any other single class of archaeological data
as conclusive evidence of ancient warfare and migration is at best problematic.
If archaeologists are to correctly identify migration and conflict, it is imperative
that we employ several lines of evidence in a conjunctive approach (Ambrosino
et al. 2003; Freidel et al. 2003). If material culture is to be considered as an ethnic
marker, in addition to providing evidence of conflict between ethnic groups, it
is necessary to first identify the social use and meanings ascribed to each artifact
class and to independently determine how variations in style were employed in
distinct social situations (Emberling 1997:319–320). This is important because
stylistic variation in artifact assemblages may sometimes only reflect social identity and status rather than ethnicity. Moreover, stylistic variation may be correlated with transformations in community structure due to regional political or
economic processes and can result from the emulation of foreign practices. At
lowland Maya sites, for example, the artifacts found in elite tombs often differ
considerably from those found in the graves of commoners. These differences are
primarily reflections of status and not of ethnicity. With these caveats in mind,

we now turn to the analysis of the ceramics and architecture of Cahal Pech in the Belize Valley to evaluate hypotheses of migration and conflict during the Middle Preclassic period.

Cahal Pech

Located on the outskirts of the modern town of San Ignacio, Cahal Pech is a medium-size Maya city situated 270 m above sea level and 2 km from the confluence of the Mopan and Macal tributaries of the Belize River (Figure 3.2).[1] This strategic hilltop location gave the occupants of the epicenter of Cahal Pech access to fertile alluvial lands and to important trade routes that linked the Caribbean coast with the large cities of the central Maya lowlands. The first permanent occupation of Cahal Pech began sometime between 1200 and 1000 BC with the establishment of a small settlement at the summit of the hill in the area of what is now Plaza B. The site was then continuously occupied for approximately

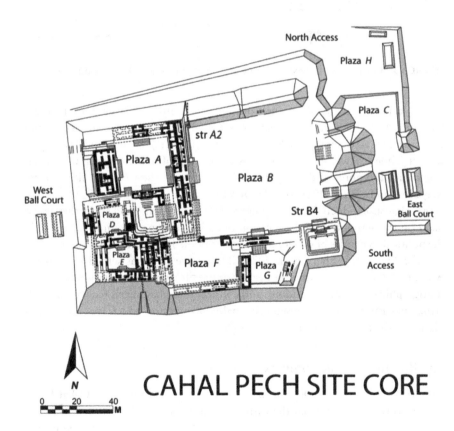

CAHAL PECH SITE CORE

FIGURE 3.2 Cahal Pech site core.

Source: Courtesy of the BVAR project.

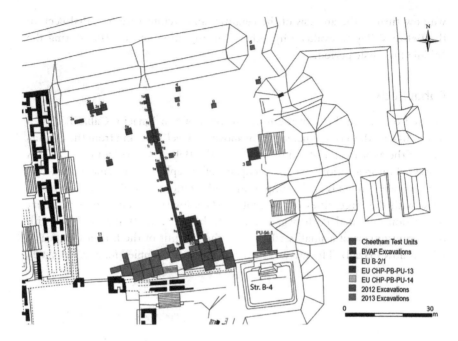

Cheetham Test Units
BVAP Excavations
EU B-2/1
EU CHP-PB-PU-13
EU CHP-PB-PU-14
2012 Excavations
2013 Excavations

0   30
m

Str. B-4

PU-04-1

N

FIGURE 3.3 Location of the excavation units opened in Plaza B by various projects.

2,000 years and finally abandoned during the Terminal Classic period ca. AD 850/900. Archaeological investigations at Cahal Pech, under the auspices of the Belize Valley Archaeological Reconnaissance (BVAR) Project and the direction of Jaime J. Awe, began in 1988 with the aim of understanding the social, economic, and political development of one of the earliest communities in the Maya lowlands. From 2011 to 2013, and then again from 2016 to 2018, BVAR archaeologists conducted extensive horizontal excavations in Plaza B, the largest plaza on the acropolis and the location of earliest occupation, in order to study the political dynamics of society during the Middle Preclassic period (Figure 3.3; Peniche May 2016; Ebert et al. 2021). These investigations served to confirm Awe's (1992) previous settlement history of the site, exposed a long and complex stratigraphic sequence of buildings and construction phases, and recovered a rich artifactual assemblage composed principally of ceramics, which we analyze and discuss in the following sections of this chapter.

The Kanluk ceramic complex

The Middle Preclassic (900–600 BC) Kanluk ceramic complex at Cahal Pech, which evolved directly from the earlier Cunil complex (1200/1100–900 BC), is relatively coeval and typologically similar to the Jenney Creek complex as defined for Barton Ramie by James Gifford (1976; also see Willey et al. 1965:325). In his seminal Barton Ramie ceramic report, Gifford (1976) argued that Jenney Creek pottery exhibits close relationships with ceramic types recovered from Middle Preclassic contexts at Uaxactun. At the same time, Gifford also recognized differences in the two ceramic assemblages. For example, he noted that the Jocote Orange-brown ceramic type, which characterizes utilitarian vessels, is unique to the Belize Valley Jenney Creek complex. On the other hand, while Sayab Daub-striated and Palma Daub represent only minor elements in the Barton Ramie assemblage, they dominate the Uaxactun assemblage. Gifford argued that these differences were technological in nature and that they likely reflected differences in regional traditions. Gifford (in Willey et al. 1965:327) further noted that Sayab Daub-striated and Palma Daub types were recovered in contexts that placed them during the latter part of the Jenney Creek phase, and therefore he proposed dividing the Jenney Creek complex into two facets. His early facet of Jenney Creek represents the pre-Mamom Xe sphere of Uaxactun, and the late facet of Jenney Creek reflects a local manifestation of the Mamom ceramic complex. Because Mamom-related pottery had been reported across much of the Maya lowland territory after 600 BC, most archaeologists at the time did not hesitate to accept Gifford's model.

Following a considerable increase in archaeological projects across the central Maya lowlands in recent decades, Gifford's conclusion that the Jenney Creek ceramic complex was affiliated with the Xe and Mamom traditions has been called into question and largely refuted. Archaeological research at the Belize Valley sites of Cahal Pech and Blackman Eddy, for example, now recognizes that ceramics of the early-facet Jenney Creek complex do not reflect a close Xe affiliation. Instead, they were derived from local Belize Valley Cunil and Kanocha pottery, which are roughly contemporaneous, and with other so-called "pre-Mamom" potteries of the Maya lowlands (Sullivan and Awe 2013; Sullivan et al. 2018). Second, Mamom ceramic types (including Joventud Red, Chunhinta Black, and Pital Cream) that were used by Gifford as late-facet markers of the Jenney Creek ceramic complex are not at all abundant in the Belize Valley (Ball and Taschek 2003:188,191). This limited distribution led Ball and Taschek (2003:196) to comment that while Mamom ceramic types in Belize Valley assemblages are "distinctive and culturally important," they are "nonetheless [a] secondary assemblage" that represents the local circulation of exotic pottery. The present consensus is that both early- and late-facet Jenney Creek ceramics are characterized by locally produced pottery of the Jocote domestic group and by the more sophisticated Mars Orange serving vessels. Ceramics recovered from our Plaza B excavations in the Cahal Pech acropolis, as well as from other site core contexts, have corroborated the predominance of the Jocote and Mars Orange pottery in the Middle Preclassic Kanluk ceramic complex, and we have documented much smaller quantities of Mamom types (Table 3.1).

The early facet of the Kanluk ceramic complex at Cahal Pech has been dated to 900–700 BC based on ceramic crossties and seven radiocarbon dates from contexts in the epicenter (Ebert et al. 2017:Table 3.2). The sample of early-facet Kanluk ceramics from Plaza B discussed here was excavated by Peniche May

TABLE 3.1 Wares, groups, types, and varieties of the early facet of the Kanluk ceramic complex observed in Middle Preclassic contexts beneath Plaza B of Cahal Pech

Ware	Group	Type-variety	N	%
Belize Valley	Uck	Uck Red: Uck	82	4.62
Dull	Cocoyol	Cocoyol Cream: Cocoyol	79	4.45
		Unnamed Red-on buff: Unspecified	2	0.11
	No identified	No identified	19	1.07
		Uck Red – Savana Orange	2	0.11
		Sikiya – Jocote	29	1.63
Mars Orange	Savana	Savana Orange: Rejolla	443	25
		Savana Orange: Savana	56	3.15
		Savana Orange: Unspecified C-1	8	0.45
		Savana Orange: Unspecified C-2	2	0.11
		Reforma Incised: Mucnal	17	0.96
		Reforma Incised: Reforma	4	0.22
		Sibun Punctated-Incised: Sibun	2	0.11
	Unnamed Black	Unnamed Black: Unspecified A	2	0.11
Undesignated	Unnamed	Unnamed Brown-black: Unspecified	34	1.92
	Brown-black	Unnamed Brown-black Incised: Unspecified	6	0.34
Uaxactun	Jocote	Jocote Orange-brown: Jocote	932	52.53
Unslipped		Chacchinic Red-on-orange-brown	34	1.92
	Sayab	Sayab Daub	1	0.06
Flores Waxy	Joventud	Sampoperro Red	2	0.11
	Chunhinta	Chunhinta Black	1	0.06
	Not identified	Not identified	17	0.96
		Total	1774	100

TABLE 3.2 Wares, groups, types, and varieties of the late facet of the Kanluk ceramic complex observed in Middle Preclassic contexts beneath Plaza B of Cahal Pech

Ware	Group	Type-variety	N	%
Belize Valley	Cocoyol	Cocoyol Cream: Cocoyol	354	1.3
Dull		Unnamed Red-on-cream: Unspecified	2	0.01
	Uck	Uck Red: Uck	297	1.11
		Baki Red Incised: Baki	4	0.02
		Kitam Incised: Kitam	6	0.02
	Chi	Chi Black: Chi	8	0.03
	Huetche	Huetche White	9	0.03
Belize Valley	Sikiya	Sikiya: Sikiya	64	0.24
Unslipped				
	No identified	Uck-Savana	37	0.14
		Sikiya-Jocote	7	0.03
		Kitam Incised – Unnamed Brown-black Incised	1	0
		No identified	56	0.21

Ware	Group	Type-variety	N	%
Mars Orange	Savana	Savana Orange: Rejolla	7848	29.29
		Savana Orange: Savana	998	3.72
		Savana Orange: Unspecified C-1	196	0.73
		Savana Orange: Unspecified C-2	201	0.75
		Savana Orange: Unspecified (Red slip)	6	0.02
		Reforma Incised: Reforma	133	0.5
		Reforma Incised: Mucnal	852	3.18
		Reforma Incised: Unspecified C-1 & C-2	33	0.12
		Sibun Punctated-Incised: Sibun	30	0.11
	Unnamed Black	Unnamed Black: Unspecified A & B	51	0.19
		Unnamed Black Incised: Unspecified B	21	0.08
	Unnamed Bichrome	Unnamed Bichrome: Unspecified B	13	0.05
		Unnamed Red-on-orange: Unspecified	7	0.03
		Unnamed Red-on-cream: Unspecified	1	0
		Unnamed Bichrome Incised: Unspecified	4	0.02
		Unnamed Bichrome Punctated-Incised: Unspecified	1	0
Undesignated	Unnamed Brown-black	Unnamed Brown-black: Unspecified	132	0.49
		Unnamed Brown-black Incised: Unspecified	29	0.10
Uaxactun Unslipped	Jocote	Jocote Orange-brown: Jocote	13974	52.14
		Chacchinic Red-on-orange-brown	719	2.68
		Palma Daub	2	0.01
	Sayab	Sayab Daub	14	0.05
Flores Waxy	Joventud	Joventud Red	259	1
		Pinola Creek Incised	4	0.02
		Sampoperro Red	104	0.39
		Black Rock Red	14	0.05
	Chunhinta	Chunhinta Black	115	0.43
		Deprecio Incised	7	0.03
	Pital	Pital Cream	15	0.05
Fort George Orange	Chicago	Chicago Orange	6	0.02
Rio Nuevo Glossy	Consejo	Consejo Red	16	0.06
	Quamina	Tower Hill Red-on-cream	3	0.01
	Not identified	Not identified	145	0.54
	Total		26798	100

(2016) and consists of 1,774 sherds (Table 3.1). The assemblage is characterized by the predominance of the Savana Orange: Rejolla Variety (24.97%) and by Jocote Orange-brown: Jocote Variety (52.53%). The sheer abundance and preponderance of these ceramic types and varieties in early-facet Kanluk contexts strongly suggests that they represent locally produced pottery (Figures 3.4 and 3.5; see also Ebert et al. 2019).

Another minor but significant component of the early Kanluk assemblage is Cunil pottery, represented by the types Uck Red: Uck Variety (4.62%), Cocoyol Cream: Cocoyol Variety (4.45%), and Unnamed Red-on-buff: Unspecified Variety (0.11%). A similar phenomenon was observed in other excavations in Structure B-4 and Plaza B (Ebert et al. 2021; Lauren Sullivan personal communication 2015). The presence of some Cunil pottery in the early-facet collection likely demonstrates the continuation of cultural practices from earlier times. A link is also noted between Cunil ash-tempered and early-facet Kanluk pottery from Cahal Pech.

Other ceramic types present in the early facet sample include Unnamed Brown-black: Unspecified Variety (1.92%), Unnamed Brown-black Incised: Unspecified Variety (0.34%), Chacchinic Red-on-orange-brown (1.92%), and Savana Orange: Savana C-1 (0.45%) and C-2 (0.11%) varieties. These last were quite rare. The Reforma Incised type in its Mucnal (0.96%) and Reforma (0.22%) varieties appeared towards the end of the early facet.

Contrary to Ball and Taschek's (2003) previous argument, Mamom ceramics represented by the Joventud and Sayab groups also appeared late in the early Kanluk contexts, but their presence is extremely rare, constituting no more than four sherds (0.22%) in our sample (Peniche May 2016). Garber and Awe (2008)

FIGURE 3.4 Savana Ceramic Group, early facet of the Kanluk phase.

FIGURE 3.5 Jocote Ceramic Group.

also previously reported Mamom ceramics in a possible early Kanluk context north of Plaza B, but more recent dating of the human remains associated with this pottery now indicates that the context is later than previously assumed and likely dates to the Late Preclassic period.

The late facet of the Kanluk ceramic complex has been dated to 700–350 BC based on ceramic crossties and four radiocarbon assays (Ebert et al. 2017:Table 3.2). We analyzed 26,798 sherds from late-facet Kanluk contexts in Plaza B (Peniche May 2016; Table 3.2). As with the early-facet assemblage, the types Savana Orange: Rejolla Variety (29.29%) and Jocote Orange-brown: Jocote Variety (52.14%) predominate (Figures 3.5 and 3.6). The ceramic types Unnamed Brown-black: Unspecified Variety (0.49%), Unnamed Brown-black Incised: Unspecified Variety (0.10%), and Chacchinic Red-on-orange-brown (2.68%) also were present in this facet, as were sherds assigned to Savana Orange: Unspecified Variety C-1 (0.73%) and Unspecified Variety C-2 (0.75%), as well as Reforma Incised: Mucnal (3.18%) and Reforma (0.50%) varieties.

Nonetheless, all these types and varieties are either minor or quite rare in the inventory. The ceramic types Chacchinic Red-on-orange-brown, Savana Orange: Savana Variety, and Reforma Incised: Mucnal Variety increased in frequency during the late facet. For example, at the beginning of the facet, the type Reforma Incised: Mucnal Variety represented just 2.6% of the collection, but at the end of the Kanluk phase it increased to 5.0%.

New types and varieties appeared that serve as markers of late-facet Kanluk, although they tend to be quite rare. These new types include Unnamed Black: Unspecified Variety (0.19%), Unnamed Black Incised: Unspecified

FIGURE 3.6 Savana Ceramic Group, late facet of the Kanluk phase.

Variety (0.08%), Unnamed Dichrome: Unspecified Variety (0.05%), Unnamed Dichrome Incised: Unspecified Variety (0.02%), Sibun Punctated-Incised: Sibun Variety (0.11%), Reforma Incised: C-1 and C-2 varieties (0.04% and 0.08%), and Savana Orange: Unspecified Red-slip Variety (0.02%). The last seems to be an imitation of the Joventud Red type of the Mamom sphere. Along with new types and forms, new decorative techniques were introduced during the late Kanluk complex to imitate non-local pottery. The decorative chamfering technique was perhaps introduced to create local copies of the Desvario Chamfered vessels of the Mamom sphere. Human effigy bottles of the Savana Orange type share modes with the Unnamed Red Modeled types of the Joventud group from Colha, and chocolate pots with lip-to-lip handles also have parallels with the pots from northern Belize.

Mamom ceramics increased in importance in late-facet Kanluk. At its inception, Mamom represented just 1% of the Kanluk ceramic inventory. By the end of the late facet of the Kanluk phase, the ceramic types Joventud Red, Sampoperro Red, Chunhinta Black, Pital Cream, and Sayab Daub-striated comprised 4% of the inventory. Ceramics from northern Belize also appear at the end of the Kanluk phase, but their presence is rare, and they represent less than 1% of the collection. Some Cunil materials persist but in very low frequency.

In our analysis of Kanluk pottery, we were able to identify the presence of three ceramic production, use, and distribution systems that roughly coincide with those proposed by Ball and Taschek (2003:196). The most common is the Jocote system, which includes the Jocote Orange-brown and Chacchinic Red-on-orange-brown ceramic types. Vessels in this system were locally produced for use in domestic contexts. The Jocote system remained almost unchanged throughout the Kanluk phase. The second system is quite heterogeneous. It includes slipped and polished-unslipped serving vessels with orange, reddish orange, red, and black surfaces. The Savana Orange ceramic type was the main element of this system, which was subject to more experimentation and innovation than the Jocote system. For example, the surfaces of vessels in this second system were generally undecorated during the early facet of Kanluk, but various decorative techniques appeared in the late facet. Some of these techniques are similar to those used to treat the surfaces of Mamom pottery. During the late facet, new vessel forms and ceramic types also appeared in this second system. Despite these innovations, the clays used to produce this second system remained constant and local throughout the Kanluk phase. Finally, the third ceramic system includes imported vessels produced elsewhere. Among them are Flores Waxy, Fort George Orange, New River Lustrous, and Uaxactun Unslipped ware.

Architecture

The Kanluk phase was a time of considerable architectural development at Cahal Pech. Structures dating to this period share forms and architectural styles with contemporary buildings in other regions of the Maya lowlands. Because so many Middle Preclassic structures have been excavated at and around Cahal Pech, we concentrate here on the Kanluk phase buildings that we have recorded in the acropolis.

During the early facet of the Kanluk phase, occupation focused primarily on four areas located to the north, northwest, south, and southeast of Plaza B. In the northwest, a domestic building and its stucco courtyard that was constructed during Cunil times continued to be in use. In the northern section, a cobble platform was built that covered earlier Cunil architecture, and, slightly to the east, the surface of a courtyard delimited by low foundations was erected. These architectural features probably constituted a residence. Both buildings were modified at least once during the Kanluk phase, but their forms, styles, and functions repeated those of earlier times (Horn et al. 2017:81–83, Figure 3.5). Subsequently, a round platform was built on the stucco surface of the northwest section using large rectangular limestone blocks (Horn 2015:263). This structure and other early buildings and floors were destroyed during the transition between the early and late facets of the Kanluk phase (ca. 650 BC) in order to build a large, square basal platform. This platform spanned approximately 307 m^2 and supported at least two structures that probably functioned as residences. Although one corner of the platform was dismantled to build another structure and a hole was excavated to deposit household waste, there was no other evidence that the platform was destroyed (Horn et al. 2017:83–84, Figure 3.6; see Horn 2015:213–214 for a discussion of the dating of this structure). This basal platform continued to be used during the late facet of the Kanluk phase.

The most significant construction sequence of the Kanluk phase was found in the southeast section, at the locus of Structure B-4 (Figure 3.7; Awe 1992:134–137; Ebert et al. 2017; Ishihara-Brito and Awe 2013:125–127). At the beginning of the Kanluk phase, after 950 BC, this structure consisted of a basal platform supporting a rectilinear platform 70 cm high. Well-faced limestone blocks covered with stucco were used for its construction. We found burned clay with the imprints of plant stalks, indicating that the basal platform supported superstructures made of wattle-and-daub walls and palm-leaf roofs. In the next construction phase, the basal platform was covered by a larger platform that reached 1.1 m in height. In 895–820 BC, the shape of the building was altered. At this time, the basal platform stood 1.5 m high, and its top was reached by a staircase located on its north side. On the east and west sides of the summit, two low foundations were built. One of them has a circular plan. This shape would be imitated in subsequent phases built during the late facet of Kanluk, although the dimensions would increase.

The southern section, on the other hand, had a completely different development pattern from the northern section (Figure 3.8). At the beginning of the Kanluk phase, two surfaces were constructed using marl. The west floor was

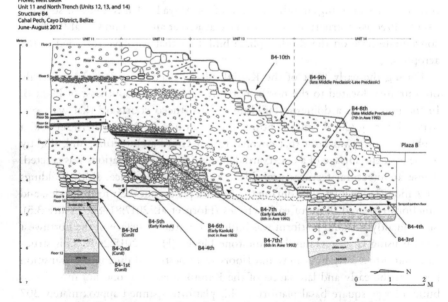

FIGURE 3.7 Profile of Structure B-4 showing its architectural sequence.

Source: After Ishihara-Brito and Awe 2013:119.

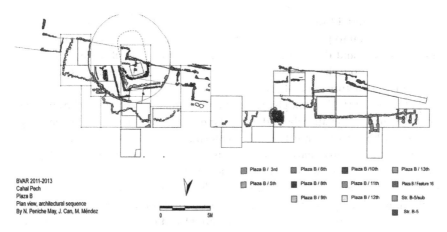

BVAR 2011-2013
Cahal Pech
Plaza B
Plan view, architectural sequence
By N. Peniche May, J. Can, M. Méndez

Plaza B / 3rd	Plaza B / 6th	Plaza B /10th	Plaza B / 13th
Plaza B / 5th	Plaza B / 8th	Plaza B / 11th	Plaza B / Feature 16
Plaza B	Plaza B / 9th	Plaza B / 12th	Str. B-5/sub
			Str. B-5

0   5M

FIGURE 3.8 Construction sequence exposed in the southern section of Plaza B.

not associated with any features, and the eastern surface supported a low foundation (Horn et al. 2017:83). To the east, two other alignments were identified
that could be the remains of residences that delimited the floor to the north
and east (Plaza B/5th; Peniche May 2016:403). Both surfaces were covered by
a rectangular platform that measured at least 52 m^2 in area. This platform was
built using rectangular limestone blocks covered with white marl (Horn et al.
2017:83, Figure 3.5). Four meters to the southeast, a circular structure was built.
This was delimited by small slabs arranged vertically (Plaza B/6th; Peniche May
2016:159). Because of their proximity to each other, these structures likely were
part of the same architectural group. During the transition between early and
late Kanluk, the rectangular structure was partially dismantled and replaced by
an apsidal structure that covered an area of 54 m^2 and whose surface was stuccoed
(Horn 2015:644; Horn et al. 2017:83, Figure 3.6). To the southeast, the circular
structure of vertical slabs was replaced by a low apsidal foundation (Plaza B/8th).

Construction activity continued during the late facet of Kanluk in the southern section, although there were changes in architectural style and the function
of the space. It is unknown if the great apsidal platform continued in use during this facet. The apsidal platform located slightly to the southeast was successively replaced by two rectangular platforms, the second of which features a
narrow terrace (Plaza B/9th and Plaza B/10th). During the next architectural
phase (Plaza B/11th), the area was reorganized. The rectangular structure was
covered by a round platform built with large well-worked blocks coated with a
thick layer of stucco. Similar structures have been interpreted as public spaces
in which rituals were carried out to venerate the ancestors (Aimers et al. 2000;
Hendon 2000). We found evidence for such rituals at this structure in the form
of associated figurine fragments. This specialized function also is suggested by
two caches (an inverted Uck Red and half a Savana Orange plate), most likely
offered during a dedication ritual, that were deposited under the base of this

construction. Just 14 m to the west, a rectangular platform was built with a different orientation to previous structures: 15° west instead of 8° west of magnetic north. Its floor and that of the associated patio were made of tamped earth. A small construction adjoined its northwest corner and may have served as a terrace or auxiliary structure. A small oval feature was built 3 m to the east.

At the end of the Kanluk phase, the circular structure was covered by a large platform made of small slabs and a courtyard that was stuccoed in its entirety (Plaza B/12th). To the north of the platform, we found a large and possibly engraved stone. It may have functioned as an altar or stela. Unfortunately, the stone is fragmented so we are unable to identify its design. The rectangular platform and oval feature were used until they both were covered by an expansion of the interlocking patio (Plaza B/12th-2). As part of this construction stage, the oval feature was dismantled, two *manos* were placed on its exterior, and it was covered by a layer of small stones. This suggests that it was the subject of reverential termination (Pagliaro et al. 2003), adding further reason to interpret it as a specialized structure. At some point during the transition between the two facets of the Kanluk phase, or within the late facet, a structure was built in the area that divided the north and south groups. This structure consisted of a plaster surface adjoining an ovoid feature. Censers were found associated with this structure, suggesting that it may have functioned as ceremonial space (Horn et al. 2017:83).

By late Kanluk times the first E-Group complex at Cahal Pech was built in Group B. Possibly constructed as early as ca. 700 BC (Ebert et al. 2021), this massive building followed a Uaxactun-style E-Group building plan, indicating significant ideological connections beyond trade and exchange between Peten and the Belize Valley. The E-Group complex consisted of a typical eastern platform that is located below the later construction phases of Structures B1, B2, and B3, and by an accompanying western structure that is located below Plaza B, just east of the eastern base of Structure A2. Designated as Structure B8, the western structure represents the largest, most elaborate Middle Preclassic construction yet documented at the site. At its base it measures 20 m north-to-south and 12.5 m east-to-west. Although the eastern façade of the building is poorly preserved, a centrally located stairway on the western side of the building is present. We estimate that the platform may have been up to 3 m in height, although the presence of megalithic blocks on top of intact architecture suggests that the upper half of the structure was dismantled and removed during Late Preclassic modifications and expansion to Plaza B.

Other areas of the acropolis also witnessed the construction of monumental architecture during the late facet of the Kanluk phase. In Plaza C, in an area now covered by the Eastern Ballcourt, a round structure 5 m in diameter was built. In Plaza G, a low structure 15 cm high was erected (Audet 2001). In Plaza F, a 50-cm-high platform was built directly on the bedrock using river stones and limestone blocks. Its walls were covered with stucco. The dimensions of the structure increased in the next construction phase, reaching 85 cm in height (Audet 2001). Like the site core, settlements in the Cahal Pech periphery witnessed increased construction during late-facet Kanluk times. This architectural activity also included the construction of both domestic and special function structures.

Discussion

According to proponents of the migration and conflict model, the Belize Valley was inhabited by two ethnic/linguistic groups during the Middle Preclassic period. Proponents of this model further suggest that although both groups may have spoken Mayan languages, it is more likely that the original inhabitants were of Mixe-Zoquean affiliation who migrated from the highlands of El Salvador or western Honduras to the central lowlands (Andrews 1990; Ball and Taschek 2003; Gifford 1970). This interpretation is based on the stylistic attributes of Jocote Orange-brown pottery, which suggest a relationship with the unslipped vessels of the Pasion River of southern Peten, western Honduras, the southeastern Maya highlands, and the Pacific coast of Chiapas and Guatemala (Andrews 1990; Demarest 1989; Gifford 1970; Lowe 1977). Proponents of the migration/conflict model suggest that around 700 BC, a group with a Mayan linguistic affiliation, possibly from northern Belize, migrated to the Belize Valley (Ball and Taschek 2003). They further propose that this population movement coincided with the introduction of Mamom ceramics and with changes to the local ceramic traditions. They posit, for example, that calcareous white ceramics with little polish appeared at this time; that plates and bowls with very everted edges were introduced; and that red, black, cream, dichromic, waxy-slipped, and highly lustrous serving vessels began to proliferate. This new pottery exhibited modes considered Maya "in the currently accepted conventional wisdom of Mesoamerican archeology" (Ball and Taschek 2003:205). The dishes with a red slip, called Yesoso Orange Paste, are quantitatively the most important and include locally produced pots of the Joventud and Sierra groups. Such vessels are characterized by a highly polished, bright red, double-slipped surface. Their surfaces are decorated with shallow pre-slip incisions that exhibit geometric patterns. The paste of this pottery is dense, compact to medium or coarse in texture, and pale orange to light orange-red in color, and it includes volcanic tuff, carbonates, or quartz as temper. Forms include shallow plates, bowls, and jugs with necks. Of particular significance to our present study, however, is that although the shapes and decorations of Belize Valley pottery share some similarities with those of the Joventud and Sierra groups, the clay and production technology of this pottery are actually quite similar to that of the local Mars Orange ware.

Migration/conflict proponents further suggest that interaction between the local and immigrant groups was not entirely peaceful. Ball and Taschek (2003) infer the presence of conflict, which caused an increase in the sociopolitical complexity of the region and resulted in the appearance of a complex chiefdom ca. 500–200 BC. According to Brown and Garber (2003), this conflict can be seen at Blackman Eddy, where the main structure of the settlement was desecrated in a termination ritual.

Our perspective, based on the chemical analysis of pottery, on our study of other artifactual remains, and on the development of architecture at Cahal Pech, supports certain aspects of this scenario but contradicts other important ones. We agree, for example, that there were three systems of ceramic production, use, and distribution: (1) the domestic Jocote system; (2) the heterogeneous system of slipped and unslipped but polished vessels that were produced locally; and (3) the limited exotic ware system that included vessels from the Mamom Lopez ceramic complex of northern Belize. These Mamom vessels were likely imports.

It also is important to note that Ball and Taschek (2003) view Yesoso Orange Paste ware as a complement to Mars Orange that later replaced it. At Cahal Pech, we identified sherds with orange-red, compact paste lacking ash temper and surfaces that are moderately polished but not waxy. The slip, when present, has a reddish-orange hue. Despite the fact that these vessels exhibit some forms and some decoration techniques similar to the Joventud group, we classify these sherds as Savana Orange: Rejolla Variety and Rejolla Incised: Mucnal Variety because of their surface treatment. Furthermore, our study did not find any materials in our Cahal Pech excavations that conform to Yesoso Orange Paste as defined by Ball and Taschek (2003:208). Besides the stylistic and technological differences between Mamom and Kanluk pottery, our more recent chemical analysis of Cahal Pech ceramics provides even more convincing evidence against the migration/conflict hypothesis. In their recent instrumental neutron activation analysis study of Preclassic pottery from Cahal Pech, Ebert and colleagues (2019:1278) identified a clear "compositional correlation between late Middle Preclassic Jocote vessels and earlier Cunil utilitarian [Sikiya] wares," strongly suggesting continuity in ceramic production, and "that both types were produced locally for domestic consumption." Furthermore, compositional overlap was noted between decorated Cunil types (Uck Red, Cocoyol Cream) and the Savana Orange pastes that dominate the Kanluk assemblage. Based on its unique composition compared to previously analyzed ceramics from throughout Mesoamerica (MURR Archaeometry Laboratory Database n.d.), decorated Cunil pottery also was found to have been produced and distributed locally in the Belize Valley, suggesting the same for Savana vessels. High frequencies of Savana Orange ceramics (approximately 18–50%) found at sites across the Belize Valley additionally indicate local manufacture (e.g., Gifford 1976:73–77; Awe 1992:236–240; Ball and Taschek 2003:195; Kosakowsky 2012:62), an observation that is also supported by Callaghan and colleagues (2017, 2018:824) who note a decreasing frequency in the distribution of Mars Orange ware as one moves westward from the Belize Valley into the central Peten.

The migration model assumes that ceramic attributes indicate identity, which in turn can be equated to ethnicity and language group. Proponents of this model, therefore, suggest that the presence of Jocote Orange-brown ceramics also implies the presence of Mixe-Zoquean populations in the Belize Valley, while the introduction of Mamom pottery implies the immigration of Mayan speakers from northern Belize or the Peten, and Yesoso Orange Paste indicates an accommodation to local resources by the ancestors of the Classic Maya of the Belize Valley. According to this model, populations did not merge or amalgamate with each other but instead lived in an environment of competition and conflict. Geochemical analyses indicate that through time ceramic types reflect stylistic change but not necessarily technological change. Instead of replacement, continuity is noted from Cunil to the later Middle Preclassic ceramic inventory. The migration hypothesis also does not explain why newly arrived Maya would decide not to produce their domestic pottery using local clays, or why they continued to produce red-slipped pottery of the Joventud group in limited frequency and only in plate and bowl forms. Also significant is that the hypothesis does not explain why locally produced black-slipped vessels are rare in the late Kanluk inventory and why red-slipped vessels are practically non-existent.

Another alternative proposal is that the original inhabitants of the region spoke a Mayan language rather than Mixe-Zoquean (Ball and Taschek 2003:204). Ball and Tasheck further consider it possible that the Mamom-shaped and -decorated vessels produced in the Belize Valley were imitations of pottery used by people from the Peten or northern Belize and that these imitations were produced for local consumption (Ball and Taschek 2003:208). We are more inclined to support this alternative line of thought. At the same time, we strongly suggest that ceramic attributes alone are insufficient to identify the presence of Mixe-Zoquean speakers as the first settlers of the Belize Valley, let alone to posit the immigration of Mayan groups during the Kanluk phase. Although we might accept the possibility that the Belize Valley was inhabited in the Kanluk phase by two or more groups with distinct identities expressed in their material culture, we stress that it is impossible to establish that they spoke distinct languages on the basis of pottery alone. In fact, the changes that we observe in the ceramics of the Kanluk phase blur more into a continuum than represent distinct and clearly different manifestations of material culture and hence, cultural practice. Although the domestic Jocote system remained practically unchanged throughout the Kanluk phase, the heterogeneous system that included slipped vessels and polished surfaces underwent significant transformation, most likely due to increasing interaction with groups from other regions of the Maya lowlands. Such interaction is evidenced not only by the import of Mamom slipped vessels, but also by the presence of lithic and shell materials from the highlands of Guatemala and the Caribbean, but it should be noted that many of these items are also present in earlier Cunil contexts. Thus, everyday pottery suggests the continuation of local populations, while the emulation and limited importation of Mamom vessels may simply have been used as status markers by emerging elites in the Belize Valley or to demonstrate their relationships with people beyond their territory.

Public and private architecture also underwent transformations throughout the Kanluk phase, but these did not coincide with the introduction of Mamom ceramics to the Belize Valley. At Cahal Pech, new architectural styles emerged around 950 BC (Ebert et al. 2017). Rectangular structures appeared first in public and later in domestic architecture. There also was an increase in the use of stucco to decorate surfaces, but this was almost exclusively used for private buildings during the Kanluk phase. The late facet saw further changes to both form and function of the built environment, but for the most part these entailed manipulating the existing attributes of architecture rather than introducing new styles. One new architectural form that emerged near the end of the Kanluk phase was the round structure. This was a public space associated with elite domestic groups (Hendon 2000). We consider that the appearance of this architectural style played an important role in the development of the political complexity of Cahal Pech because it allowed the manipulation of behaviors and symbolic systems on an elevated, open, and public stage (Peniche May 2016). These buildings ultimately may have been replaced by the E-Group complex and other larger temple structures, so that by the Late Preclassic period, communally oriented ritual space was supplanted by an elite shrine (the Eastern Triadic Assemblage) and buildings demarcating private elite space.

Burial traditions and strontium isotope analysis, which provide important insights into the identities of individuals and communities, are additional lines of evidence that can help us evaluate the migration/conflict model hypothesized for the Middle Preclassic Belize Valley. In the case of burial traditions, for example, body orientation generally conforms to local and regional patterns (Welsh 1988:55). In the Belize Valley the typical burial orientation from Preclassic to Terminal Classic times is almost always prone, extended, and oriented north to south, with heads to the south (Chapter 9). Only during Terminal Classic and Postclassic times do we see significant divergence from this established pattern.

Freiwald and colleagues (2014:111) observed that strontium, carbon, and oxygen isotope analysis of 148 individuals buried at 15 Belize Valley sites demonstrates that origin and burial treatment are related: 89% of those with strontium isotope values local to the region were buried with their heads oriented to the south, and mostly in a prone position (Chapter 9). This contrasts with the primarily northern or eastern orientation and supine or flexed body position described at sites elsewhere in the Maya lowlands. In fact, the orientation of individuals buried in northern Belize and Peten displays neither the north-south pattern nor the head-to-the-south orientation evident at the Belize Valley sites of Cahal Pech, Blackman Eddy, Xunantunich, and Baking Pot.

We return now to the notion that warfare served as a mechanism for political evolution in the Belize Valley. Competitive behavior is always present in human societies. But not all competition leads to conflict, let alone war. In fact, competition between factions is one of the mechanisms that generates social change (Brumfiel 1994). Conflict and warfare may occur as part of factional competition. Perhaps the termination ritual and desecration of Blackman Eddy Structure B1–4 at about 650 BC was the result of a violent conflict among local factions, rather than between different cultural or linguistic groups (cf. Brown and Garber 2003). In any event, there is no evidence that a similar event – let alone warfare –

occurred at contemporary Cahal Pech. Some buildings do show signs of dismantling, but this was carried out as part of various construction phases and not with the aim of desecration. The only Kanluk phase structure that evinces ritual termination is the small altar that is contemporary with the circular platform and rectangular structure (Plaza B/12th; Peniche May 2016). Moreover, this small oval feature was the subject of a reverential termination. This ritual may have been associated with the change in function of the area from private to public that occurred at the end of the Kanluk phase. The dismantling of Structure B8, the western platform of the Cahal Pech E-Group, provides yet another example of the periodic termination of early architecture to make way for subsequent modifications. Finally, although it is true that the architectural nucleus of Cahal Pech was built in a strategic and defensive location, it also may be that the population settled there seeking protection from the annual flooding of the Mopan and Macal rivers, or because the elevated location represented a sacred landscape, or simply because the hilltop provided a more pleasant and well-drained location for habitation. Indeed, early settlements across the Belize Valley and extending into Peten exhibit variable placement in relation to topography, suggesting that communities formed in areas where access to resources was plentiful.

Conclusion

The study of migration and conflict during Middle Preclassic times is an especially complex and difficult task, in large part because those behaviors did not always result in tangible and unambiguous evidence preserved in the archaeological record, but also because of the simple fact that data for this time period are very limited. Despite these considerable challenges, more than 30 years of archaeological research at Cahal Pech provides us with a relatively large data base from which to test these and other related hypotheses. Presently, the ceramic and architectural data from the site imply that the early inhabitants of the Belize Valley interacted with their contemporaries in other regions of the Maya lowlands, including those populations that inhabited the Caribbean coast, northern Belize, and eastern Peten as early as 1200–1000 BC. This situation is corroborated by other data derived from the distribution of lithic and marine shell artifacts (Awe and Healy 1994; Hohman 2002; Horn 2015; Peniche May 2016), by trace-element studies of ceramics (Callaghan et al. 2017, 2018; Ebert et al. 2019), by strontium isotope analysis (Chapter 9), and by the presence of some late Middle Preclassic architectural styles at the site (Ebert et al. 2021; Peniche May 2016). Although these data do indicate regional interaction, we argue that they do not provide incontrovertible evidence of the arrival of immigrant groups to the Belize Valley during the Middle Preclassic. As we note above, Mamom ceramics first appeared in the Belize Valley at the end of the early facet of the Kanluk phase. Mamom-related pottery increased in frequency during late-facet Kanluk, but it continued to represent just a small fraction of the ceramic inventory and appeared in a limited number of types and vessel forms. If people from other regions arrived and brought with them their pottery traditions, it remains to be determined why we see major ceramic continuities during the Middle Preclassic period and why these hypothesized migrants did not produce and use utilitarian vessels typical of their foreign tradition. Furthermore, one also needs to explain why these hypothesized immigrants limited their production to vessels from the Joventud group. It also is true that there are vessels with shapes and decorations resembling Mamom pottery, but these were mostly produced from local clays and most likely made by potters from the Belize Valley rather than by immigrants from northern Belize or Peten. We assert this because the clays and technology used to produce such imitations were the same as those used to make Mars Orange serving wares. Instead of migration and the selective preservation of certain pottery traditions, we believe that interaction with populations living in other regions provides a more accurate explanation for the limited emulation of decorative forms and techniques that were used to create vessels that are clearly copies of Mamom ceramics.

We also point out that, while it is possible that violent conflicts were part of Middle Preclassic life in the Belize Valley, incontrovertible evidence for such martial activities remains elusive, controversial, and subject to interpretation. As Sharer and Traxler (2005:143) previously noted, most Maya centers lacked military fortifications and there is little evidence for conflict for most of their history. Even at the peak of militarism in the Terminal Classic period, conflicts were very limited both in scale and in scope. For this reason, and given the limitations of ceramic data, we urge researchers to take a scientifically rigorous approach that includes multiple lines of evidence and the testing of hypotheses that link changes in ceramic styles to models of invasion and migration (cf. Cobos 2006). We further advocate that the concept of ethnicity not be applied loosely to Middle Preclassic societies, which probably were politically organized as chiefdoms. Large-scale bioarcheological and strontium isotope analyses of a meaningful sample of skeletal remains from across the Maya lowlands are required to accurately assess questions of migration. We also need to consider that ethnicity is a form of social identity that, by definition, occurs in states and remains poorly identified in pre-state societies.

Models that incorporate interaction and emulation as explanatory mechanisms for the changes in the architecture and ceramic inventory of Cahal Pech during the Kanluk phase provide far more satisfactory explanations than migration and conflict for the developments seen in the archaeological record. Such interaction models also lend themselves to evaluation that combines both processual and post-processual archaeology, and especially to rigorous scientific testing. It is the bringing together of all these approaches that leads us to conclude that the Middle Preclassic rise of social complexity in the Belize Valley was the direct result of continuous interaction between inhabitants of the valley and neighbors throughout the Maya lowlands.

Note

1 We are extremely grateful for all the contributions made by many scholars and workers who have contributed to the efforts of BVAR at Cahal Pech over more than 30 years of research. Nonetheless, we do not intend this to be a review article covering the entirety of that project. Readers interested in a summary and a complete bibliography through about 2015, including unpublished reports, are referred to Horn (2015) or Peniche May (2016). Ebert et al. (2021) includes important references to work conducted after that date. Moreover, it should be understood that much data and many observations discussed here first appeared in Awe (1992) or Peniche May (2016). Rather than repeatedly cite these two sources, in many cases we have opted to refer to more recent references.

References cited

Aimers, James, Terry G. Powis, and Jaime J. Awe 2000 Preclassic Round Structures of the Upper Belize River Valley. *Latin American Antiquity* 11:71–86.

Alcover Firpi, Omar Andrés, and Charles Golden 2020 The Politics of Conflict: War before and beyond the State in Maya Society. In *The Maya World*, edited by Scott R. Hutson and Traci Ardren, pp. 477–496. Routledge, New York.

Ambrosino, James, Traci Ardren, and Travis W. Stanton 2003 The History of Warfare at Yaxuná. In *Ancient Maya Warfare*, edited by M. Kathryn Brown and Travis W. Stanton, pp. 109–123. Altamira Press, Walnut Creek, CA.

Andrews, E. Wyllys, V 1990 Early Ceramic History of the Lowland Maya. In *Vision and Revision in Maya Studies*, edited by Flora S. Clancy and Peter D. Harrison, pp. 1–19. University of New Mexico Press, Albuquerque.

Audet, Carolyn M. 2001 Excavations of Structure F-2, Cahal Pech, Cayo District, Belize. In *The Western Belize Regional Cave Project: A Report of the 2000 Field Season*, edited by Reiko Ishihara, Cameron S. Griffith, and Jaime J. Awe, pp. 269–284. University of New Hampshire, Durham.

Awe, Jaime J. 1992 *Dawn in the Land between the Rivers: Formative Occupation at Cahal Pech, Belize and Its Implications for Preclassic Occupation in the Central Maya Lowlands*. Unpublished Ph.D. dissertation, University of London, London.

———— 2021 Archaeological Evidence for the Preclassic Origins of the Maya Creation Story and the Resurrection of the Maize God at Cahal Pech, Belize. In *The Myths of the Popol Vuh in Cosmology Art and Ritual*, edited by Holley Moyes, Allen Christenson, and Frauke Sachse. University Press of Colorado, Boulder. In press.

Awe, Jaime J., Claire E. Ebert, Julie A. Hoggarth, James J. Aimers, Christophe Helmke, et al. 2020a The Last Hurrah: Examining the Nature of Peri-Abandonment Deposits and Activities at Cahal Pech, Belize. *Ancient Mesoamerica* 31:175–187.

Awe, Jaime J., and Paul F. Healy 1994 Flakes to Blades? Middle Formative Development of Obsidian Artifacts in the Upper Belize River Valley. *Latin American Antiquity* 5:193–205.

Awe, Jaime J., Christophe Helmke, James J. Aimers, Claire E. Ebert, Julie A. Hoggarth, et al. 2020b Applying Regional, Contextual, Ethnohistoric, and Ethnographic Approaches for Understanding the Significance of Peri-Abandonment Deposits in Western Belize. *Ancient Mesoamerica* 31:109–126.

Awe, Jaime J., and Shawn G. Morton n.d. All in All, It's Not Just Another Brick in the Wall: Examining the Diverse Functions of Wall Architecture in Western Belize. In *The Ties That Bind and the Walls That Divide*, edited by Thomas Guderjan and Jennifer Mathews. University of Arizona Press, Tucson. In press.

Ball, Joseph 1993 Pottery, Potters, and Polities: Some Socioeconomic and Political Implications of Late Classic Maya Ceramic Industries. In *Lowland Maya Civilization in the Eighth Century A.D.*, edited by Jeremy A. Sabloff and John S. Henderson, pp. 243–272. Dumbarton Oaks Research Library and Collection, Washington, DC.

Ball, Joseph, and Jennifer Taschek 2003 Reconsidering the Belize Valley Preclassic: A Case for Multiethnic Interactions in the Development of a Regional Culture Tradition. *Ancient Mesoamerica* 14:179–217.

Barth, Frederick 1969 Introduction. In *Ethnic Groups and Boundaries: The Social Organization of Culture Difference*, edited by Frederick Barth, pp. 1–38. Universitetsforlaget, Oslo.

Bey, George J., III 2003 The Role of Ceramics in the Study of Conflict in Maya Archaeology. In *Ancient Maya Warfare*, edited by M. Kathryn Brown and Travis W. Stanton, pp. 19–30. Altamira Press, Walnut Creek, CA.

Braswell, Geoffrey E. 2016 The Problem of Ethnicity and the Construction of K'iche'an Identity. In *Archaeology and Identity on the Pacific Coast and Southern Highlands of Mesoamerica*, edited by Claudia García-Des Lauriers and Michael W. Love, pp. 172–184. University of Utah Press, Salt Lake City.

Brown, M. Kathryn 2008 Establishing Hierarchies in the Middle Preclassic Belize River Valley. *Research Reports in Belizean Archaeology* 5:175–184.

Brown, M. Kathryn, and James F. Garber 2003 Evidence of Conflict during the Middle Formative in the Maya Lowlands: A View from Blackman Eddy, Belize. In *Ancient Maya Warfare*, edited by M. Kathryn Brown and Travis W. Stanton, pp. 91–108. Altamira Press, Walnut Creek, CA.

Brumfiel, Elizabeth M. 1994 Ethnic Groups and Political Development in Ancient Mexico. In *Factional Competition and Political Development in the New World*, edited by Elizabeth M. Brumfiel and John W. Fox, pp. 89–102. Cambridge University Press, Cambridge.

Burke, Chrissina C., Katie K. Tappan, Gavin B. Wisner, Julie A. Hoggarth, and Jaime J. Awe 2020 To Eat, Discard, or Venerate: Faunal Remains as Proxy for Human Behaviors in Lowland Maya Peri-Abandonment Deposits. *Ancient Mesoamerica* 31:127–137.

Callaghan, Michael G., Daniel E. Pierce, and William D. Gilstrap. 2018 The First Maya Trade Ware? New Data on Middle Preclassic-Period Mars Orange Ware from Holtun, Guatemala. *Latin American Antiquity* 12:821–827.

Callaghan, Michael G., Daniel E. Pierce, Bridget Kovacevich, and Michael Glascock 2017 Chemical Paste Characterization of Late Middle Preclassic-Period Ceramics from Holtun, Guatemala and Its Implications for Production and Exchange. *Journal of Archaeological Science: Reports* 12:334–345.

Carneiro, Robert L. 1981 The Chiefdom: Precursor of the State. In *The Transition to Statehood in the New World*, edited by Grant D. Jones and Robert R. Kautz, pp. 37–79. Cambridge University Press, Cambridge.

Carr, Christopher, and Jill E. Neitzel (editors) 1995 *Style, Society, and Person: Archaeological and Ethnological Approaches*. Plenum Press, New York.

Chase, Arlen F., and Diane Z. Chase 2012 Complex Societies in the Southern Maya Lowlands: Their Development and Florescence in the Archaeological Record. In *Oxford Dictionary of Mesoamerica*, edited by Deborah L. Nichols and Christopher A. Pool, pp. 255–267. Oxford University Press, Oxford.

Cobos, Rafael 2006 The Relationship between Tula and Chichen Itza: Influences or Interactions? In *Lifeways in the Northern Maya Lowlands: New Approaches to Archaeology in the Yucatan Peninsula*, edited by Jennifer P. Mathews and Bethany A. Morrison, pp. 173–183. University of Arizona Press, Tucson.

Dahlin, Bruce H. 2000 The Barricade and Abandonment of Chunchucmil: Implications for Northern Maya Warfare. *Latin American Antiquity* 11:283–298.

Demarest, Arthur A. 1989 The Olmec and the Rise of Civilization in Eastern Meso-america. In *Regional Perspectives on the Olmec*, edited by Robert J. Sharer and David C. Grove, pp. 303–344. Cambridge University Press, Cambridge.

Demarest, Arthur A., Matt O'Mansky, Claudia Wolley, Dirk Van Tuerenhout, Takeshi Inomata, et al. 1997 Classic Maya Defensive Systems and Warfare in the Petexbatun Region. *Ancient Mesoamerica* 8:229–253.

Ebert, Claire E., and Jaime J. Awe 2020 Who Were the Early Preclassic Maya?: Reas-sessing Key Questions about the Origins of Village Life in the Belize River Valley. *Research Reports in Belizean Archaeology* 17:273–286.

Ebert, Claire E., Nancy Peniche May, Brendan J. Culleton, Jaime J. Awe, and Douglas J. Kennett 2017 Regional Response to Drought during the Formation and Decline of Preclassic Maya Societies. *Quaternary Science Reviews* 173:211–235.

Ebert, Claire E., James McGee, and Jaime J. Awe 2021 Early Monumentality in the Belize River Valley: Excavations of a Preclassic E-Group at Cahal Pech, Belize. *Latin American Antiquity* 32:209–217.

Ebert, Claire E., Daniel E. Pierce, and Jaime J. Awe 2019 Preclassic Ceramic Economy in Belize: Neutron Activation Analysis at Cahal Pech. *Antiquity* 93:1266–1283.

Emberling, Geoff 1997 Ethnicity in Complex Societies: Archaeological Perspectives. *Journal of Archaeological Research* 5:295–344.

Foias, Antonia, and Ronald L. Bishop 1997 Changing Ceramic Production and Exchange in the Petexbatun Region, Guatemala: Reconsidering the Classic Maya Collapse. *Ancient Mesoamerica* 8:275–292.

Ford, Anabel 2016 Unexpected Discovery with LiDAR: Uncovering the Citadel at El Pilar in the Context of the Maya Forest GIS. *Research Reports on Belizean Archaeology* 13:87–98.

Freidel, David A., Barbara MacLeod, and Charles K. Suhler 2003 Early Classic Maya Conquest in Words and Deeds. In *Ancient Maya Warfare*, edited by M. Kathryn Brown and Travis W. Stanton, pp. 189–215. Altamira Press, Walnut Creek, CA.

Freidel, David A., and Linda Schele 1989 Dead Kings and Living Temples. In *Word and Image in Maya Culture: Explorations in Language, Writing, and Representation*, edited by William F. Hanks and Donald S. Rice, pp. 233–243. University of Utah Press, Salt Lake City.

Freiwald, Carolyn, Jason Yaegar, Jaime Awe, and Jennifer Piehl 2014 Isotopic Insights into Mortuary Treatment and Origin at Xunantunich, Belize. In *The Bioarchaeology of Space and Place: Ideology, Power and Meaning in Maya Mortuary Contexts*, edited by Gabriel D. Wrobel, pp. 107–139. Springer, New York.

Garber, James F., and Jaime J. Awe 2008 Middle Formative Architecture and Ritual at Cahal Pech. *Research Reports in Belizean Archaeology* 5:185–190.

Garber, James F., Jennifer L. Cochran, Lauren A. Sullivan, and Jaime J. Awe 2007 Exca-vations in Plaza B at Cahal Pech: The 2006 Field Season. In *The Belize Valley Archaeo-logical Project: Results of the 2006 Field Season*, edited by James F. Garber, pp. 4–26. Texas State University, San Marcos.

Gifford, James C. 1970 The Earliest and Other Intrusive Population Elements at Barton Ramie May Have Come from Central America. *Cerámica de Cultura Maya* 6:1–10.

———— 1976 *Prehistoric Pottery Analysis and the Ceramics of Barton Ramie in the Belize Valley.* Memoirs of the Peabody Museum of Archaeology and Ethnology, Vol. 18. Harvard University, Cambridge.

Hahn, Lauren, and Geoffrey E. Braswell 2012 Divide and Rule: Interpreting Site Perim-eter Walls in the Northern Maya Lowlands and Beyond. In *Ancient Maya of Mexico: Reinterpreting the Past of the Northern Maya Lowlands*, edited by Geoffrey E. Braswell, pp. 264–281. Routledge, London.

Helmke, Christophe, and Jaime J. Awe 2016a Death Becomes Her: An Analysis of Panel 3, Xunantunich, Belize. *The PARI Journal* 16(4):1–14.

———— 2016b Sharper than a Serpent's Tooth: A Tale of the Snake-Head Dynasty as Recounted on Xunantunich Panel 4. *The PARI Journal* 17(2):1–22.

Hendon, Julia A. 2000 Round Structures, Household Identity, and Public Performances in Preclassic Maya Society. *Latin American Antiquity* 11:299–301.

Hoggarth, Julie A., J. Britt Davis, Jaime J. Awe, and Christophe Helmke. 2020 Reconstructing the Formation of Peri-Abandonment Deposits at Baking Pot, Belize. *Ancient Mesoamerica* 31:139–149.

Hohman, Bobbi M. 2002 *Preclassic Maya Shell Ornament Production in the Belize Valley, Belize*. Unpublished Ph.D. dissertation, Department of Anthropology, University of New Mexico, Albuquerque.

Horn, Sherman W., III 2015 *The Web of Complexity: Socioeconomic Networks in the Middle Preclassic Belize Valley*. Unpublished Ph.D. dissertation, Department of Anthropology, Tulane University, New Orleans.

Horn, Sherman W., III, James F. Garber, and Jaime J. Awe 2017 And Now for Something Completely Different: Architectural Variability as a Signature of Dynamic Social Relations at Middle Preclassic Cahal Pech. *Research Reports in Belizean Archaeology* 14:77–86.

Inomata, Takeshi 1997 The Last Days of a Fortified Classic Maya Center: Archaeological Investigations at Aguateca, Guatemala. *Ancient Mesoamerica* 8:337–351.

Ishihara-Brito, Reiko, and Jaime J. Awe 2013 Excavations on Cahal Pech Structure B-4. In *Belize Valley Reconnaissance Project: A Report of the 2011 Field Season*, edited by Julie A. Hoggarth, Rafael A. Guerra, and Jaime J. Awe, pp. 118–127. Institute of Archaeology, Belmopan, Belize.

Joyce, Arthur A. 2003 Imperialism in Pre-Aztec Mesoamerica: Monte Albán, Teotihuacan, and the Lower Río Verde Valley. In *Ancient Maya Warfare*, edited by M. Kathryn Brown and Travis W. Stanton, pp. 49–71. Altamira Press, Walnut Creek, CA.

Kettunen, Harri 2014 Ancient Maya Warfare: An Interdisciplinary Approach. In *Socio-Political Strategies among the Maya from the Classic Period to the Present*, edited by Verónica A. Vásquez, Rogelio Valencia Rivera, and Eugenia Gutiérrez González, pp. 95–107. BAR International Series 2619. Archaeopress, Oxford.

Kosakowsky, Laura J. 2012 Ceramics and Chronology at Chan. In *Chan: An Ancient Maya Farming Community*, edited by Cynthia Robin, pp. 42–70. University Press of Florida, Gainesville.

Lowe, Gareth W. 1977 The Mixe: Zoque as Competing Neighbors of the Early Lowland Maya. In *The Origins of Maya Civilization*, edited by Richard E. W. Adams, pp. 197–248. University of New Mexico Press, Albuquerque.

Manahan, T. Kam 2008 Anatomy of a Post-Collapse Society: Identity and Interaction in Early Postclassic Copán. In *Ruins of the Past: The Use and Perception of Abandoned Structures in the Maya Lowlands*, edited by Travis W. Stanton and Aline Magnoni, pp. 170–192. University Press of Colorado, Boulder.

Martin, Simon 2020 *Ancient Maya Politics: A Political Anthropology of the Classic Period 150–900 CE*. Cambridge University Press, Cambridge.

Masson, Marilyn A. 1997 Cultural Transformation at the Maya Postclassic Community of Laguna de On, Belize. *Latin American Antiquity* 8:293–316.

Miller, Mary E. 1986 *The Murals of Bonampak*. Princeton University Press, Princeton, NJ.

MURR Archaeometry Laboratory Database n.d. *Archaeometry Laboratory Database*. http://archaeometry.missouri. edu/datasets/datasets.html, accessed June 7, 2019.

Pagliaro, Jonathan B., James F. Garber, and Travis W. Stanton 2003 Evaluating the Archaeological Signatures of Maya Ritual and Conflict. In *Ancient Mesoamerican*

Warfare, edited by M. Kathryn Brown and Travis W. Stanton, pp. 75–90. Alta Mira Press, Walnut Creek, CA.

Palka, Joel W. 2014 *Maya Pilgrimage to Ritual Landscapes: Insights from Archaeology, History, and Ethnography*. University of New Mexico Press, Albuquerque.

Peniche May, Nancy 2012 The Architecture of Power and Sociopolitical Complexity in Northwestern Yucatan during the Preclassic Period. In *The Maya of Ancient Mexico: Reinterpreting the Northern Maya Lowlands*, edited by Geoffrey E. Braswell, pp. 65–87. Routledge Press, London.

——— 2016 *Building Power: Political Dynamics in Cahal Pech, Belize during the Middle Preclassic*. Unpublished Ph.D. dissertation, Department of Anthropology, University of California, San Diego.

Powis, Terry G. 2009 *Pacbitun Preclassic Project: Report on the 2008 Field Season*. Report submitted to the Institute of Archaeology, Belmopan, Belize.

Puleston, Dennis E., and Donald W. Callender 1967 Defensive Earthworks at Tikal. *Expedition* 9:40–48.

Ringle, William M., George J. Bey, III, Tara Bond Freeman, Craig A. Hanson, Charles W. Houck, and J. Gregory Smith 2004 The Decline of the East: The Classic to Postclassic Transition at Ek Balam, Yucatan. In *The Terminal Classic in the Maya Lowlands: Collapse: Transitions, and Transformation*, edited by Arthur A. Demarest, Prudence M. Rice, and Don S. Rice, pp. 485–516. University Press of Colorado, Boulder.

Santley, Robert S., Ponciano Ortiz, and Christopher A. Pool 1987 Recent Archaeological Research at Matacapan, Veracruz: A Summary of the Results of the 1982 to 1986 Field Seasons. *Mexicon* 11:41–48.

Sharer, Robert J., and Loa P. Traxler 2005 *The Ancient Maya*, 6th Edition. Stanford University Press, Palo Alto, CA.

Sheets, Payson D. 2003 Warfare in Ancient Mesoamerica: A Summary View. In *Ancient Maya Warfare*, edited by M. Kathryn Brown and Travis W. Stanton, pp. 287–301. Altamira Press, Walnut Creek, CA.

Stanton, Travis, and Traci Ardren 2005 The Middle Formative of Yucatan in Context: The View from Yaxuna. *Ancient Mesoamerica* 16:213–228.

Stemp, W. James, Jaime J. Awe, Keith M. Prufer, and Christophe G. B. Helmke 2016 Design and Function of Lowe and Sawmill Points from the Preceramic Period of Belize. *Latin American Antiquity* 27:279–299.

Suhler, Charles K., Traci Ardren, David Freidel, and David Johnstone 2004 The Rise and Fall of Terminal Classic Yaxuna, Yucatan, Mexico. In *The Terminal Classic in the Maya Lowlands: Collapse: Transitions, and Transformation*, edited by Arthur A. Demarest, Prudence M. Rice, and Don S. Rice, pp. 450–484. University Press of Colorado, Boulder.

Suhler, Charles K., Tracy Ardren, and David Johnstone 1998 The Chronology of Yaxuna: Evidence from Excavation and Ceramics. *Ancient Mesoamerica* 9:176–182.

Sullivan, Lauren A., and Jaime J. Awe 2013 Establishing the Cunil Ceramic Complex at Cahal Pech, Belize. In *Ancient Maya Pottery: Classification, Analysis, and Interpretation*, edited by James J. Aimers, pp. 107–120. University Press of Florida, Gainesville.

Sullivan, Lauren A., Jaime J. Awe, and M. Kathryn Brown 2018 The Cunil Complex: Early Villages in Belize. In *Pathways to Complexity: A View from the Maya Lowlands*, edited by M. Kathryn Brown and George J. Bey, III, pp. 35–48. University Press of Florida, Gainesville.

Tuerenhout, Dirk van 2001 Maya Warfare: Sources and Interpretations. *Civilisations* 50(1/2):129–152.

78 Nancy Peniche May, Jaime J. Awe and Claire E. Ebert

Webster, David 1976 *Defensive Earthworks at Becan, Campeche, Mexico: Implications for Maya Warfare.* Middle American Research Institute, Publication 41. Tulane University, New Orleans.

———— 1993 The Study of Maya Warfare: What It Tells Us about the Maya and What It Tells Us about Maya Archaeology. In *Lowland Maya Civilization in the Eighth Century A.D.*, edited by Jeremy A. Sabloff and John S. Henderson, pp. 415–44. Dumbarton Oaks Research Library and Collection, Washington, DC.

———— 2011 Warfare and the Evolution of the State: A Reconsideration. *American Antiquity* 40:464–470.

Welsh, W. Bruce 1988 *An Analysis of Classic Lowland Maya Burials.* International Series 409. British Archaeological Reports, Oxford.

Willey, Gordon R. 1990 General Summary and Conclusions. In *Excavations at Seibal.* Memoirs of the Peabody Museum of Archaeology and Ethnology, No. 4. Harvard University, Cambridge.

Willey, Gordon R., William R. Bullard, Jr., John B. Glass, and James G. Gifford 1965 *Prehistoric Maya Settlement in the Belize Valley.* Papers of Peabody Museum, Harvard University No 54. Harvard University, Cambridge.

4

SOUTHERN BELIZE FROM PALEOINDIAN TO PRECLASSIC TIMES

Introduction to the region, early origins, and identity

Geoffrey E. Braswell

The southern Maya lowlands of Central America do not constitute a uniform environmental zone. Instead, the territory stretching from Honduras to Chiapas contains cayes, beaches and mangrove coasts, lagoons, infertile peri-coastal zones, fertile and wet flatlands, transitional foothills cut with river and stream valleys, karstic hills and metamorphic mountain chains, low-canopy and scrub forests, high-canopy rainforests at various altitudes, lake zones, savannahs, and inland seasonal swamps of several types referred to as *bajos*. Given the environmental diversity of the southern Maya lowlands, it is no surprise that different adaptive strategies and discrete historical trajectories emerged in different regions. Although the villages, towns, and cities of the southern lowlands are all recognizably Maya, specific patterns are seen in architecture, pottery, visual art, hieroglyphic texts, and other aspects of material cultures across the varied landscape of the southern lowlands. Moreover, the settlement histories and political trajectories of distinct regions reflect, but were not determined by, their different environmental settings.

One such corner of the southern Maya lowlands is found in Toledo District, Belize. The geography, climate, and distinct expressions of ancient Maya culture all led Richard Leventhal (1990, 1992) to define this as the Southern Belize Region (SBR). My first goal in this chapter is to describe the architecture, artifacts, and hieroglyphic texts of Classic period culture of the SBR in general terms so that they can be understood as a distinct set of material expressions of culture and behavior within the wider Maya world. I then turn to what we know about the origins of the people of the SBR and focus on the Paleoindian through Preclassic periods in an attempt to understand how they were similar to and different from other early peoples of the Maya area and Mesoamerica. In the following two chapters, I look at the histories of each of the major "cities" (sensu Houk 2015) of the SBR, even though I believe that only one site should

DOI: 10.4324/9781351268004-4

be considered truly urban. In those chapters, I explore how during the Classic period the people of the SBR expressed distinct identities within the same bounded geographical context, and I discuss their interactions – peaceful and bellicose – with each other and beyond the region through time.

Defining the Southern Belize Region

The SBR may be defined as the area bounded to the east by the Caribbean Sea, to the south by the Sarstoon River (the current southern border of Belize) and surrounding swamp lands, and to the northwest by the Maya Mountains (Figure 4.1). The northeast and southwest corners of the SBR are less circumscribed by natural barriers. The flatlands of the former are crossed every few kilometers by creeks and rivers; one can arbitrarily choose the Bladen or the Swasey Branch, two tributaries of Monkey River, as boundaries. Alternatively, the SBR could be considered as gradually transitioning into the sparsely occupied Stann Creek region. There are some ceramic ties and significant architectural differences between the few studied sites in that frontier zone and the SBR (Jordan 2019; MacKinnon 1991). The ancient Maya centers of Nim li Punit and Xnaheb are positioned a few hundred meters west and above the natural route leading north out of the SBR to Stann Creek and, eventually, the Belize Valley and northern Belize. Similarly, the southwest corner of the SBR provides three natural passageways into southern Peten, Guatemala. The northernmost passes by the archaeological site of Uxbenka and on to the modern border village of Jalacte; the central goes through the heart of the ancient Maya city of Pusilha and the village of San Benito Poite; and the southernmost route passes no known site and reaches the modern frontier near the small village of Dolores. Just 20 years ago, all three of these routes were largely forested. Now they are cleared and commonly used to travel across the international border. Thus, although the SBR is largely defined by hard-to-cross natural boundaries, one north-south and three east-west routes connect it to other parts of the Maya region. Lubaantun, the last major site of the SBR to be occupied, is located just a few kilometers from both the north-south route and one of the three east-west corridors leading out of the SBR – a perfect spot for controlling exchange and movement along both terrestrial routes. Finally, the Caribbean itself provided a natural means of transportation that connected the SBR to all of the east coast of the Yucatan peninsula, as well as to the non-Maya north coast of Honduras. Nim li Punit, Xnaheb, and Lubaantun are all within a short walk and an easy canoe ride from the coast.

Separating the major Maya settlements of inland Toledo District from the Caribbean is a strip of flat, low land with limited agricultural potential. Except for sediments found adjacent to creeks and rivers that cross this territory, there has been little deposition during the Holocene. Soils are thin and sandy. In many places, shallow sands above red clays support palmettos and scrub conifers. In Belize, a forested area is referred to as a "ridge," hence these lowlands are locally called "pine ridge." Today, the pine ridge and other portions of the coastal strip

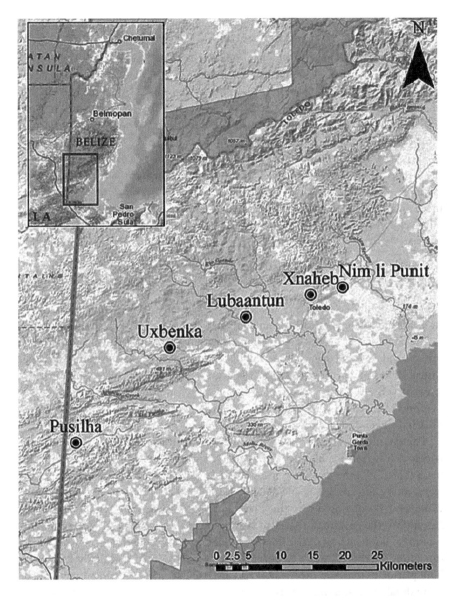

FIGURE 4.1 The Southern Belize Region showing principal archaeological sites.

Source: Figure by Mark Irish.

typified by broad-leafed forest and palms are sparsely settled except along roads, and they separate the Kriol and Garifuna people of coastal Toledo District from the Q'eqchi' and Mopan Maya who live inland. We know nothing of settlement in this region during ancient times except to say that there are no obvious major sites. For this reason, I limit my discussion largely to inland portions of the SBR.

The ancient material culture of the SBR differs from that of other parts of the southern Maya area and is in some ways unique. These differences were first noted by early explorers, but when considered together they led Leventhal (1990, 1992) to propose the SBR as a "cultural region" within the larger Maya culture area. Working at the northeastern extreme of the SBR, J. Jefferson MacKinnon (1991) questioned both the utility and reality of this concept and accentuated distinctions between the sites of southern Stann Creek and Toledo District. Nonetheless, Leventhal's catalog of traits – and a few more – do clearly distinguish inland Toledo from central Peten sites, the Quirigua and Copan regions, the Belize Valley, northern Belize, and the entire northern and western Maya lowlands. These characteristics are manifestations of what must have been one or more distinct identities that distinguished the inhabitants of the SBR from Maya living elsewhere in the lowlands.

Material cultural characteristics of the SBR: architecture and hieroglyphs

The most obvious defining characteristics of the SBR are seen in its architecture. Structures of the SBR completely lack vaulted roofs. In fact, Lubaantun is the only site with stone superstructures of any sort, and these are waist-high walls found on small special-function platforms that may have served as shrines. Instead, the stone platforms of the SBR were apparently topped with perishable structures. Stone tombs were built, but long capstones rather than vaults served as roofs. These cannot support much weight, so most of the known tombs in the SBR have been found close to the ground surface.

The quality of the masonry within the SBR differs from site to site. This is largely a function of the quality of the local stone. At Pusilha, both are quite poor. The limestone used there is remarkably hard and amorphous and does not cleave along an axis. As a result, construction blocks are all crude and not dressed. Builders at Pusilha used very thick layers of plaster to cover the rough masonry. In contrast, the building material at Nim li Punit was calcareous Toledo mud- or silt-stone, a soft material that fractures in laminar sheets and which, when wet, can almost be carved with a fingernail. Mudstone was used to face low but well-built platforms that now are greatly eroded. At Lubaantun, the limestone is much more durable yet fractures easily and in a predictable manner. In part because of the quality of the stone, the masonry of that site is the finest anywhere between Copan and the Rio Bec region of southern Campeche. Similar fine masonry is found at Uxbenka Group B.

A typical free-standing platform in the SBR consists of vertical tiers 75 cm to 1.5 m high. These were constructed as corrals and filled with earth, dry stones, or a combination of both. At Lubaantun interior retention walls are common, and these are built using cut stones. Some interior retention walls at that site were so meticulously constructed that they can be confused with substructures. Plaza platforms at Lubaantun have carefully built retention walls on a diagonal to the plan of the plazas and the structures they support, adding stability during earth-quakes. A pyramid-platform in the SBR may have one or more tiers. Higher tiers are set back like the layers of a wedding cake. At Lubaantun, the setbacks are quite standard, either two or four fingers wide. Throughout the SBR, once a platform was built to its intended height, a stair block was added that rests against and supports the outer wall of the platform. These often are flanked by stair-side outsets built against the platform and the sidewalls of the stair to buttress both. None of these distinct elements articulate with interdigitating stone.

The masonry façades of the SBR were not built with apron moldings, lack anything resembling a *talud-tablero*, and do not have inset corners. Nor was much in the way of molded plaster used to adorn structures; the only fragments I have ever recovered were small and at Pusilha. Instead, architects relied on the slightly offset bodies of platforms, sharp sloping angles, and the interplay of right angles and curved corners to produce decoration (Figure 4.2). At Lubaantun, the stones used to create these effects are often beveled or shaped into actual curves. Thomas A. Joyce and J. Eric S. Thompson differed about the existence of so-called "in and out" architecture at Lubaantun, that is, alternating vertical bodies that are outset at the bottom, inset in the middle, and then outset at the top. Thompson won the argument, stressing that the upper "out" tier is always found above the current ground level and therefore created by the pushing out of exposed blocks by tree roots, or, as I propose, by the swelling of platform fill caused by rain. Despite the logic of Thompson's argument, we did discover a single preserved example of "in and out" architecture completely sealed and buried by fill on the south side of Structure 34. It is commonly said that plaster, stucco, and lime mortar were not employed at either Lubaantun or Nim li Punit. This is false. Thin surface layers of plaster were used at both sites, but some later constructions at Nim li Punit may lack such coverings. A final oddity is that some of the tallest pyramidal platforms in the SBR lack stairs going to the top. This is true of Nim li Punit Structure 2, and Structures 10 and 12 of Lubaantun are the clearest examples (Figure 4.3). The first has no stair at all, while the sec-ond is fronted by a low *adosada* platform (see Chapter 7) with four or five steps. To reach the top of either platform, one must scramble up the low bodies or tiers. These unique structures, therefore, resemble the steep mountains that inspired Maya pyramids.

The pyramids of the SBR are quite low; only a few freestanding platforms are more than nine meters high. As Leventhal (1990) points out, many of the larger structures have "Hollywood" façades built against and on top of natural hillocks and outcroppings. This is a common pattern at many sites throughout the south-ern Maya lowlands, especially those built quickly such as Dos Pilas. One example is the acropolis of Lubaantun itself, which has a walled façade on all but its north end. Another dramatic example of façade construction is the royal acropolis of Pusilha, which rises some 79 m above the unique ancient Maya bridge spanning the Machaca (or Pusilha) River. Like the acropolis of Tonina, it was built on and against a natural hill. The effective height of this acropolis is nearly that of the

FIGURE 4.2 Masonry in the Southern Belize Region: southeast corner of Lubaantun Structure 104.

Source: Photo by the author.

FIGURE 4.3 Pyramids without stairs to the summit: (a) Lubaantun Structure 10, which completely lacks a stair; (b) Lubaantun Structure 12, with a stair leading to a low *adosada* in front of the pyramid (note radial platform altar Structure 32 in the right foreground); (c) Nim li Punit Structure 2, with a stair ending three steps up.

Source: Photos by the author.

Caana of Caracol and the Castillo of Xunantunich – the two tallest freestanding ancient buildings in Belize – combined.

Ballcourts are common in the SBR. Pusilha and Lubaantun have three each, Uxbenka has two, and Nim li Punit and Xnaheb each have one. Leventhal notes that these are either entirely enclosed by walls, as Ballcourt 1 at Pusilha (Figure 4.4), or are enclosed on at least one end.

The hieroglyphic texts of the SBR also differ somewhat from their counterparts in other regions. First, compared to anywhere else in Belize except Caracol, inland Toledo is unusually rich in hieroglyphic texts with political information. In fact, Pusilha has more hieroglyphic monuments and longer texts than all of the Belize Valley and northern Belize combined. The hieroglyphic and sculptural corpus from Pusilha consists of at least 20 stelae, four zoomorphic altars, three ballcourt markers, 17 known sculptured monument fragments (including pieces of a fourth zoomorphic altar), two miscellaneous texts, and the only intact hieroglyphic stair known in Belize. Nim li Punit, Xnaheb, and Uxbenka are small sites, yet the number and quality of carved monuments – eight at Nim li Punit, three at Xnaheb, and at least ten at Uxbenka – are quite impressive. Particularly famous is Nim li Punit Stela 14. At 9.29 m long, it is the second longest carved stela in the Maya world after Quirigua Stela E. In comparison, Lubaantun has only four known carved monuments. These are three ballcourt markers with short hieroglyphic texts and a crudely carved human head. Some mold-made figurative ceramics found at the site depict individuals in niches or on carved thrones that carry short texts, but the relative dearth of hieroglyphic texts on stone distinguishes Lubaantun from the other major sites in the SBR.

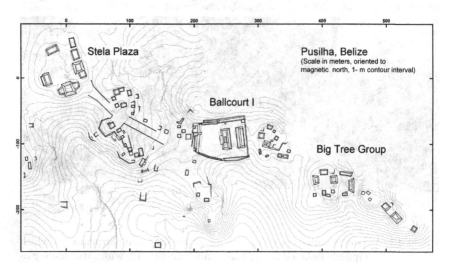

FIGURE 4.4 Pusilha Ballcourt 1: an enclosed ballcourt of the Southern Belize Region.
Source: Drawing by Beniamino Volta and the author.

Although great in number, the texts of the SBR differ from inscriptions found in other regions. First, the syntax of the monuments does not always conform to norms elsewhere. Second, the monuments may display odd or erroneous calendrical information. For example, the lunar series on Pusilha monuments is distinct from that in the rest of the Maya region, and in more than one case, lunar series data at Nim li Punit are not consonant with the accompanying Long Count or Calendar Round dates. Another glyphic oddity is found on the unique Pusilha hieroglyphic stair. It contains an "impossible" calendar round date, that is, a combination of the 260-day ritual year and 365-day solar year that under usual circumstances does not occur in inscriptions. This is the only known example in Belize, but others are known in Mexico. The best explanation for this date is that the Haab and Tz'olk'in "days" began at different hours in a 24-hour cycle, and that the dedication described on the Pusilha hieroglyphic stair took place at an unusual time after a day in one calendar had ended but before a new day began in the other. I suspect this was at night, sometime between sunset and sunrise.

Material cultural characteristics of the SBR: burial patterns and pottery

Burial patterns in the SBR are also somewhat distinctive. As mentioned, tombs were closed with long capstones rather than vaults. In the case of extended burials, the most common pattern is a supine placement with the head in the north, turned to face east. This contrasts with the prone, head-to-the-south placement common in western Belize (Somerville et al. 2016:274). Moreover, the opening of burials and placement of multiple individuals is relatively common in southern Belize (for a comparison across Belize and the southern lowlands, see Schwake 2008).

Until recently, the only scholars who have discussed the ceramics of southern Belize in any depth were Joyce (1929), who focused on the polychromes, and Hammond (1975), who described the ceramics of Lubaantun in as great detail as the relatively simple and impoverished inventory of that site requires. Some decorative motifs and forms tie Lubaantun to other regions, but the polychromes there are generally related to Tepeu ceramics of Peten dating to the Late Classic. At Lubaantun and Uxbenka, cream-slipped polychromes with red pastes predominate, while orange-slipped polychromes probably were imported and have been found mostly in tombs and special contexts (Jordan and Prufer 2020). In contrast, orange-slipped polychromes are much more common in the collection from Pusilha, and many of these display the "twist-and-bud" motif known best from Copan and eastern El Salvador (Bill and Braswell 2005). Both orange- and cream-slipped polychromes are common at Nim li Punit. Potters at Lubaantun used calcite temper, while use of such material ceased at Nim li Punit after the Early Classic. Griddles or *comales* are common at Pusilha, but rare to absent at the other sites. Unslipped jar forms at all sites in the SBR often have zoned striation on their necks or shoulders, and stamped or impressed jars are particularly noteworthy at Lubaantun and Nim li Punit. The most common stamped pattern has an "S" motif, but birds and monkeys are also present. Importantly, stamped pottery with these designs is also found at coastal Belize sites (Heather I. McKillop, personal communication 2010), demonstrating close connection between the coast and the inland sites, especially Terminal Classic Lubaantun.

Another shared pottery type is Puluacax Unslipped (Hammond 1975). This very peculiar and ugly ceramic has an extremely coarse paste with irregular inclusions up to a centimeter across and is typified by a pinkish color and out-turned rims as much as two centimeters thick. Puluacax Unslipped is known almost entirely from these thick rim sherds. The vertical bodies of the vessels taper quickly to a thickness of just a few millimeters, and base fragments are extremely rare. The most common form appears to have been a plate about five centimeters high. The few basal fragments we have are extremely thin and charred black, and at least one has a corrugated bottom. Because this pottery is so poorly made, friable, and burned on its bottom, walls and bases generally completely disintegrate. Puluacax may have antecedents at Early Classic Uxbenka and is quite commonly found in later contexts, is extraordinarily common throughout the sequence at Lubaantun, is known at Pusilha in Late and especially Terminal Classic contexts, and appears in lesser quantities at Late to Terminal Classic Nim li Punit. The Nim li Punit examples tend to have rims that are less thick and inclusions that are of smaller size than found at the other sites. Puluacax Unslipped also is found at coastal sites in southern Belize (Heather I. McKillop, personal communication 2010), and the examples I have been shown share closer affinities with sherds from Lubaantun than from Nim li Punit. Whatever this extraordinary ceramic was used for, it is characteristic of the Late and especially Terminal Classic period in the SBR and at least some sites in Stann Creek district (Jordan 2019). In addition to Puluacax, two other pottery types found commonly in the SBR are Turneffe Unslipped and Remate Red (Hammond 1975). The first is the most common utilitarian ware, while the second also frequently appears in serving forms. Jillian Jordan (Jordan and Prufer 2020) sees sufficient similarities between the pottery of Uxbenka and Lubaantun to use these names, and we probably will adopt them for Nim li Punit. Nonetheless, unslipped and red-slipped vessels can be significantly different at Pusilha, and I am unsure if Turneffe Unslipped and Remate Red should be used as names for all such pottery there.

Ties between the SBR and the Belize Valley were forged by AD 780, and the presence of imported Belize Red vessels is an important diacritic of the Terminal Classic period, especially before AD 830. At Nim li Punit, Belize Red is less common in some later Terminal Classic contexts that contain pyriform vessels of the Fine Orange supersystem, suggesting that ties between the Belize Valley and that site may have attenuated as the ninth century progressed.

In sum, the Classic pottery of the SBR displays some distinct types, forms, and decorative modes that differentiate it from the ceramics of adjacent regions. For example, until the Terminal Classic, the ceramics of the SBR shared more in common with Peten than with the inventories of the rest of what today is

Belize. At the same time, the pottery also exhibits significant site-to-site varia-tion, suggesting distinct production and consumption patterns rather than par-ticipation in the same market system that distributed the same wares. Despite the unique or otherwise distinguishing characteristics, yet another interesting aspect of inland Toledo is that two of the sites, Pusilha and Nim li Punit, had very interesting connections throughout the Maya lowlands and highlands, and even beyond the Maya area. I turn to these in discussions of individual sites presented in the next two chapters.

The Southern Belize Region in the Paleoindian and Archaic periods

Among the many questions concerning the Paleoindian and Archaic periods are: who were the first inhabitants to arrive, and how were they related to known groups from much later periods? What was the material culture of the long Archaic period like, and what does it tell us about changing patterns of human manipulation of the environment? Finally, when, why, and how did the transi-tion to agriculture and village life occur?

We do not know enough about the Paleoindian and Archaic period occupa-tions of Mesoamerica to give definitive answers to any of these questions. This is especially true for most of the Maya region, but Belize is one bright spot where research has yielded important information. The SBR is no exception, and Keith Prufer, Douglas Kennett, and their colleagues have made very significant con-tributions that are challenging our traditional interpretations of the Paleoindian period, migration models of early Americans through Central America, and the rise of horticulture and agriculture during the Archaic period. Their results are derived from careful excavations in Mayahak Cab Pek and Tzibete Yux, two rockshelters of the SBR (Kennett et al. 2020; Posth et al. 2018; Prufer et al. 2019).

Paleolithic and Archaic stone tools

To date, a single fluted fishtail point has been recovered in the SBR (Figure 4.5a), but it is an isolated find made by a farmer while plowing (Weintraub 1994; see also Lohse et al. 2006:215). This accidental find provides unequivocal evidence of a Paleoindian human presence in the SBR ca. 13,500–12,800 calendar years ago, that is, towards the end of the Pleistocene.

The next lithic artifacts known in Belize are at least two and possibly four types of chipped-stone bifaces (Kelly 1993; Lohse et al. 2006; Lohse 2010; Stemp et al. 2016). Prufer et al. (2019) argue that they should be classified together and collectively call them the "Lowe complex" even though the types have not been found within the same contexts or even at the same sites, conceivably could date to different periods, and do not represent a complete set of tools, preforms, and debitage (Lohse 2019). Nonetheless, since so few examples of two of the proposed

FIGURE 4.5 Paleoindian and Archaic bifacially worked points from the Southern Belize Region. (a) Paleoindian Fish-tail point; (b) Archaic Lowe point from Tzibte Yux rockshelter; (c) Archaic Lowe point from Mayahak Cab Pek rockshelter.

Source: After Lohse et al. 2006:Figure 4b; Prufer et al. 2019:Figure 3a & 3c.

four types have been found, lumping them together makes a certain amount of sense. What they share in common is that they are well made, have sharp barbs, have squarish bases that are thinned on just one side, and have edges that often exhibit pronounced alternate-edge beveling (Figure 4.5b–c). I agree with Lohse (2019) and other lithic specialists that this last trait probably is a resharpening or curation technology, one that is not related to production and is not particularly diagnostic of any time period.

Lowe complex bifaces are now known throughout Belize and have been found in both surface and excavated contexts within the SBR (Stemp et al. 2016). Their chronological placement is debated. Lowe complex bifaces were originally dated by members of MacNeish's Belize Archaic Archaeological Reconnaissance to 7500–6000 BC, with some examples potentially assigned to the period 9000–7500 BC (Zeitlin 1984:Figure 4.3). This assessment was made with no chronometric dates and very tenuous cross-dating to bifaces from North America. More recent research in northern Belize, where most Lowe points have been found, places them much later during the early facet of the Late Archaic (ca. 2500–1900 BC; Iceland 1997; Lohse et al. 2006). Supporting this later date range are two radio-carbon assays from a single hearth at the Ladyville site (Kelly 1993:215) and a third from Pulltrouser Swamp (Pohl et al. 1996:Table 4.1). Neither dated context has a completely satisfactory association of artifact and charcoal, underscoring both the paucity of radiocarbon dates and the difficulty of dating such isolated and early finds. Turning to the SBR, Prufer and colleagues (2019) recently have provided support for a Paleoindian date for Lowe points using a Bayesian analysis of three AMS assays determined from charcoal recovered from secondary contexts within a rockshelter. On this basis, they argue that finds of Lowe complex bifaces recovered there and in the second rockshelter are properly dated to ca. 8000 BC (Prufer et al. 2019:12). This redating – from the early Late Archaic to the end of the Paleoindian period – is the subject of disagreement with lithic specialists who work in northern Belize. All parties reject as unreasonable the possibility that Lowe complex points span the entire first half of the Holocene.

I suspect that there is *some* temporal gap between the Clovis/Fishtail traditions of the late Pleistocene and the bifaces Prufer and colleagues assign to their Lowe complex. This is because I am not yet convinced by technological and attribute analyses that try to link the Lowe complex to earlier fluted Clovis/Fishtail traditions of the Paleoindian period. Similarly, there is a temporal gap between the Lowe complex and the final Late Preceramic (ca. 1500–900 BC), characterized in northern Belize by constricted unifaces and bifacial celts used to clear the forest for horticulture and agriculture. This later temporal gap is implied by the fact that Lowe and similar bifacial points do not overlap or show significant technological continuation with the well-defined lithic complexes of the final half-millennium before the emergence of pottery and settled village life. What I do not know is how short or long each of these gaps was. For me, the various types of the Lowe complex – if such a thing should be defined – are still chronologically unmoored, floating somewhere in the many thousands of years between the end of the Pleistocene and the emergence of settled village life. Yet there is something about the form, workmanship, and technology of the points that leads me to wonder if they are more likely earlier rather than late in date. It will take more excavations, more radiocarbon assays, and, especially, more convincing associations to resolve this question. I would like to see a Lowe point found within a direct-dated burial of any period or inside the ribcage of extinct Late Pleistocene fauna, like Clovis at Blackwater Draw.

Did ancestors of the Maya make Lowe points? Other groundbreaking research refines this question but does not yet answer it definitively.

Paleoindian origins, migrations, and later populations

Who were these earliest inhabitants of the SBR? Prufer's research in the rockshelters of Toledo District also has provided important genetic data used to construct and test two models of early migration in the Americas (Posth et al. 2018). Although the models differ, they both posit migrations of genetically distinct groups through Central America into South America. The first genetic group is related to an individual called *Anzick-1*, who lived ca. 12,900–12,700 BP and whose remains were found at a Clovis site in Montana. Remains of the earliest individual known from the SBR share alleles with *Anzick-1* and also with Paleoindians from sites in Chile and Brazil. The early spread of these alleles southward, therefore, could be tied to the spread of fluted Clovis/Fishtail technology throughout Central and South America. In contrast, later remains excavated in the rockshelters of SBR show fewer affinities with *Anzick-1*, and "the overwhelming majority of the ancestry of most Central and South Americans derives from one or more lineages without the *Anzick-1* affinities" (Posth et al. 2018:1191–1192). When evaluating these conclusions, it is important to remember that they are derived from very few sets of human remains.

What we can take from this is support for the old conclusion that the fluted Clovis and Fishtail traditions of North, Central, and South America were related. Moreover, this technology may have spread as the descendants of one group of early Paleoindians migrated south through the New World. Among these were the earliest inhabitants of the SBR dating to the end of the Pleistocene. But these early occupants left an ever-attenuating genetic footprint, either as it was selected against or, much more likely, as later groups arrived. Thus, the much later inhabitants of the SBR and Maya Area as a whole may have had some relationship with the Paleoindians of the region 10 millennia earlier, but that relationship probably was quite distant and likely dates to a time before the first Paleoindians left North America and arrived in what today is Belize. Put another way, the genetic evidence that the Maya are direct descendants of the Paleoindians of Central America is very slim and much more strongly suggests that they represent a later migration that, unfortunately, has not yet been dated (Posth et al. 2018:1194). If Prufer et al. (2019) are correct and the Lowe points should be placed early, that is, at the end of the Paleoindian period, then these, like earlier fluted points, should not be associated with close ancestors of the Maya. Conversely, an Archaic date for Lowe makes such an association more likely.

The slow transition to agriculture and a maize-based diet

The third important contribution that springs from Prufer's exciting field work in rockshelters of the SBR concerns the adoption of maize agriculture. Isotopic evidence from a total of 52 individuals that were direct-dated implies that no domesticated maize was consumed before ca. 4,700 years BP, that maize constituted approximately 30 percent of the diet of some individuals during the period 4,700–4,000 BP, and that maize was a staple consumed in amounts comparable to all later periods by a date no later than 4,000 BP (Kennett et al. 2020). The total array of radiocarbon assays made by Kennett and associates for the Belize rockshelters is most impressive. Ultimately, the determination that full-time maize agriculture was practiced by 4,000 BP principally relies on just two direct AMS dates. For some this is enough; for others it is insufficient. For me, the dates are an important first step suggesting a hypothesis rather than conclusive proof demonstrating it.

There is evidence from a patchwork of sites and regions across Mesoamerica, including northern Belize (Pohl et al. 1996; Rosenswig et al. 2014), that by the third millennium BC, maize horticulture began to supplement diets previously based on hunting, fishing, foraging, and collecting wild foods. This trend increased throughout the second millennium. In a few places in Mesoamerica, such early horticulturalists began to live in villages at about the same time that they started to add maize and other domesticates to their diet. For example, just outside the Maya area, the nearest known early pottery is found at Barra-phase villages on the Pacific coast of Chiapas that date to ca. 1800 BC. But within the Maya area proper, the process of settling down occurred much later. There, a mixed subsistence pattern of foraging and horticulture, some level of seasonal mobility, and a material culture that did not include pottery persisted until quite late. In fact, the earliest permanent villages and ceramics of the Maya lowlands date to the interval 1200/1100–900 BC (Chapters 2 and 3). Yet even at that time and in those early "pre-Mamom" ceramic villages, there is no evidence for reliance on maize as a dietary staple. Within the SBR itself, we do not yet know of any village predating the dawn of the Classic period. A very sparse population could be present but would be difficult to detect in open-air sites.

The SBR isotope data, therefore, suggest that a mixed diet including some corn began at least as early as anywhere else in the Maya lowlands, and perhaps up to 800 years before such a time. To be expected during such a transition are stone axes and adzes for horticulture or forest clearance, and perhaps constricted unifaces of the sort found commonly in northern Belize contexts dating to the Late Preceramic (1500–900 BC). Such tools were needed to clear ever-larger patches of the forest for horticulture. To date, a full lithic complex of this sort has not been described for the SBR. Much more surprising is that reliance on a maize-based diet is posited for the SBR fully 1,500 years earlier than has been observed anywhere else in the Maya area. Dependence on maize at 4000 BP would require permanent villages where farmers lived year-round and where maize was stored for consumption throughout the year. Also required would be numerous large grinding stones for processing grain; we should expect at least one for each household, yet we know of no houses with *manos* or *metates* dating to this period in the SBR. Finally, it is reasonable to expect the practice of ceramic technology in the SBR during the transition to reliance on maize as the principal dietary staple. Pottery greatly aids in the storage, preparation, cooking, and serving of maize products such as tamales, tortillas, and beer. Nowhere else in Mesoamerica has consumption of maize as a dietary staple of central importance been demonstrated without pottery.

The Southern Belize Region in the Preclassic period

What we know about the Preclassic in the SBR is easily summed up in a short phrase: next to nothing. The Paleolithic through Preclassic periods of the SBR may at first seem continuous, but a fine-grained lens reveals centuries and even millennia about which we still know very little. There is no unequivocal evidence of permanent settlement or ceramics for some 2,000 years after the posited emergence of a maize-reliant diet. Until more evidence is found both within and beyond the SBR for such early dependence on maize agriculture, these data will be viewed with a healthy mixture of surprise and skepticism. The next step should be to locate and excavate an early village near the rockshelters that Prufer has discovered and carefully studied. Such a village should have pottery, because we know of no fully agricultural settlement in Mesoamerica that lacks ceramics. Levels of the rockshelters that date to all periods after 4000 BP have yielded pottery sherds and even some whole vessels, but most remain to be described and published. We know what Early Preclassic pottery looks like across much of Mesoamerica, and if there is any in the SBR it will display attributes diagnostic of that period. I will be pleasantly surprised if attribute analysis of pottery from the SBR rockshelters reveals that any of it dates to the first half of the Middle Preclassic, that is, to a time before Mamom ceramics. Such a find would rank with that of the earliest complexes described in Chapters 2 and 3. It will be a major discovery indeed if any pottery associated with burials dated to 4000–3000 BP – the first 1000 years after a maize-dependent diet is thought to have emerged in the region – is identified and described.

At present, what clear evidence there is of Preclassic activity in Toledo District is limited to caves and rockshelters where late Middle Preclassic Mamom (the earliest materials that can be assigned unambiguously to the Maya culture) and Late Preclassic Chicanel pottery have been found. We should keep in mind that these are, for the most part, located northwest of the SBR proper, and so it seems likely that the people who visited these locations came from that side of the mountains. A Middle Formative "Olmec style" jadeite spoon was found in a tomb context at Uxbenka that dates to the Classic period (Healy and Awe 2001), and this could have been an heirloom inherited from early occupants of the SBR. Alternatively, it may have been traded to the region at a much later date. Brendan Culleton (2012; Culleton et al. 2012) has dated charcoal associated with agricultural features near Uxbenka to the Middle Preclassic, but this was recovered from contexts that lack artifacts diagnostic of that time. In fact, we have yet to identify any residential sites or architecture with associated artifacts that are uniquely diagnostic of the Late – let alone the Middle or Early – Preclassic.

This underscores two different approaches and interpretive strategies. Should archaeological chronologies be built on radiocarbon dates alone? Or, since archaeology is the study of material culture, is it better to create archaeological chronologies using artifacts and to test them with radiocarbon assays? For me, chronometric dating is supplemental to artifact chronologies and cannot replace them. A radiocarbon date is an adjective that modifies a defined noun, and that noun is an artifact or feature. On their own or used to date undescribed or non-diagnostic artifacts, chronometric dates are meaningless. Radiocarbon assays help us formulate and answer questions about chronologies developed from artifacts and can anchor such material cultural chronologies in real time. But without association with described artifacts or when found in secondary contexts, carbon dates tell us only what we already know: that carbon-based life forms lived continuously as far back as we can reliably measure the decay of ^{14}C. This is true not only for complete chronologies, but also for gaps within and early or late extensions to archaeological chronologies. It certainly is reasonable to expect that fully agricultural Middle and Late Preclassic settlers lived in the SBR. But to date, we do *not* have an archaeological chronology based on material culture that demonstrates this. Early radiocarbon dates suggest that we should keep looking for early artifacts and sites but do not prove that they must exist.

Until more artifactual evidence is found – especially in the form of identifiable ceramics, houses, villages, and the lithic artifacts used for agriculture and forestry – I prefer to view the Preclassic as a time when the predominant human activity in the SBR was the periodic visiting of Maya from other areas, probably southern Peten. The ritual focus of their visits was caves and rockshelters, where they placed offerings diagnostic of the late Middle and Late Preclassic, and conducted cave burials of the sort excavated by Prufer and his colleagues. Since they left pottery within the rockshelters, such materials also must be abundant wherever they lived, yet no ceramics uniquely diagnostic of the Preclassic period have been found associated with the Preclassic radiocarbon dates so far reported for open-air contexts in the SBR. For these reasons, the full-time agriculturalists of the Preclassic buried in the excavated rockshelters seem more likely to have lived elsewhere than in villages located within the SBR itself. Isotopic analyses are not yet sufficient to pinpoint their precise origins, but it is doubtful that they lived more than a few days walk away, probably across the Maya Mountains from the SBR proper.

Why have we found no Preclassic village southeast of the Maya Mountains in the SBR? There are two possible reasons. First, it could be that we have not looked hard enough for them, concentrating instead on either intensive excavation of major sites or extensive survey by LiDAR or other means (see Chapter 5). Second, it could be that no substantial Preclassic settlement exists southeast of the Maya Mountains. For the present, I favor this second scenario but look forward to being proved wrong. Evidence for Preclassic occupation in the Maya area is most often found beneath the most substantial cities (see Chapters 2 and 3). These sites were settled first, grew to be large, and were abandoned late often because of their setting. The best locations for settlement are usually chosen first and are not abandoned unless subject to a human or natural disaster. The central groups of the four major sites of the SBR have now seen significant excavation down to bedrock. If there was anything more than the most meager of Preclassic occupations, we would have found it in the form of ceramics or architecture.

Conclusions

In the first part of this chapter, following the observations of Leventhal (1990, 1992) and others, I describe the geography and Classic period material culture of the SBR in a way that allows the SBR to be defined as a distinct region, paying particular attention to the architecture, hieroglyphic texts, burial patterns, and pottery of the major sites. The last represents a new contribution that, although there are marked differences from site to site, supports Leventhal's argument. Similarities and differences in material culture, and especially how they may be interpreted to understand local political and economic structure, are turned to in the next chapter.

I then consider evidence for occupation of the SBR during the Paleoindian through Preclassic periods. As is often the case, groundbreaking archaeological research in a new region and time period raises more questions than it answers and allows old questions to be refined. Prufer's recent work has done just this. We already knew that early Amerindians passed through the SBR during the Paleoindian period, but we did not previously have any evidence of an occupation during the Archaic. The Archaic period inhabitants of the SBR used Lowe points of the same sort known in northern and western Belize. Although a single point type cannot be relied upon to define an archaeological culture, the presence of Lowe points throughout the southeastern Maya lowlands minimally implies interaction. We need now to expand outwards from Belize to see if similar lithic forms can be found elsewhere. The chronological placement of Lowe points is still uncertain, but there now is intriguing evidence that they might be quite a bit earlier than we thought and may date to the early Holocene or possibly even to the end of the Pleistocene. What seems certain is that the answer to this question will come from the rockshelters of the SBR or western Belize rather than the shallow soils of the north. Sometime later in the Archaic period, rockshelters of the SBR were used as places of burial. Chemical analyses of skeletal materials from these caves raises the possibility that the transition from foraging to horticulture to agriculture began at a very early date, but this seems inconsistent with the lack of evidence for permanent settlement and also conflicts with data from throughout the Maya lowlands that implies village life did not begin long before 1100–1000 BC.

Beyond sharing a projectile point type, what can we say about the identity of the early inhabitants of Belize and the SBR? Genetic evidence is consistent with at least two distinct waves of migration and implies more. The first bodies to be buried in the caves of the SBR show affiliation with a Paleoindian group that elsewhere is associated with Clovis and Fishtail points of the late Pleistocene. Current data suggest that these peoples spread throughout the Americas early and rather quickly, bringing their tools and lithic technology with them. Nonetheless, genetic evidence for their presence in Belize and elsewhere diminished during the early Holocene as other groups moved southward. Until the temporal placement of Lowe points is better understood, we cannot know if they were made by descendants of the first people to arrive in southern Belize, by the ancestors of the Maya, or by some other group of nomadic people moving through Central America during the Archaic period.

To date, no "pre-Mamom" pottery of the early Middle Formative has been identified and described in the SBR. By the late Middle Preclassic period, however, the people occupying or at least visiting the SBR were almost certainly Maya. They possessed and probably made Mamom pottery, which they left in rockshelters and caves in the region. Nonetheless, given that no Preclassic village has yet been identified in the SBR, we cannot say with certainty that these Maya were ancestral to those who arrived at the dawn of the Classic period. The Maya who settled the SBR at that later time are the focus of the following chapter.

References cited

Bill, Cassandra R., and Geoffrey E. Braswell 2005 Life at the Crossroads: New Data from Pusilha, Belize. *Research Reports in Belizean Archaeology* 2:301–312.

Culleton, Brendan J. 2012 *Human Ecology, Agricultural Intensification and Landscape Transformation at the Ancient Maya Polity of Uxbenká, Southern Belize*. Unpublished Ph.D. dissertation, Department of Anthropology, University of Oregon, Eugene.

Culleton, Brendan J., Keith M. Prufer, and Douglas J. Kennett 2012 A Bayesian AMS 14C Chronology of the Classic Maya Urban Center of Uxbenká, Belize. *Journal of Archaeological Science* 39:1572–1586.

Hammond, Norman 1975 *Lubaantun: A Classic Maya Realm*. Peabody Museum of Archaeology and Ethnology, Cambridge, MA.

Healy, Paul F., and Jaime J. Awe 2001 Middle Preclassic Jade Spoon from Belize. *Mexicon* 23:61–64.

Houk, Brett A. 2015 *Ancient Maya Cities of the Eastern Lowlands*. University Press of Florida, Gainesville.

Iceland, Harry B. 1997 *The Preceramic Origins of the Maya: The Results of the Colha Preceramic Project in Northern Belize*. Ph.D. dissertation, Department of Anthropology, University of Texas, Austin. UMI Microforms, Ann Arbor.

Jordan, Jillian M. 2019 *Pottery and Practice in the Late to Terminal Classic Maya Lowlands: Case Studies from Uxbenká and Baking Pot, Belize*. Unpublished PhD Dissertation, Department of Anthropology, University of New Mexico, Albuquerque.

Jordan, Jillian M., and Keith M. Prufer 2020 Pottery Production in a Limestone-Poor Region of the Maya Lowlands: Thin Section Petrography and Scanning Electron Microscopy-Energy Dispersive Spectrometry (SEM-EDS) Analysis on Pottery from Uxbenká, Southern Belize. *Journal of Archaeological Sciences: Reports* 2020:102371.

Joyce, Thomas A. 1929 Report on the British Museum Expedition to British Honduras, 1929. *Journal of the Royal Anthropological Institute* 59:439–457.

Kelly, Thomas C. 1993 Preceramic Projectile-Point Typology in Belize. *Ancient Mesoamerica* 4:205–227.

Kennett, Douglas J., Keith M. Prufer, Brendan J. Culleton, et al. 2020 Early Isotopic Evidence for Maize as a Staple Grain in the Americas. *Science Advances* 5:eaba3245.

Leventhal, Richard M. 1990 Southern Belize: An Ancient Maya Region. In *Vision and Revision in Maya Studies*, edited by Flora S. Clancy and Peter D. Harrison, pp. 125–141, University of New Mexico Press, Albuquerque.

———— 1992 The Development of a Regional Tradition in Southern Belize. In *New Theories on the Ancient Maya*, edited by Elin C. Danien and Robert J. Sharer, pp. 145–153. University Museum Symposium, Vol. 3. The University of Pennsylvania Museum, Philadelphia.

Lohse, Jon C. 2010 Archaic Origins of the Lowland Maya. *Latin American Antiquity* 21:312–352.

———— 2019 Early Holocene Cultural Diversity in Central America: Comment on Prufer et al. (2019) "Linking Late Paleoindian Stone Tool Technologies and Populations in North, Central, and South America." *Lithic Technology*. DOI: 10.1080/01977261.2020.1713609.

Lohse, Jon C., Jaime Awe, Cameron Griffith, Robert M. Rosenswig, and Fred Valdez, Jr. 2006 Preceramic Occupations in Belize: Updating the Paleoindian and Archaic Record. *Latin American Antiquity* 17:209–226.

MacKinnon, J. Jefferson 1991 Preliminary Reconnaissance of the Quebrada de Oro Site: Implications for a Regional Model of Maya Civilization in Southern Belize. *Mexicon* 13:87–92.

Pohl, Mary D., Kevin O. Pope, John G. Jones, John Jacob S., Dolores R. Piperno, et al. 1996 Early Agriculture in the Maya Lowlands. *Latin American Antiquity* 7:355–372.

Posth, Cosimo, Nathan Kakatsuka, Iosif Lazaridis, et al. 2018 Reconstructing the Deep Population History of Central and South America. *Cell* 175:1185–1197.

Prufer, Keith M., Asia V. Alsgaard, Mark Robinson, Clayton R. Meredith, et al. 2019 Linking Late Paleoindian Stone Tool Technologies and Populations in North, Central and South America. *PLoS One* 14(7):e0219812.

Rosenswig, Robert M., Deborah M. Pearsall, Marilyn A. Masson, et al. 2014 Archaic Period Settlement and Subsistence in the Maya Lowlands: New Starch Grain and Lithic Data from Freshwater Creek, Belize. *Journal of Archaeological Science* 41:308–321.

Schwake, Sonja A. 2008 *The Social Implications of Ritual Behavior in the Maya Lowlands: A Perspective from Minanha, Belize.* Ph.D. dissertation, Department of Anthropology, University of California, San Diego.

Somerville, Andrew D., Christian M. Prager, and Geoffrey E. Braswell 2016 Political Alliance, Residential Mobility, and Diet at the Ancient Maya City of Pusilha, Belize. *Journal of Anthropological Archaeology* 41:147–158.

Stemp, W. James, Jaime J. Awe, Keith M. Prufer, and Christophe G. B. Helmke 2016 Design and Function of Lowe and Sawmill Points from the Preceramic Period of Belize. *Latin American Antiquity* 27:279–299.

Weintraub, Boris 1994 Geographica. *National Geographic* 185(4).

Zeitlin, Robert N. 1984 A Summary Report on Three Seasons of Field Investigations into the Archaic Period Prehistory of Lowland Belize. *American Anthropologist* 86:358–369.

5

THE SOUTHERN BELIZE REGION IN EARLY TO LATE CLASSIC PERIOD MESOAMERICA

First settlement, Nim li Punit, and Uxbenka

Geoffrey E. Braswell

As described in the previous chapter, research in the rockshelters of the Maya Mountains has provided a rich and extremely valuable source of information concerning the Paleoindian to Archaic people whose yearly rounds included forays into the Southern Belize Region (SBR) for ritual, subsistence, and other economic reasons. By the late Middle and especially during the Late Preclassic period, village dwellers from unidentified sites that presumably were not too distant – perhaps just northwest of the Maya Mountains – buried some of their dead in rockshelters and left pottery and other objects in caves.

Nonetheless, the first fully sedentary villages that have been identified southeast of the Maya Mountains and in the SBR proper date to the dawn of the Early Classic period. By the late eighth century AD, sites with significant masonry architecture were built across the foothills of inland Toledo District (Figure 4.1). At least seven of these Classic period sites have hieroglyphic monuments, and a few more have purely figurative, pecked, or blank stelae (for a nearly complete inventory, see Wanyerka 2003, 2009). Questions central to the archaeology of the Classic period SBR are: where did the people come from? Were each of the four or five largest sites the capitals of distinct polities, or were they part of a bigger political and economic system that shared a common identity? What role did conflict play in forming the SBR, and how did interaction with larger and more powerful polities outside southern Belize shape the region?

In this chapter and the next, I outline what is known about the four principal sites of the inland SBR. From southwest to northeast, these are Pusilha, Uxbenka, Lubaantun, and Nim li Punit. Xnaheb is a fifth important site located just a few kilometers from Nim li Punit. Very little is known about it, but I suspect it was a satellite of the latter site occupied primarily in the eighth century AD. For this reason, I briefly mention it as part of a longer discussion concerning Nim li Punit. I am not certain to what extent Classic sites in the heart of

DOI: 10.4324/9781351268004-5

the Maya Mountains (e.g., Dunham and Prufer 1998) should be considered as belonging to the SBR, and so I do not consider them here. Finally, and for reasons described in the previous chapter, I exclude from protracted discussion various sites in Stann Creek district (e.g., MacKinnon 1991), as well as coastal sites that must have been integral to the economies of the SBR. Illustrated figurines and pottery dating to the Late and especially Terminal Classic period strongly suggest that the closest ties were with Lubaantun (McKillop 2009:Figures 2 & 3). These coastal sites may have been part of what Norman Hammond (1975) referred to as the sovereign Lubaantun "realm." In contrast, McKillop (2009) has argued that suzerainty was negotiated through feasting, trading, and marriage alliances. Given that relations between the coast and the inland SBR are worthy themselves of extended discussion, I opt in this chapter to limit consideration to the two important sites of the inland SBR that were occupied in the Early Classic period: Nim li Punit and Uxbenka. The next chapter focuses on Pusilha and Lubaantun, both founded in the Late Classic period. At the end of that chapter, I synthesize what we now know about the SBR and discuss in more detail issues of economic and political structure, interaction, and identity.

The founding of the Southern Belize Region in the Early Classic

The earliest known permanent occupations in the SBR are best-documented at Nim li Punit and Uxbenka, but Early Classic occupations also have been found at Ix Kukuil (Thompson and Prufer 2019) and Kaq'ru' Ha' (Novotny 2015). Pusilha was first occupied at the very end of the Early Classic and is best considered a later site. Thus, for more than 300 years, Uxbenka and Nim li Punit were the only sizeable communities in the SBR.

At present, archaeological evidence does not tell us whether Nim li Punit or Uxbenka was settled first. This is likely to remain unknown until a much-refined artifact chronology is developed, but fortunately it is a completely unimportant question. At both sites, the earliest pottery appears in a mixture of modes and types often assigned to the Late Preclassic through Early Classic periods. These include waxy-slipped pottery such as Sierra Red, mammiform feet, Usulutan resist decoration (Figure 5.1), and polychrome bowls and plates with basal flanges. Careful analysis at both sites and years of informal discussions, debates, and Belikin have not yet revealed any single-component context in the SBR that contains types or modes diagnostic of the Late Preclassic without also including Early Classic pottery. That is, the co-association of Late Preclassic, "Protoclassic," and Early Classic diagnostics does not imply that the contexts in which they were found are temporally mixed. Instead, the earliest ceramic complexes of the SBR seem to reflect a gradual and protracted change from Preclassic to Classic, with certain popular wares and decorative modes enduring well into the Early Classic. This gradual change is familiar to Maya ceramicists who work outside of central Peten. At Copan, for example, the transition is called the Bijac phase (AD 50–400, now split into two phases at AD 200). This is a portmanteau of the earlier

FIGURE 5.1   Pottery from Nim li Punit dating to the Early Classic I phase (AD 150/250–400). Both are mammiform supports; the right example has resist Usulutan decoration. These are typical "Protoclassic" modes that date to the Late Preclassic, Terminal Preclassic, and beginning of the Early Classic period.

Source: Photos by the author.

Chabij and later Acbi phase names, reflecting initial difficulties distinguishing the pottery of the phase from what came before and after it. Similarly, a fully "Early Classic" (i.e., by central Peten standards) ceramic complex was not present in the Belize Valley until the early fifth century AD. In parts of the northern Maya lowlands, identifying ceramics between the end of the Late Preclassic and the Late Classic also is difficult. For me, the slow transition from Preclassic to Classic seen in many regions after the Preclassic Collapse of AD 150–250 (see Braswell 2021) suggests continued low population levels, a protracted rather than rapid adoption of Classic Maya kingship and statecraft, and the persistence of traditional social relations of production that did not support the specialized crafting of status-endowing polychromes. We should think of the rapid emergence of Early Classic political and economic structures at Tikal as an exception rather than the norm for the Maya lowlands.

The lack of evidence for Preclassic villages and local chiefdoms implies that the period of initial population of the SBR was during or after the Preclassic Collapse. We call this initial ceramic phase Early Classic I (EC1; Irish and Braswell 2015) and date it to ca. AD 150/250–400. It is possible that the first colonists came to the SBR during and because of the Preclassic Collapse (i.e., ca. AD 150), but we suspect that the earliest documented sites were settled in a later period of population recovery and expansion (i.e., ca. AD 250). Members of the Uxbenka project also have adopted the phrase EC1 to describe the earliest ceramics of that site and of Ix Kukuil (Thompson and Prufer 2019). Finally, EC1 pottery has been identified at the small site of Kaq'ru' Ha' (Novotny 2015).

Although the initial EC1 pottery of Nim li Punit and Uxbenka is very similar, suggesting considerable interaction or shared origins, in later phases of the Classic period the ceramics grow to become quite different. In particular, the pottery of Uxbenka is not as rich or diverse, evinces general ties with the Maya lowlands, but has fewer exotic or specific connections outside of the SBR (Jordan and Prufer 2014). In contrast, the pottery of Nim li Punit is much more diverse, has ties throughout the southern Maya lowlands, and even emulates distant Teotihuacan.

Nim li Punit: an Early to Terminal Classic dynastic center

Nim li Punit is a small but exciting site known to the inhabitants of Indian Creek Village since its founding but first reported to Belizean authorities in 1976 by oil prospectors (Figure 5.2). Joseph Palacio, Commissioner of Archaeology of Belize, gave the site its modern name upon seeing the complex headdress worn by a ruler on one of the stelae at the site. In Q'eqchi' Mayan, *nim li punit* means "The hat is big." Hammond and colleagues (1999) describe initial visits to the site soon thereafter. They drew a preliminary sketch of the center and test-pitted the Stela Plaza in search of stelae caches. Most importantly, this early work documented the carved monuments of the site (MacLeod 1981). In 1985, Richard Leventhal and members of the Southern Belize Archaeological Project conducted limited excavations at Nim li Punit. They also produced a map of the roughly 60 mounds in the site core, as well as a larger-scale settlement map (Jamison 2001). In 1986, Leventhal conducted salvage excavations in Tomb I, just west of the stair to Structure 5. This important find was documented in a newspaper article but has not been published in any detail (Manning 1986). We know that the tomb contained multiple individuals, but sources do not agree on the number. Ceramics from Tomb I are said to date to the Late Classic, but this has not been verified.

Leventhal and his students also conducted the first research at Xnaheb, a nearby site with many more low mounds than Nim li Punit and three stelae with hieroglyphic texts. Employing a gravity model weighted by population proxies, Dunham (1990) concludes that Xnaheb was located on the border between the Nim li Punit and Lubaantun polities, leaving open the question as to which it belonged. A stela at Xnaheb dates to AD 780. Given that there are no stelae at Lubaantun and that evidence for literacy is scarce at that site, it is reasonable to hypothesize that Xnaheb was part of the Nim li Punit polity and perhaps its dynastic seat for several decades in the middle of the eighth century AD. No carved monuments were erected at Nim li Punit during the period AD 741–790, which may correspond to the political and demographic peak of Xnaheb.

In 1998, members of the Mayan Archaeological Sites Development Programme (MASDP) consolidated some structures at Nim li Punit for

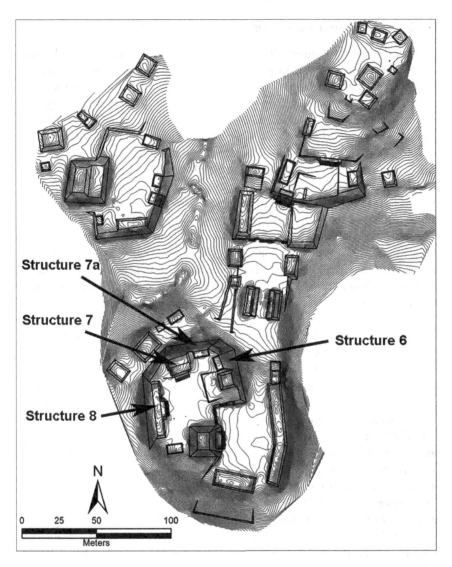

FIGURE 5.2   Map of Nim li Punit showing locations of excavated and consolidated structures.

Source: Map by James T. Daniels and the author.

preservation and tourism and also built the visitors' center (Larios Villalta 1998). An important new monument, Stela 21, was found at that time. During the consolidation of the stair block of Structure 8, Tombs II and III were discovered and excavated. These, too, probably date to the Late Classic period. Documentation of these tombs and several artifacts are presented in the new visitors' center.

The Toledo Regional Interaction Project at Nim li Punit

I created the Toledo Regional Interaction Project (TRIP), successor to the earlier Pusilha Archaeological Project, to consider issues of regional integration first posed by Leventhal (1990, 1992). How did the various sites of the SBR interact? Were they part of a single kingdom, or were they dynastic capitals of independent polities? Did the SBR articulate as an economic system rather than a political one? Do the sites share general cultural characteristics merely because of proximity? Or, following MacKinnon (1991), should we abandon entirely the culture-historical notion of the SBR as a "cultural region"? Using data from seven field seasons at Pusilha as a comparative baseline, TRIP seeks answers to these questions by conducting new investigations of Nim li Punit and Lubaantun.

Since 2010, TRIP members have worked at Nim li Punit. Our work has included a test-pit program, mapping, a ground-penetrating radar survey, palaeobotanical research, the horizontal excavation of structures, and architectural consolidation. To date, we have excavated and consolidated five structures (Figure 5.2). We have not conducted a radiocarbon dating program like that at Uxbenka (see later in this chapter) because, so far, we have been able to answer important chronological questions using the artifacts we have recovered.

Initial Settlement. Like Uxbenka, Nim li Punit was first settled as a permanent village at the dawn of the Early Classic period, during what researchers at both sites now call the EC1 phase (ca. AD 150/250–400). Occupation continued well into the Terminal Classic. Stela 3 contains the date AD 830, and there also is ample evidence of Terminal Classic construction.

In the South Group of Nim li Punit, EC1 sherds have been found directly on the buried A-horizon palaeosurface beneath plaza construction fill, as well as within Structure 6 and Structure 7-sub. These platforms were built directly on plaza fill rather than on a prepared plaza floor, implying contemporaneity of construction. Wilk (1977) reports "Preclassic" pottery from test pits at the foot of the South Group acropolis. I am almost certain that this Sierra Red should be assigned to EC1. The ceramics of this time, as described above, consist of a mixture of Late Preclassic, "Protoclassic," and Early Classic decorative modes and forms.

EC2 (ca. AD 400–500) follows EC1 and lacks pottery with Preclassic and "Protoclassic" modes and forms. To make our earlier work more understandable, an update is needed. Mikael Fauvelle defined an "EC1" and "EC2" in Braswell et al. (2012). Given the subsequent discovery of still earlier pottery, these complexes and phases have been renamed and are now referred to respectively as "EC2" and "EC3." Important diagnostics of the EC2 complex include rare Actuncan Group polychromes, suggesting contact with western Belize, and gouge incised and appliqué bowls with cream slips (Fauvelle in Braswell et al. 2012:103–104). Black and possibly, too, red-slipped monochromes are found, sometimes with coffee-bean-shaped appliqués, but are diagnostic of both EC2 and EC3. Polychrome plates belonging to the Dos Arroyos group are fairly common. During EC3 times, their basal flanges were absolutely huge, extending up to two centimeters from the base of the vessels. We have not conducted a seriation but impressionistically note that basal flanges seem to grow from EC2 to EC3 (ca. AD 400–500).

Ceramics of Nim li Punit

Three aspects of Nim li Punit ceramics deserve special note. First, a significant change occurred in ceramic production between the Early and Late Classic periods. Most Early Classic pottery from Nim li Punit contains calcite temper that reacts when HCl is placed on the paste. In contrast, very few sherds dating to the Late Classic react with HCl, indicating a lack of calcium carbonate. (I add the cautionary note that in near-surface contexts, dissolution and leaching account for some of the drop in reactivity.) Individual lots can be easily assigned to different periods by such acid tests. In fact, of the 30 lots tested by Fauvelle, 18 lots had fewer than 20 percent of the sherds react with HCl. The ceramics in these lots are assigned to Late to Terminal Classic types and groups. Eight more lots had 80 percent or more sherds that reacted to HCl and are judged to date to the Early Classic period. In contrast, only four lots exhibited mixed reactivity rates in the range of 20–80 percent (Fauvelle in Braswell et al. 2012:109, Table 4.1). Thus, it appears that the Late Classic potters of Nim li Punit switched to non-calcite tempers and clays that did not naturally include carbonate. Given that 60 percent of Late Classic pottery recovered from Lubaantun – and nearly all sherds from deeply buried and better-preserved contexts – strongly reacts to acid (Braswell and Fauvelle 2011:5), one explanation may be that the Early Classic potters of Nim li Punit extracted limestone or clays containing it from areas that came under the control of Lubaantun during the Late Classic period. Two important correlates of this observation are (1) it is easy to identify Late Classic imports at Nim li Punit because most have carbonate temper; and (2) it is easy to identify pottery made at Nim li Punit when it appears in Late Classic contexts at nearby Lubaantun because it lacks such temper. The stark differences in Late Classic reactive rates observed at Lubaantun and Nim li Punit indicate that these two sites separated by only a few miles did not engage in the heavy exchange of pottery. As we shall see, identical patterns have been observed at Uxbenka.

A second particularly notable aspect concerns the Late Classic to Terminal Classic Hondo ceramic group. This is a hard-fired, orange-to-yellow/tan paste pottery with fine and well-sorted inclusions and a hard red to mulberry slip. First defined from just 14 sherds at Lubaantun (Hammond 1975), Hondo Red is extremely rare at that site. It is similarly quite scarce at Uxbenka. In contrast, it accounts for 12 percent of the entire ceramic inventory at Nim li Punit (Braswell and Fauvelle 2011:Figure 1.3) and therefore even more of the Late to Terminal Classic pottery from the site. Jillian Jordan and colleagues (2021) have noted that even more Hondo group pottery is known from Late to

Terminal Classic Alabama in Stann Creek, and petrographic analysis of a sherd from Uxbenka reveals that it contained carbonate sand (Jordan 2019:414–415). This may imply that Hondo pottery was produced elsewhere and exported to both Nim li Punit and Alabama. Very tentatively, Jordan wonders if Quirigua could have been one place where Hondo was produced (Jillian Jordan, personal communication 2021). Whether or not Hondo pottery was produced at Nim li Punit or somewhere else, it is clear that the exchange sphere in which it circulated largely excluded both Lubaantun and Uxbenka, implying different economic relations rather than participation in the same regional market or distribution system.

Third, Hammond (1975) observed approximately 150 sherds of Belize Red at Lubaantun. This imported ash-tempered ceramic is present but similarly scarce at Pusilha and Uxbenka. In contrast, Belize Red dating to the Terminal Classic period (AD 780+) is much more common at Nim li Punit, comprising seven percent of all pottery recovered from test pits. This difference reflects the earlier decline of Pusilha and Uxbenka. Nonetheless, Lubaantun has a much stronger Terminal Classic occupation, so it seems that the larger site had much weaker external ties with western Belize than did Nim li Punit in the early ninth century. A final observation is that Puluacax Unslipped, a very crude ceramic that is quite common at both Lubaantun and Uxbenka, comprises only one percent of the total inventory at Nim li Punit (Braswell and Fauvelle 2011).

Excavations and structures of Nim li Punit

To date, TRIP members have excavated and consolidated Structures 6, 7, 7a, 8, and 50. I have described excavation of two of these structures elsewhere (Braswell 2017), so I only briefly summarize that work here.

Structure 7. The northern platform in this portion of the South Group of Nim li Punit was built in two stages. The first platform, Structure 7-sub (Figure 5.3), is rectangular and has the only bench we so far have excavated. We interpret this as the throne room of the governmental palace complex. Like almost all other platforms in the SBR, it had no stone superstructure. It is probable that a perishable structure was built on top, most likely containing a single room with the bench. At about AD 400, an elaborate crypt, which we call Tomb IV, was cut through the plaster floor. Among the five whole vessels associated with the burial were a brown bowl, a Dos Arroyos polychrome plate, and three tripod vessels of Teotihuacan style (Figure 5.4; Braswell 2017). These – and a similar set from Tomb VI – are the first three direct-rim tripod vases found in the SBR and help us place EC2 in time.

Eventually the southeastern corner of Structure 7-sub collapsed. The platform was subsequently raised higher and enlarged in the Terminal Classic to have a T-shape. The lack of a bench, its curious shape, and additional access from both the west and east sides suggest the platform no longer served as the royal throne

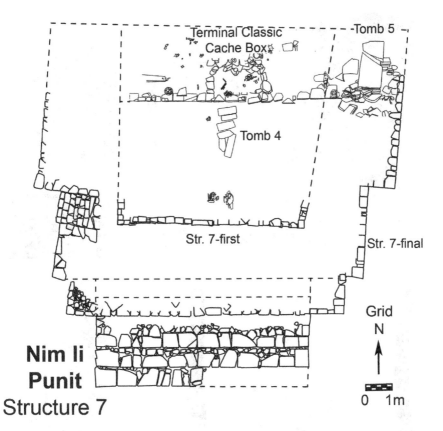

FIGURE 5.3 Nim li Punit Structure 7, "The Palace of the Wind God." Rectangular substructure dates to the Early Classic; Teotihuacan-style pottery was found in Tomb IV, cut into the floor of the substructure. The final Terminal Classic structure is T-shaped and contains Tomb V, where the wind jewel and anthropoid eccentric chert were recovered.

Source: Drawing by Chelsea Fisher, Mario Borrero, Maya Azarova, and the author.

room. At the time of repair and expansion, Tomb IV was reopened, and Early Classic items were taken out of it and redeposited along with Terminal Classic materials in a series of caches on top of the Early Classic bench. Numerous small shell beads painted green were found in the caches, but we also found some on the floor of Tomb IV, indicating that they originally were located there. The Dos Arroyos polychrome plate was removed from the crypt and placed on the old floor of Structure 7-sub near the tomb but outside of it. We found most of the plate in this location, but one large sherd was left within the burial. Many important skeletal elements, including the skull, were removed. A simple bowl placed at the waist of the individual was found empty, but it may once have

FIGURE 5.4 Nim li Punit Tomb IV and direct-rim tripod vases showing trade and emulation of Teotihuacan-style pottery. The lower composite photo-drawings are of the left two vessels in the upper photograph.

Source: Photos by the author, drawings by Luke Stroth and Mario Borrero.

included teeth, as in Pusilha Burial 3/1 (discussed in the next chapter). I suspect this because concentrations of teeth were found within the Terminal Classic caches discovered on the bench with the painted beads taken from Tomb IV, and may have been redeposited from the tomb. Before adding fill above Structure

7-sub, the capstones of Tomb IV were replaced. Closer to the stair, large fires were built, and ceramics containing ash were found.

The most exciting discovery in Structure 7 was Tomb V, which we cross-date based on ceramics to AD 825 ± 25 years (Figure 5.5). Tomb V was placed within the fill of the final version of Structure 7 during repair and expansion. The tomb is a cenotaph dedicated to a large anthropomorphic eccentric chert placed like a human body in the tomb. In form, it is very similar to the eccentric found above Ruler G's tomb at Pusilha. Placed on top of the anthropomorphic eccentric in Tomb V was the jade pectoral or wind jewel worn by kings at the site for 150 years (Figure 5.6). Its shape and position of placement are reminiscent of that of the obsidian eccentric found in Ruler G's tomb (see Figure 6.5). The T form is more serifed or lobed at Pusilha, but both resemble the wind jewel worn by a figurine found in Structure 50 at Nim li Punit. It has the more serifed form of the eccentric found buried on Ruler G of Pusilha.

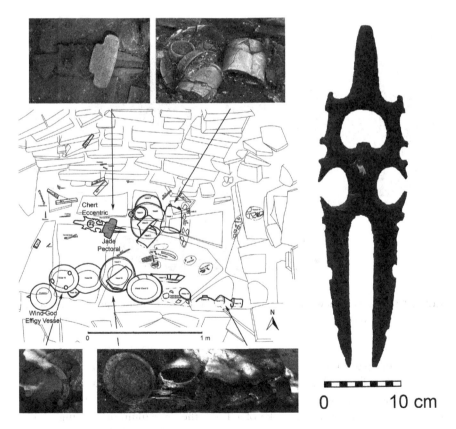

FIGURE 5.5 Nim li Punit Tomb V, a cenotaph containing an eccentric flint and objects indicating veneration of the wind god. The chert eccentric, which was wearing the wind jewel, is shown to the right.

Source: Photos by the author, drawing by Maya Azarova and the author.

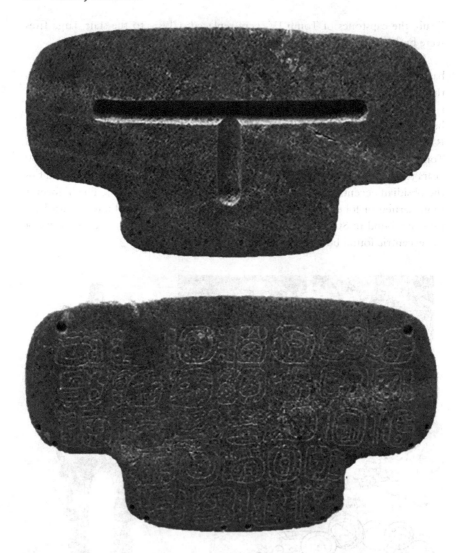

FIGURE 5.6 The wind jewel from Nim li Punit, Tomb V. Obverse (upper) and reverse (lower).

The wind jewel form is an old one. I believe it is derived from shell-shaped pectorals that date back to Preclassic times. Some of the oldest examples appear to be longitudinal sections of conch shells (Figure 5.7). The extruding central, lower element – the vertical stroke of a T – is the operculum or opening of the conch. Some Preclassic or Formative examples even have spirals and chambers. *Strombus* shells have a long and widespread tradition in Mesoamerica as being used to summon the winds that bring the rains that make the crops grow. To

FIGURE 5.7 Preclassic/Formative wind jewels are often made of jade and represent longitudinal sections of conch shells. The T-shape of later Classic Maya examples may be an abstraction of this older representative shape. Figure wearing a wind jewel on the "Shook Altar," a Middle or Late Formative sculpture from Pacific Guatemala (left); three unprovenanced wind jewels dating to the same period (right).

Source: Left: photo by the author; center right is Kerr 4115, lower right is Kerr 6433, www.research.mayavase.com.

speculate more, I wonder if the Classic Maya glyph *ik* for wind is an abstraction of this form.

The Nim li Punit wind jewel was carved in AD 672 and has the oldest known inscription at the site (Prager and Braswell 2016). It points to connections with Cahal Pech and, following some epigraphers, Caracol. I suspect that the original wearer of the pendant was a foreigner who was installed as a ruler of Nim li Punit in AD 652 as part of a political strategy to form alliances in the underpopulated region between the Copan state and that of Caracol. This man was named Janaab Ohl K'inich and is the first of four to five rulers known from hieroglyphic texts and monumental images at Nim li Punit.

Structure 8. This range structure dominates the western edge of the South Group. It was built in four stages and was extended south with each construction episode (Figure 5.8). Structure 8-first dates to either late in EC1 or early in EC2. Structure 8-second was built in EC3. Structure 8-third was built during the Late Classic, but at some time the southeast corner of the platform collapsed. Structure 8-final covered this damage and doubled the length of the platform, signaling its continued and increased importance.

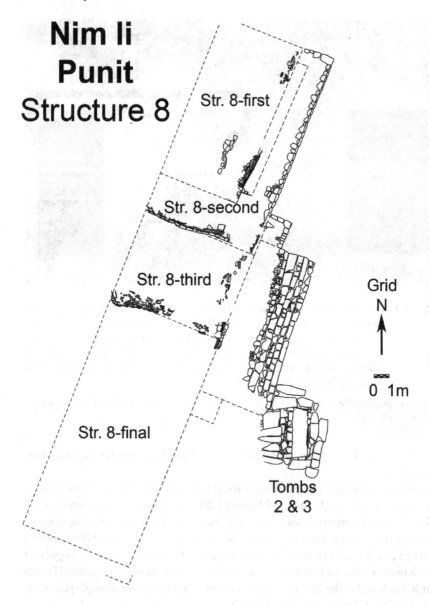

FIGURE 5.8 Plan of Nim li Punit Structure 8 and its earlier substructures.

Source: Drawing by Mikael Fauvelle and the author.

Tombs II and III were discovered by the MASDP during consolidation of the stairblock of Structure 8-final. These Late Classic tombs predate the final construction phase because the stairblock runs over a corner of one of them. In other words, they were built at a time before Structure 8 had been extended this far south. Moreover, their orientation does not conform with that of any stage of

Structure 8. I conclude that the tombs may have been placed in front of a distinct structure that now has been completely covered by Structure 8-final. The presence of a majestic fig tree on the southern half of Structure 8-final precludes its excavation.

No offerings or burials were found within the various stages of Structure 8. This suggests to us that the platform supported a public building. The especially long form and large stairblock allow us to identify Structure 8 as a *popol nah* or council house.

Structures 6 and 7a. Structure 7a is nothing more than a platform or landing at the top of the grand staircase leading up the north side of the acropolis, just east of Structure 7 (Figure 5.9). It was built at a time when Structure 7-sub was still visible and contains an earlier substructure that served the same purpose. During the Terminal Classic, after the construction of Structure 7-final, Structure 7a was attached to Structure 7 by adding a wall containing steps leading up to the summit of the latter near the east end of Tomb V. This wall also is perforated by a drain designed to keep water from pooling in this corner of the South Group.

Structure 6 is more interesting. First, it contained Tomb VI, another elaborate crypt dating to about AD 400. Tomb VI, like Tomb IV, contained three

Grid
N

0   5 m

FIGURE 5.9 Orthophoto mosaic of Nim li Punit Structures 6 (right) and 7a (upper left) after consolidation.

Source: Photogrammetric mosaic by Mario Borrero and Luke Stroth.

Teotihuacan-style slab-footed tripods and two plates. It cannot be a coincidence that the only known Teotihuacan-style vessels in southern Belize were found less than 20 m apart. Nor does it seem coincidental that, in both cases, two are polished brown vases and one is orange; nor that identical shell beads painted green to imitate jade were found inside both burials; nor that both were opened during the Terminal Classic period. We suspect that Tomb VI was first opened for objects included in the caches above the bench of Structure 7-sub, but it may also have been re-looted at an even later time. Bones were found scattered within the crypt, and a mandible, an element missing from Tomb VI, was found on the plaza floor to the west of Structure 6.

The oddest thing of all about Structure 6 is that its front wall of facing stones is completely missing, but much of the stairblock was found in place. The west wall had not merely collapsed, but the stones – including supporting footings set below the level of the plaster floor of the plaza – had all been removed. We suspect that they were used to build the final T-shaped version of Structure 7, the wall and stair connecting that platform to Structure 7a, or low walls just north of Structure 6 on the northeast corner of the acropolis.

Structure 50. In 2019, we shifted our focus to the West Group of Nim li Punit. There, we excavated and consolidated Structure 50, which was constructed during the Terminal Classic and probably supported a large, perishable house (Figure 5.10). Around it we found lots of *Strombus pugilis* shells, a small species of conch, indicating a growing reliance on seafood during the Terminal Classic period. *Manos* and *metates*, laurel-leaf-shaped and bifacially worked stone knives, and cooking vessels are much more common here than in the South Group, and figurines are abundant. Structure 50 was difficult to excavate and even harder to consolidate because it was partially destroyed and patched up in antiquity. Originally, the platform looked like a two-tiered wedding cake, but most of the front and east walls collapsed not long after it was built. Crudely stacked buttress walls, and even a buttress to a buttress, were added to keep the fill of the platform from spilling out farther beyond the original facing walls.

An earthquake in the SBR?

We now have four structures – Structure 8-third, Structure 7-sub, Structure 6, and Structure 50 – that all were severely damaged sometime around AD 800, as dated by associated ceramics. Damage to the first two was covered up in a rebuilding program. The public council house was greatly enlarged, and the royal throne room was converted into a different structure apparently dedicated to the wind god. Damage to an elite house – perhaps part of the royal residential palace – in the largest group of the site was shoddily repaired by stacking stones up against collapsing fill. Finally, although we have no proof of collapse, the entire front wall of Structure 6 was dismantled at roughly this time.

The most likely culprit of all this damage was an earthquake. The principal pyramids of Lubaantun also display evidence of massive earthquake damage (see

FIGURE 5.10 Orthophoto mosaic of Nim li Punit, Structure 50, "House of the Earthquake," after consolidation (upper). Note the buttress wall between the stair and upper level of the platform, and the low buttress wall supporting the lower level of the platform.

Source: Photogrammetric mosaic and model by Mario Borrero and Luke Stroth.

Figure 6.9), but we have had no way to date these events. The tearing down, building over, or shoring up in the early ninth century AD of all the structures at Nim li Punit that we have excavated suggests that a massive earthquake occurred in southern Belize at that time. Nonetheless, I do not argue that Nim li Punit, any other site in southern Belize, or the ancient Maya "collapsed" because of an earthquake (cf. MacKie 1961). Contrary to that position, I note that earthquakes are rather common in southern Belize and that one may have occurred early in the Terminal Classic period.

The repairs and rebuilding episodes that followed the destruction suggest that a shift in the nature of rulership took place during the Terminal Classic. Rebuilding efforts concentrated on doubling the size of the *popol nah* and converting the throne room into a platform with a different purpose. Symbols of kingship, including a massive eccentric and the wind jewel worn by rulers of Nim li Punit for 150 years, were interred during this construction. In contrast, very little energy was spent stabilizing a house platform in what we suspect was the residential group of the Nim li Punit dynasty. We speculate, therefore, that more effort was spent on public projects than on the private property of royalty. This all may indicate the end, or at least the weakening, of kingship at Nim li Punit.

The carved stelae of Nim li Punit

A total of eight carved stelae are known from Nim li Punit. These include Stela 14, the second tallest ever erected by the Maya. Six stelae were carved within two very short intervals: AD 734–741 (Stelae 1, 2, and 15) and AD 790–810 (Stelae 7, 14, and 21). Stela 4 has no date but can be attributed to the first group based on its theme. Stela 3 appears to have been a blank stela later modified for the 10.3.0.0.0 period ending in AD 830. Thus, it is useful to think of the eight carved monuments of Nim li Punit as forming two sets of four: one early and one late.

Phillip Wanyerka (2003; Helmke et al. 2018) has reported three emblem glyphs or variants for the site, including one with a main sign read as *wakam* or *kawam*. Nonetheless, we cannot be certain if all of them pertain to Nim li Punit. It is not yet entirely clear if all the lords with these titles were from the site itself or if they were from somewhere else and their deeds were commemorated at Nim li Punit.

Because of their great height, Stelae 14 and 7 of Nim li Punit are often compared to the monuments of Quirigua. Nonetheless, the stylistic depiction of the visual imagery and arrangement of text blocks on the Nim li Punit stelae in no important way resemble monuments known from Copan or Quirigua. These differences are important because the Nim li Punit monuments are interpreted by epigraphers as indicating ties, explored later in this chapter, to those sites (Helmke et al. 2018; Wanyerka 2003, 2009). Instead, the images on the monuments evince general similarities to art of the Peten and Usumacinta regions. Specifically, the thematic content, arrangement of figures, and even certain iconographic details (e.g., the inclusion of robed figures of uncertain sex in scattering scenes) resemble the stela program at Yaxchilan, albeit in a much more crudely executed form. Irregularities of syntax and other elements place the hieroglyphic texts squarely within the written tradition of the SBR. In sum, the artists and scribes who created the Nim li Punit monuments seem to have been local, shared a general aesthetic with the Peten and Usumacinta regions of the southern lowlands, and were not greatly influenced by neighbors to the south.

The Early Stelae of Nim li Punit: Events from AD 721–741. I interpret the four early monuments as forming two pairs, whose chronological reading order is Stela 15, Stela 2, and Stela 1. The placement of Stela 4 is less certain, but it is thematically paired with Stela 1, and I suggest that it is the penultimate in the series. Together, the stelae focus on a period of exactly one *k'atun* – 9.14.10.0.0 to

9.15.10.0.0 (AD 721–741) – and events during the reigns of two sequential lords of Nim li Punit. I view Stela 15 and Stela 2 as a pair because of their size, odd shape, depiction of three individuals performing a scattering ritual, portrayal of a central protagonist wearing a wind jewel, long texts, and the earlier chronological placement of the events they describe. Stela 4 and 1 form a second pair. They are smaller and more rectangular in shape, focus on the actions of a second ruler, contain shorter texts, and recount (Stela 1) or probably recount (Stela 4) somewhat later events. Although we do not know precisely when they all were dedicated, I argue all four were sponsored by the second ruler and may have been erected during the period AD 738–741+.

Stela 4 has no legible date but belongs to the early set of monuments because it shares references that link it to the others in the group. Specifically, the texts of three of these four early stelae contain the *ek' xukpi ajaw* title (Figure 5.11).[1] The main sign *xukpi* is the head of a leaf-nosed bat, which also is the main sign for Copan. Nonetheless, the prefix/superfix *ek'* ("black") was never used at the famous site. Instead, it is best-known from Quirigua. There, the king who defeated Copan in AD 738 called himself an *ek' xukpi* lord on several enormous stelae carved decades after his victory. This is often thought to be a propagandistic claim of legitimacy of the right of Quirigua to rule Copan, but it is interesting that he delayed use of this title for some time. In fact, the *ek' xukpi* title appears at Nim li Punit decades *before* the king of Quirigua began to employ the title. Most curiously, it appears twice on Nim li Punit Stela 15, a monument devoted to events entirely before the defeat of Copan.

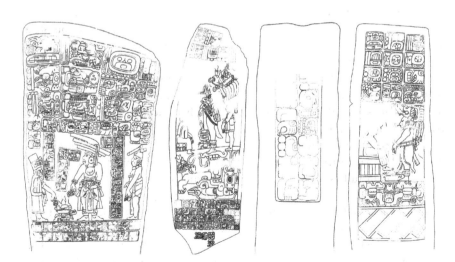

FIGURE 5.11 The early stelae of Nim li Punit: Stelae 15, 2, 4, and 1 (left to right). These describe events during the *k'atun* AD 721–741; all but Stela 1 mention *ek' xukpi* lords (monuments not presented at scale).

Source: After Wanyerka 2003:Figures 14, 15, 20, 29; original drawings by John Montgomery.

Nim li Punit Stela 2 contains two mentions of an *ek' xukpi* lord and two mentions of a "water scroll" lord. The "water scroll" main sign is now thought to be a reference to Altun Ha, an important ancient site north of Belize City and just a few miles from the Caribbean coast (Helmke et al. 2018). That identification must be considered tentative until texts that employ the "water scroll" sign are found at Altun Ha itself. Lords of foreign places are mentioned on the early stelae of Nim li Punit in four contexts: (1) participating in an uncertain event in AD 726; (2) dedicating a stela in AD 731; (3) being present at the installation of a local ruler in AD 738; and (4) partaking in various scattering events during the *k'atun*-long interval AD 721–741. These scattering rituals are the visual and textual subject of most of the monuments at Nim li Punit.

The earliest date on any of the monuments is the large Initial Series introductory date of 9.14.10.0.0 (AD 721) in the uppermost register of Stela 15. The monument depicts a retrospective scattering event that took place on that period ending. The protagonist wears the Nim li Punit wind jewel (compare Figures 5.6 and 5.11; Prager and Braswell 2016). The text caption in front of the (stage) rightmost figure on Stela 15, who is either a woman or a man dressed in a robe, states that person is named K'inich K'uk' and may have come from Copan (*u-xukpi' winik*; Wanyerka 2003:75). One possible interpretation is that this is a relative of the principal figure, perhaps a wife or robed male in-law. In either case, this first mention of a foreigner suggests to me the possibility of a royal marriage linking the Nim li Punit ruler to Copan.

The individual on the far (stage) left of Stela 15 is accompanied by the longest caption. Wanyerka (2003:75) interprets this as a truncated calendar round date of 12 Ajaw; the individual may be an ancestor from the distant past who raised a stela in AD 524. Moving forward in time, the latest date on Stela 15 – and hence the earliest date the monument could have been carved – is reconstructed by Wanyerka (2003:74) as 9.15.3.2.0 or AD 734. Importantly, this is ten *k'atuns* later than the legendary figure is said to have raised a stela. On that day in AD 734, an *ek' xukpi* lord conducted the second scattering event described at Nim li Punit, one that may have been accompanied by an act of tribute (Wanyerka 2003:75).

The narrative continues on Stela 2. The earliest date on that monument is the partial Initial Series introductory date at the top, which Wanyerka (2003:47) reconstructs in full as 9.14.15.4.14, or 16 December AD 726. The event taking place is not fully described in the hieroglyphic text but is said to have involved both *ek' xukpi* and "water scroll" lords as agents. Given that the large Long Count date floats directly above the scene that is the central figurative image, the undescribed event almost certainly was the depicted scattering ritual. The main character again is shown wearing the Nim li Punit wind jewel. Because this scene took place just five years after that of Stela 15, it is reasonable to wonder if the three individuals are the same as those depicted on that monument. The lack of a hieroglyphic caption associated with the (stage) leftmost peripheral figure and the apparent lack of a caption above the seated individual might be attributed to the fact that they already have been identified in the similar scene shown on Stela 15.

The next chronological event described on Stela 2 is the dedication of a stela for the 9.15.0.0.0 period ending in AD 731, in which lords of *ek' xukpi* participated (Wanyerka 2009:519–520). The third and final event took place precisely seven years later. This was the inauguration of a local ruler of *wakam* in AD 738 in the presence of a "water scroll" lord and is the initial subject of the large, lower register of glyphs, immediately above the signature of the artist. It is reasonable to suspect that the lord of Altun Ha oversaw or sponsored in some way this accession (Helmke et al. 2018:128; Wanyerka 2009:489). The newly inaugurated lord employed a title with the full-head variant of *k'uhul* prefixed to the presumed main sign for Nim li Punit (Wanyerka 2003:56). This installation took place less than two months after the death of the ruler of Copan at the hands of the Quirigua lord who decades later claimed the *ek' xukpi* title. It is tempting to tie these closely spaced events, but I caution that we have no evidence that such a connection was causal rather than coincidental. The text of the long lower register of Stela 2 ends with *took' pakal* (Wanyerka 2003:48), or "flint and shield." This is widely considered a metaphor for war, and the "downing of the flint and shield" is typically read as defeat in war. Does the very last phrase on Stela 2 describe a defeat of Nim li Punit? Or might it be a reference to events at Copan in AD 738 that took place shortly before the inauguration? Caution is warranted, and the glyphs are too damaged here to understand more.

Stela 4, which is not dated and whose ordinal placement in the series is therefore uncertain, describes a scattering event in which an *ek' xukpi* lord and a local ruler participated. The order of the glyphs does not conform to typical rules of syntax, but a head variant form of *k'uhul* is used here as on Stela 2, hinting that it may refer to the same individual. Stela 1 depicts a local lord performing a scattering event for the 9.15.10.0.0 period ending in AD 741. His name and titles are visible on Stela 1. Although not completely readable, these include the phrase *lajun ka'an* and, once again, a head variant form of *k'uhul* prefixed to the presumed Nim li Punit main sign. The presence of this variant on Stelae 1, 2, and 4 suggests that all three monuments may refer to the same local ruler inaugurated in AD 738, whom I call "Lord K'uhul Head." This interpretation implies that the scattering event on Stela 1 not only celebrated a period ending but also the third anniversary of Lord K'uhul Head's accession.

The central figures depicted on Stela 15 and Stela 2 both wear the Nim li Punit wind jewel during scattering rituals that date to AD 721 and 726 – a short period of just five years. It seems likely that these two figures are the same man and that the wind jewel serves an iconic purpose to identify and distinguish him visually from Lord K'uhul Head. For this reason, and the fact that his name cannot be made out completely on either stela, I refer to him as "Lord Wind Jewel." The lower glyph register of Stela 2, which begins by describing Lord K'uhul Head's inauguration under the auspices of foreigners, unites the two pairs of monuments, links their protagonists as subsequent rulers, and leads me to argue that Lord K'uhul Head sponsored at least three (Stelae 1, 2, and 4) and most probably all four monuments. Thus, I argue that Lord Wind Jewel was the ruler of Nim li Punit in the 720s and most probably the father of Lord K'uhul Head, who was inaugurated in AD 738.

The monumental group of four early stelae accomplishes several programmatic goals, but the principal one – not surprisingly – is the legitimization of rulership at Nim li Punit. First, the iconography visually glorifies a previous king and therefore legitimates his successor by nature of their relationship. Second, it visually links the two kings through the practice of scattering, a central ritual of Maya kings and especially at Nim li Punit. The (stage) leftmost individual of Stela 15 and possibly Stela 2 is a distant ancestor. His presence establishes the continuity of the royal line, monument erection, and scattering at Nim li Punit over the previous 200 years, further legitimizing the two Late Classic rulers. Third, the texts, accessible by a smaller group of literate elites, mention a "water scroll" lord on one and *ek' xukpi* lords on three monuments. These monuments provide the strongest epigraphic data indicating that elites in the SBR were allied with counterparts elsewhere in the Maya area. Monuments from other sites in the region do not provide this wealth of evidence, suggesting that external political ties were far more important to the lords of Nim li Punit than to those of the other major sites of the SBR. The references to "water scroll" and *ek' xukpi* lords may celebrate the special relationship that Nim li Punit had to those places and acknowledge the role their elites played in legitimizing the rule of two generations of local kings. Alternatively, the references could serve as reminders of a time when the lords of Nim li Punit were vassals to foreigners and paid tribute. Paired stelae at Pusilha (see the following chapter) are remarkably frank in describing unfortunate events, and perhaps Nim li Punit Stela 2 is similarly forthright. Stela 2 in fact ends with the ominous "flint and shield," implying a military defeat of someone. Finally, Stela 1 breaks from the others and omits all textual references to foreigners. Just as Stela 15 began with a scattering event in which no *ek' xukpi* lord took part, Stela 1 closes the narrative in a symmetrical manner with Lord K'uhul Head celebrating a scattering in AD 741 lacking any named foreigners. I interpret this as a final statement legitimizing Lord K'uhul Head as the ruler of Nim li Punit.

The Late Stelae of Nim li Punit: AD 790–810 and 830. The early monuments are followed by a pause of 50 years when no carved stelae were erected at Nim li Punit. At least one, and possibly all three, carved stelae were dedicated at the nearby site of Xnaheb during this period, suggesting to me that it may have been the center of royal activity in the kingdom during the middle of the eighth century. Three of the late Nim li Punit monuments describe events during a single *k'atun*, and two of them name a single king. The fourth monument was almost certainly originally blank and later modified. The chronological reading order of the late monuments is Stela 21, Stela 14, Stela 7, and Stela 3.

Stela 21, found at the south end of the Stela Plaza, has a single date of 9.18.0.0.0 or AD 790. This falls ten years after the only legible monument at Xnaheb. It is

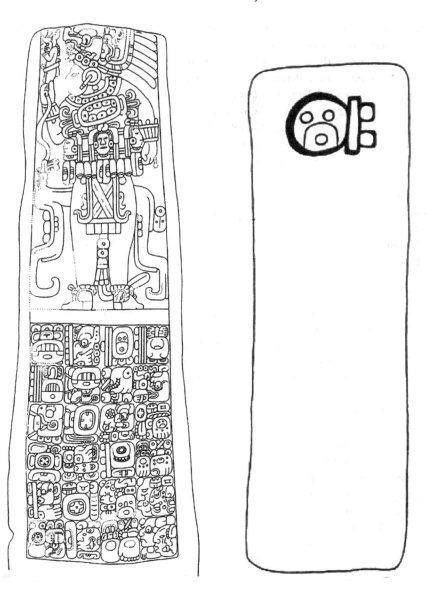

FIGURE 5.12 The late stelae of Nim li Punit: Stela 21 (left) and Stela 3 (right). With the exception of Stela 3, which contains graffiti dating to AD 830, the four monuments describe events during the *k'atun* AD 790–810 (monuments not shown to scale).

Source: After Wanyerka Figures 19 & 32; original drawings by John Montgomery.

the sole figurative stela at Nim li Punit that does not have an upper register of hieroglyphs containing an Initial Series introductory date (Figure 5.12). The image itself, too, differs from most of the others. Rather than a scattering scene, the ruler is shown holding a K'awiil manikin scepter. The king stands in front of a sinuous form labeled as made of stone that could represent the upper jaw of the underworld monster. The ruler, therefore, appears to be coming out of a cave or mouth of the underworld. The monument is well-preserved and seems to contain much more detail than was ever present on the other stelae of Nim li Punit. It also is rendered in a less cartoon-like fashion. A register of glyphs is found below the image and begins with a Long Count date and a description of a "fire" ritual (Wanyerka 2003:82). What is peculiar is that this is placed between the Long Count and the Calendar Round date instead of after the latter. This syntactic oddity creates a visual symmetry: both the two left and two right columns of glyphs begin with a date and then describe an event. Described below the Calendar Round date is yet another scattering event. The glyphs that follow contain the name and titles of the ruler conducting the scattering ritual and presumably shown in the image, and they go on to describe his parentage. Of some discussion is the beginning of this phrase. Immediately following the glyph read as "he scattered" is found *ox witik k'awiil* [position D2] *mo'* . . . [C3] *k'uhul kawam ajaw* [D3].

The glyph block found at D2 directly follows the verb and syntactically could be a direct object, an indirect object, or part of the subject that follows. *Ox witik k'awiil*, glossed as "three roots God K'awiil," therefore, could be the thing that is scattered – some sort of incense. Nonetheless, the construction of the glyph "he scatters" is an antipassive, implying the lack of a direct object. Thus, D2 could refer to an indirect object, perhaps the place where the scattering occurred. In some contexts, *ox witik k'awiil* may refer to the center of Copan. Wanyerka (2003:82) would clearly like to draw connections between that polity and Nim li Punit and so favors this interpretation. Finally, the phrase may contain no object at all, and D2 could be the first part of the subject, that is the beginning of the titular phrase that follows and identifies the king who is scattering. The phrase *ox witik k'awiil* often appears before other titles or names, so this is a distinct possibility. The truth is, we do not really know what it means.

Wanyerka glosses the ensuing nominal and titular phrase as "Macaw Jaguar Sun God of the Night, divine king of Nim li Punit." In his examination of the text on the Nim li Punit wind jewel, Christian Prager identifies a variant of the name of the Jaguar Sun God of the Night, which he tentatively reads as *k'an hix balaw* (Prager and Braswell 2016:5). Hence, the king may have been called [Ox Witik K'awiil] Mo' K'an Hix Balaw, whom I refer to as "Lord Mo." This name is extremely important because Wanyerka also identifies him as the king and protagonist of Stela 14. Potentially problematic is the emblem glyph read as *kawam* (Wanyerka 2003:82) or *wakam* (Helmke et al. 2018). This is the only example at Nim li Punit written in syllabic form, and it is not entirely clear that it is equivalent to the raptorial bird head (perhaps a harpy eagle) present on the early stela. That is, we cannot be completely certain that Lord Mo was a lord of the same polity as the earlier Lord Wind Jewel or Lord K'uhul Head.

For reasons of their extreme size, shape, layout, and iconography, Stela 14 and Stela 7 seem designed to form a visual pair (Figure 5.13.). They conform

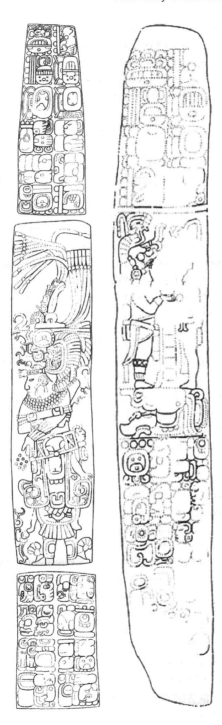

FIGURE 5.13   The late stelae of Nim li Punit: Stela 14 (left) and Stela 7 (right). These monuments describe events during the *k'atun* AD 790–810 (monuments not shown to scale).

Source: After Wanyerka 2003:Figures 25 & 21 original drawings by John Montgomery.

to the basic layout of Stela 2 and Stela 15 – other paired monuments – by having upper registers consisting of Long Count dates, figurative middle registers, and textual lower registers that describe the scene. Together, this later pair also celebrates events over the span of precisely one *k'atun*, in this case 9.18.0.0.0 to 9.19.0.0.0 (AD 790–810). The events begin on Stela 14 with a retrospective Initial Series introductory date that celebrates the same day Lord Mo scattered on Stela 21. Nonetheless, in confounding fashion, the Calendar Round date that follows appears to refer to 9.18.10.0.0, exactly ten years later. Wanyerka (2003:68) believes this is deliberate rather than a scribal error and notes that the lunar series is inconsistent with either date. I agree and wonder if the lunar miscalculation was introduced because Stela 14 may be a retrospective monument erected at the same time as Stela 7. The central image of Stela 14 displays a king wearing the eponymous "big hat" and performing a scattering ritual. Whichever date is meant – and I suspect both – the lower text describes the scattering and immediately afterwards mentions Lord Mo, implying he is the scatterer. Various titles are added but no emblem glyph is shown, and his parentage is again described. Lord Mo, then, is the protagonist of both Stela 21 and Stela 14. On both monuments, his mother is said to be a Lady of "Balam," an unidentified site perhaps somewhere in southern Peten.

Stela 7 is frustrating because so little is legible. Its upper register of glyphs contains a Long Count date of 9.19.0.0.0 or AD 810, as well as the correct *tzolk'in* date 9 Ajaw followed by an unreadable glyph. The image shows two individuals facing each other while standing upon a *witz* monster head. They are separated by an illegible glyphic text. The figures are of equal height, although the figure standing to the (stage) right sports a more complicated headdress. He also carries something in his hands. It is not clear if he has received this object from or is presenting it to the figure at (stage) left. I wonder if these individuals are Lord Mo and the next ruler, and if the scene could reflect investiture of rulership across generations. Thus, I speculate that this pair of monuments, like the early set, seeks to establish continuity and legitimacy by linking two consecutive rulers. Unfortunately, this will remain uncertain because the lower register of text is almost entirely unreadable. It begins with the *tzolk'in* date 4 Ajaw, but there is no distance number connecting it to the upper Long Count date, so we cannot know when precisely it is meant to be (Wanyerka 2003:62). The head variant of *k'uhul* once again appears in a text of Nim li Punit attached to an *ajaw* glyph, but nothing more is legible. Wanyerka notes that the text seems to degrade into a series of non-glyphic circles or spirals, but I cannot see enough on the monument to comment further.

The final dated monument at Nim li Punit is Stela 3 (Figure 5.12). It appears to be a once-blank stela to which graffito was added in AD 830 to mark the 10.0.0.0.0 period ending. The inscription is crudely pecked and consists of an *ajaw* glyph followed by a bar and two dots: *ajaw*-five-two. This is thought to represent 7 Ajaw, the name of the *k'atun*, but importantly is the mirror image of that date. Another example of a backwards 7 Ajaw date is known from the

San Juan cave in the periphery of the salt-producing site of Nueve Cerros, Guatemala. There, a backwards 7 Ajaw pictograph on a ceiling is accompanied by a negative handprint. It might celebrate the same period ending, the seating of a new *k'atun* on 11.6.0.0.0 in the Late Postclassic period, or both (Woodfill 2019:155).

The known carved stelae of Nim li Punit are limited to the eighth and early ninth centuries AD, or the second half of the Late Classic and early Terminal Classic periods. With the exception of Stela 3, the carved monuments of Nim li Punit describe the events of two distinct periods each precisely one *k'atun* in length. Most of these events were scattering rituals, and visual images of scattering appear in four of the six figurative scenes. We know of three and possibly four rulers depicted on the monuments – and can add the earlier ruler named on the Wind Jewel for a total of four or five kings – but because of differences in emblem glyphs cannot be completely certain that they all were from Nim li Punit. One of these rulers, Lord K'uhul Head, probably erected four monuments. Two of these, Stela 15 and Stela 2, celebrate acts of scattering conducted by his predecessor, Lord Wind Jewel. They also specify that foreigners – *ek' xukpi* lords and a "water scroll" lord perhaps from Altun Ha – were present at these important events, as well as at the inauguration of Lord K'uhul Head, who erected the four early monuments. After a pause of 50 years, more carved stelae were raised at Nim li Punit. The first is Stela 21, an extraordinary monument showing Lord Mo, a king whose parentage – including a foreign mother from the Balam kingdom – is mentioned. Although the stela does not show it, Lord Mo conducted a scattering event to mark the *k'atun* ending. The next two monuments, Stelae 14 and 7, form a pair, but it is not known if they were erected at the same time or ten years apart. Stela 14 shows a scattering event conducted by Lord Mo on the same day as celebrated on Stela 21. It then appears to jump forward ten years to a second scattering event that he also conducted. Stela 7 shows an event ten years later, on a date precisely one *k'atun* after the first scattering event conducted by Lord Mo. I speculate that the scene displays Lord Mo handing symbols of rulership to a fourth king, who perhaps is his son. The theme of Stelae 14 and 7, therefore, could be the legitimization of this final ruler by tying him to the actions of Lord Mo, just as the early stelae link Lord K'uhul Head to Lord Wind Jewel.

The abandonment of Nim li Punit

The Terminal Classic repairs, repurposing, and expansions to the platforms described above provide the latest evidence for construction at Nim li Punit, and Stela 3 carries the last modest inscription known from the site. To date we have no evidence of a Postclassic occupation, and the latest pottery at the site, found on top of plaza floors and against the Terminal Classic buildings, probably dates to the middle of the ninth century. For these reasons we suspect that Nim li Punit was essentially abandoned no later than AD 850.

Uxbenka: an Early to Late Classic dynastic center

Ruins in the vicinity of Uxbenka were first reported in the early 1970s by Peter Schmidt, then Archaeology Commissioner of Belize (Hammond 1975). Unfortunately, an early project had to be shut down, and many of the stelae from the site were vandalized in 1985 and then again in 1994 (Wanyerka 2003:212). Nonetheless, preliminary explorations at Uxbenka in the 1980s documented stelae, conducted salvage operations, and probed the site (Leventhal 1990; Jamison 2001). Building on these initial studies, members of the Uxbenka Archaeological Project, directed by Keith Prufer, conducted significant research at the site from 2005 to 2015. Among the important research foci of their project were settlement surveys (pedestrian and later by LiDAR; Prufer et al. 2015, 2017; Thompson 2020), an extensive radiocarbon dating program of test pits and other vertical excavations (Culleton et al. 2012), the study of ceramic production (Jordan and Prufer 2017, 2020a), and climate reconstruction (Kennett et al. 2012). Significant horizontal excavations and consolidation of entire structures were not conducted. In many respects, the methods and research foci of the Uxbenka project complement rather than duplicate those of my own projects, and therefore together our work provides a richer picture of the SBR than any one project alone.

Uxbenka is the smallest of the major sites of the SBR and is composed of several groups of structures on three hilltops separated by a gap of 400–800 m (Figure 5.14). The southeast portion consists of the Stela Plaza (Group A) and other closely associated features. The bulk of the masonry architecture at Uxbenka is located on two nearby hills connected by a saddle. In the north is Group B, with the finest architecture at the site, and Group C. Between these two linked groups is a ballcourt. Together, this largest architectural complex at Uxbenka is perhaps 225 m by 80 m. Groups D-G are made up of lower and more dispersed platforms. Group I is another concentration of significant architecture but is separated from the Stela Plaza by a distance of 2.0 km and from Groups B-G by 1.5 km.

Uxbenka grew rapidly in the Early Classic period. Earlier radiocarbon dates have been reported (Culleton et al. 2012), but the oldest known architecture at Uxbenka dates to the EC1 phase. The EC1 phase also "represents the largest investment in the site core architecture and expansion of the built environment" (Thompson and Prufer 2019:314). Approximately half the houses sampled by Prufer and his colleagues yielded carbon dates in the Early Classic period. At the end of EC1 or early in EC2, the first carved stelae were erected in Group A. To date, no Early Classic monuments have been found at other sites in the SBR, demonstrating the importance of Uxbenka as a dynastic center at that time. Uxbenka Stela 11 appears to be the oldest carved monument and is stylistically dated to the fourth or fifth centuries AD (Figure 5.15). The upper half of Uxbenka Stela 11 is missing, and the lower half depicts the feet to waist of a ruler (Fields 1989:Figure 10; Leventhal 1990:Figure 5). The front of his belt assemblage contains a jaguar paw that Wanyerka (2003:212) interprets as an iconic representation of a portion

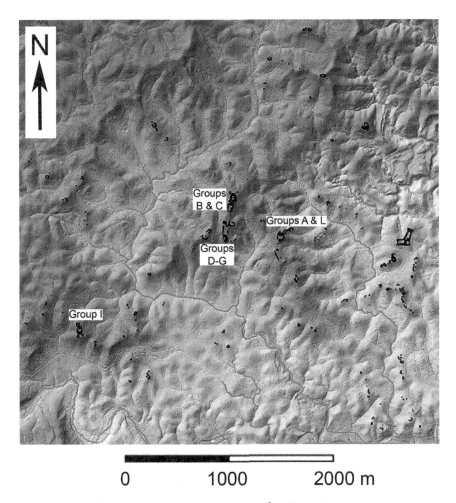

FIGURE 5.14 Uxbenka and its surrounding 16 km² residential and agricultural zone. The dispersed nature of settlement and low number of structures raises the question as to whether this is best considered a single urban site or an elite hilltop manor surrounded by scattered rural residential groups.

Source: After Prufer et al. 2015:Figure 1.

of the name Chak Tok Ich'aak, an important ruler of Tikal who died in AD 378. Moreover, Wanyerka (2003:214) is convinced that a very eroded and defaced glyph on the edge of the monument is the Tikal emblem glyph. He speculates that Uxbenka Stela 11 depicts "a member of the Tikal royal family, perhaps a brother of *Chak Tok Ich'aak* I, [who] fled Tikal for southern Belize at the beginning of the Teotihuacan 'entrada'" (Wanyerka 2003:214).

One can easily imagine that royal regalia might include a jaguar paw without serving as a reference to a fragment of a particular name. Moreover, the text is

FIGURE 5.15 Uxbenka Stela 11 carved in the First Tikal Style, dating to the late fourth or early fifth century AD.

Source: After Wanyerka 2003:Figure 93; original drawing by John Montgomery.

too defaced to read the Tikal emblem glyph with any certainty. Putting aside speculation, there is no doubt that Uxbenka Stela 11 is rendered in the "First Tikal Style" (Borowicz 2003) and shares very close similarities with Early Classic stelae at that site. Whoever the protagonist of Stela 11 was, the monument suggests some sort of connection – artistic or political – or emulation of Early Classic Tikal.

Uxbenka continued to grow during the Late Classic, and fully 98 percent of the habitation structures sampled by Prufer and his students yielded radiocarbon dates in that period (Thompson and Prufer 2019:214). They have characterized the expansion of Uxbenka using terms from human behavioral ecology. Settlement began at Uxbenka following the principles of an "ideal free distribution," where occupation evenly expanded from the most desirable to less desirable land. Later in time, relocation decisions were limited by the elite actors who controlled a disproportionate share of resources in what is termed an "ideal despotic distribution" (Prufer et al. 2017). In other words, power, status, and class differences grew with population levels over the Classic period. The initial pattern and slow transition to an ideal despotic distribution reinforces the notion that the transition to Classic Maya kingship and political and economic systems was slow in the SBR, and that it is unlikely that permanent agricultural villagers were already present before the onset of the Early Classic period.

Strontium, oxygen, and carbon isotope analyses of the remains of 27 individuals from the settlement area of Uxbenka reveal only one isotopic outlier, perhaps from the metamorphic northern Maya highlands of Guatemala (Trask et al. 2012; see also Somerville et al. 2016). What is most surprising is that the results show such little evidence of migration. Overall, such studies from the Maya region reveal that about one-fourth of all inhabitants of a site typically were isotopic outliers who came from somewhere else. Compared to other studied Maya sites, the population of Uxbenka seems to have been relatively isolated, and migration to the polity was quite limited.

Although some Terminal Classic pottery has been found and radiocarbon assays support some level of continued occupation, it seems likely that Uxbenka was the first major site of the SBR to witness decline. That decline likely began before the end of the eighth century; compared with other sites, Belize Red (AD 780–830 or so) and other Terminal Classic diagnostics are quite limited at Uxbenka, and there is little evidence of construction at that time.

Ceramics of Uxbenka

The ceramics of Uxbenka are particularly well-studied. The Uxbenka material is the only collection from the SBR to be analyzed using thin-section petrography and scanning electron microscopy (Jordan and Prufer 2020b). Excavation and the identification of artifacts used in production reveal that pottery was made by several households located in the southern portions of the settlement, close to or on the locations where red, clay-rich, sandy soils are found (Jordan and Prufer

2017). Perhaps the most important anthropological conclusion is that pottery was produced at the household level rather than by communities. The lack of community specialization seems typical of the inland SBR and stands in contrast to salt production on the nearby coast (e.g., McKillop 2005a, 2005b).

Local potters created five basic paste groups. Jillian Jordan (Jordan and Prufer 2020b) assigns nearly all domestic pottery to the "Sandstone B Fabric Group," which lacks calcareous inclusions. In contrast, pottery assigned to the "Mixed Carbonate and Sandstone A Fabric Group" has abundant crystalline calcite temper. The importance is that the practice of adding calcite temper ceased after the end of the Early Classic period. As stated above, this exact pattern also has been noted by us at Nim li Punit. Vessels assigned to the "Sandstone A Fabric Group" have been identified in just a single elite tomb and may have been made only for funerary contexts. This pottery appears to have been produced during both the Early and Late Classic periods (Jordan and Prufer 2020b).

Jordan assigns locally produced polychromes of both cream- and orange-slipped types to the "Quartz A Fabric Group" (Jordan and Prufer 2020a, 2020b). The importance of this find is that, unlike Zacatel, Saxche-Palmar, and Palmar Orange polychromes produced elsewhere in the southern Maya lowlands, these do not contain calcite. Moreover, slips at Uxbenka also were produced differently from those in Peten. Thus, local potters knew what Classic polychromes looked like but adapted their recipes to fit available local resources.

A simple takeaway is that it is easy to determine if Uxbenka polychromes are local and if locally produced domestic pottery dates to the Early or Late Classic. Locally produced polychromes should not react to HCl, and most locally produced utilitarian pottery will not react unless it dates to the Early Classic. As discussed earlier, we have used similar HCl tests to great effect at Nim li Punit since 2011.

Finally, Jordan has identified a wider range of fabric groups in three tombs (Jordan and Prufer 2020a). These include vessels from the Belize Valley ("Calcite B Group"), pottery that probably comes from Peten, and examples that might come from coastal Belize. Thus, Uxbenka had access to pottery from other areas, but that access was limited, and most imported material – with the exception of a small number of Belize Red vessels dating to the Terminal Classic – appears to be limited to tomb contexts.

Characterizing settlement at Uxbenka and other dynastic centers of the SBR

Several Maya villages of Toledo District today are more densely settled and complex than some of the ancient sites of the SBR. Should Uxbenka or these other sites be described as small cities, or were they essentially hilltop manors with a few public structures surrounded by rural farmlands? The answer to that question depends on both method and theory, and it is possible to cogently argue either position (cf. Hauk 2015).

It is important to distinguish between archaeological sites and the larger political territories they controlled. For archaeologists working in the Mediterranean, a territory could be large, but cities began and ended with a wall. Inside the wall were closely packed dwellings and public structures, while outside were spaces such as cemeteries, *tophets*, and garbage dumps. A very few Mesoamerican cities such as Mayapan were completely encircled by walls, but other features can be used to define site limits. The physical city of Teotihuacan can be said to extend as far as its grid pattern. Tenochtitlan and Monte Alban were bounded by natural features: respectively, the edges of an island and the base of a hill. City boundaries also were marked by border stelae, as at Copan, or by *sacbe* termini groups, as at Chichen Itza and Caracol. But many Maya sites seem to fade away, by which I mean their settlement densities steadily decrease to a lower limit as distance from the center increases. These sites have no sharp demarcation line but may be said to end when the density of settlement has dropped to a rural background level. In much of the Maya area, pedestrian survey has revealed that such rural inter-site settlement quite often was more than 100 people per square kilometer. In the SBR, such low density of settlement is reached within a very short distance from site-center architecture. Put another way, sprawl begins just outside the small civic cores of the SBR, and settlement there is no denser than in farmland kilometers away.

The site center of Uxbenka is minute, consisting of the two clusters of architecture formed by Groups B-G and the Stela Plaza. Beyond this, Amy Thompson's excellent pedestrian survey has revealed that the settlement density in the 35 km^2 surrounding the site center is quite sparse – only 315 "plazuela groups" consisting of at least one platform and a patio were discovered (Thompson and Prufer 2019). This is equivalent to just nine habitation groups per square kilometer. Distance between such groups can be substantial. Settlement groups SG25, -28, and -29 form another cluster of structures, but they are 1000 m or farther southeast of Group A. Similarly, SG23 and -24 form a third cluster about 800 m northwest of Groups B-G. Given that pedestrian survey has revealed little or nothing in between, should these be considered parts of a single site or as discrete sites within a low-density rural polity controlled by elites living at the principal group? To me, it seems that Uxbenka is best thought of as an elite manor with a few public structures and plazas that overlook a very rural countryside. From this manor or great house, the most important and elite lineage of Uxbenka projected political authority over the agricultural landscape, but we cannot know where de jure sovereignty ended and de facto suzerainty began. It may be that additional important lineages occupied other large settlement groups and exerted some degree of control over the "neighborhoods" and "districts" (Prufer et al. 2017) of the territory we think of as the Uxbenka polity. I view Nim li Punit and Lubaantun in the same way.

In contrast, other approaches to cities have defined urbanism in terms of social interaction and economic interdependence of the residents of a site center and people living in the hinterlands. A recent study derived in part from the

Uxbenka Archaeological Project takes this approach (Smith et al. 2020). The authors conclude that larger Maya centers had greater surrounding sprawls and lower average residential densities than did small centers. Periodic gatherings and social interactions within central architectural groups led to increasing economic returns on group labor investment, and generated economies scaled in the same general way that cities do. Nonetheless, they conclude that at small central places such as Uxbenka, the Maya interacted at a "slower temporal rhythm" (Smith et al. 2020:120). I take from this that the small centers of the SBR may have qualitatively functioned as urban places even if from a quantitative perspective they did not resemble cities. When seeking to understand the structure and function of ancient economies, the importance of this revelation may be more than it superficially seems.

But how dense was actual settlement? Once again, pedestrian survey of 35 km^2 surrounding the principal groups of Uxbenka discovered just 315 "plazuela groups," a term used by project members as roughly equivalent to the built environment occupied by a household or extended family. This translates to a population density of something on the order of 50 people per square kilometer – a very low number, indeed, and we must remember that not all structures were precisely contemporaneous. Nonetheless, various visualization techniques recently employed to inspect LiDAR survey data have revealed an additional possible 563 groups in the same territory (Thompson 2020). Thus – assuming pedestrian survey is able to verify the existence of them all – there could be a density of up to 25 plazuela groups per square kilometer, perhaps implying as many as 150 people per square kilometer. This is less than half the rural density of 340 people per square kilometer within a stretch 25–50 km north of Calakmul (Braswell et al. 2004:193). That density was calculated not from LiDAR data but from pedestrian survey, more comparable in method to the earlier terrestrial survey of Uxbenka. The density of settlement in the sustaining area of Uxbenka – and, I assume, of other major sites in the SBR – may be more than we thought. But it is still *several times less than rural settlement* quite distant from the center of a major Maya polity.

Important data from surveys around Uxbenka imply that the small centers of southern Belize could have functioned in some ways that resemble cities with "a slower temporal rhythm" of interaction. Nonetheless, to the casual modern observer, the landscape would have seemed exceedingly rural in character.

Abandonment of Uxbenka

Terminal Classic occupation of Uxbenka was limited. Small quantities of Belize Red, a Terminal Classic diagnostic ware, were recovered from some contexts, but these postdate all but the most minor of building activities. Several radiocarbon dates also support occupation during the Terminal Classic. Nonetheless, it seems likely to me that population levels began to drop no later than AD 780 and that there is very little evidence of occupation after about AD 830. A commemorative visit to the ruins of Uxbenka is demonstrated by a single Postclassic cache found in front of Stela 7 (Thompson and Prufer 2019), but no significant

Postclassic occupation of Uxbenka has been documented by archaeological materials. In fact, the only other Postclassic diagnostic artifacts found within the inland SBR come from caves and a single structure at Pusilha.

I address what happened to the inhabitants of Uxbenka in the following chapter and also consider Pusilha and Lubaantun, the last two major sites to be settled in the SBR. I end these three chapters by synthesizing what we now know about the SBR and discussing in more detail issues of economic and political structure, interaction, and identity.

Note

1 Stephen Houston (personal communication 2021) reminds me that the reading of the leaf-nosed bat glyph as *xukpi* is tentative and should not be considered definitive.

References cited

Borowicz, James 2003 Images of Power and the Power of Images: Early Classic Iconographic Programs of the Carved Monuments of Tikal. In *The Maya and Teotihuacan: Reinterpreting Early Classic Interaction*, edited by Geoffrey E. Braswell, pp. 217–234. University of Texas, Austin.

Braswell, Geoffrey E. 2017 Recent Discoveries in the Classic Maya Palace Complex of Nim li Punit, Belize. *Journal of Field Archaeology* 42:69–81.

——— 2021 The Other Maya and the Other Maya Collapse: Southern Guatemala during the Terminal Preclassic Period. In *Post-Apocalypto: Crisis and Resilience in the Maya World*, edited by Harri Kettunnen. Acta Mesoamericana Verlag, Anton Sauerwein, Markt Schwaben, Germany. In press.

Braswell, Geoffrey E., and Mikael Fauvelle 2011 *Toledo Regional Interaction Project: 2012 Annual Report*. Occasional Paper No. 5, UCSD Mesoamerican Archaeology Laboratory, San Diego, CA.

Braswell, Geoffrey E., Chelsea R. Fisher, and Mikael Fauvelle 2012 *Toledo Regional Interaction Project: 2012 Annual Report*. Occasional Paper No. 6, UCSD Mesoamerican Archaeology Laboratory, San Diego, CA.

Braswell, Geoffrey E., Joel D. Gunn, María del Rosario Domínguez C., William J. Folan, et al., 2004 Defining the Terminal Classic at Calakmul, Campeche. In *The Terminal Classic in the Maya Lowlands: Collapse, Transition, and Transformation*, edited by Arthur A. Demarest, Don S. Rice, and Prudence M. Rice, pp. 162–194. The University Press of Colorado, Boulder.

Culleton, Brendan J., Keith M. Prufer, and Douglas J. Kennett 2012 A Bayesian AMS 14C Chronology of the Classic Maya Urban Center of Uxbenká, Belize. *Journal of Archaeological Science* 39:1572–1586.

Dunham, Peter S. 1990 *Coming Apart at the Seams: The Classic Development and Demise of the Maya Civilization (A Segmentary View from Xnaheb, Belize)*. Ph.D dissertation, Department of Anthropology, State University of New York at Albany.

Dunham, Peter S., and Keith M. Prufer 1998 En la cumbre del Clásico: Descubrimientos recientes en la Montaña Maya en el sur de Belice. In *XI Simposio de Investigaciones Arqueológicas en Guatemala, 1997*, edited by Juan Pedro Laporte and Héctor L. Escobedo, pp. 165–170. Museo Nacional de Arqueología y Etnología, Guatemala.

Fields, Virginia Mary 1989 *The Origins of Divine Kingship among the Lowland Classic Maya*. Ph.D. dissertation, Department of Art and Art History, University of Texas at Austin.

Irish, Mark D., and Geoffrey E. Braswell 2015 Towards an Archaeological Chronology of Southern Belize. *Research Reports in Belizean Archaeology* 12:271–279.

Hammond, Norman 1975 *Lubaantun: A Classic Maya Realm.* Peabody Museum of Archaeology and Ethnology, Cambridge, MA.

Hammond, Norman, Sheena Howarth, and Richard R. Wilk 1999 *The Discovery, Exploration, and Monuments of Nim Li Punit, Belize.* Research Reports on Ancient Maya Writing, No. 40 & 40a. Center for Maya Research, Washington, DC.

Hauk, Brett 2015 *Ancient Maya Cities of the Eastern Lowlands.* University Press of Florida, Orlando.

Helmke, Christophe, Stanley P. Guenter, and Phillip J. Wanyerka 2018 Kings of the East: Altun Ha and the Water Scroll Emblem Glyph. *Ancient Mesoamerica* 29:112–135.

Jamison, Thomas R. 2001 Social Organization and Architectural Context: A Comparison of Nim li Punit and Xnaheb. In *The Past and Present Maya: Essays in Honor of Robert M. Carmack*, edited by John M. Weeks, pp. 73–87. Labyrithos Press, Lancaster, CA.

Jordan, Jillian M. 2019 *Pottery and Practice in the Late to Terminal Classic Maya Lowlands: Case Studies from Uxbenká and Baking Pot, Belize.* PhD Dissertation, Department of Anthropology, University of New Mexico.

Jordan, Jillian M., and Keith M. Prufer 2014 Contextualizing Uxbenká: Ceramic Analyses from Site Core and Household Contexts. *Research Reports in Belizean Archaeology* 11:317–326.

———— 2017 Identifying Domestic Ceramic Production in the Maya Lowlands: A Case Study from Uxbenka, Belize. *Latin American Antiquity* 28:66–87.

———— 2020a Identifying Local and Non-Local Pottery in Three Tombs at Uxbenká, Toledo District: Results of Thin Section Analysis. *Research Reports in Belizean Archaeology* 17:209–219.

———— 2020b Pottery Production in a Limestone-Poor Region of the Maya Lowlands: Thin Section Petrography and Scanning Electron Microscopy-Energy Dispersive Spectrometry (SEM-EDS) Analysis on Pottery from Uxbenká, Southern Belize. *Journal of Archaeological Sciences: Reports* 2020:102371.

Jordan, Jillian M., Meaghan M. Peuramaki-Brown, Sylvestro Chiac, Aurora Saqui, et al. 2021 It's What's Inside That Counts: Developing a Paste Group Typology in Belize. *Journal of Archaeological Science: Reports* 37:103019.

Kennett, Douglas J., Sebastian F. M. Breitenbach, Valorie V. Aquino, Yemane Asmerom, Jaime Awe, et al. 2012 Development and Disintegration of Maya political Systems in Response to Climate Change. *Science* 338:788–791.

Larios Villalta, R 1998 *Mayan Archaeological Sites Development Programe [sic]. Archaeology Department: Belize, C.A., January–July 1998.* Unpublished report prepared for the Department of Archaeology, Belmopan, Belize.

Leventhal, Richard M. 1990 Southern Belize: An Ancient Maya Region. In *Vision and Revision in Maya Studies*, edited by Flora S. Clancy and Peter D. Harrison, pp. 125–141. University of New Mexico Press, Albuquerque.

———— 1992 The Development of a Regional Tradition in Southern Belize. In *New Theories on the Ancient Maya*, edited by Elin C. Danien and Robert J. Sharer, pp. 145–153. University Museum Symposium, Vol. 3. The University of Pennsylvania Museum, Philadelphia.

MacKie, Euan 1961 New Light on the End of the Maya Classic Culture at Benque Viejo, British Honduras. *American Antiquity* 27:216–224.

MacKinnon, J. Jefferson 1991 Preliminary Reconnaissance of the Quebrada de Oro Site: Implications for a Regional Model of Maya Civilization in Southern Belize. *Mexicon* 13:87–92.

MacLeod, Barbara 1981 *The Hieroglyphic Inscriptions of Nim Li Punit, Toledo, Belize.* Unpublished manuscript in the library of the Institute of Archaeology, National Institute of Culture and History, Belmopan, Belize.

Manning, C. 1986 Digging into the Past: Ancient Tomb May Hold Clues to Mayan Civilization. *The Recorder.* June 7, p. 11. Amsterdam, NY.

McKillop, Heather I. 2005a Finds in Belize Document Late Classic Maya Salt Making and Canoe Transport. *Proceedings of the National Academy of Sciences* 102:5630–5634.

——— 2005b *In Search of Maya Sea Traders.* Texas A&M University Press, College Station.

——— 2009 The Geopolitics of the Coastal Maya Economy in Belize: Relations between the Coastal and Inland Maya. *Research Reports in Belizean Archaeology* 6:55–61.

Novotny, Claire 2015 *Social Identity Across Landscapes: Ancient Lives and Modern Heritage in a Q'eqchi' Maya Village.* Ph.D. dissertation, Department of Anthropology, University of North Carolina, Chapel Hill.

Prager, Christian M., and Geoffrey E. Braswell 2016 Maya Politics and Ritual: An Important New Hieroglyphic Text on a Carved Jade from Belize. *Ancient Mesoamerica* 27:267–278.

Prufer, Keith M., Amy E. Thompson, and Douglas J. Kennett 2015 Evaluating Airborne LiDAR for Detecting Settlements and Modified Landscapes in Disturbed Tropical Environments at Uxbenká, Belize. *Journal of Archaeological Science* 57:1–13.

Prufer, Keith M., Amy E. Thompson, C. R. Meredith, Jillian M. Jordan, Claire E. Ebert, et al. 2017 The Classic Period Maya Transitions from an Ideal Free to Ideal Despotic Settlement System at the Middle-Level Polity of Uxbenká. *Journal of Anthropological Archaeology* 45:53–68.

Smith, Michael E., Scott G. Ortman, José Lobo, Claire E. Ebert, Amy E. Thompson, et al. 2020 The Low-Density Urban Systems of the Classic Period Maya and Izapa: Insights from Settlement Scaling Theory. *Latin American Antiquity* 32:120–137.

Somerville, Andrew D., Margaret J. Schoeninger, and Geoffrey E. Braswell 2016 Political Alliance, Residential Mobility, and Diet at the Ancient Maya City of Pusilha, Belize. *Journal of Anthropological Archaeology* 41:147–158.

Thompson, Amy E. 2020 Detecting Classic Maya Settlements with Lidar-Derived Relief Visualizations. *Remote Sensing* 12(17):2838. https://doi.org/10.3390/rs12172838.

Thompson, Amy E., and Keith M. Prufer 2019 Archaeological Research in Southern Belize at Uxbenká and Ix Kuku'il. *Research Reports in Belizean Archaeology* 16:311–322.

Trask, Willa R., Lori E. Wright, and Keith M. Prufer 2012 Isotopic Evidence for Mobility in the Southeastern Maya Periphery: Preliminary Evidence from Uxbenká, Toledo District, Belize. *Reports in Belizean Archaeology* 9:61–74.

Wanyerka, Phillip J. 2003 *The Southern Belize Epigraphic Project: The Hieroglyphic Inscriptions of Southern Belize.* Report submitted to the Foundation for the Advancement of Mesoamerican Studies, Inc., 1 December.

——— 2009 *Classic Maya Political Organization: Epigraphic Evidence of Hierarchical Organization in the Southern Maya Mountains Region of Belize.* PhD dissertation, Department of Anthropology, Southern Illinois University, Carbondale. University Microforms, Ann Arbor, MI.

Wilk, Richard R. 1977 *Preliminary Operations at Nimli Punit, Belize, 1976.* Report on file at the Institute of Archaeology, Belmopan.

Woodfill, Brent K. S. 2019 *War in the Land of True Peace: The Fight for Maya Sacred Places.* University of Oklahoma Press, Norman.

6

THE SOUTHERN BELIZE REGION IN LATE TO TERMINAL CLASSIC PERIOD MESOAMERICA

Pusilha, Lubaantun, and identity

Geoffrey E. Braswell

The first of these three chapters on the archaeology of the Southern Belize Region (SBR) concentrates on the characteristics that define it, as well as evidence for the earliest human use of the region from the Paleoindian through Preclassic periods. The second chapter considers issues of initial settlement in permanent villages and traces the long histories of two of the major sites, Nim li Punit and Uxbenka, both settled in the Early Classic period. Along the way, I consider issues of foreign political alliances, warfare, economy, the nature of ancient cities, and identity. In this chapter, I continue these threads by turning to two major sites of the SBR that were founded in the Late Classic period: Pusilha and Lubaantun. I conclude by synthesizing what the major projects conducted in the inland SBR over the past 20 years have taught us about identity, politics, and warfare in this small corner of the Maya world.

Pusilha: a Late Classic city and dynastic capital

Archaeological fieldwork was first conducted at Pusilha from 1928 to 1930 by explorers from the British Museum (Gruning 1930; Joyce 1929; Joyce et al. 1928). They had previously worked at Lubaantun, but the discovery of a site with hieroglyphic monuments spurred them to move operations to remote Pusilha (Figures 4.1 and 6.1). Their excavations focused on the Stela Plaza, Big Tree Group, and especially within Pottery Cave. The last is a *chultun*-like feature in which large quantities of ceramics and other artifacts were deposited. The extreme soil conditions at Pusilha – indeed throughout most of the SBR – result in very poor preservation, but the ceramics from within Pottery Cave are a notable exception. Approximately 50 large wooden crates containing most of the polychrome sherds that were excavated were brought back to London and are now stored there. Monochrome and unslipped sherds were left piled in front of the collapsed side of the cave. The most important discoveries were the stelae.

DOI: 10.4324/9781351268004-6

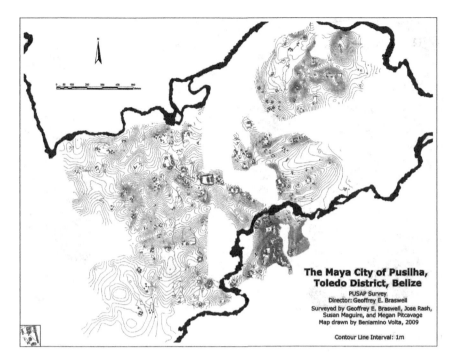

The Maya City of Pusilha,
Toledo District, Belize
PUSAP Survey
Director: Geoffrey E. Braswell
Surveyed by Geoffrey E. Braswell, Jose Rash,
Susan Maguire, and Megan Pitcavage
Map drawn by Beniamino Volta, 2009

Contour Line Interval: 1m

FIGURE 6.1   Map of Pusilha, Toledo District.

The best preserved were brought to London, where they are now kept in a storage facility (Figure 6.2). From 1930 to 1970, when Norman Hammond (1975)
visited Pusilha and re-explored Pottery Cave, no work was conducted at Pusilha.
Limited, sporadic, and largely unpublished fieldwork was conducted in 1979,
1980, and 1992. The most important discovery at that time was of the Moho
Plaza, an outlying group with a significant Terminal Classic occupation, a large
ballcourt with carved markers, and the only intact hieroglyphic stair known in
Belize (see Braswell et al. 2004).

The Pusilha Archaeological Project: 2001–2008

Our work in southern Belize began at Pusilha. Project members have published
a long summary of the results of the Pusilha Archaeological Project, conducted
from 2001 to 2008 (Prager et al. 2014). After Nim li Punit and Uxbenka, Pusilha
was the third important site to be established in the region. According to hieroglyphic texts, this occurred in AD 571 when the dynastic founder arrived at the
site (Prager et al. 2014:283). Archaeological excavations have revealed very limited and highly localized evidence of an Early Classic occupation, suggesting that
the first settlers were concentrated in the Pottery Cave group and arrived at the
time implied by the texts. Within a century, the site grew to be the largest by far
in the SBR, occupying an area of about 6 km^2 and with a population density of
about 1,100 per km^2. Given that urban studies suggest the SBR sites functioned

FIGURE 6.2 Current location of the best-preserved Pusilha stelae in a storage facility of the British Museum.

Source: Photo by the author.

like small cities with a "slower temporal rhythm" (Smith et al. 2020:120), Pusilha is the only ancient settlement in Toledo District that to my mind physically resembled a large town or city (Prager et al. 2014:250). Pusilha may have had more than 6,000 inhabitants, Lubaantun about 1,300 (Hammond 1975), while the cores of Nim li Punit and Uxbenka probably each had only a few hundred occupants.

Since the late 1920s, scholars have posited some sort of connection of Pusilha to Quirigua and Copan in the southeastern Maya region. This possible external connection stimulated our original interest in Pusilha and the SBR. The main sign of the emblem glyph for Pusilha is an avocado tree, read as *un* by Christian Prager (Prager et al. 2014:277, Figure 10.20), and sometimes is accompanied by *ehb*, meaning steps, an apparent reference to the giant staircase on the acropolis. The main sign for the Quirigua emblem glyph is similar to the avocado tree but is rotated 90 degrees, evoking a connection between the sites. The British Museum documented three zoomorphic altars at Pusilha that resemble frogs but are thought to be ocelots or jaguars (Figure 6.3). These are much smaller and cruder than examples from Quirigua or even Copan. A final connection noted by Cassandra Bill, project ceramicist, is that some polychromes from Pusilha have the "twist-and-bud" motif, known at Copan but much more frequent in eastern El Salvador (Bill and Braswell 2005). All of these seeming connections led us to focus on questions concerning the relationship between Pusilha and these two better-known sites in Guatemala and Honduras.

FIGURE 6.3 Zoomorphic altars of Pusilha.

Source: Upper left: Morley 1937–1938; upper right and lower by the author.

Beyond the use of the twist-and-bud motif, Bill's study of the pottery did not reveal other connections with Copan, except for a few sherds of Casaca Striated pottery, which is a non-Maya ceramic. Instead, she argues that the closest ties are found to sites in the southwestern Peten, especially the Rio Pasion zone (Bill and Braswell 2005). We therefore view that general region as the probable origin of most of the people who settled at Pusilha at the dawn of the Late Classic.

Some Puluacax Unslipped pottery is present in Terminal Classic contexts, but otherwise the ceramic inventory of Pusilha is distinctive and quite different from that of the rest of the SBR. Orange-slipped polychromes are most common (the opposite of the pattern at Lubaantun and Uxbenka), stamped designs on jars are very rare, and – unique for the region – *comales* (tortilla griddles) are common. This last implies a significant difference in foodways and culture. The *manos* and *metates* found at Pusilha, like most of those found at the other major SBR sites, have legs or feet, implying that they were manufactured in the Maya highlands. Again, like most other sites in the region, these grinding stones were made of a dense volcanic pumice most probably from Guatemala. Nonetheless, Pusilha also received ground stone tools of pink- and green-tinted volcanic tuff from somewhere not far from Copan, and other *manos* and *metates* from the Mountain Pine Ridge of western Belize (Brian Holland, personal communication 2007).

Obsidian procurement patterns at Pusilha indicate participation in a Late Classic trade sphere that included Peten but excluded Copan, supporting the notion that economic connections with western Honduras were never strong.

Epigraphic analysis

Christian Prager, project epigrapher, studied the dynastic history of the site (Prager et al. 2014). His work has resulted in one of the most complete dynastic histories in all of Belize, second only to that of Caracol. Prager identified 11 individuals who used the title *k'uhul un ajaw*, or holy lord of Pusilha. Seven of these can be placed into the chronology of the site. The dynastic founder was K'awil Chan K'inich Muwan Sak Tz'unun or "Ruler A." He also was an *ochk'in kalomte'*, a title generally thought to be reserved for overlord high kings, but in this and many other cases it indicates only that he was a dynastic founder. Portions of two monuments erected by Ruler A survive. These are Stela O (9.7.0.0.0) and Stela Q (9.8.0.0.0), commemorating the period endings in AD 573 and AD 593. The fragmentary Stela O was found at the focus of the Stela Plaza monuments, indicating special reverence as the oldest monument at the site. Ruler A died as an old man sometime about AD 600. One reason that we cannot pinpoint this date more exactly is that Pusilha may have suffered more than one bad military defeat during his rule, and a retrospective text claims that stelae – perhaps a reference to Stelae O and Q – were destroyed. The "water scroll" site, probably Altun Ha (Helmke et al. 2018), was the agent of this destruction in AD 595. Given that a "water scroll" lord was the suzerain of Nim li Punit a century later, we may wonder if Pusilha and that site had different external relations and alliances, or if Altun Ha once contested for hegemony of the entire SBR. Immediately following the description of this apparent defeat of Pusilha is a long description of yet another warfare event that took place under the auspices of one Chan Ek', a person from Yok'baj: an unknown place. Finally, the long and dramatic phrase ends by stating that blood was spilt (Prager et al. 2014:282–283).

Ruler A was followed by his son K'ak' u ti' Chan ("Ruler B"), who shared his name with the contemporary Ruler 11 of Copan nicknamed "Butz Chan." Following Schele and Grube (1994:118), we first suspected that they might be the same person. Nonetheless, parentage statements and dates make it clear that they were different individuals. Perhaps Pusilha Ruler B was named for the powerful Copan king, indicating a political or even a family alliance dating to the early seventh century AD.

The dramatic events of the early history of Pusilha are described on a paired set of monuments, Stelae D and P, placed one in front of the other in the Stela Plaza (Figure 6.4). Both begin with the 9.7.0.0.0 period ending, tying them explicitly to Ruler A, but these are retrospective dates and the monuments themselves were erected by Ruler B to celebrate the 9.10.15.0.0 period ending in AD 647. This set of monuments is reminiscent of later pairs erected at Nim li Punit that focus on two successive rulers. At both sites, kings are described as stelae

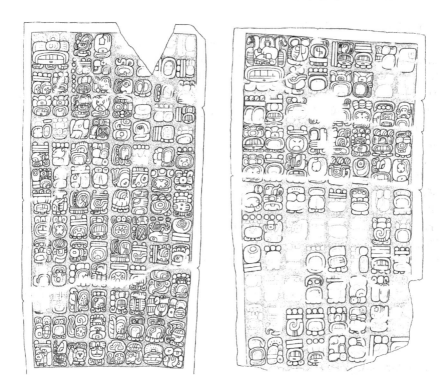

FIGURE 6.4 Pusilha Stela D (left) and Stela P (right; monuments not shown to scale).

Source: Drawings by Christian M. Prager.

dedicators and warfare is mentioned, albeit much more dramatically at Pusilha. Most importantly, all the paired monuments served to legitimize a current ruler by emphasizing continuity with his father. Although the Nim li Punit pairs of Stelae 15/2 and Stelae 14/7 have a definitive chronological reading order determined by the Initial Series date dominating their upper registers, Pusilha Stelae D and P begin with the same date, and the names of both rulers appear on each monument. Still, Stela D focuses on events during Ruler A's life, while Stela P describes Ruler B's titles and parentage. The two Pusilha texts are complementary in other ways. Stela D is concerned more with external relations and historical events, while Stela P concentrates more on the local action of monument dedication and the mythological past. Stela D also focuses on the role of warfare, while Stela P describes the ritual activities of kings. Thus, the two Pusilha monuments are thematically linked and both legitimize rulership, but they contain narratives whose complementarity can be appreciated only when they are considered together.

Following "Ruler C," there were at least two later breaks in the dynastic line suggesting political upheaval, and Pusilha "Ruler F" was a woman named Ix Ich'ak . . . K'inich. Her grandfather, who was not a ruler, is called an *ochk'in kalomte'*, suggesting that he founded the last dynastic line of Pusilha. The final king about whom we know much was "Ruler G," whose name we have reconstructed as K'ak' [u ti'] Chan K'awil (Prager et al. 2014:293–295; Somerville and Braswell 2016). He became king before AD 731 and ruled until sometime before AD 751. We excavated a tomb that we argue is his but acknowledge that it could belong to a later individual named K'ak' Kalaw, who erected the last stela at the site in AD 751. The brief text on Stela F that commemorates K'ak' Kalaw does not include the emblem glyph for Pusilha, so we do not know if he used the title *k'uhul un ajaw*.

Pusilha suffered dynastic strife and witnessed defeats in its history. A total of eight warfare events are mentioned in the texts or shown on stelae at the site (Prager et al. 2014). In some cases, the enemies of Pusilha are named. But who and where were they? With the exception of the "water scroll" site (Altun Ha; Helmke et al. 2018), none of them are archaeologically known. There is no clear reference to *ek' xukpi* lords, Copan, Quirigua, Caracol, Tikal, or Calakmul, let alone to Nim li Punit or any other known site with a legible emblem glyph. After seven years at Pusilha searching for external connections with large and famous sites, we realized that we understood even less about relations among and within the SBR.

Bioarchaeology at Pusilha

Pottery points to Peten for the origin of most people at Pusilha, and there is no claim in the hieroglyphs of a connection to Copan, but there is evidence that some elites came from that Honduran site. Strontium and oxygen isotope analyses of the teeth of the principal individual from Burial 3–1, located at the summit of the Pusilha acropolis, is consistent with a Copan origin (Somerville et al. 2016). So too are the teeth of ancestors found in a plate placed on the body of that individual. A local woman was buried to the south of Burial 3–1, but just north of Burial 3–1 was a male with teeth whose isotopic composition is consistent with the northern Maya lowlands. An additional foreigner, Burial 4–1, seems to have come from the Maya highlands. Thus, Pusilha may have had marriage ties with Copan and other regions; it was a cosmopolitan place, and about 30 percent of the individuals we sampled came from somewhere else (Somerville et al. 2016). This is in notable contrast to Uxbenka, where a similar program of study revealed just one foreigner, or about four percent.

We have described the tomb that we identify as belonging to Ruler G, dating to the range AD 731–751 (Prager et al. 2014:262–266; Somerville and Braswell 2016). In this chapter, I draw attention to just two artifacts from the tomb. The first is a tri-lobed obsidian eccentric found on the torso of the figure. It is shaped like a capital T with serifs (Figure 6.5, bottom right). Found just above the tomb of Ruler G was an anthropomorphic chert eccentric (Figure 6.5, bottom left). The serif T-shaped obsidian echoes the general form of the Nim li Punit wind jewel (Figure 5.6). Moreover, the anthropomorphic chert resembles that found

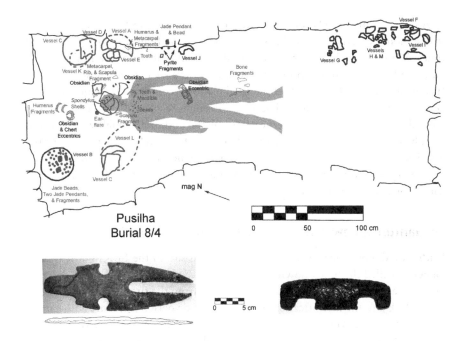

FIGURE 6.5   Pusilha Burial 8/4, thought to be the royal tomb of Ruler G. Obsidian eccentric found on body is shown (lower right); compare with the Nim li Punit wind jewel in Figure 5.6. Also shown is an anthropomorphic eccentric (lower left) found immediately above and outside the tomb, which is similar to that in Nim li Punit Tomb V (Figure 5.5 right).

Source: Drawing and photos by the author.

beneath or wearing the wind jewel in Nim li Punit Tomb V (Figure 5.5 right). Although the ceramics of Pusilha and Nim li Punit are quite different, these artifacts and their placement suggest similar practices regarding the role of rulers in summoning the winds that bring the rain and in protecting their kingdom from supernatural forces using weapons flaked in eccentric forms.

Decline and abandonment of Pusilha

The last carved stela at Pusilha dates to AD 751, suggesting an early political decline for the polity. By the beginning of the Terminal Classic about 30 years later, population levels had dropped. Terminal Classic pottery is found in several but not all major groups at the site. Elite burials continued to be placed on top of the Gateway Hill Acropolis at the foot of major structures, but garbage accumulated in the corners of its patio groups. The Moho Plaza, located southwest of other major groups at Pusilha, emerged as a center of elite activity at that time. Although we cannot be certain because it contains only a Calendar Round date, it seems likely that the hieroglyphic stair there was constructed in AD 798.

A once-significant platform that we call the Bulldozed Mound, located next to the modern Catholic church, was greatly expanded during Terminal Classic times. We excavated the nearly destroyed western half when the building was bulldozed in 2002 and consolidated what was left of the earlier substructure (Braswell et al. 2004). The fill of the final platform contained large quantities of Belize Red, a Terminal Classic diagnostic. Even more exciting, the surface of the mound and the patio floor underneath the platform slump and fall were covered with broken pottery that is later still, dating to the Postclassic period. We cannot date this material precisely, but it maintains no clear ties to earlier Classic ceramic types and modes. This is the latest ancient pottery so far recovered at a habitation site in the inland SBR.

Lubaantun: a new center of the Late to Terminal Classic

Without a doubt, Lubaantun is the most famous site in the SBR, but it can no longer be called the best-known. Hammond (1975) provides a complete description of the early work conducted at Lubaantun, from the first reports by Thomas Gann (1905), to the identification of the first Classic period ballcourt with carved markers by R.E. Merwin, through the British Museum project directed by Thomas A. Joyce, and to his own ground-breaking excavations, ceramic analysis, and theoretical interpretation of the Lubaantun "realm." Despite all this work, Lubaantun will always be infamous as the place where the crystal skull is claimed to have been discovered in 1924. It needs to be stated and re-affirmed that there is no evidence that the young Anna Mitchell-Hedges, who decades later claimed to have found the skull, was in Belize at that time. Nor did she or her family mention the skull until the late 1940s. Even more importantly, there is very clear proof in the form of a receipt that her stepfather, the explorer and sensationalist writer Frederick Mitchell-Hedges, purchased a crystal skull at Sotheby's in 1943 from the son of Sydney Burney, an antiquities dealer (https://en.wikipedia.org/wiki/F._A._Mitchell-Hedges). The credulous public desire to believe against all evidence that the crystal skull is extremely ancient and has magical abilities, but it was most likely made in Germany in the nineteenth century using rock crystal exported from Brazil. Like Baron Bliss, the crystal skull has never touched the soil of Belize but has nevertheless become a part of the history of the nation.

In 2009, I established the Toledo Regional Interaction Project with the goal of trying to understand if the four to five major sites of the SBR were capitals of independent polities, as the hieroglyphs seem to imply, or were politically and economically tied together. We began our work at Lubaantun, perhaps the oddest site in the region. As mentioned in the previous chapter, it has the finest masonry between Copan and the Rio Bec region. Yet there are no carved stelae and practically no hieroglyphs. Moreover, no royal tomb – or really any other sort of burial – has been found in the site center.[1] Did Lubaantun have a different kind of rulership that lacked the divine kings of the Classic period? Where did these people come from? Lubaantun has very few artifacts, and the only caches that have been found consist of shells or human teeth. The architecture is quite beautiful, but the artifacts suggest very few external ties, except limited connections with the Belize Valley during the Terminal Classic.

Hammond's (1972:Figure 20.4) excellent map of Lubaantun provides important details about the site (Figure 6.6). He found the earliest construction activity

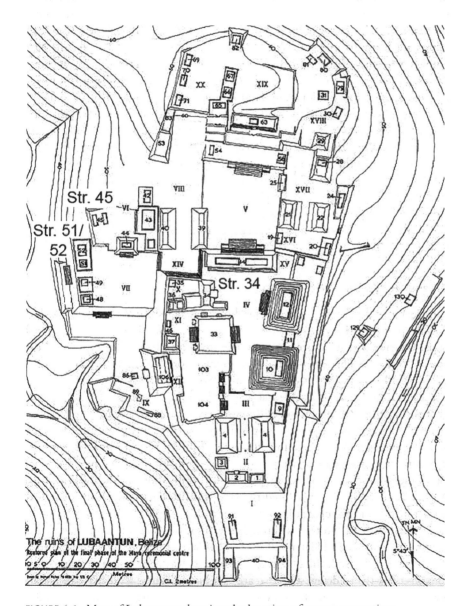

FIGURE 6.6 Map of Lubaantun showing the location of recent excavations.

Source: After Hammond 1972:Figure 20.4.

below the level of Plaza IV, the area between the two largest pyramids (Structures 10 and 12) and what may have been either an administrative building or a third temple of some kind (Structure 33). Structure 10 has no stair at all to its summit, and Structure 12 has a short stair leading to a low *adoratorio*. Access to their superstructures was achieved from any angle or approach by scrambling up the bodies of these pyramidal platforms. Structure 33 faces them and, in contrast, has long, wide, and easy-to-climb stairs in the front and the back. This triangular arrangement of tall structures is inscribed within a larger triangle formed by three ballcourts: Structure 4, Structures 21–22, and Structures 39–40. The last of these ballcourts is exceptionally wide and was left unfinished. I speculate that this inner and outer triangle may represent the cosmic hearth of creation, the elevated heavens (the inner pyramidal structures), and the underworld (the three ballcourts). Facing Structure 10 and just south of Structure 33 is an area that no one has yet mapped in an adequate fashion; Hammond labels this as Platforms 103 and 104. While they look flat on a site plan, they are filled with architecture including passageways, walls, a drain feature, and stairs leading to what may have been a second level. Unfortunately, this area has been badly disturbed by a combination of looters, early explorers, and members of the British Museum project. It will take a significant excavation project to clarify this region, but I suspect that it may have been part of an administrative-residential palace that also included Structure 33.

Recent excavations at Lubaantun

At Lubaantun, we excavated and consolidated four numbered platforms and a very deep test-pit (Figure 6.6). Our first excavated building was a Late to Terminal Classic range structure once assumed to be two distinct platforms (Structures 51 and 52). This misidentification derives from a looter's trench through its center. The southern half of the platform (Structure 51) was constructed first, and the northern half was added at a second stage. We found a whole conch shell buried in a platform on top of the addition. Both platforms have very well-constructed retention pens made of cut masonry. These relieve pressure on the outer-facing walls. We encountered the edges of a midden-like deposit beneath the southern, earlier half of the platform. It is probable that Hammond (1975) found more of this deposit when he excavated into the core of Structure 49. Within the deposit, we discovered the largest collection of figurine fragments we have yet found at Lubaantun.

Exposed bedrock protrudes through the floor of Plaza VII immediately in front of the northern and later half of the platform created by Structures 51 and 52. On the other hand, the stairway across Plaza VII that leads up to Plaza XIV contains more than a dozen steps that are now buried. These were exposed when the MASDP dug down in that location before consolidating the stair. I conclude that this stair formed the original western boundary of the Lubaantun acropolis and that the low ground of a natural saddle was later infilled to create Plaza VII.

It should be noted that a crude human head carved in the round, the only known stone sculpture at Lubaantun other than the three ballcourt markers, was once placed in the wall immediately north of this stair, that is, between Structure 44 and Structure 40, and south of Structure 43. It was dug out at night by a troubled North American who believed that golden plates were buried behind it. The wall remains in partially fallen condition because of this looting, but the head has been recovered and is in storage in Belmopan.

The second structure we excavated was Structure 45, which appears on Hammond's map as a miniature ballcourt. In reality, it too is a single platform. We think the misconception was caused not by looting but by a fallen tree. Excavations revealed this to be a beautifully constructed house platform with curved corner stones (Figure 6.7). All the ceramics associated with it date to the Late Classic period, supporting Hammond's (1975) conclusion that Plaza VI was built at an earlier time than the lower Plaza VII supporting Structures 51 and 52.

We placed a deep test pit in Plaza IV immediately south and west of the centerline of Structure 14 and dug it down below the level of the much lower Plaza V. We encountered no previous plaza level or floor, suggesting this section of Plaza IV was constructed in a single phase. Like elsewhere at Lubaantun, we found well-built retention walls within the fill that were placed at a diagonal to the axis of the site. By building fill-retention cells that were not parallel with the structures built upon the plazas, the Maya of Lubaantun provided sturdy and earthquake-proof support for their buildings.

The final platform that we have excavated and consolidated to date is Structure 34 (Figure 6.8). It is a complex temple built in six major stages and at least three minor construction "moments" (Braswell et al. 2011). The temple is the largest structure at the site never to have seen previous excavation or looting. The earliest stage was only partially exposed in the southwestern portion of the building and extends outward at a right angle from later-stage constructions. A later-stage parallel with the final structure was built at its north end. This is a small Lubaantun-style shrine consisting of a low platform with a stair and a very small stone superstructure less than one meter high, open at both the front and the back. A fully exposed shrine of the same measurements can be found near the southwest corner of Structure 33. Later stages of Structure 34 greatly expanded its size. At some point in the Terminal Classic period, people came to live in the gap between Structures 33 and 34. A low wall or threshold of just one course was built to connect the two platforms, and I imagine that the gap between them was roofed over with thatch. We found large amounts of Terminal Classic domestic trash in this area, but it was not associated with any other earlier use of the structure. Most interestingly, we recovered a large number of *Strombus pugilis* shells here and nowhere else at Lubaantun. This marine resource seems to have made up a significant portion of the diet of final inhabitants of Lubaantun as it did at Nim li Punit. No such shells were recovered in our excavations at Pusilha, located considerably further inland.

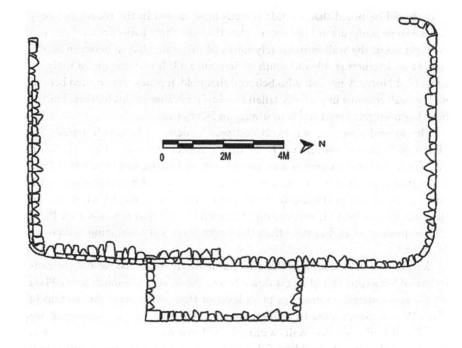

FIGURE 6.7 Lubaantun Structure 45, a Late Classic elite house platform.

Source: Drawing by Kiri Hagerman, photo by the author.

Comments are worth making about three more structures that we did not excavate. In 1998, I visited Lubaantun when Rudi Larios and the MASDP were consolidating structures for tourism. He had supervised the excavation of Structure 32, a particularly interesting altar located in the middle of Plaza IV (right foreground of Figure 4.3b). This small radial platform has steps on all four sides. Within it were a few sherds of Fine Orange (or imitations) as well as both black and green obsidian. The first was probably from the Ucareo, Michoacan, source and the second definitely came from Pachuca, Hidalgo. The radial form of the platform, the pottery, and the obsidian all suggest at least indirect ties with Chichen

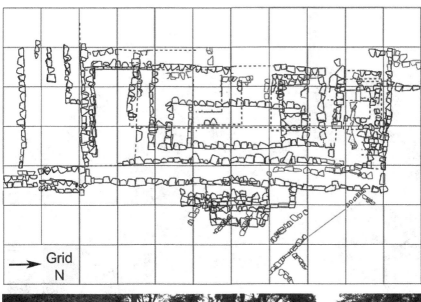

FIGURE 6.8 Plan and photograph of Lubaantun Structure 34, a Late Classic temple built in many stages and converted to a living place during the Terminal Classic period. Scale of the grid is 2 m × 2 m; diagonal features in the lower 4 m of the grid are retaining walls in the fill of the platform supporting Structure 34.

Source: Drawing by Nancy Peniche May, photo by the author.

Itza during the tenth century AD. By that time, it is possible that Lubaantun was no longer inhabited and may have been a place occasionally visited by pilgrims. Given that coastal sites and cayes in the SBR continued to be inhabited during Postclassic times and that Mexican obsidian has been found at these sites, I suspect that the visitors came from the nearby coast by paddling up river.

FIGURE 6.9 South side of Lubaantun Structure 10, showing extensive earthquake damage. The façade appears to have been thrown upward and then fell as a unit.

Source: Photo by the author.

Finally, the south sides of Structures 10 and 12, the two tallest structures of Lubaantun, exhibit violent earthquake damage. In both cases, the façades were thrown upward and then settled down with vertical displacement of more than a meter (Figure 6.9). Although we cannot date this damage, it must have occurred sometime after the structures were built, perhaps in the early ninth century and contemporary with similar damage observed only a few miles away at Nim li Punit.

Lubaantun ceramics: a continuation of Uxbenka

Norman Hammond's (1975) excellent work at Lubaantun yielded a single ceramic complex for the site, which he calls the Columbia complex. He portrays this as having early and late facets, and we wanted to see if this could be expanded into distinct phases. Moreover, his description of the pottery is remarkably simple, with only eight groups and a total of 14 types; the vast majority of pottery was assigned to just three types. We wondered if this work represented ceramic "lumping" rather than splitting and if we could improve upon it. We were able to split the complex into two phases – Early Columbia and Late Columbia – corresponding to the Late and Terminal Classic (Irish and Braswell 2015), but we were wrong to doubt Hammond's classification. The pottery is very simple, impoverished in variety and decoration, and almost entirely local.

Polychromes at Lubaantun are characterized by an extremely thick cream slip, while many to most polychromes at Pusilha and Nim li Punit are orange-slipped. Hammond (1975) assigns these to the Louisville Group, but we see little reason not to include them within the Zacatel Group. Polychrome forms and modes of the Early Columbia phase echo Tepeu 2 polychromes from Peten. Unlike Hammond, we found significant quantities of Terminal Classic Louisville polychrome, characterized by Tepeu 3 forms and modes including tripod bowls and plates with notched basal flanges. Compared to Nim li Punit, Belize Red is quite uncommon and seems to be limited to Late Columbia contexts. Puluacax Unslipped is extraordinarily common throughout. Whatever this bizarre pottery was used for, Lubaantun was a center of its consumption and I assume production. The stamped or impressed designs observed at Lubaantun on Remate Red dating to the Late Columbia phase are also found at coastal sites, which suggests to me that these were affiliated with Lubaantun during the Terminal Classic period (Figure 6.10).

Working in parallel but independently, Jillian Jordan and I have concluded that Early Columbia Lubaantun pottery is virtually identical to the Late Classic materials from Uxbenka but that Lubaantun has much more Terminal Classic pottery. The latter is present but uncommon at Uxbenka (Jordan and Prufer 2014).

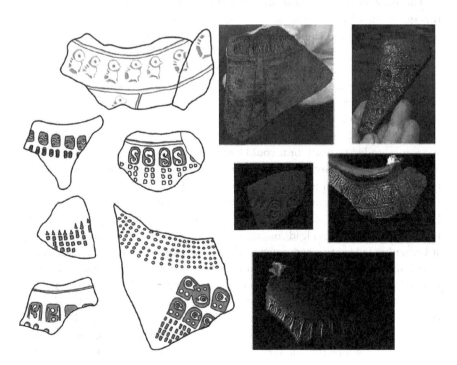

FIGURE 6.10 Unit-stamped pottery from Lubaantun (left) and coastal Toledo District, Belize.

Source: Left: drawings by Mark Irish; right: McKillop 2009:Figure 3.

Occupation history of Lubaantun

Hammond (1975) argued that Lubaantun was settled sometime in the eighth century AD, and our analysis of ceramics supports this. Our pottery shares forms and modes with Tepeu 2 and Tepeu 3 pottery but nothing earlier. Given the general lack of materials, a short occupation seems likely, so I speculate that that the site was first inhabited no earlier than AD 750. There is little evidence that Lubaantun was populated later than AD 900. In sum, I would be surprised if Lubaantun was occupied for more than 150 years.

The finest architecture at Uxbenka Group B resembles that of Lubaantun, and the Late Classic ceramics of Uxbenka and Lubaantun are extremely similar. It therefore seems quite likely that Lubaantun was founded as a satellite of Uxbenka. A conjecture worth pursuing is that Lubaantun and Xnaheb were set up by the two older polities of Uxbenka and Nim li Punit to strengthen claims to land and resources between those two older capitals. Whatever the reason for its founding, Lubaantun rapidly grew in importance and size, and within two generations surpassed the mother site. The lack of royal monuments and writing at Lubaantun might indicate that it was a secondary center beneath Uxbenka until that site ceased to be important around AD 780 or so.

The mystery of Lubaantun does not involve the crystal skull. Instead, it is this question: why does the site have such exceptionally fine architecture yet so few carved monuments? This suggests the persistence of one specialization sponsored by the ruling class but not another. Three ballcourt markers are the only hieroglyphic monuments known from the site. Morley (1937–1938:IV:8–9) dates them on stylistic grounds to the period AD 780–790. Ballcourt Marker 3 contains an apparent emblem glyph, but the main sign is the head variant of *k'uhul* (Wanyerka 2003:23). This may be a unique emblem glyph for Lubaantun, it could also be the emblem glyph of the rulers of Uxbenka (an example at that site is too eroded to read), or it could be a generic way of indicating a holy lord. The paucity of royal monuments and inscriptions at Lubaantun is uncharacteristic of the SBR and might indicate that it began as a secondary center beneath Uxbenka. No royal tombs have yet been found at Lubaantun; perhaps they are located deep within the unstable fill of Structures 10 or 12, or perhaps they do not exist. Together, this leads me to wonder if after the end of divine kingship at Uxbenka, Lubaantun continued to thrive and expand without dynastic rule.

It is important to stress that the location of Lubaantun is much more advantageous than that of Uxbenka in terms of access to the Caribbean and its resources (Figure 4.1). The decline of both Pusilha and Uxbenka in the second half of the eighth century may be related to problems with agriculture during a time period of climatic instability. Unlike the mother site of Uxbenka, Lubaantun is located at a spot below which the Rio Grande is navigable year-round and is only four to five hours by canoe from the Caribbean. We have ample evidence that *Strombus pugilis*, a small species of conch, was consumed in great quantities at Lubaantun and Nim li Punit during their last phases of occupation. By the end of the eighth century, the remaining large sites of inland Toledo required considerable maritime resources to supplement their terrestrial diets, and this was much harder to accomplish farther inland at Uxbenka and Pusilha. Because of their location closer to coastal resources and trade networks, Lubaantun and Nim li Punit were able to survive later into the Terminal Classic. Lubaantun was the last major site of the SBR to be abandoned, sometime around AD 900.

Conclusions: identity, politics, and warfare in the Southern Belize Region

Since the commencement of our two projects at Pusilha, Nim li Punit, and Lubaantun, and as a result of the great work of Keith Prufer and his students at Uxbenka, we have learned a lot about the inland SBR. Although a Paleoindian point has been known for some time, Prufer and his colleagues have begun the enormous task of fleshing out seasonal occupation of the region from roughly 12,000 years ago, through the long Archaic period, to the arrival of the first Maya in the late Middle Preclassic as ritual pilgrims, and to the establishment of the earliest permanent villages in the SBR proper at the dawn of the Classic period.

The first permanently settled communities that relied on agriculture, used pottery, and built stone architecture were Uxbenka and Nim li Punit. Although Uxbenka has suggestive carbon dates, excavations at neither site have yielded artifactual or architectural evidence that unequivocally dates to before about AD 250. Instead, the earliest datable artifacts are pottery sherds that demonstrate a slow transition from Late Preclassic to Early Classic types, forms, and modes. I attribute this to the gradual development of a local elite class that supported specialized production and to the slow emergence of divine rulership in a peripheral region of the southern Maya lowlands. It could be that the first permanent villagers arrived at the beginning of the Preclassic Collapse around AD 150, or they could have arrived as conditions improved a century later. The archaeological chronologies of the two sites do not allow us at present to determine which was established first, and I could not care less.

From the beginning, the pottery of Uxbenka and Nim li Punit was related yet distinctive, and those differences were maintained throughout the history of both sites. A stela at Uxbenka may suggest a political connection to Tikal in the fourth century AD, but ceramic analysis does not provide direct evidence of site-specific economic relations with any particular Early Classic Peten city (Jordan and Prufer 2014). Nim li Punit enjoyed more connections outside of the region throughout its long history and is the only site in southern Belize known to have participated in Teotihuacan emulation. In the Early Classic, most of its obsidian came from Ixtepeque, the dominant source at Copan and throughout El Salvador. But by the Late Classic, the inhabitants of Nim li Punit relied more on obsidian from El Chayal, demonstrating a shift to participation in a more Peten-oriented procurement sphere after about AD 600. Could this economic shift reflect strengthening ties to the north and west (e.g., Caracol), or the emergence of a local supplier (e.g., Pusilha)?

Of course, pots and obsidian are not people, but the differences in these aspects of material culture signify discrete production and distribution systems, and almost certainly divergent identities. Elsewhere, I have described why the concept of ethnicity should not be applied to the ancient Maya (Braswell 2016), and the distinctions among the Maya of the SBR almost certainly were not at that level. They may have been linguistic or simply based on history, rights to place, and claims to resources. Today in the SBR, these last three are often more important than language in maintaining differences between the Mopan Maya and Q'eqchi'. Moreover, contemporary highland Maya identify more by *municipio* than by language. I view the small kingdoms of the ancient SBR as being not that different in size from many highland *municipios*, and identity may also have been determined by the polity to which one was ascribed.

Pusilha was founded in AD 571 at the dawn of the Late Classic period. Utilitarian pottery there suggests that the strongest ties were with the southwestern Peten and, indeed, is quite different from that of either Uxbenka or Nim li Punit. The presence of *comales* at Pusilha implies they ate tortillas, something unknown at the other sites (Bill and Braswell 2005). Different foodways imply distinct identities. Pusilha was by far the largest site in the region and the only one that I feel comfortable calling urban. The scale and complexity of Pusilha, along with the fact that its inhabitants were much more numerous and arrived much later than those of Uxbenka or Nim li Punit, also must have created marked differences in identity. The establishment of a new dynastic line – the only one in the SBR about which much is known – and the use of a distinct emblem glyph would have added political dimensions to the distinct identity of the new arrivals.

Pusilha certainly had connections. At least two individuals buried in the acropolis likely came from the Copan region, a third from the northern lowlands, and a fourth from the Maya highlands. Nonetheless, the lengthy hieroglyphic texts of Pusilha do not once employ either the Copan or Quirigua emblem glyphs, and they make no clear reference to any person known from those sites. Moreover, there is little evidence for significant economic interaction with Copan. Obsidian at Pusilha came almost exclusively from the El Chayal source, while obsidian found at Copan was procured almost exclusively from the Ixtepeque source. Obsidian is much more common at Pusilha than at any of its Late Classic contemporaries in the SBR, and so I wonder if it could have become a local supplier that procured El Chayal obsidian and entered it into local market systems. The ceramics of Pusilha do show minor connections to Copan – the use of the "twist-and-bud" motif and a few sherds of a non-Maya type made at Copan – but again, the strongest ties are with southwestern Peten. Finally, most of the sculpture at Pusilha consists of flat, low-relief carvings in a Peten style, but there are four small and crude zoomorphic altars that are reminiscent of examples from Copan and Quirigua. In sum, I see marriage connections between the royal house of Pusilha and Copan during the seventh century but few indications of significant economic or cultural interaction.

Pusilha fought at least eight battles, some they lost and some they won, but for the most part we do not know with whom. We assume they were mostly smaller sites in the SBR or southeastern Peten. Nonetheless, a particularly bad defeat at the hands of the "water scroll" site – probably Altun Ha – is described on the earliest intact stela, which dates to the life of Ruler B. The monument states that two stelae were broken, and indeed, fragments of two earlier monuments erected by Ruler A have been found. Why was distant Altun Ha involved in a battle so far from home? Could it be that the establishment of Pusilha represented a threat to one of the existing polities in the SBR that was allied with the northern site? Stepping further into conjecture, I wonder if connections with Copan were strengthened during the lifetime of Ruler B because of the devastating defeat at the hands of the "water scroll" site. Except for this brief period, Pusilha seems to have been a polity that deliberately chose a "third way" that eschewed alliances with external powers (Braswell et al. 2004).

The Nim li Punit wind jewel suggests that a new dynasty was established at that already centuries-old site in AD 652. The new ruler came from somewhere else, perhaps Caracol. Nearly a century later, a stela at Nim li Punit mentions that a lord of the "water scroll" site participated in the inauguration of a different Nim li Punit ruler. Altun Ha, therefore, continued to play a role in the politics of the SBR. Three early stelae at Nim li Punit also mention lords of *ek' xukpi*, a reference to alliances with Quirigua or some other site or confederation. Compared to Pusilha, the texts of Nim li Punit indicate that site dabbled considerably in foreign alliances with polities to both the north and the south. We do not know if this was a matter of choice, was forced upon the small site, or – most likely of all – was a bit of both. Despite these political connections at Nim li Punit and more limited ones evinced at Pusilha, the SBR seems to be politically distinct. Moreover, evidence of economic interaction with external regions is limited for Pusilha and quite uncommon for Uxbenka.

Leventhal (1990, 1992) defined the SBR as an archaeological region, but there is no reason to suspect that it was politically or economically bound together. During the Late Classic, I see the SBR as consisting of three small petty kingdoms centered at Pusilha, Uxbenka, and Nim li Punit. Each was autonomous, underpopulated, and to varying degrees peripheral to the rest of the Maya lowlands. Moreover, evidence of trade among the three kingdoms is not abundant. The ceramics of all three Late Classic sites are distinctive, and the use or lack of calcite temper reveals that there was little exchange of utilitarian wares among them. The lack of economic integration mirrors the political independence of each petty kingdom expressed in the hieroglyphic texts. The Pusilha emblem glyph does not appear at any of the other sites, nor do texts at Pusilha mention any of the possible Nim li Punit emblem glyphs. Wanyerka (2003:24) argues that a variant of the Nim li Punit emblem glyph may appear on a ballcourt marker at Lubaantun, but I do not see it at all. We therefore lack texts describing warfare and intermarriage among the major sites of the SBR, even though both are mentioned in conjunction with unknown places.

Sometime in the mid-eighth century AD, Lubaantun was founded, almost certainly by colonists from Uxbenka. It may be that trade routes with Peten were already closing down, or it may be that a location on a large year-round water source that afforded easy access to the Caribbean and its resources was desired. I wonder if Xnaheb was founded at about this time by Nim li Punit as a way to mark its territory and also to maintain access to the Rio Grande downstream from Lubaantun. The only hieroglyphic monuments at Lubaantun date to around AD 780–790, but construction and occupation continued well into the Terminal Classic period. No royal tombs or stelae have been found, which leads me to wonder if Lubaantun was governed by a council rather than ruled by an *ajaw* after the collapse of Uxbenka. There is ample evidence of at least one major earthquake at both Nim li Punit and Lubaantun, and it appears to have happened around or shortly after AD 800. Faced with climate instability, access to both terrestrial and marine resources may have been especially important at the very end of the Late Classic period.

By AD 850, there were very few people left at any of the major sites except Lubaantun, and by AD 900, that site, too, was largely abandoned. Remaining peoples moved to the coast and lived as fisherfolk, salt producers, and maritime traders. They flourished in small numbers at these coastal settlements throughout the rest of the Terminal Classic and Postclassic periods. The only places in the inland SBR where Postclassic ceramics have been definitively identified are on top of and around the "Bulldozed Mound" of Pusilha, in various caves, as an offering in the Stela Plaza at Uxbenka, and associated with the small radial platform Structure 32 of Lubaantun. The first is consistent with a limited occupation, but the other contexts suggest ritual pilgrimages to the natural features and once-great sites of the interior. Thus, use of the inland SBR during the Postclassic period was not that different from that in the Preclassic period.

When the Spanish came, they were met by the Manche Chol on the coast. That encounter led to the extinction of the ancient Maya people of southern Belize. The Manche Chol quite likely were the descendants of the builders of at least some of the great sites, which were rediscovered centuries later when first Mopan Maya, and later Q'eqchi', European, Kriol, East Indian, and Garifuna settlers moved into and recolonized inland Toledo District, Belize.

Acknowledgments

I wish to thank the Institute of Archaeology of NICH for their support. This chapter and portions of the two that precede it are a summary of 19 years' work. Without the permission and help of the Institute of Archaeology, none of this work would have been possible. I also thank the many members of the communities of San Benito Poite, Indian Creek, and San Pedro Columbia who have collaborated on our projects. I also wish to acknowledge the many graduate students and other scholars who have worked on these projects over the last *k'atun*. They are too numerous to mention by name, but most appear as authors and co-authors in the papers listed in the references section and in the previous chapter. The research was supported by grants, fellowships, and multiple awards from the National Science Foundation, the National Geographic Society, the School for American (now Advanced) Research, and the Faculty Senate of the University of California, San Diego. I also wish to thank Keith Prufer, Jillian Jordan, Amy Thompson, and Valerie Aquino for years of conversations about the Southern Belize Region. Finally, I thank Joyce Marcus for her helpful comments on earlier drafts of all three chapters.

Note

1 Hammond et al. (1975) report a family tomb found outside the site center of Lubaantun. During the MASDP consolidation activities, a cist burial containing a flexed individual with no accompanying grave goods may have been found behind Str. 33, but this remains unpublished.

References cited

Bill, Cassandra R., and Geoffrey E. Braswell 2005 Life at the Crossroads: New Data from Pusilha, Belize. *Research Reports in Belizean Archaeology* 2:301–312.

Braswell, Geoffrey E. 2016 The Problem of Ethnicity and the Construction of K'iche'an Identity. In *Archaeology and Identity in Southeast Mesoamerica*, edited by C. Garcia-Des Lauriers and Michael Love, pp. 172–184. University of Utah Press, Salt Lake City.

Braswell, Geoffrey E., Nancy Peniche May, and Kiri L. Hagerman 2011 Revisiting the Kingdom of the Crystal Skull: New Investigations at Lubaantun. *Research Reports in Belizean Archaeology* 8:115–126.

Braswell, Geoffrey E., Christian M. Prager, Cassandra R. Bill, Sonja A. Schwake, and Jennifer B. Braswell 2004 The Rise of Secondary States in the Southeastern Periphery of the Maya World: A Report of Recent Archaeological and Epigraphic Research at Pusilhá, Belize. *Ancient Mesoamerica* 15:219–233.

Gann, Thomas W. F. 1905 The Ancient Monuments of Northern Honduras and the Adjacent Parts of Yucatan and Guatemala, the Former Civilisation in These Parts, and the Chief Characteristics of the Races Now Inhabiting Them: With an Account of the Visit to the Rio Grande Ruins. *Journal of Anthropology Institute of Great Britain & Ireland* 35:103–112.

Gruning, Edward L. 1939 Report on the British Museum Expeditiuon to British Honduras, 1930. *Journal of the Royal Anthropological Institute* 60:477–483.

Hammond, Norman 1972 Locational Models and the Site of Lubaantún: A Classic Maya Centre. In *Models in Archaeology*, edited by David L. Clarke, pp. 757–800. Methuen, London.

——— 1975 *Lubaantun: A Classic Maya Realm*. Peabody Museum of Archaeology and Ethnology, Cambridge, MA.

Hammond, Norman, Kate Pretty, and Frank P. Saul 1975 A Classic Maya Family Tomb. *World Archaeology* 7:57–78.

Helmke, Christophe, Stanley P. Guenter, and Phillip J. Wanyerka 2018 Kings of the East: Altun Ha and the Water Scroll Emblem Glyph. *Ancient Mesoamerica* 29:112–135.

Irish, Mark D., and Geoffrey E. Braswell 2015 Towards an Archaeological Chronology of Southern Belize. *Research Reports in Belizean Archaeology* 12:271–279.

Jordan, Jillian M., and Keith M. Prufer 2014 Contextualizing Uxbenká: Ceramic Analyses from Site Core and Household Contexts. *Research Reports in Belizean Archaeology* 11:317–326.

Joyce, Thomas A. 1929 Report on the British Museum Expedition to British Honduras, 1929. *Journal of the Royal Anthropological Institute* 59:439–459.

Joyce, Thomas A., Thomas Gann, Edward L. Gruning, and Richard C. E. Long 1928 Report on the British Museum Expedition to British Honduras, 1928. *Journal of the Royal Anthropological Institute* 58:323–350.

Leventhal, Richard M. 1990 Southern Belize: An Ancient Maya Region. In *Vision and Revision in Maya Studies*, edited by Flora S. Clancy and Peter D. Harrison, pp. 125–141, University of New Mexico Press, Albuquerque.

————— 1992 The Development of a Regional Tradition in Southern Belize. In *New Theories on the Ancient Maya*, edited by Elin C. Danien and Robert J. Sharer, pp. 145–153. University Museum Symposium, Vol. 3. The University of Pennsylvania Museum, Philadelphia.

McKillop, Heather I. 2009 The Geopolitics of the Coastal Maya Economy in Belize: Relations between the Coastal and Inland Maya. *Research Reports in Belizean Archaeology* 6:55–61.

Morley, Sylvanus G. 1937–1938 *The Inscriptions of Peten*, 5 vols. Carnegie Institution, Washington, DC.

Prager, Christian M., Beniamino Volta, and Geoffrey E. Braswell 2014 The Dynastic History and Archaeology of Pusilha. In *The Maya and Their Central American Neighbors*, edited by Geoffrey E. Braswell, pp. 245–307. Routledge Press, London and New York.

Schele, Linda, and Nikolai Grube 1994 *Tlaloc-Venus Warfare: The Peten Wars 8.17.0.0.0–9.15.13.0.0*. Notebook for the XVIII Maya Hieroglyphic Workshop, March 12–13. University of Texas, Austin.

Smith, Michael E., Scott G. Ortman, José Lobo, Claire E. Ebert, Amy E. Thompson, et al. 2020 The Low-Density Urban Systems of the Classic Period Maya and Izapa: Insights from Settlement Scaling Theory. *Latin American Antiquity* 32:120–137.

Somerville, Andrew D., and Geoffrey E. Braswell 2016 The Life, Death, and Afterlife of an Ancient Maya King: A Study of Pusilha Ruler G. *Contributions in New World Archaeology* 10:183–296.

Somerville, Andrew D., Margaret J. Somerville, and Geoffrey E. Braswell 2016 Political Alliance, Residential Mobility, and Diet at the Ancient Maya City of Pusilha, Belize. *Journal of Anthropological Archaeology* 41:147–158.

Wanyerka, Phillip J. 2003 *The Southern Belize Epigraphic Project: The Hieroglyphic Inscriptions of Southern Belize*. Report submitted to the Foundation for the Advancement of Mesoamerican Studies, Inc., December 1.

7

QUEENS AND STATECRAFT

Royal women in the heart of the Fire
Shrine at El Perú-Waka'

*Olivia C. Navarro-Farr, Damien Marken,
Mary Kate Kelly, Keith Eppich, Griselda Pérez Robles,
and Juan Carlos Pérez*

Ian Graham's initial 1968 expedition to Waka' (also called El Perú), Guatemala, provided extraordinary documentation of its complex political history as
recorded on the stelae remaining at the site. His work yielded important historical narratives that informed some of the initial research design of the Proyecto
Arqueológico Waka' (PAW) and definitively situated Waka' as an important
political center in the geopolitics of the Classic period in western Peten (Graham
1988). The history as understood from those early investigations and what has
since emerged indicates that Waka' was a critical staging ground for some of the
most pivotal military events in the region. The *kaloomte'* Sihyaj K'ahk' engaged
in a ceremony at an "origin house" at Waka' only eight days before his famed
arrival at Tikal (Stuart 2000). Centuries later, under the auspices of Kaanul – a
major kingdom then based at Calakmul – Waka' was again a staging ground
for military incursion into Tikal through the political unions of Waka' rulers
with successive generations of Kaanul-affiliated queens. Ongoing investigations
at the central public shrine of the city offer insights into the enduring political
significance of Waka' through history and the ways in which generations of royal
women of Kaanul sowed their authority and influence in the region and shaped
the nature of politics and diplomacy. In this chapter, we explore the significance
of this political history as revealed through excavation of the shrine and examine
its importance within the greater site zone and region.

Waka' sits atop a defensible escarpment near the intersection of the San Juan
and San Pedro Mártir rivers (Figure 7.1). Scholars argue that the interest of Kaanul
in the Waka' kingdom, a medium-sized monumental center enveloped within a
highly nucleated residential core, derived from its strategic location along important intersecting trade routes. Waka' is positioned along a north–south artery that
Demarest and Fahsen (2002; see also Woodfill and Andrieu 2012) call the "Great
Western Trade Route." Freidel and colleagues (2007) have referred to this route

DOI: 10.4324/9781351268004-7

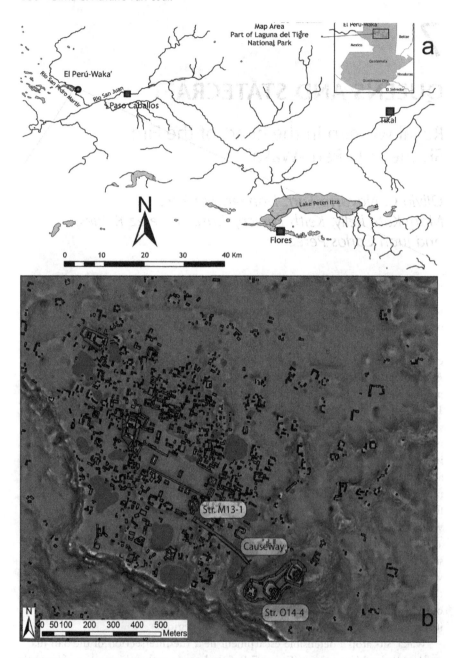

FIGURE 7.1 Location (a) and map (b) of Waka'.

Source: By Evangelia Tsesmeli and Damien Marken.

as a "royal road" connecting Calakmul to Cancuen via a chain of sites loyal to the Kaanul dynasts. Canuto and Barrientos (2013:Figure 7.1) point out that this was a route rather than a formally constructed road. The route was a dominant feature of the western Peten regional economy throughout the Classic period.

Thus, the Kaanul lords were in an ideal position to control critical trade through their loyal allies at Waka' along the route that passed through the site. This, with the conquest of Naranjo and Caracol to the east, allowed Kaanul to implement a strategy designed to slowly dominate the region and to encircle and subdue their long-term rivals at Tikal. One central focus of our research has been how royal Kaanul women who married into the Waka' royal family figured in this strategy (Navarro-Farr and Eppich et al. 2020, Navarro-Farr and Kelly et al. 2020).

In spite of epigraphic and archaeological advances in recent decades, much remains uncertain regarding the varied forms of the Kaanul hegemony across northern Guatemala and southeastern Mexico. Understanding that the manner of control exerted by Kaanul was complex and potentially varied, the nature of its relationships with patron sites requires greater clarification. Rich archaeological and epigraphic evidence from Waka', particularly regarding the end of the Early Classic and the Late Classic periods, speaks to how the relationship between the Kaanul and Waka' royal families developed and was maintained for multiple generations. We argue that at Waka' – and likely elsewhere – the queens who came from Kaanul heavily emphasized marriage diplomacy (Teufel 2008). Specifically, they built on the political capital established by their high-ranked positions within their marriage connections with Waka' nobility. They maintained marriage alliances through careful and strategic diplomacy focused on the specialized use of sorcery, divination, and oracle mediation. These efforts helped cement the loyalty of Waka to Kaanul through multiple generations. The implications for this strategy at Waka', La Corona (Canuto and Barrientos 2013), and other sites along the "royal road" inform the underexplored intersection of gender and statecraft (Martin 2008; Navarro-Farr and Kelly et al. 2020). People at Waka' memorialized two royal Kaanul women, Lady K'abel and Ix Ikoom, for having actively participated in a multigenerational strategic alliance that solidified the political and economic relationship between the two polities (Navarro-Farr and Kelly et al. 2020). It is notable that Lady K'abel politically outranked her husband, the ruler of Waka'; she bore the *ix kaloomte'* title as a sign of her elevated status and military power on her famous monument, El Perú (i.e., Waka') Stela 34 (Green Robertson 2007; Navarro-Farr 2016:Figure 11.4). More broadly than this single observation, we examine the position of these two royal women from the vantage of the polity they ruled. We consider how the complex layers of evidence from Structure M13-1 – the central shrine of Waka' where Lady K'abel was interred and the earlier Ix Ikoom was commemorated on two different monuments (Navarro-Farr and Eppich et al. 2020; Navarro-Farr et al. 2021) – situate them within historical events stretching back to the Early Classic "*entrada*" era of Sihyaj K'ahk' and underscores the enduring political and ritual significance of the site.

In order for Kaanul to secure the western route without resorting to conquest, its rulers needed to establish hegemonic relationships with vassal polities in ways that transcended coercion. Loyalty was not imposed but deeply rooted in identity and blood ties, allowing allegiance to be successfully maintained over the course of generations. The women of Kaanul who married into the Waka' polity, and therefore cemented its vassal position, were not mere pawns in service to Kaanul but were deeply aware of their diplomatic obligations and also had personal goals. They achieved these in distinct ways. Our evidence suggests the two women were remembered by the local populace as key actors in diplomatic negotiations and were embraced and revered for centuries (Navarro-Farr and Eppich et al. 2020; Navarro-Farr and Kelly et al. 2020). That these diplomatic efforts were successful is demonstrated by the ways the two foreign royal women were incorporated into the social memory and political fabric of Waka'. We have discussed evidence from Structure M13–1, the Northwest Palace, and the restricted Mirador Group of Waka' (Structure O14–04) elsewhere (Navarro-Farr and Eppich et al. 2020). In this chapter, we build on this body of data and interpretation by describing a major Late to Terminal Classic architectural feature of Structure M13–1 that we identify as a monumental hearth. We re-consider Structure M13–1 as the notably public and highly visible locus of the hearth within the site, the nearly true north alignment of the building (a feature that sets it apart from the rest of the monumental core architecture), and the role the structure played in the political landscape of the city.

Evidence from the Fire Shrine

Excavations at Structure M13–1 (Figure 7.2), which we refer to as the Fire Shrine because of its monumental hearth, reveal that Terminal Classic occupants ritually enshrined this place over generations with abundant and diverse offerings dating to the eighth and early ninth centuries AD (Navarro-Farr 2009, 2016). They also dragged, deposited, intentionally repositioned, and even re-set fragments of previously broken Early and Late Classic stelae into the final terrace walls of the building (Figure 7.3). One of the fragments embedded within these offering deposits is Stela 9. It features the feet and legs of a ruler standing atop a *k'ahk' witz*, or fire-mountain effigy (Navarro-Farr et al. 2008:Figure 5). On one side of the standing legs is a finely incised text that references a *wiinte' naah* (Guenter 2005). This term is glossed as "origin house" by David Stuart (2004) and proposed by him to be a shrine associated with fire rituals, supporting our designation of Structure M13–1 as the Fire Shrine (see also Fash et al. 2009; Taube 2004).

The design of this building, embedded with deposited materials, features a grand central structure with lower flanking additions to the north and south. Together, the central structure and its two additions span the entire eastern width of Plaza 2. The building presents an asymmetrical configuration that is also notably very nearly aligned to true north (Figure 7.2b). This alignment distinguishes it from the rest of the monumental architecture within the Waka' epicenter, which is oriented perpendicularly to Maya north. It appears that the north and south flanks of Structure M13–1, particularly as they were subjected to increased architectural modifications along its base, rendered the entire building less symmetrical over time, increasingly shifting its orientation towards true

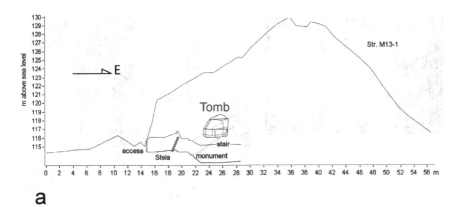

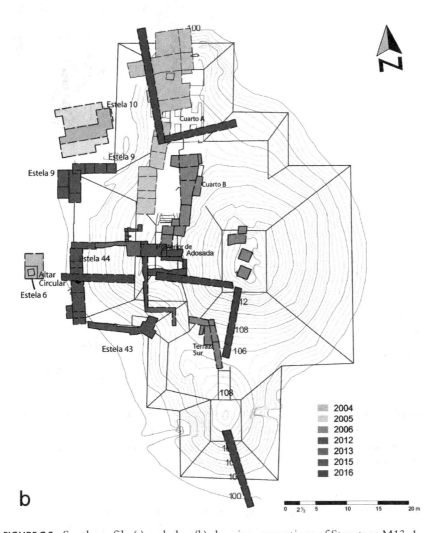

FIGURE 7.2 South profile (a) and plan (b) showing excavations of Structure M13–1.

Source: By André Rivas, Evangelia Tsesmeli, Damien Marken, Olivia Navarro-Farr, Juan Carlos Pérez, Griselda Pérez, Ana Lucía Arroyave Prera, Damaris Menéndez, David Freidel, and Danilo Hernández.

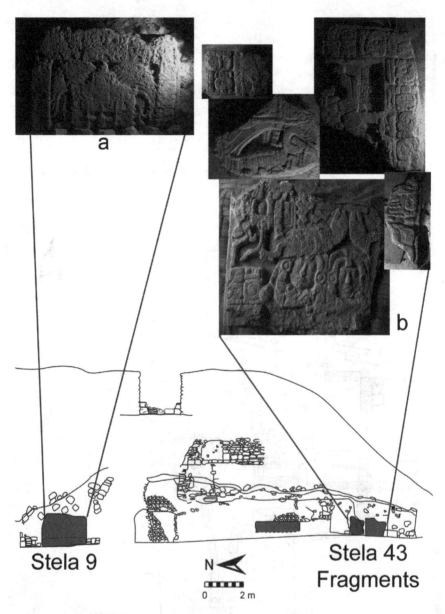

FIGURE 7.3 East profile of terminal phase *adosada* façade of Structure M13–1, including (a) the upper section of Stela 9 and (b) fragments of Stela 43.

Source: By Juan Carlos Pérez, Olivia Navarro-Farr, and Griselda Pérez Robles, Francisco Castañeda, and Stanley Guenter.

north. One test-pit into the northern terrace indicates that feature dates to the Early Classic. It is therefore possible that these flanking additions and their true north alignment also date to that period. The northern addition is the longer of the two flanks, and it is topped with a series of rooms. The southern addition features a north-facing stair that leads to a ranging superstructure oriented east-west, that is, perpendicular to the rest of the building. Although this superstructure has received limited excavation, we know that it is laid out differently than the upper rooms of the north terrace.

The central pyramid of Structure M13–1 is taller than the flanking additions and is surmounted by a temple standing 16 m above the plaza floor. In addition to having north and south wings, the central pyramid is fronted on the west by a *plataforma adosada* (attached platform). This *adosada* platform is topped by an unroofed U-shaped masonry superstructure open to the plaza below. The *adosada* is an architectural feature characteristic of the Early Classic city of Teotihuacan. William Fash and colleagues (2009) identify the stairway shrine *adosada* on the Pyramid of the Sun at Teotihuacan as the original and primary *wiinte' naah*. It is important to remember that Stela 15 states that Sihyaj K'ahk', a foreigner with Teotihuacan affiliation, came to Waka' in January AD 378, one week before he arrived in Tikal (Stuart 2000). That text declares that he carried out a ritual in a *wiinte'* place. Given the presence of an *adosada* platform in front of Structure M13–1, the image of a *k'ahk' witz* and reference to a *wiinte' naah* on the associated Stela 9, and the reference to a *wiinte'* place at Waka' on Stela 15, we infer that this historical event refers to Structure M13–1.

Fash et al. (2009) also have linked textual references to the *wiinte' naah* and its meaning as an "origin place" to archaeological evidence for shrines where Early Classic rituals similar to the New Fire Ceremonies of the Aztecs were conducted. These much later Mexica rites are well-documented in the *Codex Borbonicus*. Their argument suggests that the first of these fire ceremonies was carried out atop the *adosada* of the Sun Pyramid at Teotihuacan. Specifically, they note the discovery by Leopoldo Batres (1906) of relief sculpture on the *adosada* that depicts a fire shrine with flames emerging from it and a fire-drill cord in the doorway. Fash and colleagues (2009), therefore, argue that the lowland Maya of the fourth and fifth centuries AD referenced and likely built *wiinte' naah* shrines in the transformational wake of the arrival of Sihyaj K'ahk'. Nonetheless, none of the Maya-area examples they propose feature this kind of attached fronting platform. Two examples of such an *adosada* that are known in the lowlands are found at Waka'; these are Structure M13–1 and Structure O14–04 of the Mirador Group (cf. Figure 4.3b for a potential example at Lubaantun).

A third Early Classic *adosada* in the Maya area, Structure B-4 of Kaminaljuyu, is located in highland Guatemala (Kidder et al. 1946). That platform contained many elaborate tombs and burials with Teotihuacan-style offerings in the stairway and under the shrine. Michelle Rich (2011) and colleagues discovered a similar pattern at Waka' Structure O14–04. What is particularly striking, beyond the fact that the only known *adosada*-style buildings in Peten both occur at Waka', is that their initial spatial design was connected. The two structures are physically linked by a causeway confirmed to have been built in the Late Preclassic (Figure 7.1b). Thus, since their inception, these two buildings were likely ritually and symbolically tied as the two predominant monumental structures of the ancient city. They differ in that while Structure M13–1 had public access, Structure O14–04 was private. This underlying monumental layout endured for centuries despite near constant shifts in urban residence and form (Eppich et al. 2022).

To test our hypothesis that *wiinte' naah* ceremonialism was practiced at Structure M13–1 during the Early Classic period, we initiated tunnel excavations along the central axis of the platform in order to explore earlier construction phases. This methodology also satisfied the goal of understanding the long-term significance of, and changes to, the monumental platform. This was especially important because of the dense evidence for complicated ritual activities that typified the final phases of the building. In other words, we were keen to understand what the later inhabitants of Waka' were ritually invoking about this place and why, and what persevered or changed through time.

While defining the final terrace walls of Structure M13–1, we discovered two additional fragments of Stela 9 (Figure 7.3a). Together, these suggest that Stela 9 originally was a large monument typical of Waka', with more than 3 m² of carved surface. One of these additional fragments features the Maize God emerging from a ceremonial bar bundle, and the second constitutes the upper third of the stela. It displays the top of a headdress that was part of a large back-rack incorporating Principal Bird Deity imagery. The upper portion of this fragment and its sides have hieroglyphic texts that may name the ruler as Chan Yopaat. Based on the style of the carving, we estimate Stela 9 to date to about AD 500, most probably to the half-*k'atun* period ending of 9.3.10.0.0 in AD 504.

Farther south along that same terminal phase terrace wall, we discovered re-assembled fragments of the anciently shattered Stela 43 (Figure 7.3b). Its fragments were positioned in the wall and display various elements of the regalia of a Late Classic ruler. These include a portion showing a headdress that was re-positioned upside down and a fragment featuring the arms of a ruler holding an ancestor bundle. Two additional fragments were embedded in the south face of the fronting terrace wall of the platform. One is a small block with text and part of a headdress. The other, larger fragment includes a shoulder, parts of a head-dress, and the earspool of a ruler looking left; the face is not present. As in the case of Stela 9, the fragments display elements of royal ritual performance but few identifying features of the ruler.

Stelae 9 and 43, which date respectively to the Early and Late Classic, were broken before being re-set in Structure M13–1. These acts of destruction, which likely took place at different historical moments, evoke the fluctuating political loyalties Waka' maintained over the centuries and how opposing factions took aim at monuments that may have represented earlier political conflicts. It is even more interesting that the Terminal Classic people who reset the monuments selected fragments of both Early and Late Classic stelae to adorn the final phase of the building. Of particular importance to them were the symbolic elements of regalia and office, rather than portions that identified the depicted individuals. Likewise, the elements of Stela 9 promote the symbolic importance of rulership and the significance of the fire mountain.

Having defined the full base of the final terrace pertaining to the *adosada*, we initiated a center-line excavation. This was quickly halted because of the dangerous instability of the poorly consolidated final phase architecture. After this, we shifted our excavations to the summit of the *adosada* platform where a wide U-shaped and unroofed masonry superstructure was discovered. The U opens to the west towards the vast plaza below. The resulting excavated area was approximately 4.5 m (E-W) × 2.5 m (N-S) × 2 m deep, and 25 m³ of materials were removed. Excavators of this space discovered that it had been totally in-filled with layers of modeled stucco fragments that appear to have been detached from an architectural façade, perhaps the Late to Terminal façade of Structure M13–1. This deposit constitutes the second largest accumulation of modeled stucco yet excavated at Waka' (Figure 7.4). The deposit included numerous fragments of figures that are discernably anthropomorphic. Specifically, we recovered fragments of arms, regalia, a torso, and numerous heads (Figure 7.4a). The destruction of these stucco façade elements and their deposition in this space were carried out in order to ritually terminate the U-shaped superstructure atop the Late to Terminal Classic version of the *adosada* of Structure M13–1. Excavations beneath the massive stucco deposit revealed a distinct masonry feature that exhibited heavy burning. Rather than recount the order of discovery, we discuss the manner in which the feature was used according to reconstruction of the recorded stratigraphic sequences.

The monumental hearth

The space initially functioned as a massive, monumental hearth (Figure 7.5), which discernible layers of ash and prepared surfaces reveal was subject to frequent and repeated use. The hearth is situated along the eastern wall of the U-shaped room atop the *adosada* and was built as a low-walled masonry feature at least 1.8 m high. It consists of two short stepped benches flush with the north and south walls of the U-shaped feature that were placed atop the associated floor. Traces of painted stucco remain on the west-facing surfaces of these low stepped benches. Halfway between and parallel to the benches we recorded a low-lying alignment of roughly shaped stones creating a partition; this resulted in two distinct and parallel west-facing niches (Figure 7.5a). This slightly elevated central alignment running east-west through the center of the feature is unattached to the stepped side walls. It retained a fine layer of stucco, suggesting that it was a distinct architectural element. This elevated alignment between the niches, which measures about 40 cm in width, was not used in the same manner as the niches. The northern niche remains intact for future excavation and analyses, but the southern niche was fully excavated and measures 54 cm in diameter and 40 cm in height. When the monumental hearth was in use, these side walls plus the unattached, raised middle section gave the appearance of two apertures with a space between. These apertures, when filled with fire, would have appeared as the inflamed eyes of the *k'ahk' witz* portrayed on the lower section of Stela 9.

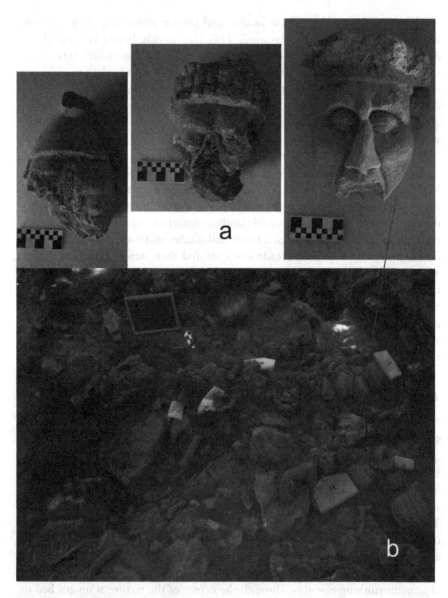

FIGURE 7.4 Stucco head fragments (a) from the stucco deposit (b) infilling the final phase of the U-shaped masonry superstructure of the Structure M13–1 *adosada*.

Source: Photos by Juan Carlos Pérez and Olivia Navarro-Farr.

This would have been particularly impressive when witnessed from the plaza below, which is one of the largest public spaces at the site. The overall design of this monumental hearth bears a striking resemblance to the *wiinte' naah* recorded in the *Codex Borbonicus* (see DiCesare 2009:Figure 5.5).

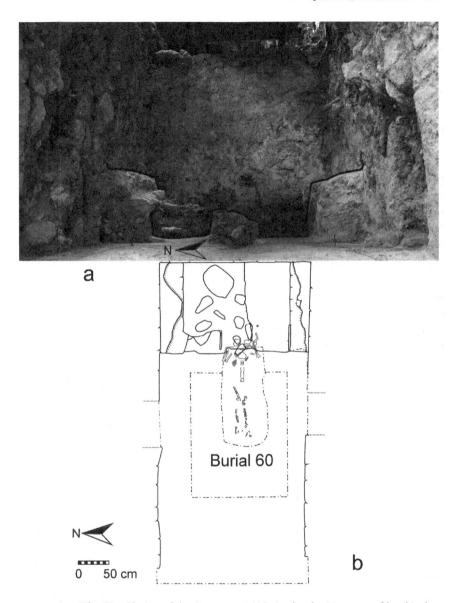

FIGURE 7.5 The Fire Shrine of the Structure M13–1 *adosada*: (a) east profile; (b) plan of exposed architecture and Burial 60.

Source: By Juan Carlos Pérez, Olivia Navarro-Farr, Damaris Menéndez, and Griselda Pérez Robles.

The hearth feature contained great quantities of charcoal, ash, and clay rubified from intense heat exposure. The walls and side benches and frontal pediment also showed intense burning use. Excavations within the north sector of the hearth demonstrate a sequence of burnt strata between seemingly prepared stucco surfaces, suggesting a series of burning events. All sediments were collected and analyzed by paleoethnobotanist Clarissa Cagnato. She reports that varied macrobotanicals such as grassy weeds, maize plants, and even painted wooden objects were chosen for ritual burning (Cagnato 2016; Cagnato et al. 2017). Cagnato (2016) has noted the selection of grassy weeds mimics those found in fallow fields between cultivation cycles. She argues that the choice of such plants for ritual burning in the site center suggests an emphasis on agriculture and its inherent seasonal cycles.

Dating the monumental hearth with its complex use-life has been tricky. Associated ceramics appear to place this use in the Late to Terminal Classic periods, which is a rather broad timespan. Stratigraphically, we know the construction of the final phase *adosada*, the U-shaped superstructure, and the monumental hearth itself all post-date the interment of Lady K'abel, whose tomb was built into an earlier phase of the *adosada* (as discussed later in this chapter) and whose associated funerary offerings date from between the late seventh and early eighth centuries (Navarro-Farr et al. 2013, 2021). She herself likely died in the early eighth century (Guenter 2014). Given that her tomb construction was followed by two subsequent architectural phases (detailed below), the monumental hearth, which was part of that final phase, had to have been commissioned well after her early eighth-century interment. This burial and construction sequence places the hearth feature in the Late to Terminal Classic, which is consistent with our ceramic chronology. Interestingly, the painted wooden objects identified by Cagnato date to the seventh century AD (Cagnato et al. 2017), which, according to our current understanding of the construction history of the *adosada*, is at least a century and a half earlier than the construction and use of the hearth. It also means those objects are roughly coeval with Lady K'abel's lifespan. As Cagnato (2016) points out, the painted wooden objects may have been relics selected for ritualized burning in this monumental ceremonial hearth.

Excavations through the fill of the floor associated with the monumental hearth further underscore the importance of this feature. An intrusive interment (Burial 60; see Figure 7.5b) was discovered immediately west of the feature. Despite poor preservation that did not allow determination of sex, project bioarchaeologist Erin Patterson (2013) determined, based in part on a lack of osteoarthritic lesions, that the individual likely died at middle age. Additionally, Patterson noted the lack of cranial elements except 12 teeth. The teeth indicate relatively good health, and the lack of other cranial elements implies that they were removed. The individual was not accompanied by burial furniture or offerings save for a large effigy hearth stone carried in the arms like a bundle (Patterson 2013). This individual was likely interred as a dedication to the Fire Shrine.

After multiple uses, the complex hearth feature was built over and refashioned as a throne. The re-purposing of the space into a throne is evidenced by a layer of numerous dressed stones concentrated in the east. This throne-like feature, which may have been short-lived, was subsequently broken into, and numerous dressed stones from it were found in disarray in a concentration to its east. Having ruptured the throne, which itself postdates the ceremonial hearth, a fire was set inside the area. That this fire was hot and intense is evidenced by abundant and sizeable carbonized wood torches, scorched dressed stones, significant quantities of ash, and rubified clay. After the fire, the entire area was infilled with the stucco deposit (Figure 7.4). No further modifications were conducted to the *adosada*.

Unequivocal archaeological evidence for a monumental hearth atop a Late Classic construction designed to mimic an Early Classic Teotihuacan-style *adosada* demonstrates the hypothesis suggested by Stelae 9 and 15 that this feature was a *wiinte' naah* and justifies our naming Structure M13–1 the Fire Shrine. This Fire Shrine, built as an eighth-century Maya version of a fifth-century Teotihuacan structure, certainly indicates strong social memories of an earlier period. Although we found no iconographic depictions of fire drills associated with this feature, the hearth was purposefully commissioned and used multiple times to ceremonially and very publicly burn a wide range of botanical materials and painted relics.

The Late Classic Fire Shrine was likely commissioned by the final rulers of the site before the structure was terminated with the infilling of stucco during the Terminal Classic period. We argue this monumental Fire Shrine is a revival of earlier *wiinte' naah* ritual practice dating back to the Early Classic arrival of Sihyaj K'ahk'. Even amid dramatic political changes sweeping the Peten throughout the Terminal Classic, the Fire Shrine of Waka' continued to be the site of ritual visits and pilgrimage (Navarro-Farr 2009), demonstrating continuity of ceremonial significance and the persistence of memory. Moreover, the impact of such a feature when viewed from one of the largest plazas in the heart of the city would have been considerable because the dramatic appearance of two niches as burning eyes operated as a physical metaphor of the *witz* earth monster aflame. This familiar and enduring Mesoamerican iconographic construction demonstrates how monumental structures, like caves, mountains, and other earthly features, are metaphors for supernatural entities embodying the potency of the earth (Brady and Ashmore 1999).

Burial 61

Underneath the final Fire Shrine, we discovered a series of earlier construction phases (Figure 7.6). The sub-phase prior to the Fire Shrine included a double I-shaped chamber at the summit of a stair; our excavation revealed the eastern room of that double chamber. Its entrance is on the west. We dubbed this earlier phase Structure M13–1 *Adosada* Sub I (henceforth Sub I). Below it, we encountered the northwest corner of the stair of M13–1 *Adosada* Sub II (henceforth Sub II). This earlier phase of construction expanded farther south, indicating that the centerline of this earlier phase also was to the south and, therefore, that the subsequent Sub I served to move the centerline axis farther to the north. Sub II included a partially preserved superstructure feature with 13 steps leading to a façade shorn along its upper half and capped with a separate floor. We located

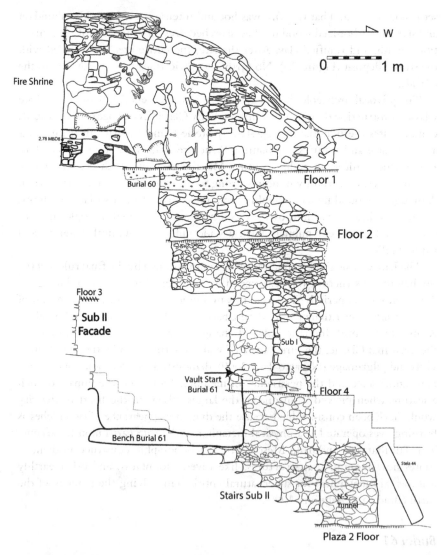

FIGURE 7.6 North profile of Structure M13–1 *adosada* showing the locations of the Fire Shrine, Burial 60, Sub I, Sub II, Burial 61, and Stela 44.

Source: By Juan Carlos Pérez, Griselda Pérez, Cyrus Hulen, and Olivia Navarro-Farr.

one doorway with its southern jamb intact and the northern jamb missing. It was cut away and infilled with substantial concentrations of charcoal and ash. Although this area remains unexcavated, we believe it likely was the location of a re-entry event.

Further tunneling revealed Burial 61, a masonry tomb chamber placed in a trench cut through the stairway of Sub II. Burial 61 contained a single mature individual laid on a stone bench (Figure 7.7). Biological sex could not be

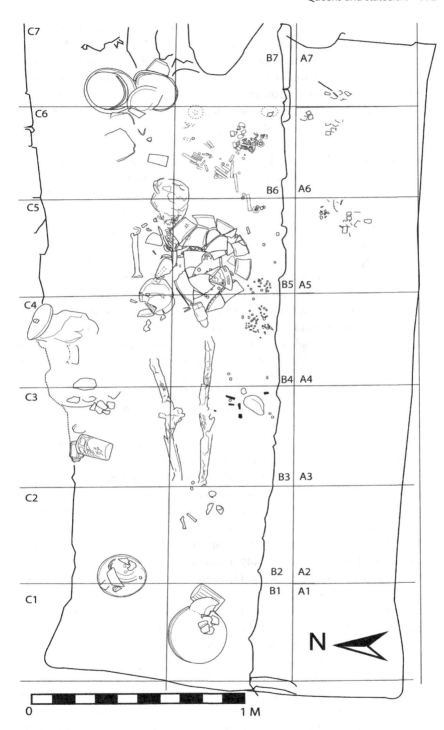

FIGURE 7.7 Plan of Waka' Burial 61, Structure M13–1 *adosada*.

Source: By Francisco Castañeda and Olivia Navarro-Farr.

conclusively determined because of the poor condition of the pelvis and certain ambiguities of other skeletal features (Patterson 2013). Nonetheless, other lines of evidence underscore that the remains are likely those of Lady K'abel. The associated ceramics date the interment to between the late seventh and early eighth centuries AD, consistent with the chronology of her death (Guenter 2014). Of the various materials included in the assemblage, notable items include a Tikal-style drinking cup decorated with the royal god K'awiil (Figure 7.8a). Next to this drinking cup was a Copador-style bottle (Figure 7.8b), possibly for powdered tobacco, and a small carved alabaster jar (Figure 7.8c). The interior of the jar contained significant levels of mercury (Loughmiller-Cardinal and Cagnato 2016), indicative of cinnabar. Its incised lines were infilled with red, probably also cinnabar paint. The iconography on the vessel depicts an aged individual emerging from a shell and text composed of four hieroglyphs identifying the owner as Lady K'abel (Navarro-Farr et al. 2013, 2021).

A large *Spondylus* shell adorned the groin of the individual interred in the tomb. This echoes the pelvic *xoc* shell with which Lady K'abel is portrayed on Stela 34 and is consistent with female regalia in general (Josserand 2002). Over the left arm, the interred bore a large Palmar Orange Polychrome serving platter with the central circular base removed (Figure 7.8d), which we interpret as a large kill hole. Although it is a plate with a serving function, it was placed on her arm to mimic a shield. This shield-bearing position is reminiscent of the two known images of her: Stela 34 and the queenly figurine in the tableau interred within Burial 39 (Navarro-Farr and Kelly et al. 2020:Figure 7.4). It is noteworthy that this scene was found in the only other *adosada* building at Waka', Structure O14–04 (Rich 2011).

Among the remains of Lady K'abel's headdress, we found numerous jades including a large earflare with a smaller earflare inside. Also present in this area were the remains of a small mosaic jadeite mask (Navarro-Farr et al. 2021:Figure 7i) about the size of an average human palm. This would have been attached to the headdress. The small mask also is visible on the Waka' Burial 39 figurine we believe depicts Lady K'abel. Another salient jadeite jewel adorning the remains in Burial 61 is a small piece shaped as a human head (Figure 7.8e). We think this is either a portrait of the young Lady K'abel or some other idealized female form such as a youthful Moon Goddess. The common identification of such jewels is that they depict the Maize God, which suggests its function as a jewel of majesty. This particular jewel could represent both the Maize and Moon Deity, given the multi-referential nature of such powerful images (Looper 2002).

Lady K'abel's mortuary assemblage reflects ceramic traditions from across the Maya world. This underscores the cosmopolitan nature of her approach to diplomacy. In total, we found more than 1,000 pieces of worked jade, some 280 pieces of worked shell, a pyrite mirror, two figurines, stingray spines, evidence of textiles, and a woven mat (Navarro-Farr et al. 2021). That this important royal woman was interred here supports the hypothesis that the dense Late and Terminal Classic deposits blanketing the building were the result of commemorative

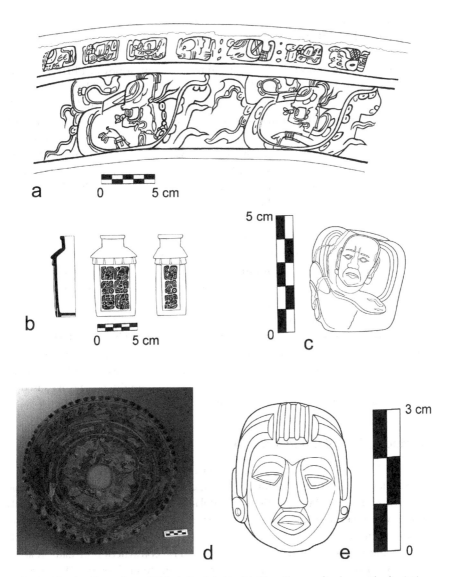

FIGURE 7.8 Artifacts from Waka' Burial 61: (a) Kanalkan cylinder with depiction of K'awiil; (b) Copador snuff bottle; (c) alabaster jar; (d) Palmar Orange Polychrome platter; (e) jadeite effigy bead.

Source: Illustrations by René Ozaeta, photo by Juan Carlos Pérez.

ritual enshrinement by Waka' inhabitants rather than post-occupational debris (Navarro-Farr 2009). We also argue that Lady K'abel's offerings convey her as an important sorceress adopting characteristics associated with the Moon Goddess (Navarro-Farr, Kelly et al. 2020). These include the paint pot, her adornments of jadeite and shell, items associated with divination such as the snuff jar and a pyrite mirror, and various representations of her as a shield bearer. The presence of such ritual paraphernalia in her mortuary assemblage speaks to Lady K'abel's power in life and her critical geopolitical role at Waka'.

Lady K'abel was most likely the daughter of the most powerful Kaanul ruler in history, Yuhknoom Ch'een the Great. Certain ceramic evidence, therefore, also visually links her interment with that of his successor and her probable brother, Calakmul ruler Yuhknoom Yich'aak K'ahk', whose burial is on display at the Fuerte de San Miguel, Campeche, Mexico. The vessels in Waka' Burial 61, such as the killed plate, multiple stuccoed vessels painted in Maya blue, and a Late Classic black-slipped cylinder, bear a striking visual resemblance to Yuhknoom Yich'aak K'ahk's mortuary assemblage. This suggests Lady K'abel's mortuary assemblage was selected to convey cosmopolitanism while simultaneously reflecting deep Kaanul cultural ties.

Lady K'abel's funerary chamber was constructed almost immediately prior to her interment. This is evident from the fact that some of the vessels on the dais surface were cemented to it, meaning the mortar was still wet when they were placed in the tomb. Impressions of both abundant cloth and a woven mat made of perishable materials also indicate that the mortar was still wet at the time of their placement in the chamber. The individual was laid upon the woven mat which, in turn, was placed atop a wooden pallet. Stanley Guenter (2014) suggests that Lady K'abel died ca. AD 711. He also notes there may be some association between her demise and that of Calakmul itself. Thus, we speculate that the hasty nature of her interment within a still-wet tomb might have been caused by political strife at Waka' linked to the decline of the Kaanul kingdom.

Ix Ikoom, Stela 43, and Stela 44

Stelae 43 and 44 and their incorporation into Structure M13–1 also enhance our understanding of the important multigenerational link between Waka' and women of Kaanul. Specifically, both Stelae 43 and 44 reference a previously unknown Kaanul-affiliated female ruler at Waka', Ix Ikoom. Investigations of the various *adosada* phases have demonstrated clear linkages between Lady K'abel and Ix Ikoom in these constructions. The construction of Lady K'abel's tomb was part of a larger building program meant to enclose Sub II; her burial chamber is situated within the center of the later Sub I construction. Stela 44 (Figure 7.9), dating to the sixth century, was re-set in the stair risers fronting Sub I (Pérez Robles and Navarro-Farr 2013). It marked the newly established centerline of that *adosada* platform and was deliberately and symbolically linked to Lady K'abel's interment. The third and final *adosada* platform, incorporating the monumental Fire Shrine, was added after the burial and establishment of a new central axis.

Later still, probably during the very late eighth or, more likely, the early ninth century, builders with inferior resources refurbished the final walls of the *adosada* platform of Structure M13–1. This refurbishment of the *adosada* may have been

FIGURE 7.9 Waka' Stela 44.

Source: Photo by Juan Carlos Pérez.

one of the final mandates of the waning royal court of Waka'. Fragments of Late Classic Stela 43 were incorporated into the structure during this final construction stage.

The fragments of Stela 43 display important emblems of the office of rulership but not the face of the ruler. The text dates to 23 January AD 702 and the monument likely portrays K'inich Bahlam II of Waka' celebrating the 7 Ahau half-*k'atun* ending (9.13.10.0.0). The monument relates this date back to an earlier 7 Ahau date celebrated by Ix Ikoom on 9.7.0.0.0 (AD 573), as well as a much earlier 7 Ahau date on 8.14.0.0.0 (AD 317). Although the exact nature of the ceremonies performed on these 7 Ahau dates is uncertain, K'inich Bahlam's prominent commemoration of this date and the association with Ix Ikoom suggests that he regarded her as an ancestress to whom he anchored his own legitimacy.

Stela 44 provides multiple details that demonstrate Kaanul affiliation, including an additional reference to Ix Ikoom. The eroded front of Stela 44, dedicated in AD 564, depicts a front-facing king in a typically sixth-century pose with his arms cradling a ceremonial bundle (Pérez Robles and Navarro-Farr 2013). The inscription indicates Stela 44 was dedicated by a Waka' dynast named Wa'oom Uch'ab Ahk, who acceded under the overlordship of the Kaanul ruler K'ahk' Ti' Ch'ich' (Martin and Beliaev 2017). The Waka' king came to the throne in AD 556, presumably right after the death of his father, Chak Tok Ich'aak, *wak ajaw* ("Great/Red Misty Claw, the Waka' Lord"). Chak Tok Ich'aak is also mentioned on La Corona Altar 5 two decades earlier (AD 544) and there is given the title *sak wahyis*. This suggests he was at that time ruling over La Corona, which by AD 520 had already become a vassal of Kaanul (Martin 2008; Stuart et al. 2018). Stela 44 indicates Wa'oom Uch'ab Ahk's accession was witnessed by his mother Ix Ikoom, who bears the royal epithets *ix sak wahyis* and *k'uhul* "cha"*tahn winik*. According to Canuto and Barrientos (2013) and Martin (2008), these titles are closely associated with Kaanul. Thus, Ix Ikoom was the queen consort of Chak Tok Ich'aak of Waka' and the mother of the ruler portrayed on Stela 44. Like Lady K'abel of later times, Ix Ikoom was a Kaanul-affiliated wife and mother whose marriage cemented the vassal status of Waka' to Kaanul. Freidel and Guenter (2003) also point to an emphasis on female elites in the texts of Waka'. These include not only references to the mothers of kings, but also to consort queens. Reese-Taylor and colleagues (2009) have also noted a pattern in which the Kaanul kingdom and its allies emphasized female royalty. This may indicate cultural influence from the northern lowlands, where references to royal women have a longer history dating back to the Early Classic period.

Taken together, a number of key elements link Stelae 43 and 44. They each were meaningfully and purposefully re-incorporated into the same structure, albeit during distinct construction episodes in the eighth to early ninth centuries. These distinct construction phases of the *adosada* platform attached to Structure M13–1 were both built on the location wherein Lady K'abel was interred. Finally, the two monuments both refer to the sixth-century Kaanul-affiliated Ix Ikoom. Given the purposeful re-arrangements of these monuments, their linked textual references, and the physical context, we argue for active and multigenerational "memory work" (Mills and Walker 2008) that was clearly associated with Kaanul. That these two monuments mentioning Ix Ikoom were chosen for incorporation in the funeral monument of Lady K'abel underscores the shared legacy of these important Kaanul-affiliated queens. Moreover, the persistence of ritual activity at this locale suggests to us that the memorialization of Lady K'abel and Ix Ikoom as ancestors was a purposeful focus of ritual even after the decline of the political institution of divine rulership (Navarro-Farr 2009).

Conclusions

In sum, the evidence for commemorative ritual acts linking Lady K'abel and Ix Ikoom to the sacred political landscape of Waka' include: (1) the Late to Terminal Classic ritual enshrinement of Structure M13–1, which already housed the remains of Lady K'abel; (2) the construction of a Late to Terminal Classic Fire Shrine atop that same building, indicating the revival of Early Classic Teotihuacan-centered *wiinte' naah* ceremonialism; (3) the interment of Lady K'abel featuring rich and cosmopolitan mortuary offerings that underscore her Kaanul roots, her broad diplomatic ties, and her likely role as an important diviner and sorceress at Waka'; (4) the commemorative caching of Stela 44 and the purposeful re-setting of Stelae 43 fragments in ways and in places that meaningfully underscored the relationship between Lady K'abel and Ix Ikoom through the enduring tradition of Kaanul marriage diplomacy; and (5) the fact that Structure O14–04 and Structure M13–1, the only two buildings with *adosadas* at Waka', were spatially linked in the sacred landscape of the city since Preclassic times by means of a causeway, further indicating that the ceremonial importance of the building we dub the Fire Shrine is ancient.

We have presented various data from the prominent civic-ceremonial Fire Shrine of Waka' in order to examine how foreign Kaanul royal women were integrated into the ritual landscape of the city and invested with local political power and authority. The current lack of attention to the centrality of women in Classic Maya politics impedes recognition that they actively understood and engaged in their political roles. Instead, they are characterized as passive commodities forced into hypogamous marriages. In contrast, the rich evidence from the vast and multi-faceted ritual use of the Fire Shrine throughout the final two centuries of occupation of Waka' underscores the profound social memory surrounding two women and this locale. We argue that the ritual importance of this building long predates Lady K'abel and Ix Ikoom, and therefore was well-known and understood by them. In fact, that is why we believe Lady K'abel chose this locale for her interment and why two monuments featuring her predecessor were selected for inclusion in subsequent re-building episodes.

The material evidence for the commemorative ritual acts discussed here suggests that Lady K'abel and Ix Ikoom were remembered by ancient Waka' inhabitants for successfully negotiating their political roles in the fortunes of the city and for making their marks on its history. The burial of Lady K'abel and the repeated mentions of Ix Ikoom commemorated on Stelae 43 and 44, each built into distinct phases of the Fire Shrine, underscore their posthumous associations with the revived *wiinte' naah* tradition at Waka'. This also suggests the possibility that fire ceremonialism had been carried out in that spot during the generations preceding them, a hypothesis we hope to test through further excavations into earlier substructures. This possibility is given support by the association of Structure M13–1 with the only other *adosada* building at the site, Structure O14–04, via the Late Preclassic causeway. Given the ancient connection between these two large ritual structures – each prominent but one decidedly public and the other with far more limited access – it makes sense that the Kaanul queens marked their association with Fire Shrine ceremonialism to justify their sociopolitical status and influence. The burial of Lady K'abel in the *adosada* of Structure M13–1 and references to the earlier Ix Ikoom therefore demonstrate their political maneuvering, as well as the later manipulation of social memory to engender the status of these women at Waka' long after their deaths. The choice of a monumental building, perhaps steeped in ritual significance since Preclassic times, further underscores their importance.

Our goal has been to introduce a new path for considering not just the Kaanul strategy at Waka', but also how royal women were more than mere tokens exchanged to cement political alliances. They were powerful and influential rulers and clearly were remembered as such by subsequent generations of Waka' inhabitants. With her *ix kaloomte'* title, Lady K'abel is afforded a hierarchically higher position in terms of political ranking than her royal husband. As a princess of Kaanul, one of the most powerful Late Classic kingdoms, her marriage to K'inich Bahlam II solidified the vassal status of Waka' to that polity. We think Ix Ikoom was similarly powerful and regarded as such based on the inscriptions of Stelae 43 and 44. We argue that these women and others like them across the Maya region, particularly those affiliated with Kaanul during the Late Classic period, were political actors in their own right. The power and influence of these women should not be questioned, and it is time to consider the fullest possible implications of a Classic Maya political stage that included mothers, wives, and daughters. The multiple ways that Kaanul women acted and were later commemorated at Waka' accentuates how greatly valued royal women were in the past, urgently emphasizing our own need to better understand them as agents.

Acknowledgments

Ongoing research carried out by the Proyecto Arqueológico Waka' (PAW) is supported by the Instituto de Antropología e Historia de Guatemala, the Ministerio de Cultura y Deportes, and the Departamento de Monumentos Prehispánicos. All figures are presented courtesy of the Ministry of Culture and Sports of Guatemala and the Proyecto Arqueológico Waka'. We also are grateful for the support of Jerry Glick, the Waka' Foundation, and all members of the PAW and research associates who supported this research. They include David Freidel, Stanley Guenter, Francisco Castañeda, Erin Patterson, Michelle Rich, Clarissa Cagnato, David McCormick, René Ozaeta, and Jennifer Loughmiller-Cardinal. We are grateful for reviewer comments that have strengthened this chapter and to College of Wooster research assistant Alyssa Henss for her editorial assistance. This research was generously supported by the Alphawood Foundation, the Fundación Patrimonio Cultural y Natural Maya, the Division for Equity and Inclusion of the University of New Mexico, the Department of Anthropology of the University of New Mexico, a Henry Luce III Fund for Distinguished Scholarship awarded by College of Wooster, a College of Wooster Faculty Research Leave, and the Hitz Foundation.

References cited

Batres, Leopoldo 1906 *Teotihuacan ó la Ciudad Sagrada de los Toltecas*. Imprenta de Hull, Mexico City.

Brady, James E, and Wendy Ashmore 1999 Mountains, Caves, Water: Ideational Landscapes of the Ancient Maya. In *Archaeologies of Landscape: Contemporary Perspectives*, edited by Wendy Ashmore and A. Bernard Knapp, pp. 124–145. Blackwell Publishing, Malden.

Cagnato, Clarissa 2016 *A Paleoethnobotanical Study of Two Classic Maya Sites, El Perú-Waka' and La Corona*. Unpublished PhD dissertation, Department of Anthropology, Washington University, St. Louis.

Cagnato, Clarissa, Olivia Navarro-Farr, Griselda Pérez Robles, Juan Carlos Pérez Calderón, and Damaris Menéndez 2017 Feeding the Mountain: Plant Remains from Ritual Contexts on and Around Structure M13-1 at El Perú-Waka'. *Paper presented at the 82nd Annual Meeting of the Society for American Archaeology*, Vancouver, British Columbia.

Canuto, Marcello A., and Tomàs Barrientos Q. 2013 The Importance of La Corona. *La Corona Notes* 1(1):1–5.

Demarest, Arthur, and Federico Fahsen 2002 Nuevos datos e interpretaciones de los reinos occidentales del clásico tardío: Hacia una visión sintética de la historia Pasión-Usumacinta. *Paper presented at the XVI Simposio de Investigaciones Arqueológicas en Guatemala*, Guatemala City.

DiCesare, Catherine 2009 *Sweeping the Way: Divine Transformation in the Aztec Festival of Ochpaniztli*. University Press of Colorado, Boulder.

Eppich, Keith, Damien B. Marken, and Elsa Damaris Menéndez 2022 A City in Flux: The Dynamic Urban Form and Functions of El Peru-Waka', Guatemala. In *Building an Archaeology of Maya Urbanism: Flexibility and Planning in the American Tropics*, edited by Damien B. Marken and M. Charlotte Arnauld. University Press of Colorado, Boulder.

Fash, William L., Alexandre Tokovinine, and Barbara W. Fash. 2009 The House of New Fire at Teotihuacan and its Legacy in Mesoamerica. In *Art of Urbanism: How Mesoamerican Kingdoms Represented Themselves in Architecture and Imagery*, edited by William L. Fash and Leonardo López Luján, pp. 201–229. Dumbarton Oaks Research Library and Collection, Washington, DC.

Freidel, David A., Héctor L. Escobedo, and Stanley Guenter 2007 A Crossroads of Conquerors: Waka' and Gordon Willey's "Rehearsal for the Collapse" Hypothesis. In *Gordon R. Willey and American Archaeology: Contemporary Perspectives*, edited by Jeremy A. Sabloff and William L. Fash, pp. 187–208. University of Oklahoma Press, Norman.

Freidel, David A., and Stanley Guenter 2003 Bearers of War and Creation. *Archaeology.* January 23. www.archaeology.org/online/features/siteq2/, accessed March 13, 2018.

Graham, Ian 1988 Homeless Hieroglyphs. *Antiquity* 62(234):122–126.

Greene Robertson, Merle 2007 The Lost Field Notebook Restored. *The PARI Journal* 8(2):1–12.

Guenter, Stanley Paul 2005 Informe Preliminar de la Epigrafía de El Perú. In *Proyecto Arqueológico El Perú-Waka': Informe No. 2, Temporada 2004*, edited by Héctor L. Escobedo and David Freidel, pp. 359–400. Instituto de Antropología e Historia, Guatemala City.

——— 2014 The Epigraphy of El Perú-Waka'. In *Archaeology at El Perú-Waka': Performances of Ritual, Memory, and Power*, edited by Olivia C. Navarro-Farr and Michelle Rich, pp. 147–166. University of Arizona Press, Tucson.

Josserand, J. Kathryn 2002 Women in Classic Maya Hieroglyphic Texts. In *Ancient Maya Women*, edited by Traci Ardren, pp. 114–151. Altamira Press, Walnut Creek.

Kidder, A. V., J. D. Jennings, and E. M. Shook 1946 *Excavations at Kaminaljuyu with Technological Notes by Anna O. Shepard*. Pennsylvania State University Press, University Park.

Looper, Matthew G. 2002 Women-Men (and Men-Women): Classic Maya Rulers and the Third Gender. In *Ancient Maya Women*, edited by Traci Ardren, pp. 171–202. Altamira Press, Walnut Creek.

Loughmiller-Cardinal, Jennifer, and Clarissa Cagnato 2016 Análisis del contenido de las vasijas del Entierro 61. In *Proyecto Arqueológico El Perú-Waka': Informe No. 13, Temporada 2015*, edited by Juan Carlos Pérez and Griselda Pérez Robles, pp. 219–249. Instituto de Antropología e Historia, Guatemala City.

Martin, Simon 2008 Wives and Daughters on the Dallas Altar. *Mesoweb.* www.mesoweb. com/articles/martin/Wives&Daughters.pdf, accessed March 13, 2018.

Martin, Simon, and Dmitri Beliaev 2017 K'ahk' Ti' Ch'ich': A New Snake King from the Early Classic Period. *The PARI Journal* 17(3):1–7.

Mills, Barbara, and William Walker (editors) 2008 *Memory Work: Archaeologies of Material Practices*. School of Advanced Research Press, Santa Fe.

Navarro-Farr, Olivia C. 2009 *Ritual, Process, and Continuity in the Late to Terminal Classic Transition: Investigations at Structure M13–1 in the Ancient Maya Site of El Perú-Waka', Petén, Guatemala*. PhD dissertation, Department of Anthropology, Southern Methodist University, Dallas.

——— 2016 Dynamic Transitions at El Perú-Waka': Late Terminal Classic Ritual Repurposing of a Monumental Shrine. In *Ritual, Violence, and the Fall of the Classic Maya Kings*, edited by Gyles Iannone, Brett A. Houk, and Sonja A. Schwake, pp. 243–269. University Press of Florida, Gainesville.

Navarro-Farr, Olivia C., Keith Eppich, David A. Freidel, and Griselda Pérez Robles 2020 Ancient Maya Queenship: Generations of Crafting State Politics and Alliance Building from Kaanul to Waka'. In *Approaches to Monumental Landscapes of the Ancient Maya*, edited by Brett A. Houk, Barbara Arroyo, and Terry G. Powis, pp. 196–217. University Press of Florida, Gainesville.

Navarro-Farr, Olivia C., David A. Freidel, and Ana Lucía Arroyave Prera 2008 Manipulating Memory in the Wake of Dynastic Decline at El Perú-Waka': Termination Deposits at Abandoned Structure M13–1. In *Ruins of the Past: The Use and Perception of Abandoned Structures in the Lowland Maya Area*, edited by Travis W. Stanton and Aline Magnoni, pp. 113–146. University Press of Colorado, Boulder.

Navarro-Farr, Olivia C., Mary Kate Kelly, Michelle Rich, and Griselda Pérez Robles 2020 Expanding the Canon: Lady K'abel the Ix Kaloomte' and the Political Narratives of Classic Maya Queens. *Feminist Anthropology* 1:38–55. DOI: 10.1002/fea2.12007.

Navarro-Farr, Olivia C., Griselda Pérez Robles, and Damaris Menéndez Bolaños 2013 WK-01: Excavaciones en la Estructura M13–1. In *Proyecto Arqueológico El Perú-Waka': Informe No. 10, Temporada 2012*, edited by Juan Carlos Pérez Calderón, pp. 12–100. Instituto de Antropología e Historia, Guatemala City.

Navarro-Farr, Olivia C., Griselda Pérez Robles, Juan Carlos Pérez Calderón, Elsa Damaris Menéndez Bolaños, et al. 2021 Burial 61 at El Perú-Waka's Structure M13–1. *Latin American Antiquity* 32(1):188–200.

Patterson, Erin 2013 Análisis preliminar de restos óseos humanos. Temporada 2012. In *Proyecto Arqueológico El Perú-Waka': Informe No. 10, Temporada 2012*, edited by Juan Carlos Pérez Calderón, pp. 92–105. Instituto de Antropología e Historia, Guatemala City.

Pérez Robles, Griselda, and Olivia Navarro-Farr 2013 WK01: Excavaciones en M13–1 y el descubrimiento de la Estela 44. In *Proyecto Arqueológico El Perú-Waka': Informe No. 11, Temporada 2013*, edited by Juan Carlos Pérez Calderón, pp. 3–26. Instituto de Antropología e Historia, Guatemala City.

Reese-Taylor, Kathryn, Peter Mathews, Julia Guernsey, and Marlene Fritzler 2009 Warrior Queens among the Classic Maya. In *Blood and Beauty: Organized Violence in the Art and Archaeology of Mesoamerica and Central America*, edited by Heather Orr and Rex Koontz, pp. 39–72. Cotsen Institute of Archaeology, University of California, Los Angeles.

Rich, Michelle E. 2011 *Ritual, Royalty and Classic Period Politics: The Archaeology of the Mirador Group at El Perú-Waka', Petén, Guatemala*. PhD dissertation, Department of Anthropology, Southern Methodist University, Dallas.

Stuart, David 2000 *Mesoamerica's Classic Heritage: From Teotihuacan to the Aztecs*. University Press of Colorado, Boulder.

——— 2004 The Beginnings of the Copan Dynasty: A Review of the Hieroglyphic and Historical Evidence. In *Understanding Early Classic Copan*, edited by Ellen E. Bell, Marcello A. Canuto, and Robert J. Sharer, pp. 265–296. University of Pennsylvania Museum of Archaeology and Anthropology, Philadelphia.

Stuart, David, Marcello Canuto, Tomás Barrientos, and Alejandro González 2018 A Preliminary Analysis of Altar 5 from La Corona. *The PARI Journal* 19(2):1–13.

Taube, Karl 2004 Structure 10L-16 and Its Early Classic Antecedents: Fire Shrines and the Evocation and Resurrection of K'inich Yax K'uk' Mo'. In *Understanding Early Classic Copan*, edited by Ellen E. Bell, Marcello A. Canuto, and Robert J. Sharer, pp. 265–295. University of Pennsylvania Museum of Archaeology and Anthropology, Philadelphia.

Teufel, Stefanie 2008 Marriage Diplomacy: Women at the Royal Court. In *Maya: Divine Kings of the Rain Forest*, edited by Nikolai Grube, pp. 172–173. Könemann, Cologne.

Woodfill, Brent K. S., and Chloé Andrieu 2012 Tikal's Early Classic Domination of the Great Western Trade Route: Ceramic, Lithic, and Iconographic Evidence. *Ancient Mesoamerica* 23:189–209.

8

ARCHITECTURE AS A MATERIAL REPRESENTATION OF SOCIOPOLITICAL STRUCTURE

An analysis of lowland Maya palace complexes in the late eighth century

Tomás Barrientos Q.

The archaeology of the Maya lowlands, especially research that focuses on the development of cities during the Classic period (AD 250–900), constitutes an important field for the analysis of the sociopolitical organization of ancient states. The study of geopolitics in this region concentrates on hieroglyphic inscriptions that have made it possible to identify the presence of well-defined political entities governed by a monarchical and dynastic system headed by rulers who held titles such as *k'uhul ajaw* (sacred lord). This system originated during the Preclassic period, and there is strong evidence of the presence of such rulers from the first century BC onward. Nonetheless, the political system of the sacred lords consolidated in the Classic period. Although written records are the main source of information used to reconstruct the political environment, archaeological research in Maya cities has provided material evidence of the complexity achieved by these centers. This was expressed through monumental architecture and fine art, as well as complex settlement patterns that allowed the sustained use of the tropical forest environment for more than a thousand years.

Given the long history of this sociopolitical system, it is no surprise that its characteristics evolved over time. Although all Maya cities contained elements in common and shared the same ideological basis, each one also developed its own characteristics that were the expression of the variability that existed within the system of the sacred lords. Therefore, we can identify what may be called "regimes" specific to particular cities or regions, which in turn created a complex network of interaction throughout the lowlands (Canuto and Lamoureux-St-Hilaire 2017). As many studies have shown, this political system began to collapse in the late eighth century AD and eventually disappeared in the late ninth century, only to be replaced by new forms of government during the Postclassic period (Demarest et al. 2005; Iannone 2014).

DOI: 10.4324/9781351268004-8

My work attempts to explain the changing nature of the political system of the Maya cities of the Classic period, specifically in the second half of the eighth century. This was the moment that preceded the collapse of the regimes centered on the figure of the *k'uhul ajaw*. Given that only some cities of this time have detailed epigraphic records, I argue that the interpretation of sociopolitical structures may be based on architectural studies. In specific, I propose that palatial architecture constitutes one of the best sources of data for understanding the processes of political change.

I present data from the ancient city of Cancuen, whose palace complex is one of the most monumental and best preserved in the central Maya lowlands. Its construction corresponds precisely to the moment prior to the collapse of the sacred lord political system. The analysis and interpretation of this building complex, therefore, provide an important window on the nature of Maya cities at the time when monarchical government began to undergo dramatic changes that would eventually lead to its complete transformation as a political system.

The concept of social structure

When studying past societies, such as lowland Maya civilization, it must be remembered that the evidence recovered through archaeology and related disciplines is always incomplete. Interpretations of these data are largely based on the application of theoretical models developed from the studies of contemporary or historical societies. These models create a frame of reference for analyzing material remains as a reflection of social practices.

One of the most important theoretical currents in anthropology explains human behavior based on the existence of social structures, which are nothing more than the organized network of relations between entities (Smith 1998). Although social structures are invisible, they are symbolically expressed in the interaction between people and institutions (Eisenstadt 1982).

Functionalist and structuralist approaches have studied human relationships from both individual and collective perspectives (Bauman 1999; Crothers 1996; Rossi 1982). Although social systems were once conceived as hegemonic, human action and agency are increasingly viewed as the basis for the creation and reproduction of these structures. For this reason, social structures are now seen as dynamic and viewed from a multidirectional perspective that takes into account the diversity of actors, variables, and the particular historical processes involved in their creation and constant modification. Nonetheless, individual agency and practice do not necessarily negate the importance of patterns and regularities that take the form of social institutions (Bourdieu 1990, 1977, 1998; Cohen 1989; Parker 2000; Sewell 1992; Téllez 2002). The latter are defined as the forms of organized action that maintain social order and continuity and which link the individual with collective rationalities. On a larger scale, social systems are created by grouping together related social structures from the economic, political, ideological, and kinship spheres that are collectively defined by a particular group of people. In complex societies, this group is generally small and closed and has a high degree of power over the rest. This allows it to exercise a "collective agency" over other systems and individuals (Haugaard 1992; Kontopoulos 1993).

In archaeological interpretation, those structures that last through time and leave a recognizable material footprint are the easiest to observe and are assigned the most relevance. These include the ideological structures that underpin government systems, including that of the sacred lords of the Classic period.

The reconstruction of Classic Maya sociopolitical systems and regimes has been one of the greatest challenges since the beginning of archaeological investigation in the region. Unfortunately, data is limited both in quantity and scope and biased towards that which relates to the structural basis of the ideologies that governed society. This information allows us to make inferences concerning the social ideals of the time, but little is known about the social practice of the inhabitants of ancient Maya cities. In the realm of material remains, the best-preserved architecture – especially palace complexes – represents a material expression of social and political structures that archaeologists can readily study.

The built environment: architecture and social structure

Architectural design reflects the goals and intentions of the people and their leaders. This is why buildings can be conceived as an expression of language, the semiotic study of which allows the interpretation of the social structures from which they have originated (Moore 2005; Preziosi 1979a, 1979b, 1983; Raskin 1974). A sociopolitical theory of constructed space defines public architecture as a stage for the production and reproduction of sociopolitical structures for the individual and collective (Locock 1994). It is in division and delimitation of physical space where human action is modeled, organized, predicted, and restricted according to ideological patterns that, in turn, create power strategies which reinforce social hierarchies. For this reason, the evolution of architecture at an archaeological site can be an important diachronic indicator of political processes, one that reflects changes in material representations (Kent 1990).

The structural and semiotic analysis of architecture also is an important complement to functional interpretation, because it questions the argument that form always reflects utilitarian function. Careful analysis of architecture can reveal design details in a building relating to territoriality and privacy, as well as other features related to environmental psychology, including proxemics and kinesics. Furthermore, the contextual distribution of constructed features defined movement and behavioral patterns of those who used those spaces (Amerlinck 2001; Hitchcock1990; Rapoport 1969, 1980, 1990; Sanders 1990). My work focuses on the application of structural concepts to the analysis of the constructed spaces that constituted the palatial complexes of the Late Classic period. I use this approach to understand Maya politics of the eighth century AD.

The concept of palace in classic lowland Maya civilization

The term "palace" is often associated with the sumptuous buildings that function as the official residence of a head of state, but Maya palaces were multifunctional in nature and were the main physical expression of political power in each city (Martin 2001; Houston and Stuart 2001; Inomata 2001:344; Inomata and Triadan 2003:175; Webster 1998).

Maya palace structures have been studied since the first archaeologists began to work in Central America and southeast Mexico, but early scholars debated whether these buildings actually housed rulers (see Adams 1974:286; Christie 2003; Kowalski 1987:780–781). It was not until investigations of the Central Acropolis of Tikal that their residential nature was confirmed (Harrison 2003a, 2003b). This work also made evident that palace structures were complex and monumental buildings, with multiple spaces that had different functions. Moreover, these often were located in central, elevated, restricted, and circumscribed places that facilitated visual, physical, and social separation (Andrews 1975; Traxler 2001). As built spaces, Maya palace complexes were important means of expressing the ideology of rulership and were places where structural power relations developed (Christie 2006; Jackson 2013:73; Kurjack 2003:286).

Maya palaces were not built based on any single, specific pattern or design, but their planning indicates that they shared functions and, therefore, that they were all part of the same political system focused on sacred lords. They share several elements of form and arrangement in common that can be considered contextual variants of the same concept. This is why each palace complex has a certain individuality that reflects the variability that existed between different political regimes or the differences that resulted from the evolution of cities in distinct periods (Figure 8.1; Chase and Chase 2001; Harrison and Andrews IV 2004; Houston and Stuart 2001; Prem 2000:63).

Archaeological, ethnohistorical, epigraphic, and iconographic investigations have been able to identify a wide range of activities that were carried out in palace complexes. These include the permanent residence of the ruler and his family, the residences of specialists (priests, guards, and providers of other court services), temporary residences of guests, artistic and crafting workshops, schools, banquets, and places for storage, dances, speeches, marriages, coronations, the presentation of tribute or prisoners, and self-sacrifice rituals (Barrientos Q. 2014:203–240).

In terms of shape or form, the term "palace" has been applied to a wide variety of buildings, especially those with an elongated rectangular plan and a large number of chambers and entrances (Kowalski 1987:77). In this study, I consider to be polyfunctional all those acropolis-type complexes that comprise several individual structures of different shapes and sizes, as well as several open spaces that also vary in their area and access (Harrison and Andrews 2004; Inomata and Houston 2001:17; Webster 2001:141). In the perimeter of such acropolis complexes are elongated buildings with multiple doors. These are directly

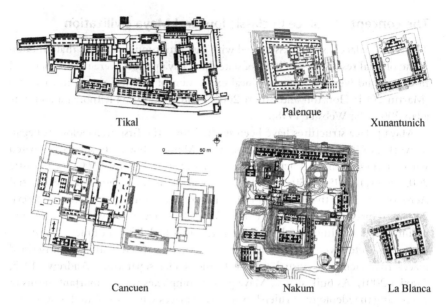

Tikal

Palenque

Xunantunich

Cancuen

Nakum

La Blanca

FIGURE 8.1   Comparison of Maya palaces.

Source: After Andrews 1975:Figure 13; Andrews 1989:Figure 127; Yaeger 2010:Figure 7.1; Źrałka and Hermes 2012:Figure 3; Muñoz 2010:online figure.

associated with monumental stairs that provide access to the interior courtyards. Such structures are called "passage palaces" (Harrison 1999), "gateway palaces" (Runggaldier 2009), or "long houses" (Arnauld 2001). Their main function was to restrict access to areas reserved for the most important members of the court. In this way, they functioned not only as visual and physical blocks, but also as social filters that put into practice the hierarchical relationships between the different groups that made up the population. Moreover, I will show that these buildings also played an important role in the negotiation that took place between the royal court and the social groups that gradually gained political power in the Maya cities at the end of the Classic period.

Variation in Maya palaces also can be considered from a diachronic point of view because their chronological development reflected the evolution of polities in the Maya lowlands (Barrientos Q. 2014:241–322; Lacadena and Ciudad Ruiz 1998:53–54). In their beginnings during the Late Preclassic period, cities did not reflect a system in which palaces played a preponderant role. Instead, most monumental constructed space consisted of large temples, triadic acropolises, and E-groups. All these had functions that were largely ceremonial in nature. To date, not one important Late Preclassic center has been documented as having what may be interpreted as administrative or royal residential spaces, let alone a multifunctional palace complex.

It was not until the Early Classic that palaces began to develop from structures of modest size that appear originally to have been restricted to residential use by the ruler (e.g., Tikal Structure 5D-46, Calakmul Structure III, Uaxactun Structure A- 4; Ciudad Ruiz 2001). Later, palace complexes began to appear in the sixth century AD, but the golden age of these buildings was the eighth century. At that time, small independent states proliferated in areas that previously were within the domains of the large hegemonic states of Tikal and Calakmul. The new regional capitals expressed their position of power through the use of their own emblem glyph (i.e., the *k'uhul ajaw* title with a polity-specific main sign). They also constructed monumental acropolises, as at sites such as Nakum (Żrałka and Hermes 2012), Xunantunich (Yaeger 2010), La Blanca (Muñoz 2010), San Clemente, Aguateca, La Milpa, El Chal, Pueblito, La Corona, and Cancuen, to mention just a few examples. Farther north, rulers of sites such as Becan, Ek Balam, Sayil, and Santa Rosa Xtampak also erected large palace complexes, although the more decentralized settlement patterns of these places often included more than one center of power. In contrast, at cities such as Uxmal, Edzna, and Dzibilchaltun, huge "long houses" were built. These long houses suggest important differences in the form of government because the buildings could have functioned as council houses, indicating that power did not reside in a single person (Figure 8.2; Arnauld 2001:396; Ciudad Ruiz and Iglesias 2001:27). This process of the decentralization of power culminated in the construction of the large galleries that characterize Postclassic sites such as Chichen Itza, the proliferation of long houses with columns at Mayapan, and the construction of long houses at most of the Postclassic centers in highland Guatemala.

The evolution of palaces from the Preclassic to the Postclassic clearly reflects the emergence of highly centralized monarchical states, as well as the gradual transformation of palaces to spaces where power was distributed outside the royal court and high nobility. This transformation is evidenced by the proliferation of small spaces in the palace complexes, especially in the "passage palaces" found on their main façades, and which often were the product of late modifications that divided large spaces into many chambers. Given that these architectural changes date to the late eighth century AD at the vast majority of Maya cities, I propose that this was the time when the sociopolitical system of the *k'uhul ajaw* began to lose prominence and when the process of sociopolitical collapse began. To illustrate this argument, I present data corresponding to the growth and evolution of the Cancuen palace complex.

The palace complex of Cancuen

For 20 uninterrupted years, the Cancuen Archaeological Project has investigated the palace complex of that site. This work has provided one of the most extensive databases concerning this type of building. The investigations carried out since 1999 have allowed the creation of a detailed plan of the acropolis, and more than 650 units have been excavated, corresponding to approximately 10% of the surface of the structure. Also, scholars have analyzed the ceramic and lithic artifacts (obsidian, chert, and jadeite), bone, and stucco sculptural fragments recovered by

FIGURE 8.2   Edzna Structure 424 "Nohoch Na" (above) and Dzibilchaltun Structure 44 (below).

Source: Photos by Tomás Barrientos Q.

our excavations. Moreover, the hieroglyphic texts and associated iconographic elements have been interpreted (Barrientos Q. 2014:53–65).

Cancuen is a site of modest dimensions. Its epicenter, located on a peninsula formed by the Pasión River, is about 3 km² in area. Towards the northwest and northeast, the site stretches for an additional 4 km, following the high, well-drained areas on both sides of the river (Wolf and Bracken 2013). This location at the head of navigation of the Pasión River was strategic. At this point, land communication routes leading north out of the Maya highlands were connected with the canoe routes of the Maya lowlands (Figure 8.3). At least six small bays or inlets around the peninsula could have functioned as the ports of the site (Demarest et al. 2013). Cancuen was founded at the onset of the Late Classic (seventh century AD) and was abandoned at the beginning of the ninth century. This short occupation is divided into four ceramic phases (Forné et al. 2011), which are correlated with the historical events contained in the Cancuen inscriptions and the other sites with which it was related, as well as with the architectural sequences of the main buildings, especially the palace complex (Figure 8.4).

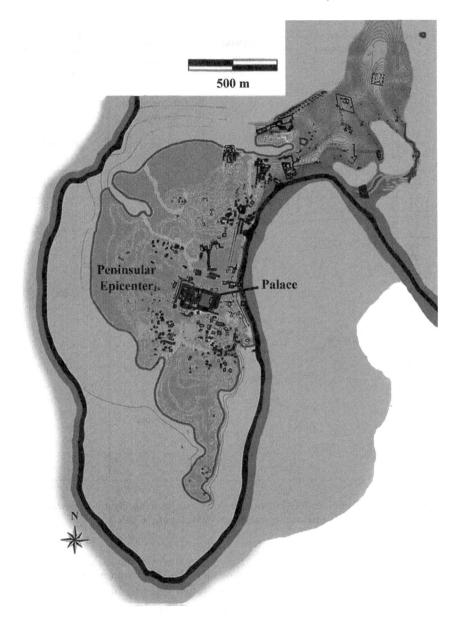

FIGURE 8.3 Cancuen and location of the palace complex.

Source: By Tomás Barrientos Q. after Marc Wolf, VCAP.

Excavations carried out in the palace complex have revealed important details that allow a detailed functional analysis (Barrientos Q. 2014:790–849). The base of the acropolis covers a total area of 32,000 m² (235 m east-west by 135 m north-south) and is oriented between 12 and 14 degrees east of north. The plinth supports 23 buildings of various types, distributed in 12 patios and three levels.

Year AD	Cancuen Ceramic Phase	Cancuen Ruler	Political Events	Cancuen Palace Architectural stages
800		Kan Ma'ax		Episode 6
795	Late Chaman			
790			Domination over Machaquila	Episode 5
785				
780	Early Chaman	Tajal Chan Ahk		
775				Episode 4
770				
765	Los Laureles			
760				Episode 3
755				
750	Concordia			
745				
740				
735				
730		Lady G1-K'awiil	Dos Pilas hegemony	
725				
720				
715				Episode 2
710				
705				
700				
695				
690				
685		Itzam Chan Ahk Wi' Taak'an Chay		
680				Episode 1
675			Calakmul hegemony	
670		K'iib' Ajaw		
665				
660				
655				
650				

FIGURE 8.4 Chronology of Cancuen in years AD, showing ceramic phases, rulers, major events, and construction episodes of the palace.

The highest courtyard rises 11.5 m above the plaza level, and its tallest building once stood 17 m above the plaza. The individual structures measure up to 50 m long and are 6–8 m high. In total, it is estimated that the entire complex housed up to 130 vaulted chambers (Figure 8.5).

Because of its location in the peninsular epicenter and the presence of two large public squares to the north and east, the palace complex figures prominently at Cancuen. It also communicates with the principal port of the site via a small causeway. The exterior of the palace is quite visible to the rest of the site and to the entire region, but its interior contains highly private areas. We have identified four large sections of the acropolis: the central portion (comprising the Patio Sur, Patio Central, Patio Norte, and Patio Norte Bajo), the west acropolis (with

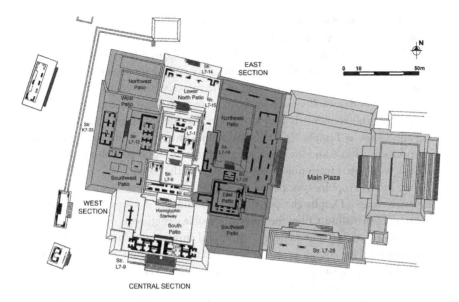

FIGURE 8.5 The Cancuen palace, showing its four spatial sections, patios, and structures.

Source: By Tomás Barrientos Q. and Luis Fernando Luin, VCAP.

the Patio Noroeste, Patio Oeste, and Patio Soeste), the eastern section (Patio Noreste, Patio Este, Patio Sureste, and Corredor Sureste), and the Main Plaza (adjacent to the eastern side of the acropolis). At the western end of the acropolis there are three residential structures and a defensive wall. To the south is a masonry pool or cistern that was fed by a water source.

The palace complex was built using diverse construction techniques and materials, some of which correspond to certain stages while others were employed throughout its history. In the initial phases, some buildings were constructed with adobe and mud fill, but dressed stones also were employed to make walls of soft, white limestone. The later monumental stages are characterized by walls built of hard limestone blocks placed on their sides (*mamposteria canteada* in Spanish, literally "edged masonry"), as well as the use of slabs for plaza floors. The fill and drains were made mainly with irregular limestone and gray or yellow sandstone, generally from the banks of the Pasión River. In some cases, river pebbles also were used for stucco floor fillers. Masonry buildings are characterized by the use of rectangular blocks and small wedges, and reddish mud was used as a binder or mortar. As for the false arch vaults, most were made with thin slabs, similar to the style found in the Usumacinta and Palenque region. Other buildings had flagstone roofs supported by wooden beams.

An important feature of the palace complex is its decoration with stucco sculpture. So far, nine of the 23 buildings have revealed remains of stucco relief, and Structure L7–9 has the most and most important fragments (Figure 8.7).

In it, more than 5,000 fragments of modeled stucco were recovered. These come from a frieze with complex designs and at least 10 human portraits placed directly above the lintels of chamber doors. These characters were dressed as ball players, and we have identified elements associated with sacred mountains and water. These indicate the association of the palace with the sacred geography of the Maya worldview. It is important to note that the technique used to make these sculptural elements is very similar to that identified in some buildings in Palenque, such as Temple XIX. The palace has only two in situ monuments with inscriptions: Altar 6 and the Hieroglyphic Stair. It also is probable that Cancuen Panel 1 was looted from one of the chambers of the palace.

Like other acropolis-type palace complexes, the palace of Cancuen was built in successive stages. Despite the fact that some buildings overlie others, it is important to note that almost all of the currently visible structures correspond to a single main construction event subject to later and minor modifications. This differs from other palace complexes, such as the Central Acropolis of Tikal, where the visible buildings correspond to different stages that were added over a period of more than 400 years (Ashmore and Sabloff 2000:30). The developmental complexity of such palaces has generally limited their spatial analysis to the final visible stage (Folan et al. 2001; Martin 2001). In contrast, most of the monumental acropolis was built during Stage 4 of the six construction stages identified at the Palace of Cancuen (Figure 8.6), making it an exceptional case in that it allows a synchronic analysis of its entire architectural design at a specific moment.

Stage 1: The first palace (AD 657–ca. 700)

This first version of the acropolis includes at least three mud platforms covered with stucco and masonry walls (Structures L7–1–Sub-2, L7–1–Sub-3, and L7–8–Sub-3). These platforms measure from 0.5 to 1.5 m high and are placed on a small platform that is directly below the North and Central Patios. A dedicatory burial (Burial 83) under Structure L7–1–Sub-2 included an offering of a Mataculebra-type vase, which dates this construction to the seventh century AD (Figure 8.8). In the epigraphic record of Cancuen, the oldest date corresponds to AD 657 (Panel 1), when K'ii'b Ajaw took power in Cancuen under the auspices of Yuknoom Ch'en of Calakmul. Therefore, this first acropolis could have been the site of the Cancuen dynastic foundation, as part of the "Camino Real" that linked Calakmul to the entire southern lowlands and highlands (see Chapter 7; Canuto and Barrientos Q. 2013). The occupation of these buildings is also quite likely to extend to the reign of Chan Ahk Wi 'Taak Kay, who acceded to the throne in AD 682 and who also was a vassal of Yuknoom Ch'een of Calakmul.

Stage 2: The First Monumental Acropolis (ca. AD 700–757)

This is the least understood period in the history of Cancuen. There are no historical records, and characteristic ceramic markers have not been identified

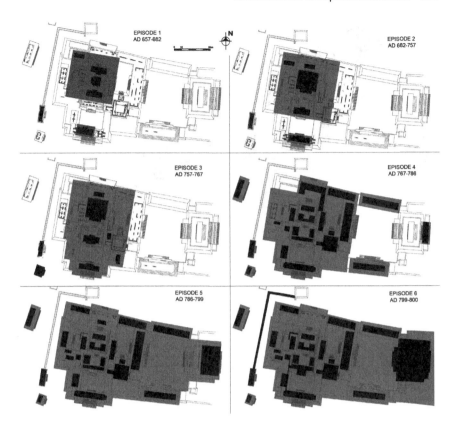

FIGURE 8.6 The Cancuen palace, showing the location of structures corresponding to its six construction episodes.

Source: By Tomás Barrientos Q. and Luis Fernando Luin, VCAP.

for this time span. Instead, it is identified from sealed contexts that precede the Los Laureles phase, defined by the appearance of the Fine Gray Chablekal type in AD 760. The greatest constructive activity in this episode was in the Central and Lower North courtyards, where Structures L7–8-Sub-2 and L7–14-Sub-3 were built. The main building of this time was Structure L7–1-Sub-1, which covered the first acropolis (Figure 8.8). This structure was made of soft limestone masonry and consisted of a pyramidal platform with a front stair, which rose at least 7 m above the plaza level. It is possible that this structure was built between AD 740 and 750, when Cancuen was subject not to Calakmul but to Dos Pilas. This is reflected in the marriage of Ruler 3 of Dos Pilas to Lady G1-K'awiil from Cancuen. Structure K7–3 also has been dated to this period. It corresponds to a small temple that housed Panel 2 and Burial 50. The latter consisted of a domed chamber containing the remains of a ruler, possibly the father of Taj Chan Ahk. We think this because the theme of Panel 2 is the enthronement of Taj Chan Ahk at the hands of his predecessor.

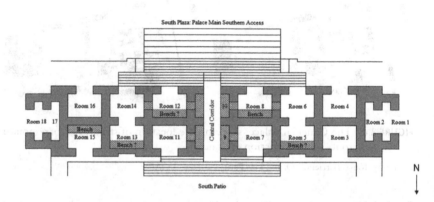

FIGURE 8.7 Hypothetical reconstruction of Structure L7–9 south facade (by Luis Fernando Luin, VCAP) and plan of Structure L7–9 indicating added benches and blocked doorways.

Source: By Tomás Barrientos Q.

Stage 3: Taj Chan Ahk's First Palace (AD 757–767)

The history of Cancuen changed dramatically with the enthronement of Taj Chan Ahk in AD 757 under the auspices of Ruler 4 of Dos Pilas. As is well-known, the regional hegemony of Dos Pilas was broken in AD 761. This allowed the young ruler of Cancuen to take advantage of his position to control the upper Pasión region through very successful political and commercial strategies. During his rule, the palace grew to an unprecedented scale, indicating that this architectural program was part of the political strategies that made Cancuen one

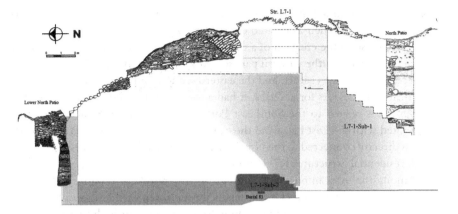

FIGURE 8.8 West profile of the central axis of the Cancuen palace, showing known substructures.

Source: By Tomás Barrientos Q. and Luis Fernando Luin, VCAP.

of the most prosperous kingdoms of the time. We can recognize this moment in the material record by the appearance of the Fine Gray Chablekal ceramics, which came from the far northwest of the Maya area. At this time, the platform of the acropolis was expanded upward, reaching a height of 4 m above plaza level in some areas. Although we have identified few new buildings for this stage, the area with the most construction activity was the Patio Norte Bajo. In the Corredor Sureste, Structure L7–17-Sub-1 was built on a 1.4-m-high platform. Its superstructure had masonry walls built of soft limestone that rose 1.6 m above the basal platform.

Stage 4: Taj Chan Ahk's monumental palace complex (AD 767–786)

The ruler Taj Chan Ahk consolidated his power in the upper Río Pasión region by conquering Machaquila around AD 775. He also constructed the monumental palace complex, which possibly was inaugurated in AD 767 according to the text of Panel 1. This is a date that marks a new architectural tradition at the site characterized by the use of flagstones for the construction of plaza floors, walls built of *mamposteria canteada*, the construction of corbelled vaults and ceilings with flat slabs and beams, and the incorporation of modeled stucco as decorative elements for walls and cornices. Since no direct antecedents of these elements or techniques have been documented in Cancuen, the rapid construction of the new palace is explained by the presence of foreign architects and artists, possibly from the Usumacinta region. This hypothesis is supported by the import of ceramic types from the northwestern lowlands, as well as the introduction of techniques and styles of modeled stucco that are related to the Palenque region.

In spatial terms, the palace complex of Taj Chan Ahk maintained some previous patterns, such as the centrality of the North and Central courtyards.

Nonetheless, as an architectural ensemble it had a new design, made up of 20 new buildings and their associated courtyards. Therefore, I propose that Stage 4 was a response to the creation of a new sociopolitical regime at Cancuen. Of its three main sections, the western part served for residential activities, the central to receive important visitors, and the eastern section for less-restricted ritual and political activities. As for accesses, it had a south entrance (Structure L7–9) that possibly was related to the Southeast Port, an east entrance (Structure L7–27) associated with the East Plaza and the causeway leading to the East Port, a north access directly connected to the North Plaza, and a possible west access associated with residential Structures K7–1 and K7–2.

Among the most important buildings in this episode, Structure L7–1 stands out. It may have functioned as the main throne room of the palace. Structure L7–9 consisted of an elongated building 40 m long by 8 m high that was richly decorated with stucco friezes and 10 sculptures of ball players. Its south façade includes a monumental stair that functioned as the southern access to the entire complex, so the presence of a gallery of interconnected chambers places this building as a typical passage palace. The north façade of L7–9 looks towards the South Patio, where the Hieroglyphic Stair served as access to Structure L7–8 and the Central Patio. Structure K7–33 is located in the West Patio. Together with Structure L7–12, it probably functioned as the residence of the ruler and his family. Although there are no inscriptions or remains of housing activity that can corroborate this hypothesis, its spatial characteristics suggest a high degree of privacy and restriction that is typical of clearly identified royal residences in the Maya lowlands. The temporal placement of Structure K7–33 has not yet been resolved; it could have been added as a second royal residential structure during the subsequent construction phase.

Stage 5: The multi-roomed palace complex (AD 786–799)

Construction activity decreased during the second half of Taj Chan Ahk's reign, but the importation of raw materials from the Maya highlands increased. These decades also saw the increased production and redistribution of obsidian blades, jade preforms, and other artifacts (Andrieu et al. 2012; Demarest et al. 2014). The population of Cancuen grew, to a large degree because of the influx of groups of diverse identities from different regions. Evidence for this includes the presence of pottery belonging to ceramic complexes from the Alta Verapaz region, southern Veracruz, and Peten, on top of or additional to the local complex of the site (Forné et al. 2011). Outside the acropolis, secondary small palaces associated with residential and craft production areas were built (Structures M9–1, N11–1, K8–1, and K9–1). These indicate the decentralization of power and with it a new change in the sociopolitical regime of the site. The political shift also is represented in the palace complex itself. Modifications of this stage are mainly limited to accesses, façades, and interior elements of existing buildings, but two or three new buildings (Structures K7–33, K7–35, and L7–10) may have been built during this stage. Examples of modifications include the blocking of at least eight interior entrances in Structure L7–9, thus creating 18 separate chambers. Five raised benches also were added, as was a wall linking Structure L7–9 to Structure K7–36. It was precisely at this time when most of the known inscriptions of Cancuen were carved, beginning with the Hieroglyphic Stair in AD 786. The sculpted monuments portray Taj Chan Ahk interacting with other members of the court (Panel 3 and Altar 6), with allies from other places (Altar/Marker 2), with prisoners (Stela 2), and with his son and successor Kan Ma'ax (Altar/Marker 1 and Stela 1).

Stage 6: The unfinished palace of Kan Ma'ax (AD 799–800)

The last modifications to the Cancuen palace correspond to the short reign of Kan Ma'ax, son and successor of Taj Chan Ahk. When Kan Ma'ax took power in AD 799, he inherited an already weak kingdom on the brink of collapse. The decline is noticeable architecturally in the cessation of stucco decoration and the use of hard limestone in masonry. Many buildings from the previous stage, including Structure L7–9, were intentionally dismantled and infilled in termination rituals. Structure L7–27 was transformed into a huge masonry-covered mud platform that never was completed. This return to the construction techniques of the earliest stages of the acropolis is possibly due to the absence of foreign architects and artists. Finally, walls were added in the western section, possibly to defend the entrances to the residence of the ruler.

The history of Cancuen ended abruptly in AD 800 when the family and the royal court were killed. Their bodies were deposited in the water reserves, including the pool/cistern located at the south entrance of the palace. There we found the remains of 32 individuals. Another 41 individuals have been identified at the Main Port and north pool/cistern, indicating that people outside of the royal court also met a violent end. The ruler Kan Ma'ax was placed in a rapidly constructed burial on top of Structure L7–27 (Burial 77), next to the body of another person who may have been his wife (Burial 96).

Spatial and functional analysis of the Cancuen palace complex

Unlike other similar palace complexes in the Maya lowlands, the interpretation of architectural features and spaces at the Cancuen palace has been limited by the lack of archaeological contexts such as dumps, burials, activity areas, and abandonment deposits. This seems to be the result of several factors. First, there was a fairly efficient court and chamber cleaning system, which removed physical evidence of ceremonial and diplomatic activities (Pillsbury and Leonard 2004; Kowalski 1987:76). Second, garbage collection and temporary storage, as well as burials and interments, may have taken place off the acropolis. Third, the ritual termination of architecture may have included the cleaning of interior spaces in the building. Finally, the palace complex and site may have been rapidly abandoned after termination, and so the gradual deposition of materials left by later occupants did not occur.

For these reasons, I carried out an analysis that moved beyond establishing a simple morphological typology for the acropolis buildings. I conducted a contextual analysis based on structural concepts, which allowed me to define spatial relationships among the courtyards, buildings, chambers, and other functional areas that were in use at the completion of Stage 4 construction. I chose that moment in time because it was then that the vast majority of the buildings that comprise the palace complex were designed and built. Each patio and its associated structures were analyzed according to 14 variables: permanence, scale, centrality, singularity, visibility, access, proxemics, privacy, territoriality, archaeological context, modifications, allusive function, territorial function, and aesthetic function.

As part of this analysis, I calculated the exact capacity of each patio and defined their access routes. With these data and archaeological information, I proposed a functional typology for all the structures (Figure 8.9). In total, the palace has 8,710 m^2 of open area. If we include the internal space of all the rooms, it could have accommodated a theoretical maximum of 650 people at the same time. More realistically, it could have held up to 250 people in the main square, 160 people in the central section, and 120 people in the east and west sections. Similarly, I identified patios that may have had a residential function. These could have held a maximum of 65 permanent and 90 to 120 temporary residents (Figure 8.10). In other special analyses, I identified a central route for the entire

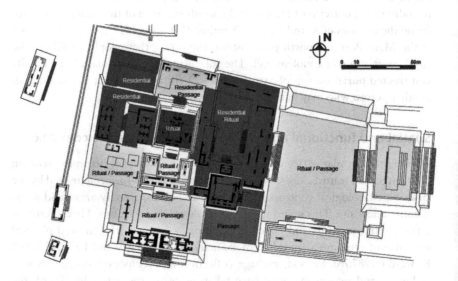

FIGURE 8.9 The Cancuen palace, showing the proposed function of each patio.

Source: By Tomás Barrientos Q. and Luis Fernando Luin, VCAP.

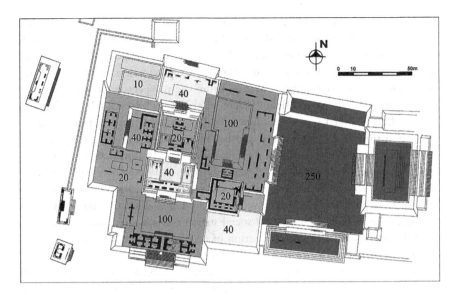

FIGURE 8.10 The Cancuen palace, showing the calculated capacity for each patio.

Source: By Tomás Barrientos Q. and Luis Fernando Luin, VCAP.

palatial complex, which could be used for the entrance of important guests or for ceremonial processions.

One of the most important results of the structural analysis of the built spaces that make up the Cancuen palace complex was the identification of major modifications that took place to the "passage palaces" during Stage 5. In particular, doors and gates were closed or sealed, and benches were added. Evidence for such changes is common at other cities in the Maya lowlands that date to the end of the eighth century, but little so far has been written about the increase that occurred at that time in the number of rooms and other private spaces within palace complexes and the elongated buildings that may have had administrative or residential functions.

Palace architecture and political order in the Maya lowlands during the late eighth century

The political system or structure that existed at Cancuen and other polities of the Maya lowlands during the second part of the eighth century AD was centered on the figure of the ruler, who carried the title of *k'uhul ajaw*, or holy lord. In practice, each polity developed its political system in a unique historical context, so it is possible to identify particular regimes for each city or region. The social practice of each regime was expressed through different hierarchical structures that included different social groups. These are reflected in hieroglyphic texts and material expressions such as architecture.

Constructed spaces can be viewed as the stage and scenery where power structures were produced and reproduced. The actors generally were members of the highest social strata but also could include the rest of the population. A palatial palace complex like Cancuen, therefore, is a reproduction or material manifestation of its sociopolitical structure. From the perspective of what Bourdieu defined as a "sociocultural field" (Webb et al. 2002; Téllez 2002) or what Giddens called a "social locale" (Cohen 1989:109) these constructed spaces shaped the opportunities for interaction and behavior between power groups and the rest of the social actors, through the organization and coordination of an official social practice. My study, analysis, and interpretation of data we collected at the Cancuen palace complex suggest that it did not function as a coercive institution that restricted the interaction between elites and non-elites. On the contrary, the complex seems to have fostered a social structure with a reciprocal nature that laid the foundations for the interaction of groups at different levels. The palace institutionalized and made official the behavior of the nobility and their interaction with the rest of the population, which at Cancuen acquired a multi-ethnic nature during the last decades of the eighth century AD. The increase at that time in the production of lithic artifacts seems to indicate the existence not only of a growing export economy (which also could have included perishable products), but also the emergence of a group of merchants. These consolidated and became an important agent in the power structure of Cancuen (Demarest et al. 2016). In fact, this change to a more mercantile economic regime could be an important factor in the collapse and transformation of the *k'uhul ajaw* system (Demarest et al. 2017, 2020).

Thus, the Cancuen palace complex served as an important tool that introduced changes to the political regime. By AD 760, the Stage 4 monumental palace complex became the main representation of the political independence acquired early in the reign of Taj Chan Ahk. Its design reflects the need to house a growing court and its new allies. Somewhat later, around AD 780, the regime was transformed again at a time characterized by exponential economic growth. This new era also saw the incorporation of new populations that participated in artisanal production, as well as merchants dedicated to importing raw materials and exporting finished and semi-finished artifacts. To meet the evolving conditions and to incorporate the growing merchant elite, the modifications of Stage 5 provided the main stage for new practices that were vital for economic growth. In particular, participation in rituals and ceremonies was expanded to a greater number of actors, which was expressed in the increase of space within the "passage palaces" that surround various perimeter areas of the complex. It is important to note that despite this opening of space in the main accesses of the acropolis, its interior retained a high degree of privacy. In some places, access was even further restricted by constructing walls that closed the doors that communicated between courtyards and buildings. Although there is no evidence of the type of activities that were carried out in front of the structures that have many individual doors and chambers, I speculate that these could include the presentation of tribute or surplus production. It also is possible that these rooms facing the outer façades functioned like loges or boxes, where members of the growing secondary elite could accompany the royal court in ceremonies and events that had a public nature. This would demonstrate their rise in the political hierarchy.

The comparative analysis of complexes contemporary with the Cancuen acropolis makes it possible to identify this period as the Golden Age of Maya palaces. It was in the late eighth century that the monumental scale and complexity of these palaces reached their peak. Moreover, their spatial distribution was greatest at that time; almost all the independent kingdoms – as identified by the presence of emblem glyphs – focused their construction efforts on building palaces. Although the spatial design of each palace complex is particular to each site, they share many characteristics. Among these is the presence of the "passage palaces" with many doors and interior chambers. Based on the attributes that other palaces share with the Cancuen royal complex, I suggest that many small and independent kingdoms underwent similar political processes at the end of the Late Classic period. First, they disassociated themselves from the domination of large hegemonic states – especially Tikal, Calakmul, and their principal allies – and emerged as new political entities. This was followed by great, albeit short-lived, local economic booms. Key to this later step was a process of political decentralization that transformed the system of the sacred lords. Power was shared with new and emerging groups, such as the merchant class at Cancuen, or with existing groups, such as the *sajales* and other members of the non-royal nobility.

In the southern Maya lowlands, this process of transformation ended with collapse and abandonment. The end was abrupt at cities like Cancuen (Demarest 2013, 2014; Demarest et al. 2016), but others waned more slowly. In the northern Maya lowlands, the transformation continued in the Terminal Classic. Many sites, such as those of the Río Bec region, had already developed less centralized regimes (Nondédéo et al. 2013). At cities like Sayil and Ek Balam, multifunctional acropolises were built. Other cities, including Dzibilchaltun and Edzna, constructed monumental "long houses." Eventually, these range structures evolved into the council houses characteristic of the Postclassic period.

To summarize, I propose that monumental palace complexes appeared in the late eighth century AD at small sites like Cancuen as the material expressions of changes to the sociopolitical structure. This change in political regime was characterized by a trend towards the decentralization of authority and to new forms of hierarchy. The growing secondary nobility required access to their own spaces within the palace complexes that served as the main symbols of institutionalized power. For this reason, new palaces with greater capacity were built, and existing ones were expanded to house more people.

I hope that investigation of other palace complexes may provide more data to test my broader hypothesis concerning political reorganization at the end of the Late Classic period. Cancuen clearly indicates that the structural analysis of built spaces is an important tool for understanding the nature of the political regimes that developed in the lowlands from the Preclassic to Postclassic periods. The diachronic and synchronic interpretation of this palace complex has revealed the constant construction and redefinition of its design, thus indicating that sociopolitical structures were highly dynamic rather than rigid systems.

References cited

Adams, Richard E. 1974 Trial Estimation of Classic Maya Palace Populations at Uaxactun. In *Mesoamerican Archaeology: New Approaches*, edited by Norman Hammond, pp. 285–296. University of Texas Press, Austin.

Amerlinck, Mari-Jose 2001 *Architectural Anthropology*. Bergin & Garvey, Westport, CT.

Andrews, George 1975 *Maya Cities: Placemaking and Urbanization*. University of Oklahoma Press, Norman.

———— 1989 *Comalcalco, Tabasco, México*. Labyrinthos, Culver City.

Andrieu, Chloé, Melanie Forné, and Arthur Demarest 2012 El Valor del jade: Producción y distribución del jade en el sitio de Cancuén. In *El Jade y otras piedras verdes: perspectivas interdisciplinarias e interculturales*, edited by Walburga Wiesheu and Gabriela Guzzy, pp. 145–180. Colección Científica, Instituto Nacional de Arqueología e Historia, Mexico City.

Arnauld, Marie Charlotte 2001 "Casa grande": evolución de la arquitectura del poder del Clásico al Postclásico. In *Reconstruyendo la ciudad maya: el urbanismo en las sociedades antiguas*, edited by André Ciudad Ruiz, María Josefa Iglesias, and María del Carmen Martínez, pp. 363–401. SEEM Publication No. 6. Sociedad Española de Estudios Mayas, Madrid.

Ashmore, Wendy, and Jeremy Sabloff 2000 El orden del espacio en los planes cívicos Mayas. In *Arquitectura e Ideología de los Antiguos Mayas Vol. 2: Memoria de la Segunda Mesa Redonda de Palenque*, edited by S. Trejo, pp. 15–33. Conaculta, Inah, México, DF.

Barrientos Q., Tomás 2014 *The Royal Palace of Cancuen: The Structure of Lowland Maya Architecture and Politics at the end of the Late Classic Period*. Ph.D. Dissertation, Department of Anthropology, Vanderbilt University.

Bauman, Zygmunt 1999 *Culture as Praxis*. Sage Publications, Thousand Oaks.

Bourdieu, Pierre 1977 *Outline of a Theory of Practice*. Cambridge: Cambridge University Press.

———— 1990 Structures, Habitus, Practices. In *The Logic of Practice*, edited by P. Bourdieu, pp. 52–79. Stanford University Press, Stanford.

———— 1998 *Practical Reason: On the Theory of Action*. Stanford University Press, Stanford.

Canuto, Marcello, and Tomás Barrientos Q. 2013 The Importance of La Corona. *La Corona Notes* 1(1). Mesoweb. www.mesoweb.com/LaCorona/LaCoronaNotes01.pdf.

Canuto, Marcello, and Maxime Lamoureux-St-Hilaire 2017 From Polities to Regimes: Towards Recognizing Ancient Maya Regimes. *Paper presented at the Round-Table Regimes of the Classic Maya*, Middle American Research Institute, Tulane University, New Orleans.

Chase, Arlen, and Diane Chase 2001 The Royal Court of Caracol, Belize: Its Palaces and People. In *Royal Courts of the Ancient Maya, Volume Two: Data and Case Studies*, edited by Takeshi Inomata and Stephen Houston, pp. 102–137. Westview Press, Boulder.

Christie, Jessica 2003 Introduction. In *Maya Palaces and Elite Residences: An Interdisciplinary Approach*, edited by Jessica Christie, pp. 1–13. University of Texas Press, Austin.

———— 2006 Introduction. In *Palaces and Power in the Americas: From Peru to the Northwest Coast*, edited by Jessica Christie and P. Sarro, pp. 1–20. University of Texas Press, Austin.

Ciudad Ruiz, Andrés 2001 Los palacios residenciales del Clásico Temprano en las ciudades del sur de lasTierras Bajas Mayas. In *Reconstruyendo la ciudad maya: el urbanismo en las sociedades antiguas*, edited by Andrés Ciudad Ruiz, Marí Josefa Iglesias, and María del Carmen Martínez, pp. 305–340. SEEM Publications No. 6. Sociedad Española de Estudios Mayas, Madrid.

Ciudad Ruiz, Andrés, and María Josefa Iglesias 2001 Un mundo ordenado: La ciudad Maya y el urbanismo en las sociedades antiguas. In *Reconstruyendo la ciudad Maya: el urbanismo en las sociedades antiguas*, edited by Andrés Ciudad Ruiz, María Josef Iglesias, and María del Carmen Martínez, p. 1140. SEEM Publications No. 6. Sociedad Española de Estudios Mayas, Madrid.

Cohen, Ira 1989 *Structuration Theory: Anthony Giddens*. St. Martin's Press, New York.

Crothers, C. 1996 *Social Structure*. Routledge, London.

Demarest, Arthur 2013 Ideological Pathways to Economic Exchange: Religion, Economy, and Legitimation at the Classic Maya Royal Capital of Cancuen. *Latin American Antiquity* 24(4):371–402.

———— 2014 Collapse and Non-Recovery in the "Wet Zone": The Aborted Economic and Political Transition at the Far Southern Border of the Classic Maya World. In *The Great Maya Droughts in Cultural Economy, Exchange, and Power Context: Case Studies in Resilience and Vulnerability*, edited by Gyles Iannone, pp. 177–206. University Press of Colorado, Boulder.

Demarest, Arthur, Chloé Andrieu, Paola Torres, Mélanie Forné, and Tomás Barrientos Q. 2014 Economy, Exchange, and Power: New Evidence from the Late Classic Maya Port City of Cancuen. *Ancient Mesoamerica* 25:187–219.

Demarest, Arthur, Horacio Martínez, Paola Torres, Carlos Alvarado, and Douglas Quiñónez 2013 Los puertos de la capital real de Cancuén y su papel en la economía y política Clásica Maya. In *XXVI Simposio de Investigaciones Arqueológicas en Guatemala, 2012*, edited by Bárbar Arroyo and Luísa Méndez, pp. 75–86. Museo Nacional de Arqueología y Etnología, Guatemala.

Demarest, Arthur, Claudia Quintanilla, and José Samuel Suasnávar 2016 The Collapses in the West and the Violent Ritual Termination of the Classic Maya Capital Center of Cancuen. In *Ritual, Violence, and the Fall of the Classic Maya Kings*, edited by Gyles Iannone, Brett Houk, and Sonja Schwake, pp. 159–186. University Press of Florida, Gainesville.

Demarest, Arthur, Prudence Rice, and Don Rice (editors) 2005 *The Terminal Classic in the Maya Lowlands: Collapse, Transition, and Transformation*. University Press of Colorado, Boulder.

Demarest, Arthur, Bart Victor, Chloe Andrieu, Edward Fischer, and Paola Torres 2017 Changing Classic Maya Economic Regimes, Networks, and Strategies on the Eve of Collapse. *Paper presented at the Round-Table Regimes of the Classic Maya*. Middle American Research Institute, Tulane University, New Orleans.

Demarest, Arthur, Bart Victor, Chloe Andrieu, and Paola Torres 2020 Monumental Landscapes as Instruments of Radical Economic Change: Innovation, Apogee, and Collapse. In *Monumental Landscapes: How the Maya Shaped their World*, edited by Brett Houk, Bárbara Arroyo, and Terry Powis, pp. 242–267. University Press of Florida, Gainesville.

Eisenstadt, Shmuel 1982 Symbolic Structures and Social Dynamics with Special Reference to Studies of Modernization. In *Structural Sociology*, edited by I. Rossi, pp. 149–179. Columbia University Press, New York.

Folan, William H., Joel Gunn, and María del Rosario Dominguez 2001 Triadic Temples, Central Plazas, and Dynastic Palaces: A Diachronic Analysis of the Royal Court

Complex, Calakmul, Campeche, Mexico. In *Royal Courts of the Ancient Maya, Volume Two: Data and Case Studies*, edited by T. Inomata and S. Houston, pp. 223–265. Westview Press, Boulder.

Forné, Melanié, Silvia Alvarado, and Paola Torres 2011 Cronología cerámica en Cancuen: historia de una ciudad del Clásico Tardío. *Estudios de Cultura Maya* 38:11–39.

Harrison, Peter 1999 *The Lords of Tikal: Rulers of an Ancient Maya City*. Thames & Hudson, London.

——— 2003a The Central Acropolis of Tikal. In *Tikal: Dynasties, Foreigners, & Affairs of State*, edited by Jeremy Sabloff, pp. 171–206. School for Advanced Research Press, Santa Fe.

——— 2003b Palaces of the Royal Court at Tikal. In *Maya Palaces and Elite Residences: An Interdisciplinary Approach*, edited by Jessica Christie, pp. 98–119. University of Texas Press, Austin.

Harrison, Peter, and E. Wyllys Andrews IV 2004 Palaces of Tikal and Copan. In *Palaces of the Ancient New World*, edited by Susan T. Evans and Joanne Pillsbury, pp. 113–147. Dumbarton Oaks, Washington, DC.

Haugaard, Mark 1992 *Structures, Restructuration, and Social Power*. Avebury, Aldershot.

Hitchcock, Louise 2000 *Minoan Architecture: A Contextual Analysis*. P. Åströms förlag, Jonsered.

Houston, Stephen, and David Stuart 2001 Peopling the Classic Maya Court. In *Royal Courts of the Ancient Maya. Volume 1: Theory, Comparison, and Synthesis*, edited by Takeshi Inomata and Stephen Houston, pp. 54–83. Westview Press, Boulder.

Iannone, Gyles (editor) 2014 *The Great Maya Droughts in Cultural Context: Case Studies in Resilience and Vulnerability*. University Press of Colorado, Boulder.

Inomata, Takeshi 2001 Classic Maya Palace as a Political Theater. In *Reconstruyendo la ciudad maya: el urbanismo en las sociedades antiguas*, edited by Andréa Ciudad Ruiz, María Josefa Iglesias, and María del Carmen Martínez, pp. 341–361. SEEM Publications No. 6. Sociedad Española de Estudios Mayas, Madrid.

Inomata, Takeshi, and Stephen Houston 2001 Opening the Maya Royal Court. In *Royal Courts of the Ancient Maya. Volume 1: Theory, Comparison, and Synthesis*, edited by Takeshi Inomata and Stephen Houston, pp. 3–26. Westview Press, Boulder.

Inomata, Takeshi, and Daniela Triadan 2003 Where Did Elites Live? In *Maya Palaces and Elite Residences: An Interdisciplinary Approach*, edited by Jessica Christie, pp. 154–183. University of Texas Press, Austin.

Jackson, Sarah 2013 *Politics of the Maya Court: Hierarchy and Change in the Late Classic Period*. Oklahoma University Press, Norman.

Kent, Susan 1990 Activity Areas and Architecture: An Interdisciplinary View of the Relationship between Use of Space and Domestic Built Environments. In *Domestic Architecture and the Use of Space*, edited by Susan Kent, pp. 1–8. Cambridge University Press, Cambridge.

Kontopoulos, Kyriakos M. 1993 *The Logics of Social Structure*. Cambridge University Press, Cambridge.

Kowalski, Jeffrey 1987 *The House of the Governor*. University of Oklahoma Press, Norman.

Kurjack, Edward 2003 Palace and Society in the Northern Maya Lowlands. In *Maya Palaces and Elite Residences: An Interdisciplinary Approach*, edited by Jessica Christie, pp. 274–290. University of Texas Press, Austin.

Lacadena, Alfonso, and Andrés Ciudad Ruiz 1998 Reflexiones sobre la estructura política maya clásica. In *Anatomía de una civilización: Aproximaciones interdisciplinarias a la Cultura Maya*, edited by Andrés Ciudad Ruiz, et al., pp. 31–64. Sociedad Española de Estudios Mayas, Madrid.

Locock, Martin 1994 *Meaningful Architecture: Social Interpretations of Buildings*. Avebury, Aldershot.

Martin, Simon 2001 Court and Realm: Archaeological Signatures in the Classic Maya Lowlands. In *Royal Courts of the Ancient Maya. Volume 1: Theory, Comparison, and Synthesis*, edited by Takeshi Inomata and Stephen Houston, pp. 168–194. Westview Press, Boulder.

Moore, Jerry 2005 *Architecture and Power in the Ancient Andes: The Archaeology of Public Buildings*. New Studies in Archaeology. Cambridge University Press, Cambridge.

Muñoz, Gaspar 2010 Arquitectura de La Blanca. *Proyecto La Blanca*. www.uv.es/arsmaya/ proyecto.html, accessed January 24, 2018.

Nondédéo, Philippe, M. Charlotte Arnauld, and Dominique Michelet 2013 Río Bec Settlement Patterns and Local Sociopolitical Organization. *Ancient Mesoamerica* 24:373–396.

Parker, John 2000 *Structuration*. Open University, Buckingham.

Pillsbury, Joanne, and Banks Leonard 2004 Identifying Chimu Palaces: Elite Residential Architecture in the Late Intermediate Period. In *Palaces of the Ancient New World*, edited by Susan Evans and Joanne Pillsbury, pp. 247-298. Dumbarton Oaks, Washington, D.C.

Prem, Hans 2000 Detrás de qué esquina se esconde la ideología? In *Arquitectura e ideología de los antiguos mayas, Mesa Redonda de Palenque 1997*, edited by S. Trejo, pp. 55–77. Inah-Conaculta, Mexico.

Preziosi, Donald 1979a *Architecture, Language, and Meaning*. Mouton Publishers, The Hague.

——— 1979b *The Semiotic of the Built Environment: An Introduction to Architectonic Analysis*. Indiana University Press, Bloomington.

——— 1983 *Minoan Architectural Design: Formation and Signification*. Mouton, Berlin.

Rapoport, Amos 1969 *House Form and Culture*. Prentice-Hall, Englewood Cliffs.

——— 1980 Vernacular Architecture and the Cultural Determinants of Forms. In *Building and Society*, edited by A. King, pp. 283–305. Routledge and Kegan Paul, London.

——— 1990 Systems of Activities and Systems of Settings. In *Domestic Architecture and the Use of Space*, edited by Susan Kent, pp. 9–19. Cambridge University Press, Cambridge.

Raskin, Eugene 1974 *Architecture and People*. Prentice-Hall, Englewood Cliffs.

Rossi, Ino (editor) 1982 *Structural Sociology*. Columbia University Press, New York.

Runggaldier, Astrid 2009 *Memory and Materiality in Monumental Architecture: Construction and Reuse of a Late Preclassic Maya Palace at San Bartolo, Guatemala*. Ph.D. dissertation, Department of Archaeology, Boston University.

Sanders, Donald 1990 Behavioral Conventions and Archaeology: Methods for the Analysis of Ancient Architecture. In *Domestic Architecture and the Use of Space: An Interdisciplinary Cross-Cultural Study*, edited by Susan Kent, pp. 43–72. Cambridge University Press, Cambridge.

Sewell, W. H 1992 A Theory of Structure: Duality, Agency and Transformation. *American Journal of Sociology* 98:1–29.

Smith, Michael E. 1998 *The Study of Social Structure*. Research Institute for the Study of Man, New York.

Téllez Iregui, Gustavo 2002 *Pierre Bourdieu, conceptos básicos y construcción socioeducativa: claves para su lectura*. Universidad Pedagógica Nacional, Bogotá.

Traxler, Loa 2001 The Royal Courts of Early Classic Copan. In *Royal Courts of the Ancient Maya. Volume 2: Data and Case Studies*, edited by Takeshi Inomata and Stephen Houston, pp. 46–73. Westview Press, Boulder.

Webb, Jen, Tony Schirato, and Geoff Danaher 2002 *Understanding Bourdieu*. SAGE Publications, London and Thousand Oaks.

Webster, David 1998 Classic Maya Architecture: Implications and Comparisons. In *Function and Meaning in Classic Maya Architecture*, edited by Stephen Houston, pp. 5–47. Dumbarton Oaks, Washington, DC.

———— 2001 Spatial Dimensions of Maya Courtly Life. In *Royal Courts of the Ancient Maya. Volume 1: Theory, Comparison, and Synthesis*, edited by Takeshi Inomata and Stephen Houston, pp. 130–167. Westview Press, Boulder.

Wolf, Marc, and Justin Bracken 2013 Investigaciones en la zona urbana del sitio de Cancuén: dinámica de patrones de a sentamiento y topografía natural afuera del epicentro. In *Proyecto Arqueológico Cancuén, informe # 13, temporada 2013*, edited by A. Demarest and H. Martínez, pp. 283–290. Annual report submitted to DGPCN, Guatemala.

Yaeger, Jason 2010 Shifting Political Dynamics as Seen from the Xunantunich Palace. In *Classic Maya Provincial Politics: Xunantunich and Its Hinterlands*, edited by Lisa LeCount and Jason Yaeger, pp. 145–160. The University of Arizona Press, Tucson.

Źrałka, Jarosław, and Bernard Hermes 2012 Great Development in Troubled Times: The Terminal Classic at the Maya Site of Nakum, Peten, Guatemala. *Ancient Mesoamerica* 23:161–187.

9

AS THE *B'AK'TUN* TURNED

Reconstructing Classic to Postclassic population dynamics in the Belize River Valley

Julie A. Hoggarth, Carolyn Freiwald, Claire E. Ebert,
Christophe Helmke, Jaime J. Awe, Kirsten Green Mink,
Patricia Powless, and Ashley H. McKeown

Archaeological studies of the Classic Maya collapse have broadly characterized the changes that transformed the Maya lowlands from Classic to Postclassic times. The disintegration of Classic Maya political systems linked with the *k'uhul ajaw* institution (divine kingship) and associated great traditions are well-documented by the cessation of glyphic texts detailing dynastic histories on carved stone monuments. Yet, the disintegration of these systems is not directly described in the written texts, leaving other lines of evidence to serve as proxies for the cessation of institutionalized kingship and the abandonment of sites. Archaeological studies focusing on the abandonment of royal palaces provide one source of such evidence (Chapters 8 and 10). Research also has focused on ideological changes from Classic to Postclassic times, including political transformations surrounding kingship, as well as the spread of new ritual and iconographic traditions (e.g., Ringle et al. 1998). Large-scale economic transformations also have been documented for this critical period, including a shift from interior, over-land trade routes to maritime exchange (e.g., Gunn et al. 2017; Masson 2002; Turner and Sabloff 2012).

The most poorly understood aspect of the Classic Maya collapse is the demographic decline documented in the central and southern Maya lowlands during the eighth and ninth centuries AD. Evidence for large-scale demographic transformations is apparent when comparing Classic and Postclassic settlement histories (Culbert and Rice 1990:Table 1.4). Although medium-sized Classic Maya centers, such as those in the Belize River Valley (Figure 9.1), possessed populations in the low thousands (Awe et al. 2014:Table 1; Yaeger 2003:Figure 5.6; Willey et al. 1965:576), large and influential Maya cities, such as Calakmul, Caracol, and Tikal supported populations estimated in the tens to hundreds of thousands (Braswell et al. 2004:170; Chase et al. 2011:389; Rice and Culbert 1990:11). By Postclassic times, archaeological data indicate that most settlements

DOI: 10.4324/9781351268004-9

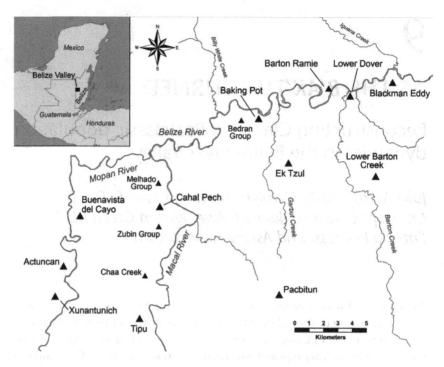

FIGURE 9.1 Map of the Belize River Valley showing sites and settlement groups discussed in the text.

in the central and southern Maya lowlands had been abandoned, with smaller populations persisting in resource-rich zones along the margins of lakes, rivers, lagoons, and the Caribbean coast (Graham 2004; McKillop 1996; Pendergast 1990; Rice and Rice 2009). One of the biggest mysteries surrounding the Classic Maya collapse is why inland regions never experienced a demographic rebound (Webster 2012:329).

We examine Classic to Postclassic population dynamics throughout the tenth *b'ak'tun* (9.0.0.0.0 to 10.0.0.0.0, AD 435–830) in the Belize River Valley to explore the topic of demographic decline in greater depth. Because the area of our study is adjacent to large Classic Maya kingdoms to the south (Caracol) and west (Naranjo), evidence for population decline and migration in the Belize Valley can more broadly elucidate the demographic processes associated with the Classic Maya collapse. We examine patterns in archaeological, epigraphic, and isotopic data from human remains to understand changing population dynamics in the Belize Valley at the end of the Classic period. We identify evidence for rapid population decline that corresponds to an increase in atypical burial patterns and non-local strontium isotope signatures at the sites of Baking Pot, Barton Ramie, and Cahal Pech. We contextualize our data within the broader processes of demographic decline that occurred across the Maya Lowlands at the end of the Classic period.

Culture history of the Belize River Valley

The Belize Valley (Figure 9.1) is best-known as the location of Gordon Willey's pioneering settlement archaeology research of the 1950s. Excavations by Willey and his colleagues (1965) at the sites of Barton Ramie, Baking Pot, Spanish Lookout, and the smaller Melhado settlement group at Cahal Pech set the stage for advances in household and community-scale archaeology, the study of regional political interaction between major and minor centers, and broader discourse on Belize Valley culture history. Over half a century later, extensive archaeological research continues in this area, revealing cultural sequences associated with the rise and fall of ancient Maya civilization that span more than two millennia. Excavations at several sites in the Belize Valley have produced ceramic and radiocarbon evidence for the earliest permanently settled communities dating to ca. 1200–900 BC at Cahal Pech (Awe 1992; Ebert et al. 2017), Blackman Eddy (Garber et al. 2004), Xunantunich Group E (Brown et al. 2011), and Actuncan (Mixter et al. 2014; see also Ebert and Awe 2020). Formally organized civic centers and monumental architecture appeared during the Late Preclassic at sites throughout the Belize Valley. These include Cahal Pech (Awe 2013), Baking Pot (Audet 2006:167–337), and Blackman Eddy (Brown et al. 2013). Excavations at Barton Ramie and the residential settlement outside the Lower Dover civic-ceremonial core have similarly revealed evidence for Late Preclassic growth. Recently acquired data, however, suggest that major construction at the Lower Dover site core was not initiated until about AD 500, in the middle of the Classic period (Guerra and Awe 2017).

Early Classic occupation (AD 150/430–600)

The Early Classic period is not well-understood in the Belize River Valley, to a great degree because local Preclassic ceramics were not rapidly or completely replaced by Tepeu sphere pottery (Awe and Helmke 2005). In this regard, the Belize River Valley resembles Copan, the northern Maya lowlands, and the Southern Belize Region (Chapter 5). Limited settlement data suggest that an increase in population began in the Early Classic period (Willey et al. 1965:281–285). An increase in building activity was seen during those centuries at several sites including Cahal Pech (Awe and Helmke 2005), Buenavista (Ball and Taschek 2004), and Pacbitun (Healy et al. 2004). At Cahal Pech, monumental buildings within public plazas were constructed and remodeled. Pottery from some of the most elaborate royal burials from Cahal Pech has been dated to the Early Classic period (Awe 2013). Settlement research and AMS ^{14}C dating document the Early Classic establishment of several new residential groups around the Cahal Pech site core (Ebert et al. 2016). Although archaeological evidence suggests that Baking Pot experienced a decline or hiatus in monumental construction throughout the Early Classic period, texts on ceramic vessels recovered from a burial at the Bedran settlement group imply that the Baking Pot royal dynasty had already been long established and endured into the Classic period (Colas et al. 2002; Helmke and Awe 2012:65–66).

Late Classic occupation (AD 600–800)

The Late Classic period saw the height of Classic Maya society in the Belize Valley, with expansive monumental construction efforts identified at nearly all regional major centers. At Cahal Pech, a lavish royal burial included a series of carved objects such as bone rings and incised turtle plastrons bearing the name K'awiil Chan K'inich, one of the Late Classic rulers of the site who employed the local title *K'an Hix . . . w* (Awe and Zender 2016). The same title has recently been documented on a jadeite plaque at the site of Nim li Punit that describes the mother of the original owner as *K'an Hix [Bala]w*, strongly suggesting that she was related to the Cahal Pech lineage (Chapter 6; Prager and Braswell 2016:5).

An impressive number of elaborate Late Classic royal and elite tombs containing a wealth of imported grave goods also have been identified at Baking Pot (Audet 2006:175–214). These include two tombs located atop the central structure of the eastern triadic architectural assemblage of Group A. These finds, as well as extensive evidence for monumental construction dating to the Late Classic period from the royal palace complex (Audet 2006:295), suggest that sites such as Baking Pot reached their economic and political apogees between AD 600 and 750. Monumental construction at Lower Dover appears to have consisted of one or two major construction episodes at the end of the Classic period, suggesting the expansion of competing political regimes in the Belize Valley as populations grew.

Terminal Classic occupation (AD 800–900)

The end of mortuary and construction activity occurred at most Belize Valley sites ca. AD 850–900, during the Terminal Classic period. One formally constructed Terminal Classic tomb at Cahal Pech housed the remains of a prominent individual (Awe, Ebert et al. 2020). Nonetheless, this is the only primary Terminal Classic interment recorded to date at the site. An examination of construction sequences at Cahal Pech suggests that building activity at the site rapidly declined after AD 750, with little evidence of occupation into the tenth century in either the settlement or ceremonial areas (Awe 2013; Ebert et al. 2016). Evidence for political fragmentation can also be identified in the form of peri-abandonment deposits at several Belize Valley sites (Awe, Helmke et al. 2020; Burke et al. 2020; Hoggarth et al. 2020). These features, which include broken ceramics (especially decorated serving vessels including polychromes and molded-carved vases), musical instruments, figurines, faunal remains, and other materials are often found on terminal plaza and courtyard floors within civic-ceremonial centers of major Belize Valley centers. Excavations of peri-abandonment deposits suggest that these features formed in elite ceremonial areas after they fell into disuse, or as a result of poor maintenance during the final phases of political and ritual activity at individual sites. A pattern of intrusive burials containing Terminal Classic ceramics (late-facet Spanish Lookout complex) within peri-abandonment contexts has been noted in multiple plazas within the Cahal Pech site core (Awe 2013; Awe, Ebert et al. 2020).

At Baking Pot, one royal burial that previously had been interpreted as dating to the Terminal Classic was radiocarbon dated to AD 660–765, that is, to the Late Classic period (UCIAMS-132226, 1315 ± 20 years BP; Hoggarth et al. 2014:Table 9.1). This has led to a re-assessment of the ceramic diagnostics for the late Spanish Lookout complex, particularly for Daylight Orange: Darknight Variety ceramics included in the burial. Although previous work suggested large-scale continuity in occupation from the Classic to Postclassic periods (Aimers 2003; Hoggarth 2012:Tables 3–5; Willey et al. 1965:292), recent research focused on AMS ^{14}C direct dating of human burials from the site shows a distinct gap in occupation corresponding to the Early Postclassic period (AD 900–1200; Hoggarth et al. 2014:Figure 9.4). The degree and rate of depopulation that occurred during and after the Terminal Classic period are currently unknown. AMS ^{14}C dates on human burials indicate an expansion of activity at Baking Pot during the period AD 1290–1420, suggesting that the site was reoccupied during the Late Postclassic period.

Political geography

Central Belize does not have an abundance of carved monuments or glyphic texts. One cause may be the relatively small size of polities in the area (Helmke and Awe 2012). Nevertheless, carved monuments have been found at a number of sites, and portable objects with texts that date to two major periods have been recovered. Because the monuments celebrate important historical turning points and portable artifacts bearing texts are records of historical and sociopolitical processes, we present a chronological outline to better track the actions of particularly charismatic and influential kings and their royal courts.

Some of the oldest known monuments in the central Maya lowlands come from the Belize Valley. The two earliest are carved Preclassic stelae found at Cahal Pech and Actuncan (Table 9.1). Although both lack glyphic texts, they are carved in an early style. Stela 9 from Cahal Pech, perhaps the earlier of the two, depicts a ruler emerging from the maw of a supernatural feline, replete with a serpentine bifid tongue. Subsequent to its breakage, this stela was reverentially buried in a Late Classic masonry tomb at the Zopilote causeway terminus complex, located 670 m south of the site core (Awe et al. 2009). The Actuncan stela reflects the iconography of the Classic period, depicting a ruler brandishing a ceremonial bar, although the dynamic stance, with legs apart, is analogous to the earliest Preclassic monuments of the region (Fahsen and Grube 2005), including the carved stelae of Cival and Nakum (Grube and Martin 2004:5; Źrałka et al. 2018). Both of these stone monuments provide evidence for the birth and expansion of centralized rulership across the region.

The first monuments to bear Long Count dates and glyphic texts are the Early Classic stelae of Blackman Eddy and Pacbitun. During this period, polities of the Belize Valley participated in the same tradition of monument erection as their neighbors in the central lowlands, yet this process was interrupted at the close of the fifth century. The earliest monument of the period is the fully glyphic Stela 1 of Blackman Eddy that carries the Long Count date of 8.17.5.?.10, corresponding to a date of AD 381 or 382 (Helmke et al. 2003; see also Garber 1992). This is followed approximately a century later by Stela 6 at Pacbitun, which commemorates the half-*k'atun* ending of 9.2.10.0.0 that occurred in AD 485 (Helmke et al. 2006; see also Healy 1990). This stela depicts a seated king, possibly at his accession, commemorating the celebration of the appropriate calendrical station. The small caption is most remarkable, since it may record the first *ukabjiiy* "agency expression" (Martin and Grube 1995). This implies that the accession of the local Pacbitun king, as a vassal, took place under the aegis of a superordinate king (Helmke et al. 2006:74). Although eroded, faint traces of the name of this contemporaneous king can be discerned in the text. Based on the dynamic political environment across the Maya lowlands at that time, Tikal is the most likely candidate for the polity of the superior ruler. Thus, Pacbitun probably was a vassal of Tikal at this early date, in much the same way as the kings of Caracol pleaded fealty to Tikal until the marked reversals of the sixth century AD (Martin and Grube 2000:88; Houston 1991). Altar 3, thought to have been originally paired with Stela 6, presents the local king of Pacbitun standing upon the ancient toponym of the site (Helmke and Awe 2008:73–74; Skaggs et al. 2017).

The Belize Valley is geographically positioned between the competing superordinate centers of Naranjo to the west and Caracol to the south. A variety of portable objects and glyphic evidence suggests that sites in the Belize Valley were caught in a tug-of-war between these two large centers. Close scrutiny of this evidence indicates that the power and influence of Caracol are discernible in the Early Classic, but that of Naranjo is readily apparent during the Late Classic, especially from the seventh century AD onwards (Helmke and Awe 2008:78–86).

Two beautifully inscribed ceramic vessels dated to the middle to late fifth century were discovered in a burial at the Bedran Group, in the western periphery of Baking Pot (Colas et al. 2002). These ceramics are remarkable for the quality of their glyphic texts, representing some of the earliest examples of dedicatory inscriptions (i.e., Primary Standard Sequences) in the entire Maya lowlands. The texts indicate that the vessels were both intended for *kakaw*-based beverages and that one of them was owned by a royal figure who may have been named Lem? Tz'unun Tok Suutz'. What is most interesting is his regnal name, the name received upon his accession, which can be read in part as ? . . . m Yohl K'inich – a regnal name favored by the kings of Caracol (Helmke and Awe 2008:85–86).

A sherd from a Saxche Orange-polychrome bowl (ca. AD 550–650), recovered in the eastern periphery of Baking Pot, also is remarkable. It may bear the eroded dynastic title of the Caracol dynasty along its rim. Based on present evidence, this could be the third example of a ceramic vessel to bear this title. Use of this title suggests that a king of Caracol may have been the original owner of the bowl and that its presence at Baking Pot implies a relationship, perhaps an alliance, between the two sites.

The connection between Baking Pot and Caracol is expressed not only in the realm of ceramics and royal onomastics, but also by the appearance of certain ritual features such as "finger-bowl" caches. Offerings containing one or more phalanges or finger bones deposited within small, purpose-made offering vessels are typical for Caracol and appear for the first time in the Belize Valley at Baking Pot. An Early Classic finger-bowl cache there was placed within a carved circular masonry altar at the southern causeway terminus group of the site (Audet and Awe 2005).

Similar finger bowls were found in the entombment of Stela 9 at Cahal Pech (Awe 2013), suggesting a Late Classic phase of Caracol influence in the Belize Valley (Helmke and Awe 2008:84–85). The reappearance of this typical Caracol ritual feature may be the direct result of martial incursions made into the area by Caracol at the start of the eighth century AD. This is suggested by Stela 21 at Caracol, which shows a triumphant king standing above a bound captive who may be the king of Pacbitun, as identified in the accompanying glyphic caption (Helmke and Awe 2008:74–75). Stela 6 and Altar 3 at Pacbitun were both smashed and displaced from their original contexts in antiquity. It is tempting to see this destruction as wrought by Caracol during the same military incursion (Skaggs et al. 2017).

Despite the prominence of Caracol, the influence of Naranjo in the Belize Valley increased by the end of the seventh century. Perhaps the best evidence for direct alliances between sites in the Belize Valley and Naranjo comes from the carved monuments found at Xunantunich. The recent discovery of Panels 3 and 4 offers important information about Late Classic geopolitics in the central Maya lowlands (Helmke and Awe 2016a, 2016b), especially as these panels once were part of a hieroglyphic stairway that had been raised at Caracol in AD 642 during the reign of K'an II (AD 618–658). After the defeat of Caracol at the hands of Naranjo in AD 680, the monuments of K'an II were battered and broken, the hieroglyphic stair dismantled, and pieces transported to allied sites including Ucanal, Xunantunich, and Naranjo during the triumphal return to that city.

The decades that followed were tumultuous, but Naranjo maintained ties with sites in western Belize. Among other lines of evidence, this is suggested by a cream-polychrome vase bearing the Calendar Round date of 8 Ajaw 8 Woj, corresponding to the important period ending of 9.13.0.0.0 (AD 692). This vase was found in a cave near the modern town of Benque Viejo (Gann 1925:72). Crafted in the style of Naranjo, the vase may be attributable to the regency of Lady Six Sky and suggests that she already exerted some influence on sites in the area (Helmke 2019), even before the accession of her son, K'ahk' Tiliw Chan Chaahk, the 38th king of Naranjo, in AD 693 (Martin and Grube 2000:75). The political landscape of the Belize Valley changed radically with his accession. The first few years of the reign of this young king were characterized by warfare and conflict. Between AD 693 and 716, a series of neighboring sites were duly toppled or set to the torch, and adversaries were captured. Although martial accounts of K'ahk' Tiliw Chan Chaahk can be read as "a conflagration of the eastern Peten" (Martin and Grube 2000:76), many of these triumphs may have been intended to reassert vassalage over adjoining polities that had once been in the political orbit of Naranjo rather than true territorial expansion. With the reaches of the realm under firmer control, we can see the king setting out to maintain his hard-won martial prizes by devoting himself to more diplomatic relations. The beautiful "Jauncy Vase" discovered in a burial at Buenavista del Cayo exemplifies this. That vase had been the personal drinking cup of the king of Naranjo and was gifted to a ruler of Buenavista to cement an alliance between the two centers (Houston et al. 1992). Similarly, a Naranjo-style vase was made specifically for an early eighth-century king of Ucanal (Helmke, Polyukhovych et al. 2017:11, 20–21, Figure 9.9). Sherds of precisely the same type of ceramic as the Jauncy Vase also have been discovered at Xunantunich and Baking Pot, suggesting that all three of these sites were allied with Naranjo during the reign of K'ahk' Tiliw Chan Chaahk (Helmke et al. 2015).

That allegiances endured beyond the reign of a single king is suggested by a miniature vase found in a tomb at the summit of Structure A1 in the northern group at Baking Pot. This small vase is typical of the royal workshops of Naranjo, and the name of the original owner is written as K'ahk' . . . Chan Chaahk, a distinctive regnal name of Late Classic Naranjo kings, especially between AD 693 and 780 (Martin and Grube 2000:75–81). Based on the remaining features of the name as well as ceramic associations, we believe that this is a vase that once belonged to K'ahk' Ukalaw Chan Chaahk – the son of K'ahk' Tiliw – who ruled from AD 755 until about AD 780 (Helmke and Awe 2008:79–80; Martin and Grube 2000:80–81). Thus, the gifting of royal ceramics shows that the rulers of Baking Pot maintained allegiance to the kings of Naranjo for almost a century.

Baking Pot also maintained relations with other peers. These included the kings of Komkom, as revealed by a fully glyphic vase recovered from a peri-abandonment deposit in Baking Pot Group B (Helmke, Hoggarth et al. 2017). Glyphic references at Naranjo imply that Komkom was a subsidiary court of that polity. The owner of the vase was the son of a Komkom king named Sak Witzil Baah and of Ixchanal Lem?, a princess of Naranjo (Helmke, Polyuk-hovych et al. 2017:231). The lengthy glyphic text is an unparalleled account of war and conflict in the central Maya lowlands, detailing events in the first half of AD 799 (Figure 9.2). This was a period of intense warfare between Naranjo and Yaxha. The Komkom Vase describes the involvement of that court in this conflict in a fast-paced and enthralling narrative. The contemporaneous king of Naranjo, "Itzamnaaj" K'awil, is nowhere named in the narrative, although near

FIGURE 9.2 The Komkom Vase discovered in a peri-abandonment deposit at Baking Pot.

Source: After Helmke, Hoggarth et al. 2017:Figure 1.

identical events are related on Stela 12 at Naranjo. There, credit for victory is given not to the king of Komkom but instead to the ruler of Naranjo. In sum, the vase presents a riveting account of warfare and political intrigue involving Baking Pot and other polities of the Belize Valley.

Allegiances between Baking Pot and Naranjo continued, demonstrated by a polychromatic barrel-shaped vase bearing the name Waxaklajun Ubah K'awil that was found in peri-abandonment deposits in the palatial complex of Baking Pot Group B (Helmke et al. 2015; Hoggarth et al. 2014). This is the last known ruler of Naranjo, who erected Stela 32 of that site to commemorate the period ending of AD 820. Stela 8 at Xunantunich also mentions him in connection with a dance ritual celebrated with the local lord on the same date. This may suggest that the king of Naranjo celebrated this important period ending not at his own capital but at that of a vassal (Helmke et al. 2010). If so, this would have fostered bonds with a vassal during a time of increasingly decentralized and fractured royal power. The kings of Xunantunich endured for only a few decades until the erection in AD 849 of Stela 1 and its pair Altar 1. After this date, the historical record ceased (Yaeger 2010).

Environmental context

An environmental reconstruction of the Classic and Postclassic central Maya lowlands provides context for the sociopolitical transformations that occurred during this critical period. To conduct this reconstruction, we rely on several speleothem records from the central Maya lowlands. The first, the Macal Chasm speleothem (MC01), provides the most detailed local paleoclimate record concerning the Belize Valley (Akers et al. 2016). It documents over 6,000 years of climatic change from the Archaic period to modern times. The MC01 record features roughly 3-year analytical resolution of oxygen isotope ($\delta^{18}O$) measurements throughout the Classic, improving to about 1.7-year resolution during the Terminal Classic period. The record is anchored with 21 uranium-thorium series dates, with average measurement errors between 250 and 380 years. After AD 1200, the analytical resolution drops to 12-year intervals, making reconstructions of Late Postclassic climatic changes less precise. A second analyzed speleothem (YOK-I) comes from Yok Balum Cave, located in far southern Belize, approximately 1.5 km from the Classic period site of Uxbenka (Chapter 5). The Yok-1 record features sub-annual (0.49/yr) analytical resolution of $\delta^{18}O$ measurements, with dating uncertainties averaging ± 9.6 years across the Classic and Postclassic periods (Kennett et al. 2012). Finally, an additional speleothem record from Box Tunich cave, located south of Baking Pot in the karstic foothills of the Maya Mountains, offers another local view of climatic changes in the Belize Valley. Although this speleothem contained little uranium, leading to difficulties in dating, the record was tuned to the Yok-I record and shows similar trends as the Macal Chasm and Yok-I records. All three speleothems document multi-decadal droughts during the ninth and eleventh centuries (Figure 9.3).

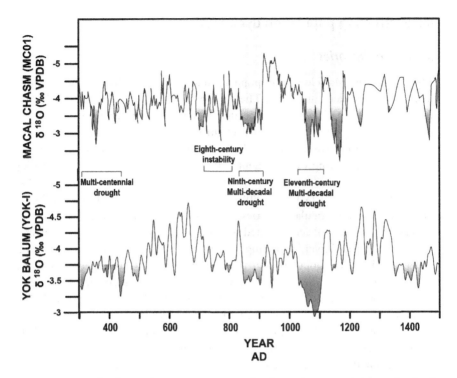

FIGURE 9.3 Speleothem climate proxy records from the central Maya lowlands, showing the Macal Chasm (MC01; Akers et al. 2019) and Yok Balum (Yok-I; Kennett et al. 2012) records. Both show multi-decadal droughts at the end of the Classic period during the ninth and eleventh centuries AD.

The transition from the Late Preclassic to the Early Classic period was characterized by wetter conditions after an extended drought. Shorter dry intervals can be identified in both speleothem records during the fifth century. A period of high precipitation from approximately AD 550 to 640 favored stable environmental conditions and fostered agricultural production. This allowed population expansion during the Late Classic period. A drying trend occurred after AD 640. Climatic instability, including a series of short but recurrent droughts, is identified in the late seventh century, culminating in severe multi-decadal droughts during the ninth century (AD 820–900) and eleventh century (AD 1020–1100). The MC01 record shows an intermittent wet period between two distinct droughts from AD 1100–1130, although this period falls well within the dating uncertainties associated with the record. Overall, this likely represents the same drought episode in both speleothem records, showing some degree of regional variability with a brief (<30 year) return to stable climatic conditions in the mid-twelfth century (Akers et al. 2019). The Yok Balum record shows a return to favorable climatic conditions from the mid-twelfth through fourteenth centuries, associated with the transition from the Early to Late Postclassic period.

Reconstructing population dynamics

Settlement histories

Throughout the Maya lowlands, population histories typically have been reconstructed from settlement studies. These methods use systematic survey and excavation data corrected to calculate occupancy rates of houses. Such studies in the Belize Valley have yielded two different chronological reconstructions for population decline and abandonment at the end of the Classic period. Research using relative ceramic dating of settlement patterns suggests that most Belize Valley centers reached their demographic peak during the Spanish Lookout (AD 700–900)/Late Classic I-II (AD 580–780) ceramic phases (Figure 9.4; Yaeger 2008). Nonetheless, the particular histories of the abandonment of major sites appear to vary after AD 800. Reconstructed settlement histories suggest that major sites along the Mopan River, including Xunantunich, Buenavista, and Actuncan, experienced rapid depopulation at the end of the Late Classic period. For the Xunantunich polity, Yaeger (2008) proposes that 72% of identified settlements were occupied during the eighth century, but only 19% were populated after about AD 800. Research at Buenavista del Cayo records a decline in occupancy from 87% of excavated settlement sites (*n*=15) in BVS Cluster 1 during the Late Classic II phase (AD 670–780) to 27% during the Terminal Classic period (calculated from Peuramaki-Brown 2012: Table 4.14). In contrast, LeCount and colleagues (2011) and Mixter and colleagues (2014) have identified significant Terminal Classic activity at Actuncan. Mixter (2013) reports that approximately 78% of houses there were occupied during the Late Classic II phase and into the Terminal Classic. After that, Postclassic settlement declined in the Actuncan core to around 22%.

The systematic survey and excavation of settlement groups around Cahal Pech is ongoing. Initial assessments of excavated settlement groups there suggest nearly 100% occupation between AD 600 and 900, with no evidence for a Postclassic occupation. The BRASS survey (Ford 1990), extending north of the Mopan and Belize rivers and encompassing the major center of El Pilar, also recorded evidence of large-scale abandonment at the end of the Late Classic period. Population declined from 98% occupation during the Late Classic to approximately 48% during the Terminal Classic (AD 800–900). Ford notes a further drop to just 21% during the Postclassic period. At Pacbitun, populations reached their height in the Late Classic Tzib phase (AD 700–900) at 100% occupation (Healy et al. 2007). No Postclassic occupation has been noted.

In contrast, a longer and more gradual depopulation during the Early Postclassic period (AD 900–1200) has been proposed for some settlements along the Belize River. The presence of Postclassic ceramics at Barton Ramie (Sharer and Chase 1976; Willey et al. 1965) and Baking Pot (Aimers 2003; Audet and Awe 2005; Ricketson 1931:4–5) has been interpreted as evidence for continuous Classic to Postclassic occupation (Aimers 2004; Willey et al. 1965:568). Excavations

PERIOD		Gifford 1976	Barton Ramie	Baking Pot	BRASS	XSS	Buenavista BVS C1	Actuncan Core	LeCount 1996
	─1500								
POSTCLASSIC Late 1400 1300									
─1200 Early 1100 1000	New Town	95%	68%	21%	0%	0%	22%	PC
900					19%	27%	78%	TC
Terminal ─ 800	Spanish Lookout	100%	95%	48%	n/a	n/a	n/a	LCIIB
			100%					
CLASSIC Late 700				98%	72%	87%	78%	LCII
600	Tiger Run	85%	94%		59%	87%	44%	LCI
500 Early 400	Hermitage	77%	78%	49%	41%	87%	89%	EC
─ 300								
Protoclassic 200 100	Floral Park	77%	59%		34%	60%	78%	PP
─ AD/BC	Mount Hope	37%	55%	91%				
Late 100 200	Barton Creek	23%	36%		29%	40%	44%	LP
PRECLASSIC 300 400 500 600 Middle 700 800 900	Jenney Creek	28%	22%	51%	50%	33%	22%	MP
1000 1100 ─1200 Early 1300 1400	None defined in Gifford but see Awe 1992	0%	0%	0%	0%	%	0%	

FIGURE 9.4 Population histories from settlement surveys of Belize Valley sites, showing the percent of settlement occupied by ceramic phase.

Source: After Yaeger 2008:Figure 4.

at Barton Ramie recorded maximum (100%) occupation between AD 700 and 900, with a slight decline to 95% during the New Town ceramic phase. Gifford's (1976) ceramic typology classified the Postclassic ceramics into the early facet of the New Town ceramic phase (AD 950–?) based on comparisons with types in the nearby Peten Lakes area. Nonetheless, the temporal distinction between the facets and the duration of the New Town phase remain undefined (Chase and Garber 2004:8–9). Postclassic ceramics also have been identified at Baking Pot. Settlement studies there suggest that population fell from 95% occupation during the late facet of the Spanish Lookout phase (AD 800–900) to 68% during the Postclassic period (Hoggarth 2012:Table 3–5). Based on a sample (n=182) of Postclassic ceramic sherds from the site core of Baking Pot, Aimers (2004) notes a high proportion (98%) of early-facet New Town ceramics (dated by him to AD 900–1050). He argues that this provides evidence for a gradual depopulation at Baking Pot, with no ceramics postdating AD 1050 at the site core itself (Aimers 2003:160).

The conclusion based on ceramic data that the transition from Terminal Classic to Early Postclassic at Baking Pot was gradual contrasts sharply with recent AMS ^{14}C dates taken directly from human burials (Hoggarth et al. 2014). These imply that a large-scale depopulation event occurred at the end of the Classic period and that there was no substantial reoccupation until after AD 1200 in the Late Postclassic period.

Mobility through the lens of strontium isotope values in tooth enamel

Strontium isotope data allow us to measure population movement within the Belize Valley. These are recorded from tooth enamel formed during infancy and childhood; values that are statistical outliers represent migrants or individuals who relocated at least once between enamel formation and burial. In central Belize, nearly a quarter of the population appears to have moved at least once (Freiwald 2011; Green 2016; Mitchell 2006; Spotts 2013). Most movement seems to have been within the region, because more than half of the non-local isotope values in Belize Valley burials fall into ranges typical of places less than 20 km away. These data also provide very little evidence for long-distance movement into the area from more distant regions. This finding has implications for the political and social conditions that restrict or drive mobility and also may reflect the influence that rulers had over the general population and polity size (Helmke and Awe 2012; Inomata 2004).

The bedrock geology of the Maya Mountains is distinct from the ancient limestone seabed that underlies the Belize River floodplain (Cornec 1986; Wright et al. 1959). This is reflected in ^{87}Sr/^{86}Sr isotope values exceeding 0.711 in the mountains to the south and values of ~0.7086 at most archaeological sites within the region. Sites located in the foothills of the mountains have intermediate values of 0.709–0.710 ^{87}Sr/^{86}Sr or higher (Freiwald 2011; Hodell et al. 2004; Wrobel et al. 2014, 2017), likely because soils there are derived in part from sediments carried by rivers and streams flowing from the mountains. Differences in the chronology of marine limestone formation of the Yucatan Peninsula create a decrease in ^{87}Sr/^{86}Sr values from the northern Maya lowlands to the south, and inland from the Belize coast to the central lowlands. The concept of strontium "isoscapes" (e.g., West et al. 2009) does not work well in Mesoamerica, however, because ^{87}Sr/^{86}Sr values can vary among sites located only 5–10 km apart. This is documented in the Belize Valley, where individuals buried at Chaa Creek have values distinct from those interred at the sites of San Lorenzo and Xunantunich, located less than 10 km away (Freiwald 2020). Similarly, individuals buried in Actun Uayazba Kab Cave southeast of the Belize Valley also have values distinct from those at Pook's Hill, despite the fact that they are located 5 km from each other in the foothills of the mountains (Freiwald 2020; Wrobel et al. 2017). Similar variability also may exist in the terrain of the western Maya lowlands near Palenque, Bonampak, and Yaxchilan (Freiwald 2011; Price et al. 2008). Average values exceeding 0.702 ^{87}Sr/^{86}Sr in human populations, however, are unique to Belize and can be used to identify movement within central Belize.

Population movement in the Belize Valley region was greatest during the Late Classic period when populations were at their peak. Strontium isotope values in the tooth enamel of 88 individuals at three Belize Valley sites – Cahal Pech, Baking Pot, and Barton Ramie – and peripheral settlement groups in this study reflect this pattern. Sample preparation and methods are described in Freiwald (2011) and follow Price et al. (2002), who use faunal baseline values and statistical analyses to differentiate local from non-local values. The ^{87}Sr/^{86}Sr values range from 0.70729 for one individual buried at Baking Pot to 0.70987 for an individual in a Zubin Group burial in the periphery of Cahal Pech. Most values fall within the range of baseline fauna collected along the Belize River floodplain (Figure 9.5), ranging from 0.70821 to 0.70908 ^{87}Sr/^{86}Sr (Freiwald 2011:86). This range reflects much – but not all – of the expected variation of ^{87}Sr/^{86}Sr values for human populations using the same catchments. In all, the values of seven individuals are statistical outliers that fall more than two standard deviations

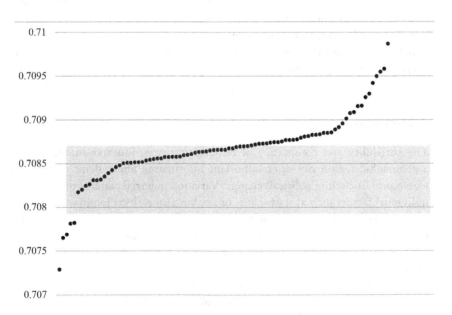

FIGURE 9.5 Strontium isotope values from the sites of Cahal Pech, Baking Pot, and Barton Ramie.

from the mean for each site. An additional six more values are identified as outliers when these seven are removed and standard deviations are recalculated. Thus 13 individuals or 14.8% of the total sample are interpreted as having non-local values (Table 9.1).

At each site, individuals with non-local isotope signatures came from multiple locations, but most came from the vicinity of the Maya Mountains, the only known location in the Maya region with values in the range of 0.7095 $^{87}Sr/^{86}Sr$ and higher in human populations (Freiwald 2020; Wrobel et al. 2017). In some cases, this may represent a move of only a few kilometers and demonstrate population movement within the Belize Valley. Each site also had in-migration from the central or southern Maya lowlands, which could represent movement from neighboring areas over short distances of only 20–30 km, or, alternatively, from hundreds of kilometers away. Identifying more specific places of origin, however, is not possible due to the similarity in isotope values for multiple areas across the Maya lowlands.

Table 9.2 shows the highest mobility at each site during the Late Classic, the period with peak population levels, as well as the largest number of samples included in this study. The decrease in non-local strontium isotope values during the Terminal Classic period likely stems from both a reduction of in-migration to the region and from the small size of the sample. There are very few Terminal Classic burials at most sites in the region.

As noted above, Classic to Postclassic occupational continuity has been argued for Baking Pot and Barton Ramie based on the presence of New Town complex ceramics (AD 900–1050+). If this were the case, we also would expect a continuity in local strontium isotope ratios. Instead, two of the three Late Postclassic burials from Baking Pot demonstrate in-migration (Tables 9.1 and 9.2). The sample is small, but the combination of direct AMS ^{14}C and stable isotope data from Baking Pot presents a compelling argument against large-scale occupational continuity into the Postclassic period at Baking Pot and Barton Ramie.

Burial patterns

The variability and consistency of burial patterns within and among sites in a geographic region can offer important information about demographic and ideological (including political) change. Variation in burial patterns may relate to individual factors such as status, age, or sex but also reflects longstanding traditions and beliefs that help define regional identity. In this section, we show that the position and orientation of the body were highly consistent through the Late Classic, with variability increasing as cities were depopulated during the Terminal Classic period (Table 9.3).

The mortuary tradition of the Belize Valley features prone extended burials with the head oriented to the south (Schwake 2008:Table 6.1; Welsh 1988:77–79; Willey et al. 1965:544–558). Table 9.3 shows that this tradition was fully in place by Late Preclassic times (Chapter 3). This pattern persisted for over a millennium,

TABLE 9.1 Chronology of hieroglyphic texts on carved stone monuments and portable objects in the Belize River Valley (compiled by Helmke and Hoggarth)

Site Monument/Object	Maya Date	Long Count	Date	Dating Basis
Cahal Pech, Stela 9	–	–	Late Preclassic	Iconographic style
Actuncan, Stela 1	–	–	400 BC–AD 100	Iconographic style
Blackman Eddy, Stela 1	–	8.17.5.?.10	AD 381–382	Long Count
Baking Pot, Bedran Group, Vessels 1 and 2	–	–	Early Classic AD 450–500	Ceramic association and paleography
Pacbitun, Stela 6	3 Ajaw 8 Kumk'u	9.2.10.0.0	AD 485	Long Count
Pacbitun, Altar 3	–	–	Fifth century (AD 485?)	Paleographic style
Baking Pot, Fragmentary bowl	–	–	AD 550–650	Ceramic dating
Cave near Benque Viejo, Polychrome vase	8 Ajaw 8 Woj	9.13.0.0.0	AD 692	Calendar round
Baking Pot, Str. A1, Cylinder vase	–	–	AD 693–780	Naranjo regnal name
Xunantunich, Panel 1	#	#	ca. AD 670–870	Paleographic style
Caracol, Stela 21	7 Ajaw 3 Kumk'u	9.13.10.0.0	AD 702	Long Count
Xunantunich, Panel 2	#	#	ca. AD 780–820	Paleographic style
Xunantunich, Panel 3	13 Ajaw 18 K'ank'in	9.10.10.0.0	AD 642	Calendar round
Xunantunich, Panel 4	13 Ajaw 18 K'ank'in	9.10.10.0.0	AD 642	Calendar round
Cahal Pech, Str. A1, Graffiti	–	–	AD 700–800	Paleographic style
Baking Pot, Group B, Komkom Vase	–	9.19.1.15.8	AD 812	Long Count
Xunantunich, Stela 8	8 Ajaw 8 [Xul]	9.19.10.0.0	AD 820	Calendar round
Baking Pot, Group B, Polychrome barrel-shaped vase	8 Ajaw 8 Xul	9.19.10.0.0	AD 820	Calendar round
Xunantunich, Stela 9	7 [Ajaw] [18 Sip]	10.0.0.0.0	AD 830	Long Count
Xunantunich, Stela 1	5 Ajaw [3 K'ayab]	10.1.0.0.0	AD 849	Calendar round
Xunantunich, Altar 1	5 Ajaw [3 K'ayab]	10.1.0.0.0	AD 849	Long Count

TABLE 9.2 List of strontium isotope values interpreted as non-local to Baking Pot, Barton Ramie, and Cahal Pech, and regions where these values are found by time period

Site and burial #	87Sr/86Sr value	Similar values in the Maya region	Time period
Baking Pot 30 individuals sampled (mean 0.708631 ± .00039)			
B101–1	0.707824	Vaca Plateau, southern lowlands	Late Postclassic
B99E-1	0.707815	Vaca Plateau, southern lowlands	Late Postclassic
Atalaya Group Burial 1 Individual B	0.709259	Maya Mountain foothills	Late Classic
M-190 Burial 5	0.708174	Central, western, or northern lowlands	Late Classic
M-215 Burial 4	0.709549	Maya Mountain foothills	Terminal Classic
Excavation 9 (after Ricketson 1929)	0.707289	Southern lowlands, Copan region	Unknown
Barton Ramie 20 individuals sampled (mean 0.708676 ± .00019)			
BR-123 Burial 9	0.709584	Maya Mountain foothills	Late Classic
BR-123 Burial 18	0.709160	Maya Mountain foothills	Late Classic
BR-144 Burial 2	0.707650	Vaca Plateau, southern lowlands	Late Classic/ Postclassic
Cahal Pech 38 individuals sampled (mean 0.708674 ± .00024)			
Plaza B Burial 1	0.709297	Maya Mountain foothills	Early Classic
Zopilote Group Tomb 1 Individual 2	0.709418	Maya Mountain foothills	Late Classic
Zubin Group Burial A1-B3 Individual 6	0.709500	Maya Mountain foothills	Late Classic
Zubin Group Burial A1-B3 Individual 3	0.709816	Maya Mountain foothills	Late/Terminal Classic
Plaza G Burial 1	0.707651 0.707725	Vaca Plateau, southern lowlands	Historic

spanning the Late Preclassic, Early Classic, and Late/Terminal Classic periods. Although this was the dominant pattern, there are a few examples of variability in burial practices. For example, at Early Classic Barton Ramie, 25% of burials were flexed or seated. One potential explanation for this difference may lie in the distinct developmental trajectory of Barton Ramie and its ceremonial center of Lower Dover. Baking Pot and Cahal Pech, where burial patterns were remarkably stable, were established by at least the beginning of the Middle Preclassic period. In contrast, Lower Dover exhibits minimal construction or activity before the formal establishment of the site core in the middle of the Classic period. We hypothesize that people might have migrated from other centers or regions to live at Lower Dover in and after the sixth century AD.

TABLE 9.3 Breakdown of local vs. non-local isotopic signatures for analyzed burials at Cahal Pech, Baking Pot, and Barton Ramie. Three Barton Ramie burials were described as Late Classic or later based on ceramic analyses

Time period	n Burials	Local	Non-local
Cahal Pech			
Middle/Late Preclassic	0	0%	0%
Late Preclassic	5	100%	0%
Early Classic	3	100%	0%
Late Classic	9	78%	22%
Late/Terminal	2	50%	50%
Terminal Classic	1	100%	0%
Baking Pot			
Middle/Late Preclassic	1	100%	0%
Late Preclassic	1	100%	0%
Early Classic	5	80%	20%
Late Classic	6	67%	33%
Late/Terminal	2	50%	50%
Terminal Classic	6	100%	0%
Late Postclassic	3	33%	67%
Barton Ramie			
Middle/Late Preclassic	0	0%	0%
Late Preclassic	0	0%	0%
Early Classic	0	0%	0%
Late Classic	17	82%	18%

Source: Willey et al. 1965

We identify an increase in atypical burial practices across all three sites during the Terminal Classic period. This started shortly after the beginning of the eleventh *b'ak'tun* in AD 830. At Cahal Pech and Baking Pot, flexed interments represent 17% and 14% of the burial samples dating to this period. At Lower Dover/Barton Ramie, no flexed burials have been identified, but 14% of individuals buried during the Terminal Classic were found in a seated position. Schwake (2008:Table 6.1), following Healy et al. (1998), identified a shift from single to multiple interments at the end of the Classic period, demonstrating another change in regional burial practices. Another example of Terminal Classic mortuary practice is apparent at Tutu Uitz Na, a sizeable minor center 600 m south of the Lower Dover site core (Biggie et al. 2019). There, an intrusive burial pit was cut through the central staircase of the eastern triadic structure at Tutu Uitz Na around the time of abandonment (AD 750–850). Excavation of this feature revealed five individuals interred in the three burials (SG1-Bu 2, 3 and 4). The pit contained a seated individual with an andesite celt with bright olivine inclusions between the legs, 22 *Olivella* tinklers around the wrists and neck, the right foot placed in a manner consistent with the raised heel motif, a large upturned Vaca Falls bowl over the head, and a chert ceremonial biface placed parallel through the mouth. Above this individual were two ventrally placed, legs flexed (VPLF) burials. These individuals had their hands at their sides. The uppermost of the two individuals dated to AD 780–880 (PSUAMS#3464), while the one immediately beneath dated to AD 770–890 (PSUAMS#3365). Nine individuals placed in the VPLF position also have been found in Terminal Classic contexts at Lower Dover itself (Biggie et al. 2019). The VPLF position is common at Terminal Classic Marco Gonzalez and at Early Postclassic Lamanai and Chau Hiix (Wrobel and Graham 2015). Together, the evidence for an increase in non-standard interments suggests that this was a highly unstable period characterized by atypical mortuary treatment and high mobility. In fact, out-migration is one possible cause for the drastic population decline at these centers at the end of the Classic period.

Mortuary activity during the Postclassic period has been identified at only two sites in the Belize River Valley: Baking Pot and Barton Ramie. At Barton Ramie, 20 burials were excavated that date to the Spanish Lookout/New Town ceramic phases (Willey et al. 1965:532–533). Of these, none contained Postclassic ceramics to definitively tie the burials to that period and none have published radiocarbon dates. In contrast, three Postclassic burials, all direct dated, have been excavated at Baking Pot. Despite arguments for Classic to Postclassic continuity at that site, not one of these is Early Postclassic. Instead, all three burials date to Late Postclassic times (AD 1290–1490), suggesting a gap in the occupation of Baking Pot. Each of the Late Postclassic burials is distinct. The two adult primary burials from M-101 and M-99 in the eastern settlement area at Baking Pot are flexed with heads oriented to the north (Hoggarth 2012:214–227). The other burial is in a less secure context, a midden with mixed ceramic types that span both the Classic and Postclassic periods (Audet and Awe 2005). Although the Barton Ramie Late Classic/Postclassic burials are of uncertain date, it very well may be that some of them are Postclassic. Of this group, approximately 7% have heads oriented to the north, but not one of them is in a flexed position.

In sum, Postclassic population levels were much lower than in the Classic period, and Postclassic burials exhibit distinct mortuary practices that were uncommon in earlier times. Moreover, Postclassic populations appear to have been limited to sites located along the rich fluvial bottomlands of the Belize River. Rather than arguing for a continuity of cultural traditions and occupation, this suggests great cultural change and, quite likely, in-migration and the reoccupation of abandoned Classic sites during the Late Postclassic period.

Discussion

Data from settlement histories, burial patterns, and strontium isotope analyses of human remains provide the basis for reconstructing ancient Maya population dynamics during the late ninth to early eleventh b'ak'tuns in the Belize River Valley. Settlement histories suggest that most sites in the region reached peak

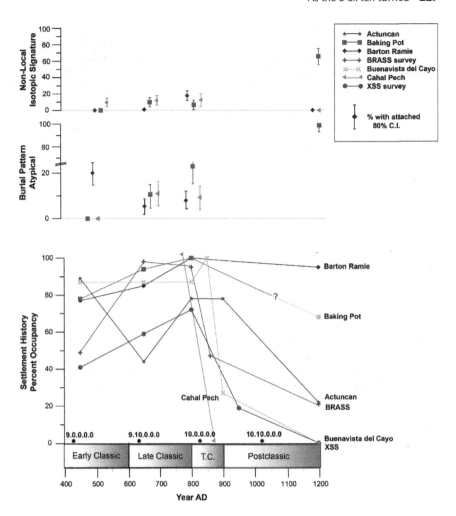

FIGURE 9.6   Comparison of settlement histories across Belize Valley sites (below), with burial patterns (middle) and percent of non-local isotopic signatures (above) at Baking Pot, Barton Ramie, and Cahal Pech.

populations around AD 750–850, with marked population decline thereafter (Figure 9.6). Limited information is available for Cahal Pech, but the population peak there likely occurred earlier than at other sites, with decline beginning around AD 800. In contrast, models based on the ceramic studies suggest a gradual depopulation from Classic to Postclassic times at Baking Pot and Barton Ramie. Nonetheless, this does not align with radiocarbon evidence from human burials at Baking Pot, which indicates that populations declined after AD 800 and that Postclassic occupation resumed after AD 1250. Additional direct-dated human skeletal remains from burials will help us to better evaluate gradual versus rapid depopulation scenarios.

TABLE 9.4 Burial patterns, including primary position (extended, flexed, seated) and orientation (north, south, east, west) for Cahal Pech, Baking Pot, and Barton Ramie. Temporal assignments are based on ceramic associations with burials, unless direct AMS ^{14}C dates have been reported (Ebert et al. 2019; Hoggarth et al. 2014). These include all burials recovered, not just those subject to isotopic assay. Note that not all percentages total 100% because some lack appropriate data and are not included in this summary list.

Period	Extended	Flexed	Seated	North	South	East	West	Total
Cahal Pech								
Middle/Late Preclassic	0%	0%	0%	0%	100%	0%	0%	1
Late Preclassic	100%	0%	0%	14%	86%	0%	0%	14
Early Classic	100%	0%	0%	0%	100%	0%	0%	3
Late Classic	75%	8%	0%	0%	100%	0%	0%	24
Late/Terminal Classic	100%	0%	0%	25%	75%	0%	0%	4
Terminal Classic	86%	14%	0%	0%	71%	0%	0%	7
Late Postclassic	0%	0%	0%	0%	0%	0%	0%	0
								45
Baking Pot								
Middle/Late Preclassic								
Late Preclassic								
Early Classic	100%	0%	0%	0%	100%	0%	0%	5
Late Classic	100%	0%	0%	8%	92%	0%	0%	12
Late/Terminal Classic	100%	0%	0%	0%	82%	0%	18%	11
Terminal Classic	83%	17%	0%	0%	50%	33%	0%	6
Late Postclassic	0%	100%	0%	100%	0%	0%	0%	2
								36
Barton Ramie								
Middle/Late Preclassic	100%	0%	0%	75%	25%	0%	0%	4
Late Preclassic	100%	0%	0%	25%	75%	0%	0%	4
Early Classic	75%	12.5%	12.5%	13%	75%	0%	0%	8
Late Classic	93%	0%	7%	0%	99%	0%	1%	68
Late/Terminal/ Postclassic	86%	0%	14%	7%	93%	0%	0%	14
								100

The examination of burials, in both elite ceremonial contexts as well as the residential platforms of commoners, also sheds light on changing population dynamics in the Belize River Valley at the end of the Classic period. This research shows that the typical burial tradition of primary interments, extended with the head oriented southward, was established no later than the Late Preclassic period and persisted for nearly a millennium throughout the ninth, tenth, and into the eleventh *b'ak'tun*. At Baking Pot, burials not oriented to the south account for only 8% of the mortuary sample dating to the Late Classic period. During the Late to Terminal Classic transition, this increased to 18%, and to 33% during the Terminal Classic period. Variation in mortuary practices also is evident at Cahal Pech during the Late Classic and Terminal Classic periods, with at least 25% of the burials oriented to the north rather than the south. We do not see this same trend at Barton Ramie but currently lack burials dated to the Terminal Classic period. The observed change in burial practices at the end of the tenth *b'ak'tun* may have been the result of at least two distinct processes. First, atypical burial practices might indicate increased mobility and the in-migration of non-local populations who retained their native traditions. If this were the case, we also would expect an increase in non-local isotope values. This has been noted at Baking Pot but only during the Late Postclassic period. A second possibility is that political and environmental changes, as well as other societal factors, contributed to decreased adherence to traditional mortuary practices in the Belize Valley during the Terminal Classic period. In this case, we would not necessarily expect to identify more non-local isotopic signatures. This could explain the increased variation in burials despite reduced in-migration during the Terminal Classic period.

The data from Cahal Pech, Baking Pot, and Barton Ramie show different isotopic patterns. At Baking Pot, 33% of burials were characterized as "non-local" during the Late Classic period. The proportion of non-local burials increased to 50% for the Late to Terminal Classic burial population. These values include both elite and commoner burials, more indicative of movement of the entire population rather than simply segments or certain social tiers. Unfortunately, the sample size is small for the Terminal Classic period. A significant change is seen during Late Postclassic times. Fully 66% of the burial population shows non-local origins. Thus, evidence from Baking Pot supports the first hypothesis that in-migration and population replacement account for changes in interment patterns.

At Cahal Pech, isotopically non-local burials constitute approximately 22% of the burial population during Late Classic times. This amount increased to approximately 50% during the Late to Terminal Classic, supporting the supposition that population movement increased overall during this period. Fewer Terminal Classic burials have been identified, but those that have been analyzed all show local origins. No Postclassic burials have been identified at Cahal Pech, although one early colonial burial has been documented (Awe et al. 2017).

The Terminal Classic period is poorly represented at Barton Ramie, so we can only estimate Late Classic population trends at that site. Approximately 18% of burials there are characterized by non-local isotopic signatures, lower than at Baking Pot but similar to Cahal Pech. Although several burials could date to later times, no definitive Postclassic burials have yet been identified at Barton Ramie.

Together, the burial and isotope data from Belize Valley sites suggest that, even though a substantial portion (18–33%) of the population was of non-local origin during the Late Classic, there was strict conformity to burial traditions. Burial patterns became variable as populations declined. These data may support models for high population mobility in association with increased political and environmental stress at the end of the Classic period. Nonetheless, the disparity between burial patterns and isotopic signatures among sites is an interesting one. Although Baking Pot burial and isotopic data strongly align, data from Cahal Pech and Barton Ramie do not seem to show an increase in atypical burials during periods where higher non-local isotopic signatures are recorded. Unfortunately, we lack robust samples clearly dating to the Terminal Classic and Postclassic periods for these two sites. It may be that at Cahal Pech and Barton Ramie, cultural assimilation and group cohesion caused Late Classic migrants to conform to local burial practices. But we caution that some of the in-migration, as recorded by strontium isotopes, reflects movement over relatively short distances, perhaps only from other locations within the Belize Valley that already shared the same burial tradition. That is, "non-local" is a relative term, and isotopes do not necessarily reflect identity or cultural practices.

Although the temporal resolution of settlement histories based on ceramic chronologies is rather coarse, existing data are consistent with a dramatic population decline during the ninth century AD. In those cases where evidence of Postclassic occupation exists – including at Baking Pot and Barton Ramie – the degree of Classic to Postclassic continuity continues to be questioned. This underscores the need for greater chronological resolution to assess population change. We still are uncertain if population decline was continuous and gradual, spread across one or several centuries, or whether waves of population decline correlate with specific drought episodes or political events. High-precision AMS ^{14}C dates on human burials allow for population reconstructions that are independent of ceramic chronologies. These data also can be combined with existing settlement histories to gain a more thorough view of depopulation in distinct sub-regions of the Maya lowlands.

Conclusions

A contextual understanding of population dynamics at the end of the Classic period is essential if we are to decouple the demographic and political aspects of the Classic Maya collapse. It is clear that political and economic systems were transformed during the transition from the tenth to eleventh b'ak'tun. The documented population decline that occurred at that time also was dramatic. The depopulation and abandonment of settlements in the central and southern Maya lowlands was more than a transformation – it was nothing short of a demographic collapse. The causes and consequences of this dramatic change are still debated, but documented climatic stress during the latter half of the eighth century, followed by severe multi-decadal droughts throughout most of the ninth century, certainly contributed to existing political and economic stress. At that time and in the Belize Valley, the Late Classic glyphic evidence on monuments and portable objects implies that the area was largely influenced by, if not incorporated within, networks of alliances regulated by the Naranjo court. The presence across the Belize Valley of regal serving vessels made at workshops tied to

Naranjo demonstrates the extent of this Late Classic network. The Komkom Vase, found in the Belize Valley, describes how sites in the region participated in alliances during periods of increasing warfare in the eighth century. But the political authority of Naranjo appears to have waned by the beginning of the eleventh b'ak'tun (AD 830). The rulers of Xunantunich mentioned the final ruler of Naranjo while employing for the first time a local emblem glyph. These are signs of political decentralization and increasing autonomy for Xunantunich during the Terminal Classic.

From this political vantage, Belize Valley population dynamics can be contextualized as part of broader demographic changes within the central Maya lowlands. Across the Belize Valley, populations reached their apogees during the early to mid-eighth century, and most sites were significantly depopulated (below 25% of maximum) or abandoned by the tenth century. The trajectory of riverine settlements, including Baking Pot and Barton Ramie, may differ from other centers in the Belize Valley. They show occupation during the Late Postclassic, but it is not clear if they held significant populations during the Early Postclassic period. More AMS ^{14}C dating of human burials and additional systematic settlement excavations are needed to resolve the persisting problem of Early Postclassic occupation.

Acknowledgments

Archaeological excavations at Baking Pot, Cahal Pech, and Xunantunich were conducted under the auspices of the Belize Valley Archaeological Reconnaissance (BVAR) Project, directed by Jaime J. Awe, Julie A. Hoggarth, and Claire E. Ebert. Epigraphic research was conducted by Christophe Helmke under the auspices of the Tourism Development Project and the BVAR project. Funding for research came from the BVAR field school, the Tilden Family Foundation, the National Science Foundation, and the Institute of Cross-cultural and Regional Studies of the University of Copenhagen. Isotope assays were conducted at the University of North Carolina at Chapel Hill in collaboration with the T. Douglas Price Laboratory for Archaeological Chemistry with additional funding provided by a SDE/GWIS Eloise Gerry Fellowship. We thank Dr. John Morris and the Belize Institute of Archaeology for the permitting of BVAR Project research, as well as their continued support of the project.

References cited

Aimers, James J. 2003 Abandonment and Non-Abandonment at Baking Pot, Belize. In *The Archaeology of Settlement Abandonment in Middle America*, edited by Takeshi Inomata and Robert W. Webb, pp. 149–162. University of Utah Press, Salt Lake City.

——— 2004 *Cultural Change on a Temporal and Spatial Frontier: Ceramics of the Terminal Classic to Postclassic Transition in the Upper Belize River Valley.* BAR International Series. Archaeopress, Oxford.

Akers, Pete D., George A. Brook, L. Bruce Railsback, Alex Cherkinksy, Fuyuan Liang, Claire E. Ebert, Julie A. Hoggarth, Jaime J. Awe, Hai Cheng, and R. Lawrence Edwards 2019 Integrating U-Th, 14C, and 210Pb Methods to Produce a Chronologically Reliable Isotope Record for the Belize River Valley Maya from a Low-Uranium Stalagmite. *The Holocene* 29:1234–1248.

Akers, Pete D., George A. Brook, L. Bruce Railsback, Fuyuan Liang, Gyles Iannone, et al. 2016 An Extended and Higher-Resolution Record of Climate and Land Use from Stalagmite MC01 from Macal Chasm, Belize, Revealing Connections between Major Dry Events, Overall Climate Variability, and Maya Sociopolitical Changes. *Palaeogeography, Palaeoclimatology, Palaeoecology* 459:268–288.

Audet, Carolyn M. 2006 *Political Organization in the Belize Valley: Excavations at Baking Pot, Cahal Pech and Xunantunich*. Unpublished Ph.D. dissertation, Department of Anthropology, Vanderbilt University, Nashville.

Audet, Carolyn M., and Jaime J. Awe 2005 The Political Organization of the Belize Valley: Evidence from Baking Pot, Belize. *Research Reports in Belizean Archaeology* 2:357–364.

Awe, Jaime J. 1992 *Dawn in the Land between the Rivers: Formative Occupation at Cahal Pech, Belize and Its Implications for Preclassic Development in the Maya Lowlands*. Unpublished Ph.D. dissertation, University College London, London.

—— 2013 Journey on the Cahal Pech Time Machine: An Archaeological Reconstruction of the Dynastic Sequence at a Belize Valley Maya Polity. *Research Reports in Belizean Archaeology* 10:33–50.

Awe, Jaime J., David Cheetham, and Nikolai Grube 2009 Cahal Pech Stela 9: A Preclassic Monument from the Belize Valley. *Research Reports in Belizean Archaeology* 6:179–189.

Awe, Jaime J., Claire E. Ebert, Carolyn Freiwald, and Kirsten Green 2017 The Dead Do Tell Tales: Unravelling the Case of Cahal Pech's John or Jane Doe. *Research Reports in Belizean Archaeology* 14:213–225.

Awe, Jaime J., Claire E. Ebert, Julie A. Hoggarth, James J. Aimers, Christophe Helmke, et al. 2020 The Last Hurrah: Examining the Nature of Peri-Abandonment Deposits and Activities at Cahal Pech, Belize. *Ancient Mesoamerica* 31:175–187.

Awe, Jaime J., and Christophe G. B. Helmke 2005 Alive and Kicking in the 3rd to 6th Centuries AD: Defining the Early Classic in the Belize River Valley. *Research Reports in Belizean Archaeology* 2:39–52.

Awe, Jaime J., Christophe G. B. Helmke, James J. Aimers, Claire E. Ebert, Julie A. Hoggarth, et al. 2020 Applying Regional, Contextual, Ethnohistoric, and Ethnographic Approaches for Understanding the Significance of Peri-Abandonment Deposits in Western Belize. *Ancient Mesoamerica* 31:109–126.

Awe, Jaime J., Julie A. Hoggarth, and Christophe Helmke 2014 Prehistoric Settlement Patterns in the Upper Belize River Valley and Their Implications for Models of Low-Density Urbanism. *Acta Mesoamericana* 27:263–286.

Awe, Jaime J., and Marc Zender 2016 K'awiil Chan K'inich, Lord of K'an Hix: Royal Titles and Symbols of Rulership at Cahal Pech, Belize. *Mexicon* 38:157–165.

Ball, Joseph W., and Jennifer Taschek 2004 Buenavista del Cayo: A Short Outline of Occupational and Cultural History at an Upper Belize Valley Regal-Ritual Center. In *The Ancient Maya of the Belize Valley: Half a Century of Archaeological Research*, edited by James F. Garber, pp. 149–179. University Press of Florida, Gainesville.

Biggie, Michael, John P. Walden, Rosie Bongiovanni, and Lauren Garcia 2019 The 2018 Lower Dover Settlement Survey and Excavations in the Tutu Uitz Na Neighborhood. In *The Belize Valley Archaeological Reconnaissance Project: A Report of the 2018 Field*

Season, edited by Claire E. Ebert, John P. Walden, Julie A. Hoggarth, and Jaime J. Awe, pp. 186–226. Department of Anthropology, Northern Arizona University and Institute of Archaeology, Baylor University, Waco, TX.

Braswell, Geoffrey E., Joel D. Gunn, María del Rosario Domínguez Carrasco, William J. Folan, et al. 2004 Defining the Terminal Classic at Calakmul, Campeche. In *The Terminal Classic in the Maya Lowlands: Collapse, Transition, and Transformation*, edited by Arthur A. Demarest, Prudence M. Rice, and Don S. Rice, pp. 162–194. University Press of Colorado, Niwot.

Brown, M. Kathryn, Jennifer Cochran, Leah McCurdy, and David Mixter 2011 Preceramic to Postclassic: A Brief Synthesis of the Occupation History of Group E, Xunantunich. *Research Reports in Belizean Archaeology* 8:209–219.

Brown, M. Kathryn, Leah McCurdy, Whitney Lytle, and Thomas Chapman 2013 Mopan Valley Preclassic Project: Results of the 2011 Field Season. *Research Reports in Belizean Archaeology* 10:137–146.

Burke, C. C., K. K. Tappan, G. B. Wisner, Julie A. Hoggarth, J. B. Davis, and Jaime J. Awe 2020 To Eat, Discard, or Venerate: Faunal Remains as Proxy for Human Behaviors in Lowland Maya Peri-Abandonment Deposits. *Ancient Mesoamerica* 31:127–137.

Chase, Arlen F., Diane Z. Chase, John F. Weishampel, Jason B. Drake, Ramesh L. Shrestha, et al. 2011 Airborne LiDAR, Archaeology, and the Ancient Maya Landscape at Caracol, Belize. *Journal of Archaeological Science* 38:387–398.

Chase, Arlen F., and James F. Garber 2004 The Archaeology of the Belize Valley in Historical Perspective. In *The Ancient Maya of the Belize Valley: Half a Century of Archaeological Research*, edited by James F. Garber, pp. 1–14. University Press of Florida, Gainesville.

Colas, Pierre Robert, Christophe Helmke, Jaime J. Awe, and Terry G. Powis 2002 Epigraphic and Ceramic Analyses of Two Early Classic Maya Vessels from Baking Pot, Belize. *Mexicon* 24:33–39.

Cornec, Jean H. 1986 *Provisional Geological Map of Belize at the Scale of 1:250,000*. Petroleum Office, Ministry of Natural Resources, Belmopan, Belize.

Culbert, T. Patrick, and Don S. Rice (editors) 1990 *Precolumbian Population History in the Maya Lowlands*. University of New Mexico Press, Albuquerque.

Ebert, Claire E. 2017 *Preclassic Maya Social Complexity and Origins of Inequality at Cahal Pech, Belize*. Unpublished Ph.D. dissertation, Department of Anthropology, Pennsylvania State University, State College.

Ebert, Claire E., and Jaime J. Awe 2020 Who Were the Early Preclassic Maya?: Reassessing Key Questions about the Origins of Village Life in the Belize River Valley. *Research Reports in Belizean Archaeology* 17:273–286.

Ebert, Claire E., Brendan J. Culleton, Jaime J. Awe, and Douglas J. Kennett 2016 AMS [14]C Dating of Preclassic to Classic Period Household Construction in the Ancient Maya Community of Cahal Pech, Belize. *Radiocarbon* 58:69–87.

Ebert, Claire E., Julie A. Hoggarth, Brendan J. Culleton, Jaime J. Awe, and Doug J. Kennett 2019 The Role of Diet in Resilience and Vulnerability to Climate Change among Early Agricultural Communities in the Maya Lowlands. *Current Anthropology* 60:589–601.

Fahsen, Federico, and Nikolai Grube 2005 The Origins of Maya Writing. In *Lords of Creation: The Origins of Sacred Maya Kingship*, edited by Virginia M. Fields and Dorie Reents-Budet, pp. 74–79. Scala, London.

Ford, Anabel 1990 Settlement and Environment in the Upper Belize River Area and Variability in Household Organization in the Central Maya Lowlands. In *Prehistoric*

Population History in the Maya Lowlands, edited by T. Patrick Culbert and Don S. Rice, pp. 167–182. University of New Mexico Press, Albuquerque.

Freiwald, Carolyn 2011 *Maya Migration Networks: Reconstructing Population Movement in the Belize River Valley during the Late and Terminal Classic.* Unpublished Ph.D. dissertation, University of Wisconsin-Madison, Madison.

———— 2020 Migration and Mobility in the Eastern Maya Lowlands. In *The Maya World,* edited by Scott Hutson and Traci Ardren, pp. 203–222. Routledge, New York.

Gann, Thomas A. 1925 *Mystery Cities: Explorations and Adventures in Lubaantun.* Duckworth, London.

Garber, James F. 1992 A Baktun 8 Carved Stela from the Lowland Maya Site of Blackman Eddy, Belize. *Paper presented at the 57th Annual Meeting of the Society for American Archaeology,* Pittsburgh.

Garber, James F., M. Kathryn Brown, Jaime J. Awe, and Christopher J. Hartman 2004 Middle Formative Prehistory of the Central Belize Valley: An Examination of Architecture, Material Culture, and Sociopolitical Change at Blackman Eddy. In *The Ancient Maya of the Belize Valley: Half a Century of Archaeological Research,* edited by James F. Garber, pp. 25–47. University Press of Florida, Gainesville.

Gifford, James C. (editor) 1976 *Prehistoric Pottery Analysis and the Ceramics of Barton Ramie.* Memoirs of the Peabody Museum of Archaeology and Ethnology, Harvard University, Cambridge.

Graham, Elizabeth A. 2004 Lamanai Reloaded: Alive and Well in the Early Postclassic. *Research Reports in Belizean Archaeology* 1:223–242.

Green, Kirsten A. 2016 *The Use of Stable Isotope Analysis on Burials at Cahal Pech, Belize, in Order to Identify Trends in Mortuary Practices over Time and Space.* Unpublished Ph.D. dissertation, Department of Anthropology, University of Montana, Missoula.

Grube, Nikolai, and Simon Martin 2004 Patronage, Betrayal, and Revenge: Diplomacy and Politics in the Eastern Maya Lowlands. In *Notebook for the XXVIIIth Maya Hieroglyphic Forum at Texas,* pp. 1–95. University of Texas, Austin.

Guerra, Rafael A., and Jaime J. Awe 2017 Recent Investigation at the Major Center of Lower Dover in the Belize River Valley. *Research Reports in Belizean Archaeology* 14:241–248.

Gunn, Joel, Vernon Scarborough, William Folan, Christian Isendahl, Arlen Chase, et al. 2017 A Distribution Analysis of the Central Maya Lowlands Ecoinformation Network: Its Rises, Falls, and Changes. *Ecology and Society* 22:20.

Healy, Paul F. 1990 An Early Classic Maya Monument at Pacbitun, Belize. *Mexicon* 12:109–110.

Healy, Paul F., Jaime J. Awe, and Hermann Helmuth 1998 An Ancient Maya Multiple Burial at Caledonia, Cayo District, Belize. *Journal of Field Archaeology* 25:261–274.

Healy, Paul F., Christophe Helmke, Jaime J. Awe, and Kay S. Sunahara 2007 Survey, Settlement, and Population History at the Ancient Maya Site of Pacbitun, Belize. *Journal of Field Archaeology* 32:17–39.

Healy, Paul F., Bobby Hohmann, and Terry G. Powis 2004 The Ancient Maya Center of Pacbitun. In *The Ancient Maya of the Belize Valley: Half a Century of Archaeological Research,* edited by James F. Garber, pp. 207–227. University Press of Florida, Gainesville.

Helmke, Christophe 2019 An Analysis of the Imagery and Text of the Cuychen Vase. In *The Realm Below: Speleoarchaeological Investigations in the Macal River Valley, Belize,* edited by Christophe Helmke, pp. 122–159. Precolumbian Mesoweb Press, San Francisco.

Helmke, Christophe, and Jaime J. Awe 2008 Organización territorial de los antiguos mayas de Belice Central: confluencia de datos arqueológicos y epigráficos. *Mayab* 20:65–91.

———— 2012 Ancient Maya Territorial Organization of Central Belize: Confluence of Archaeological and Epigraphic Data. *Contributions in New World Archaeology* 4:59–90.

———— 2016a Death Becomes Her: An Analysis of Panel 3, Xunantunich. *The PARI Journal* 16(4):1–14.

———— 2016b Sharper Than a Serpent's Tooth: A Tale of the Snake-Head Dynasty as Recounted on Xunantunich Panel 4. *The PARI Journal* 17(2):1–22.

Helmke, Christophe, Jaime J. Awe, and Nikolai Grube 2010 The Carved Monuments and Inscriptions of Xunantunich. In *Classic Maya Provincial Politics: Xunantunich and Its Hinterlands*, edited by Lisa J. LeCount and Jason Yaeger, pp. 97–121. University of Arizona Press, Tucson.

Helmke, Christophe, Jaime J. Awe, and Harri J. Kettunen 2003 Hieroglyphic Inscriptions of the Belize Valley: Implications for Socio-Political Landscape and Dynastic Interaction. *Paper presented at the XXVIIIth Annual Texas Maya Meetings*, University of Texas at Austin, March 11.

Helmke, Christophe, Claire E. Ebert, Jaime J. Awe, and Julie A. Hoggarth 2015 The Lay of the Land: A Political Geography of an Ancient Maya Kingdom in West-Central Belize. *Contributions in New World Archaeology* 12:9–54.

Helmke, Christophe, Nikolai Grube, Jaime J. Awe, and Paul F. Healy 2006 A Reinterpretation of Stela 6, Pacbitun, Belize. *Mexicon* 28:70–75.

Helmke, Christophe, Julie A. Hoggarth, Jaime J. Awe, Sarah E. Bednar, and Amber Lopez Johnson 2017 Some Initial Comments on the Komkom Vase Discovered at Baking Pot, Belize. *Research Reports in Belizean Archaeology* 14:227–240.

Helmke, Christophe, Yuriy Polyukhovych, Dorie J. Reents-Budet, and Ronald L. Bishop. 2017 A Bowl Fit for a King: A Ceramic Vessel of the Naranjo Court Bearing the Komkom Emblem Glyph. *The PARI Journal* 18(1):9–24.

Hodell, David A., Rhonda L. Quinn, Mark Brenner, and George D. Kamenov 2004 Spatial Variation of Strontium Isotopes ($^{87}Sr/^{86}Sr$) in the Maya Region: A Tool for Tracking Ancient Human Migration. *Journal of Archaeological Science* 31:585–601.

Hoggarth, Julie A. 2012 *Social Reorganization and Household Adaptation in the Aftermath of Collapse at Baking Pot, Belize.* Unpublished Ph.D. dissertation, Department of Anthropology, University of Pittsburgh, Pittsburgh.

Hoggarth Julie A., Brendan J. Culleton, Jaime J. Awe, and Douglas J. Kennett 2014 Questioning Postclassic Continuity at Baking Pot, Belize, Using Direct AMS ^{14}C Dating of Human Burials. *Radiocarbon* 56:1057–1075.

Hoggarth, Julie A., J. Britt Davis, Jaime J. Awe, and Christophe Helmke 2020 Reconstructing the Formation of Peri-Abandonment Deposits at Baking Pot, Belize. *Ancient Mesoamerica* 31:139–149.

Houston, Stephen D. 1991 Appendix: Caracol Altar 21. In *Sixth Palenque Round Table, 1986*, edited by Merle Greene Robertson and Virginia M. Fields, pp. 38–42. University of Oklahoma Press, Norman.

Houston, Stephen D., David Stuart, and Karl Taube 1992 Image and Text on the Jauncy Vase. In *The Maya Vase Book*, edited by Justin Kerr, Vol. 3, pp. 504–523. Kerr Associates, New York.

Inomata, Takeshi 2004 The Spatial Mobility of Non-Elite Populations in Classic Maya Society and Its Political Implications. In *Ancient Maya Commoners*, edited by Jon Lohse and Fred Valdez, Jr., pp. 175–196. University of Texas Press, Austin.

Kennett, Douglas J., Sebastian F. M. Breitenbach, Valorie V. Aquino, Yemane Asmerom, Jaime Awe, et al. 2012 Development and Disintegration of Maya Political Systems in Response to Climate Change. *Science* 338:788–791.

LeCount, Lisa, Angela Keller, and John Blitz 2011 Common House, Elite House, Council House: Report of the 2010 Field Season of the Actuncan Archaeological Project. *Research Reports Belizean Archaeology* 8:19–30.

Martin, Simon, and Nikolai Grube 1995 Maya Superstates. *Archaeology* 48(6):41–46.

———— 2000 *Chronicle of the Maya Kings and Queens: Deciphering the Dynasties of the Ancient Maya*. Thames & Hudson, London.

Masson, Marilyn 2002 Community Economy and the Mercantile Transformation in Postclassic Northeastern Belize. In *Ancient Maya Political Economies*, edited by Marilyn A. Masson and David A. Freidel, pp. 335–364. Altamira Press, Walnut Creek, CA.

McKillop, Heather I. 1996 Ancient Maya Trading Ports and the Integration of Long-Distance and Regional Economies: Wild Cane Cay in South-Coastal Belize. *Ancient Mesoamerica* 7:49–62.

Mitchell, Patricia T. 2006 *The Royal Burials of Buenavista del Cayo and Cahal Pech: Same Lineage, Different Palaces?* Unpublished M.A. thesis, Department of Anthropology, San Diego State University, San Diego.

Mixter, David W. 2013 The Memory of Collapse: Considering the Role of Cultural Trauma in Societal Reorganization Following the 9th Century Maya Collapse at Actuncan, Belize. *Poster Presented at the 29th Annual Visiting Scholar Conference*, Center for Archaeological Investigations, Southern Illinois University, Carbondale.

Mixter, David W., Kara A. Fulton, Lauren Hahn Bussiere, and Lisa J. LeCount 2014 Living through Collapse: An Analysis of Maya Residential Modifications during the Terminal Classic Period at Actuncan, Cayo, Belize. *Research Reports in Belizean Archaeology* 11:55–66.

Pendergast, David M. 1990 Up from the Dust: The Central Lowlands Postclassic as Seen from Lamanai and Marco González, Belize. In *Vision and Revision in Maya Studies*, edited by Flora S. Clancy and Peter D. Harrison, pp. 169–177. University of New Mexico Press, Albuquerque.

Peuramaki-Brown, Meagan M. 2012 *The Integration and Disintegration of Ancient Maya Urban Centres: Charting Households and Community at Buenavista Del Cayo, Belize*. Unpublished Ph.D. dissertation, Department of Anthropology, University of Calgary, Calgary.

Prager, Christian M., and Geoffrey E. Braswell 2016 Maya Politics and Ritual: An Important New Hieroglyphic Text on a Carved Jade from Belize. *Ancient Mesoamerica* 27:267–278.

Price, T. Douglas, James H. Burton, and R. Alexander Bentley 2002 The Characterization of Biologically Available Strontium Isotope Ratios for the Study of Prehistoric Migration. *Archaeometry* 44:117–135.

Price, T. Douglas, James H. Burton, Paul D. Fullagar, Lori E. Wright, Jane E. Buikstra, et al. 2008 Strontium Isotopes and the Study of Human Mobility in Ancient Mesoamerica. *Latin American Antiquity* 19:167–180.

Rice, Don S., and T. Patrick Culbert 1990 Historical Contexts for Population Reconstruction in the Maya Lowlands. In *Precolumbian Population History in the Maya Lowlands*, edited by T. Patrick Culbert and Don S. Rice, pp. 1–36. University of New Mexico Press, Albuquerque.

Rice, Prudence M., and Don S. Rice 2009 *The Kowoj: Identity, Migration, and Geopolitics in Late Postclassic Petén, Guatemala*. University Press of Colorado, Boulder.

Ricketson Jr, Oliver G. 1929 *Baking Pot, British Honduras*. Carnegie Institution of Washington, Publication no. 403, Contributions to American Archaeology 1, Washington, DC.

Ricketson, Oliver G. 1931 *Excavations at Baking Pot, British Honduras*. Carnegie Institution of Washington, Publication No. 304, Washington, DC.

Ringle, William M., Tomás Gallareta Negrón, and George J. Bey 1998 The Return of Quetzalcoatl: Evidence for the Spread of a World Religion during the Epiclassic Period. *Ancient Mesoamerica* 9:183–232.

Schwake, Sonja A. 2008 *The Social Implications of Ritual Behavior in the Maya Lowlands: A Perspective from Minanha, Belize*. Unpublished Ph.D. dissertation, Department of Anthropology, University of California at San Diego, La Jolla.

Sharer, Robert J., and Arlen F. Chase 1976 The New Town Ceramic Complex. In *Prehistoric Pottery Analysis and the Ceramics of Barton Ramie*, edited by James C. Gifford, pp. 420–445. Memoirs of the Peabody Museum of Archaeology and Ethnology, Harvard University, Cambridge.

Skaggs, Sheldon, Christophe Helmke, Jon Spenard, Paul F. Healy and Terry G. Powis 2017 Some Observations and New Discoveries Related to Altar 3, Pacbitun, Belize. *Mexicon* 39:115–123.

Spotts, John Michael 2013 *Local Achievers or Immigrant Elites? Ancestral Relics or Warrior Trophies?: Some Classic Period Cultural Historical Questions Addressed through Strontium Isotope Analysis of Burials from Western Belize*. Unpublished M.A. thesis, San Diego State University, San Diego.

Turner, B. L., and Jeremy A. Sabloff 2012 Classic Period Collapse of the Central Maya Lowlands: Insights about Human: Environment Relationships for Sustainability. *Proceedings of the National Academy of Sciences* 109:13908–13914.

Webster, David 2012 The Classic Maya Collapse. In *The Oxford Handbook of Mesoamerican Archaeology*, edited by Deborah L. Nichols and Christopher A. Pool, pp. 324–334. University of Oxford Press, Oxford.

Welsh, W. Bruce M. 1988 *An Analysis of Classic Lowland Maya Burials*. BAR International Series 409. British Archaeological Reports, Oxford.

West, Jason B., Gabriel J. Bowen, Todd E. Dawson, and Kevin P. Tu (editors) 2009 *Isoscapes: Understanding Movement, Pattern, and Process on Earth through Isotope Mapping*. Springer Science & Business Media, New York.

Willey, Gordon R., William R. Bullard, Jr., John B. Glass, and James C. Gifford 1965 *Prehistoric Maya Settlements in the Belize Valley*. Peabody Museum, Cambridge, MA.

Wright, A. C. S., D. H. Romney, R. H. Arbuckle, V. E. Vial. 1959 *Land in British Honduras: Report of the British Honduras Land Use Survey Team*. The Colonial Office, Colonial Research Publication 24. Her Majesty's Stationery Office, London.

Wrobel, Gabriel D., Carolyn Freiwald, Sherry Gibbs, Amy Michaels, and Jaime Awe 2017 Social Identity and Geographic Origin of Maya Burials at Actun Uayazba Kab, Roaring Creek Valley, Belize. *Journal of Anthropological Archaeology* 45:98–114.

Wrobel, Gabriel D., and Elizabeth Graham 2015 The Buk Phase Burials of Belize: Testing Genetic Relatedness among Early Postclassic Groups in Northern Belize Using Dental Morphology. In *Archaeology and Bioarchaeology of Population Movement among the Prehispanic Maya*, edited by Andrea Cucina, pp. 85–95. Springer, London.

Wrobel, Gabriel D., Christophe Helmke, Carolyn Freiwald, and Jaime Awe 2014 Caves of the Ancestors: A Case Study of Reverential Cave Use from Je'reftheel, Central Belize. In *The Bioarchaeology of Space and Place: Ideology, Power and Meaning in Maya Mortuary Contexts*, edited by Gabriel D. Wrobel, pp. 77–106. Springer Press, New York.

Yaeger, Jason 2003 Small Settlements in the Upper Belize River Valley: Local Complexity, Household Strategies of Affiliation, and the Changing Organization. In *Perspectives on Ancient Maya Complexity*, edited by Gyles Iannone and Samuel V. Connell, pp. 42–58. Monograph 49, Cotsen Institute of Archaeology, University of California, Los Angeles.

——— 2008 Charting the Collapse: Late Classic to Postclassic Population Dynamics in the Mopan Valley, Belize. *Research Reports in Belizean Archaeology* 5:13–21.

———— 2010 Shifting Political Dynamics as Seen from the Xunantunich Palace. In *Classic Maya Provincial Politics: Xunantunich and Its Hinterlands*, edited by Lisa J. LeCount and Jason Yaeger, pp. 145–160. University of Arizona Press, Tucson.

Źrałka, Jarosław, Christophe Helmke, Simon Martin, Wiesław Koszkul, and Juan Luis Velásquez 2018 The Monolithic Monuments of Nakum, Guatemala. *The PARI Journal* 19:1–28.

10

DZEHKABTUN

Crisis and violence in the Terminal Classic

Iken Paap

The Dzehkabtun Archaeological Project was dedicated to the investigation of socio-cultural changes towards the end of the Classic Period in the central area of the Yucatan peninsula. For Dzehkabtun – as for other sites on the peninsula with so-called "Epiclassic" architecture (Prem 2003) – there are convincing indicators that parts of the population present at the site during the Late Classic continued to live and build there into the late Terminal Classic (Paap 2017:96), albeit under radically different conditions. In addition to increasing environmental pressure during the late Terminal Classic, which in the archaeological record is manifested in burials as stress and evidence for malnutrition, as well as in offerings associated with water or rain, we documented traces of violence against buildings and individuals.

Dzehkabtun

The archaeological site of Dzehkabtun is located in the State of Campeche, Mexico, in the area of a former cattle hacienda, about eight kilometers southwest of the present town of Hopelchén (Figure 10.1). Research conducted since 2007 reveals that Dzehkabtun was inhabited from at least Middle Preclassic to late Terminal Classic times. The architectural features of the center of the site – once rich in vaulted buildings, elaborate facades, and sculpted monuments – combine elements of the Puuc and Chenes architectural styles of the Classic Maya together with regional features that clearly reference Santa Rosa Xtampak, located about 35 kilometers to the east.

Beginning in the Late Classic, if not earlier, Dzehkabtun obtained raw materials and luxury goods by participating in interregional exchange networks. This is indicated by large quantities of obsidian and non-local ceramics found at the site. Our recent excavations imply that the local population that occupied the site

DOI: 10.4324/9781351268004-10

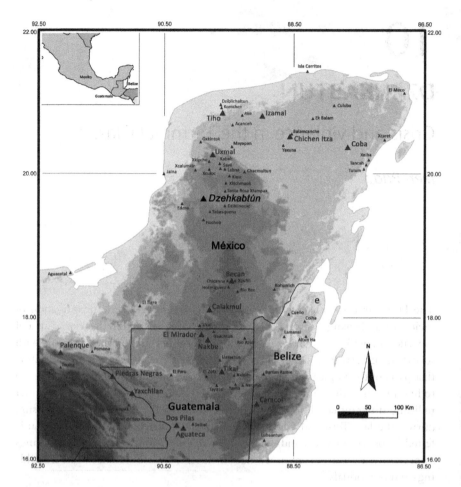

FIGURE 10.1 Location of Dzehkabtun.

during the Late Classic also was responsible for the substantial remodeling of the site center during the Terminal Classic. The spatial organization of the settlement is characterized by courtyard groups that are loosely distributed around the monumental center (Figure 10.2), and some of them are dominated by palace-pyramid buildings (Andrews 1996:22).

During the 19th and 20th centuries, central Dzehkabtun was affected to the point of destruction by the continuous removal of stones from the ancient buildings. In addition to materials for house and road construction, several monuments have been looted and can be traced to museums and private collections around the world (Grube 2009). The best-preserved buildings in Dzehkabtun were first documented by Teobert Maler in 1887 (Maler 1902:228–230, Fig. 20–21; 1997:97–99, 35–39). During the 20th century, Dzehkabtun was briefly visited by several Mexican and foreign archaeologists, who published descriptions of

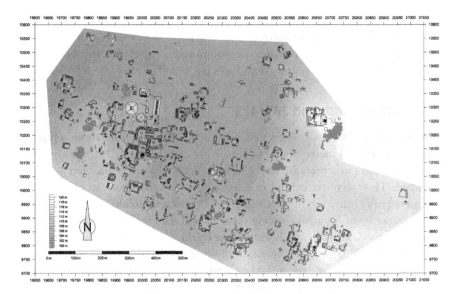

FIGURE 10.2 Map of Dzehkabtun.

the main structures and monuments (e.g., Andrews 1985:31–36; Dunning 1987; Michelet and Becquelin 2001:224; Pollock 1970:40; Ruz Lhuillier 1945:38–41; Seler 1912:32).

In 2007, survey, excavation, and consolidation work started at the site and continued until 2018. The main goal was to better understand the socio-cultural processes at the end of the Classic in the central Yucatan peninsula (Ancona Aragón and Paap 2018; Benavides Castillo and Paap 2015; Paap 2017).

Chronology

Based on the analysis of the ceramic finds recovered in stratigraphic excavations, a chronology was established for Dzehkabtun that stretches from the Middle Pre-classic to the Terminal Classic. Postclassic materials have been found only in iso-lated deposits, and we have no evidence of permanent settlement at Dzehkabtun at that time. In the Chenes region, the Late Classic is characterized by the Pich ceramic horizon and the Terminal Classic by the Habin horizon. In previous stud-ies, the Pich horizon has been dated to AD 600–800 (Góngora Cetina 2010; Góngora Cetina and Jiménez Álvarez 2009). We prefer to date it to AD 600–750/800 in order to better separate Pich and Habin and make the latter more comparable with the Cehpech horizon of the Puuc and other sites in the northern lowlands. Robles Castellanos (2006) broadens the concept of the Cehpech ceramic complex and defines it as a fairly large ceramic sphere that encompasses many sites in the northern lowlands and is dated to AD 730–900. Nonetheless, in several regions of the northern Maya lowlands, the Cehpech ceramic sphere continues after

AD 900 (Ancona Aragón, Benavides Castillo and Paap 2017:348). Thus, we date the Terminal Classic Habin horizon to AD 750/800–900+. Our excavation strategy focused on understanding the later occupation and collapse of Dzehkabtun, and so Terminal Classic Habin pottery dominates our ceramic sample from Dzehkabtun.

Habitation compound 269/425

From 2014 to 2018, we excavated a large portion of a habitation compound located about 500 meters southeast of the site center (Figure 10.3). It consists of two buildings (Structures 269 and 425) of several rooms each that were originally vaulted. They were remodeled in a late phase with the intention of converting them together into a small "pyramid-palace." This is an architectural type known from Santa Rosa Xtampak, among other sites in the area. Eight buildings of this type (largely destroyed) were identified in Dzehkabtun. Some of them, including Building 269/425, give the impression of never having been finished. Unfinished elite structures present one of the key features for the understanding of the processes at the end of the Classic (Prem 2007), as do so-called "C-shaped structures."

Building 269/425 is a central edifice surrounded by several low-walled structures. These were erected in part using carved stones taken from other nearby collapsed structures. The most obvious of these later constructions is the platform of Building 271, which was built using molding stones. Many of these appear to have been taken from Building 269/425. We know this because these specialized stones were almost completely absent from the debris of the collapsed walls of Building 269/425.

Building 269/425 was constructed in three phases. The first dates to the Late Classic, when Building 425 and Building 269 Room 3 were raised. Early in the Terminal Classic, Rooms 269–1 and 269–4 were added. In the last phase, also dating to the Terminal Classic period, Rooms 269–2 and 269–5 were added

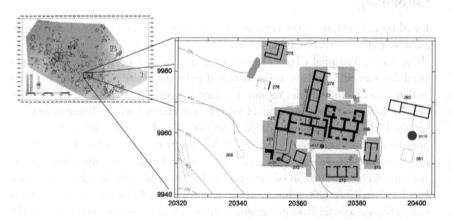

FIGURE 10.3 Building 269/425 with the surrounding structures. Areas excavated between 2014 and 2018 are shaded.

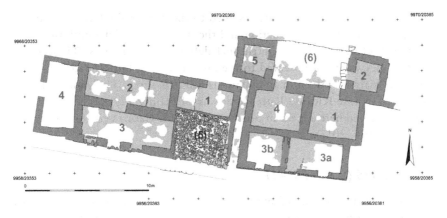

FIGURE 10.4   Buildings 269 (right) and 425 (left). Room 5 of Building 425 was filled in, in order to support a second storey that was never completed.

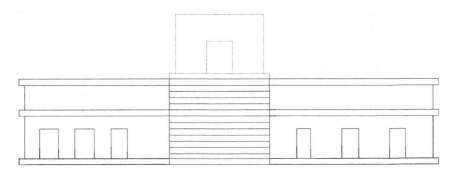

FIGURE 10.5   Buildings 269 (right) and 425 (left) remodeled to form a pyramid-palace type structure (269/425) during the Terminal Classic period. Schematic reconstruction of the southern façade with central staircase and second floor (hypothetical), without Room 425–4.

as was the entrance area to Rooms 269–1, -2, -4, and -5 (Figure 10.4). At a later stage, the corridor between Buildings 269 and 425 and the eastern part of Building 425 was filled and covered with rough stones, probably as a base for a staircase and a second floor (Figure 10.5). Frequent field-clearing fires and the theft of stones have left exposed architecture in a poor state of conservation. For this reason, we have been unable to definitively determine whether the second floor and associated staircase were left incomplete or were finished and later dismantled, as has been noted in buildings in the neighboring Puuc region (José Huchim Herrera, personal communication 2014).

Burials

Sixteen burials were found beneath Building 269/425. These can be linked to distinct construction phases and dated by means of the associated ceramic offerings. Nine individuals are assigned to the Terminal Classic period, that is, the last phases of construction and the destruction of the building. Some of the dead show signs of nutritional deficiencies and stress. These paleo-pathologies were not observed to the same extent in burials dated to earlier phases. Analysis of the human remains is still in progress. Preliminary data are provided by José Ricardo Ruiz Cazares of SEMEFO, Campeche. Interpretations presented here appear in fuller form in Ruiz Cazares (2018) and Ancona Aragón (2016, 2017).

Feature 435 (Room 269–1)

The individual is an adult of undetermined sex. Traces of possible spongy hyperostosis in the skull, moderate osteophyte growth on the edges of the vertebral bodies, and bony outgrowths on the first metatarsal and phalanx of the right foot were noted. Tooth wear and caries and alveolar bone resorption also occurred. The associated offering was a tripod plate assigned by group/type/variety to Pizarra/Muna/-.

Feature 436 (Room 269–1)

This burial contained a probable male adult. Paleopathologies include a con-solidated stress fracture zone in the proximal third of the left fibula. Tooth wear, dental calculus, and caries to a slight to moderate degree on the cement-enamel junction and the interproximal surface also were noted, as were traces of periodontal resorption. The associated offering was a tripod plate assigned to Pizarra/Muna/Yaxnic Modeled.

Feature 448 (Room 269–4)

An adult individual of undetermined sex was found in this burial. Its teeth exhibit moderate dental calculus and caries. The associated offering was a tripod plate assigned to Pizarra/Muna/Muna Pizarra.

Feature 547 (Room 269–2; figure 10.4)

This burial contained an adult of undetermined sex. The associated offering was a tripod bowl (*cajete* in Mexican Spanish) assigned to Pizarra/Sacalum Black on Pizarra/Incised.

Feature 637 (Room 269–4)

Feature 637 contained the remains of a probable male adult. His remains exhibit grade 1 growth of osteophytes on vertebral bodies, patellas, and phalanges. He also has signs of a consolidated stress fracture in the third metatarsal of the right foot. His teeth exhibit grade 4 to 5 tooth wear on their incisal and occlusal surfaces. Oral pathologies consist of grade 1 caries in the molars, presence of dental calculus, and bone resorption in the upper jaw. Alveolar resorption indicates the antemortem loss of M1 and M2 respectively. Grave goods include two tripod plates classified as Pizarra/Muna/Muna Pizarra.

Feature 981 (Room 269–5)

Remains were of an adult individual of undetermined sex. Two tripod plates classified as Pizarra/Muna/Muna Pizarra were recovered from the burial.

Feature 666 (Room 269–3b)

The remains of two individuals were found in this burial, but no grave goods were recovered. Individual 1 was an adult male. Occlusal wear and decay were observed on his teeth. Both upper central incisors exhibit possible intentional filing on the lingual side, and a notch possibly produced by intentional filing was observed on the distal edge of the left upper central incisor. The second and third lower left molars were absent antemortem and there is evidence of alveolar resorption.

Individual 2 was an adult of undetermined sex. Moderate occlusal wear and caries were observed on his teeth. In the right femur and tibia fragment, we observed alterations to the surface consistent with an advanced periosteal reaction.

Feature 1069 (Room 425–2)

This burial contained the remains of an adult male. Dental taphonomic effects that we observed include fragmentation, erosion, and the adhesion of sandy sediment. These allow us to infer contact with hard substances during the chewing of food, occupational activity, or other cultural behavior. There were no associated offerings.

The state of preservation of these remains is generally poor, due – among other factors – to the fact that most individuals at Dzehkabtun were buried directly in the ground rather than in prepared cists during the late Terminal Classic period. Although the sample size does not allow us to make statistically meaningful statements, paleopathologies appear to be more common on these remains than those buried during earlier times. They might indicate a serious deterioration of living conditions during the Terminal Classic.

Offerings

Of the deposits of ritual character dating to the end of the Late Classic and to the Terminal Classic periods at Dzehkabtun, several have a clear connection to water. These can be interpreted very cautiously as indications of deteriorating climatic conditions.

Feature 1761

This is an offering deposited in an altar in the central courtyard of Dzehkabtun, east of the great pyramid (Figure 10.2). It consists of a whitewashed pot with the modelled shape of a frog on the western side (Figure 10.6). The deposit was carefully

FIGURE 10.6 Offering 1761 *in situ* (above); the nine chert bifaces and Chencan vessel of offering 1761 (below).

placed in a small cist of stones and calcareous earth that protected it. To the east of the vessel, nine chert projectile points were arranged in a fan shape. Inside the pot, we found three conch shells each no longer than 4 cm, as well as abundant olive snail shells less than a centimeter long. The entire offering was covered with lime. Its stratigraphic location dates the offering to the Terminal Classic period. Moreover, the vessel, assigned to the Chencan group with modeled and applied decoration, also dates to the Terminal Classic (Ancona Aragón 2018). This offering was surrounded by several other deposited vessels that contained remains of sea snails and small fish.

Feature 2031

South of Building 269, we discovered a deposit of four large marine gastropod mol-lusks (*Pleuroploca gigantea* and *Turbinella angulata*) in a stratigraphic context dating to the transition from the Late Classic to the Terminal Classic (Figures 10.4 and 10.7).

The destruction of Building 269/425

Where the state of conservation of the floors allowed it, traces of fire – in the form of thin layers of ash and charred stains in the plaster – could be observed

FIGURE 10.7 Two of the four mollusks from Feature 2031, south of Building 269.

in the rooms. All vaults of Building 269, except for that of Room 269–3, were deliberately destroyed and stones were taken away. We know this because all the rooms were filled with a sandy limestone material mixed with some building stones from the vaults. But the vault stones were not found in an order consistent with collapse, and a great many were missing. In fact, the quantity of building stones documented in the rubble of all the rooms was insufficient to account for the original structure. Moreover, we found isolated stones from other contexts, such as fragments of *metates*, that were not part of the original structures. We also observed that many of the dressed stones from the north façade of Building 269 were neither found in their place nor among the fallen stones.

In no areas were there any traces of a prolonged abandonment preceding the collapse of the building. With the exception of the ash, which did not contain traces of other accumulated organic material, the floors were found to be clean. Only in Room 269–1 did we find ceramics and carved stone, obviously deposited directly on the floor (Figure 10.8).

In Rooms 269–3 and 425–3 – unlike the other rooms – the stones of the collapsed vault were found in the original positions in which they had fallen. These vaults had collapsed downward and to the south, apparently as a consequence of the dismantling of the south wall. We believe this to be the case because the required amount of building stones from the south wall was not encountered

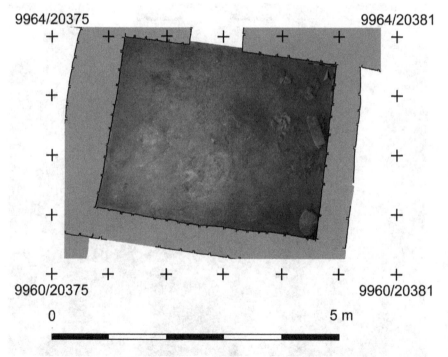

FIGURE 10.8 Room 269–1 with traces of fire and ashes, and various objects encountered directly on the floor.

50 cm

FIGURE 10.9 The collapsed vault of Room 269–3 (view to the north) as revealed by excavation in 2014; the location of the capstone is indicated by the white arrow (above); the mutilated capstone (below).

underneath the collapsed vault. Among the specialized stones found in the debris was the central capstone (Figure 10.9), which fell face down and was found a few centimeters above the floor of the collapsed room. The stucco cover of this capstone was originally painted in bright colors, but the central image of an individual had been deliberately scraped off, leaving a rectangular empty space. The capstone also contains a short inscription on the outer, lower left side. It consists of three hieroglyphic blocks painted in black most probably on the original stucco. The inscription seems to be detached from the rest of the painting, something that recalls scribal signatures on carved monuments. Thus, it probably records the titles of the person who painted the capstone. This person is said to be an *aj nik?-la aj k'uhun*. The last part of the title refers to an

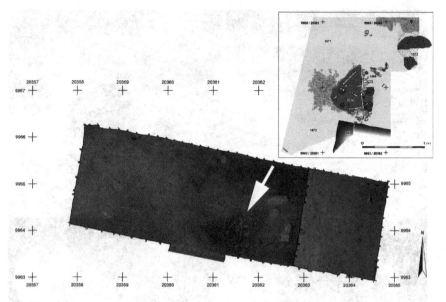

FIGURE 10.10 Human remains (Feature 1069) on the floor next to the entrance to Room 425–2.

individual considered to be a "bookkeeper" (Daniel Grana Behrens, personal communication 2019).

In Room 425–2, we found the remains of an adult male on the floor. He was surrounded by ashes and residual amounts of charred wood (Figure 10.10). The skeletal elements were incomplete, but the extremities were still articulated, placing the individual in a direct context with the destruction of the room.

Interpretation of the destruction of Building 269/425

Most of the rooms in Building 269/425 appear to have been dismantled in one or more deliberate acts, which seem to have been executed with some planning. This is demonstrated by the mutilated capstone, the burnt but swept floors, and the filling of the collapsed rooms with material that does not originate from the collapsed vaults. One probable exception to the planning is the discovery in Room 425–2 of a body in the ash layer that was crushed by the collapse of the vault, just inside the entrance to the room. We also found projectile points that could possibly be associated with the destruction of the building around it and in some rooms.

The act of bringing down the building seems to have been significantly different in the northern and southern parts of the structure. The rooms accessible to the north (Rooms 269–1, 269–2, 269–4, 269–5, and 425–1) are characterized by burnt floors with little ash and were filled with material from contexts other than the collapsed vault and roof. Moreover, many stones were taken away, and others were moved from their fall position. In the rooms with the entrances facing south (Rooms 269–3, 425–2, and 425–3), the destruction was more violent and immediate. There, the complete rubble of the collapsed vaults and roofs was found *in situ*. These differences lead us to argue that there were two distinguishable acts of destruction.

Conclusions

Analyses of the Dzehkabtun material indicate an increase in environmental stress and internal conflicts within the site. We see this reflected in offerings that are concerned with water and include the remains of aquatic animals. Moreover, although the sample size is quite small, we also have qualitative evidence suggesting that paleopathologies may have increased during the Terminal Classic period. These stresses were accompanied by a strong regionalization of ceramics during the Terminal Classic period (see Ancona Aragón 2016, 2017). In contrast, the Early Classic and Late Classic were characterized by a large variety of imported pieces from areas in the north and south of the peninsula (Ancona Aragón and Paap 2018).

When investigating phenomena of crisis and aggression in an archaeological context, one key question is: who were the actors? Identifying by archaeological means the perpetrators of these acts at Dzehkabtun is extremely difficult. There is a complete lack of clearly foreign or non-local elements in the archaeological record associated with the destruction of the building and also in other late Terminal Classic contexts at the site. If structures at Dzehkabtun were razed by people from elsewhere, we have yet to find any evidence diagnostic of their presence.

I emphasize that the current state of research in the Chenes zone does not allow comparison and clear differentiation of material culture at a regional scale, hampering our ability to answer basic questions like this. This is due to the lack of stratigraphic excavations and analyses of materials from other other sites that would allow meaningful comparisons to be made. For example, important reference data from the large city of Santa Rosa Xtampak and other key sites in the region are missing. Santa Rosa Xtampak is often stated to be the capital, and its influence on the architecture of Dzehkabtun and other sites is evident. Nonetheless, the lack of ceramic ceramic data from that huge city and many smaller settlements impedes comparative research and the construction of testable hypotheses on a regional level.

Acknowledgments

The Dzehkabtun Archaeological Project (www.dzk-online.de) is a joint undertaking of the Ibero-American Institute – Prussian Cultural Heritage Foundation and the Centro INAH Campeche. The author and Antonio Benavides Castillo have collaborated on all aspects of research. Generous sponsorship has been provided by the German Science Foundation, DFG.

References cited

Ancona Aragón, Iiana 2016 *Informe del análisis cerámico, Dzehkabtún (Campeche), temporada 2015.* Manuscript on file, Instituto Nacional de Antropología e Historia, Mexico City.

———— 2017 *Informe del análisis cerámico, Dzehkabtún (Campeche), temporada 2016.* Manuscript on file, Instituto Nacional de Antropología e Historia, Mexico City.

Ancona Aragón, Iliana, Antonio Benavides Castillo, and Iken Paap 2017 Dzehkabtún, Campeche: avances de la temporada 2015. Recorrido, excavación, consolidación y análisis cerámico. In *Los Investigadores de la Cultura Maya. El comercio y otros temas,* edited by María del Rosario Domínguez Carrasco, Miriam Judith Gallegos Gomora, Ricardo Armijo Torres, and Miriam Edith León Méndez, pp. 343–355. Universidad Autónoma de Campeche, San Francisco de Campeche.

Ancona Aragón, Iliana, and Iken Paap 2018 La estructura cirular No. 84 de Dzehkabtún, Campeche: implicaciones cronológico-culturales. In *Los investigadores de la cultura maya,* edited by María del Rosario Domínguez Carrasco, Miriam Judith Gallegos Gomora, Ricardo Armijo Torres, and Miriam Edith León Méndez, pp. 415–429. Universidad Autónoma de Campeche, San Francisco de Campeche.

Andrews, George F. 1985 Chenes-Puuc Architecture: Chronology and Cultural Interaction. In *Arquitectura y arqueología: metodologías en la cronología de Yucatán.* Collection Etudes Mesoaméricaines, Serie II, edited by George F. Andrews and Paul Gendrop, pp. 10–39. Centre d'Etudes Mexicaines et Centraméricaines, Mexico City.

———— 1996 Arquitecturas Río Bec y Chenes. *Arqueología Mexicana* 3(18):22.

Benavides Castillo, Antonio, and Iken Paap 2015 Dzehkabtún y Edzná, Campeche: edificios de planta circular. *Mexicon* 37:29–33.

Dunning, Nicholas 1987 Monuments in Yucatan and Campeche. *Mexicon* 9:99.

Góngora Cetina, Dulce Aurora 2010 *Informe tipológico de los materiales cerámicos recuperados en los tramos carreteros Hopelchén-Konchén 2007, Konchén-Pacchén 2008 y Pacchén-Dzibalchén 2010.* Manuscript on file, Archivo de la Sección de Arqueología del Centro INAH Campeche, San Francisco de Campeche.

Góngora Cetina, Dulce Aurora, and Socorro Jiménez Álvarez 2009 Aspectos cronológicos y metodológicos en la cerámica de la región de los Chenes. *Los Investigadores de la Cultura Maya* 7(2):140–160.

Grube, Nikolai 2009 Los monumentos esculpidos de Dzehkabtun, Campeche: epigrafía e iconografía. *Los Investigadores de la Cultura Maya* 18(2):27–39.

Maler, Teobert 1902 Yukatekische Forschungen. *Globus. Illustrierte Zeitschrift für Länder- und Völkerkunde* 82(13–14):197–230.

———— 1997 *Península Yucatán. Aus dem Nachlass hrsg. von Hanns J. Prem. Mit Beitr. von Ian Graham.* Monumenta Americana, Vol. 5. Gebr. Mann, Berlin.

Michelet, Dominique, and Pierre Becquelin 2001 De Río Bec a Dzibilchaltún. Interrogaciones acerca de la ciudad maya clásica desde la perspectiva del Yucatán central y septentrional. In *Reconstruyendo la ciudad maya. El urbanismo en las sociedades antiguas.* Publicaciones de la S.E.E.M, Vol. 6, edited by Andrés Ciudad Ruiz, María Josefa Iglesias Ponce de León, and María del Carmen Martínez Martínez, pp. 211–251. Sociedad Española de Estudios Mayas, Madrid.

Paap, Iken 2017 Archaeological Fieldwork in the Transitional Zone between Puuc and Chenes (Campeche, Mexico). In *Recent Investigations in the Puuc Region of Yucatán.* Pre-Columbian Archaeology Series, edited by Meghan Rubenstein, pp. 87–98. Archaeopress, Oxford.

Pollock, Harry E. D. 1970 Architectural Notes on Some Chenes Ruins. *Papers of the Peabody Museum of American Archaeology and Ethnology* 61:3–87. Harvard University, Cambridge, MA.

Prem, Hanns J. 2003 *Xkipche: una ciudad Maya clásica en el corazón del Puuc. Vol 1. El asentamiento.* Con contribuciones de Nicholas P. Dunning. Instituto Nacional de Antropología e Historia (INAH)/Universität Bonn, México, DF and Bonn.
———— 2007 Un escenario del Clásico Terminal en Yucatán. In *Culturas en movimiento: contribuciones a la transformación de identidades étnicas y culturas en América,* edited by Wiltrud Dresler, Bernd Fähmel, and Karoline Noack, pp. 131–161. Universidad Nacional Autónoma de México and the Ibero-Amerikanisches Institut, Mexico City and Berlin.
Robles Castellanos, Fernando 2006 Las esferas cerámicas Cehpech y Sotuta del apogeo del Clásico Tardío (c. 730–900 d.C.) en el norte de la península de Yucatán. In *La producción alfarera en el México antiguo III.* Colección Científica, Vol. 502, edited by Beatriz Leonor Merino Carrión and Angel García Cook, pp. 281–343. Instituto Nacional de Antropología e Historia, Mexico City.
Ruiz Cazares, Ricardo 2018 *Informe: Análisis antropofísico en los restos óseos del sitio arqueológico Dzehkabtún. Informe técnico.* Manuscript on file, Instituto Nacional de Antropología e Historia, Mexico City.
Ruz Lhuillier, Alberto 1945 *Campeche en la arqueología maya.* Acta Antropológica, Vol. 1. Instituto Nacional de Antropología e Historia, Mexico City.
Seler, Eduard 1912 Anexo No. 3: Informe del primer Director de la Escuela, Sr. Dr. D. Eduardo Seler, al Presidente de la Junta Directiva de la misma. In *Escuela Internacional de Arqueología y Etnología Americanas. Año escolar de 1910 a 1911. Informe del presidente de la junta directive,* pp. 27–32. Müller Hnos., México, DF.

11

FOREIGN ENCOUNTERS

Warfare, trade, and status at Chichen Itza

Annabeth Headrick and John W. Hoopes

The foundations of academic discourse on Chichen Itza are profoundly shaped by a transregional perspective. The title of Alfred Tozzer's (1957) seminal two-volume tome, *Chichen Itza and Its Cenote of Sacrifice: A Comparative Study of Contemporaneous Maya and Toltec*, introduced the city as a place entrenched in two identities.[1] His assertion that the city first had a Yucatan-Maya phase that was followed by a Toltec-Maya period shaped discussions of Chichen Itza until Schele and Freidel (1990) began to challenge this perspective, pressing a Maya-centric vision of the city. We do not attempt to resolve the Maya-Toltec problem, a topic that has generated a wealth of diverse opinions, but instead we address how Chichen Itza recognized a variety of identities, both friend and foe, in its artwork and how this diversity characterized the efforts of the city dwellers to formulate a multivalent, hybrid identity. Furthermore, we explore who the principal actors were in this expansive quest, probing the role of military agents as both warriors and merchants.[2]

Two locales within Chichen Itza form the basis for our discussion of identity at this city. The first is the Temple of the Warriors and its earlier manifestation, the Temple of the Chacmool, and the second is the Sacred Cenote. In the case of the first, these structures with their numerous carved and colored columns, painted murals, and other free-standing sculpture offer a wealth of images. Many were intended as portraits, even if they do not precisely meet the criteria of portraiture on all levels (Charlot 1931; Schele and Freidel 1990:502, note 42). The Cenote of Sacrifice is famous for the many offerings deposited in its waters, including well-known gold disks. These disks portray narrative scenes in which the Itza pictured themselves juxtaposed with people perceived as quite different from themselves. The very medium upon which these scenes appear indicates that trade and resource acquisition were an essential motivator behind foreign interaction.[3] Building upon the themes of identity and violence discussed

DOI: 10.4324/9781351268004-11

in this volume, the materials of Chichen Itza suggest that identity was firmly intertwined with violence. Moreover, the perception that someone was foreign enhanced the value of directing violence toward that individual.

The Temple of the Warriors

The sculpture: wealth, status, and the military

The Temple of the Warriors (Figure 11.1) is one of the most important structures for understanding the socio-economic organization of Chichen Itza. In addition, it offers clues to the vast extent that the Itza engaged in international trade as they sought to expand resources, including the exotic goods so coveted by elites.[4] We demonstrate that the military played an important role in, and appears to have been one of the main benefactors of, what we loosely call trade. In some cases, visual imagery suggests that these encounters are best described as warfare, and the Itza military often may have taken what it wanted as it overpowered those who resisted. Furthermore, there is evidence that the Itza celebrated such forced acquisitions, thereby normalizing this strategy in their efforts to expand the luxury goods accessible to their population.

It is a curious aspect of archaeology that the names applied to precolumbian architecture often are fanciful and romantic and do not accurately reflect their true function. Nonetheless, in the case of the Temple of the Warriors, the name is not unwarranted because members of the military figure prominently in its decoration.[5] The many columns that once held up the roof of its hypostyle hall are replete with militant figures (Figure 11.2). Relief carvings decorate each of the square columns in front of the temple, with a different figure depicted on all four sides. Originally finished with a coating of plaster followed by pigments applied

FIGURE 11.1 Temple of the Warriors, Chichen Itza.

Source: Photo by Annabeth Headrick.

FIGURE 11.2 Column 40, Northwest Colonnade, Temple of the Warriors, Chichen Itza.

Source: After Morris et al. 1931:Plate 106.

to the various details, the relief sculptures would have presented an incredible variety of figures with an impressive array of color that made the features easier to see, particularly in the darkened hall when the roof was intact.[6] Of the 55 sculpted columns in the Northwest Colonnade in front of the Temple of the Warriors, Charlot (1931:268) identified 161 of the 220 portraits, that is, 73 percent, as images of warriors. Given that an additional 30 portraits depict prisoners who may have been warriors captured in battle, the percentage of columns representing warriors may be higher.[7] Column 40 of the Northwest Colonnade offers a rather typical depiction of the military figures on the columns.[8] The artists depicted each figure with one foot before the other, and this, in combination with the mass of figures carved on the columns, suggests that the figures walk in a procession (Charlot 1931; Schele and Freidel 1990:36).

The framing elements above and below each figure indicate that the Itza perceived this procession as a sacred one, surrounded by a supernatural aura. Above each figure, militant beings portrayed in profile wield atlatls and darts – the weapons of warfare. These warriors only appear half-bodied, as they descend from the sky through an early manifestation of a solar disk. The feathered circumference and the triangular rays are markedly similar to the solar disks seen in Late Postclassic art.[9] Because of their partial nature and their emanation from the solar element, these figures arguably represent ancestral figures who have a dual human aspect and supernatural essence.[10] If Aztec myths emerged from earlier traditions, it is possible that these figures represent deceased warriors who died either on the battlefield or as sacrificial victims and have the honor of accompanying the sun from dawn to dusk each day.[11] They may therefore represent a cosmological model.

Below the processing individuals are frontal figures who squat with their forearms bent at the elbow. These forelimbs end in bird claws, and feathers extend from the tops of their heads and fall to either side. A human face festooned with large earflares, and sometimes with goggle-like Tlaloc eyes, emerges from the mouth of a fantastic being whose nostrils have distinct emanations or beaded projections. This figure appears frequently at Chichen Itza, including on the upper façade of the Temple of the Warriors and on the Venus platforms associated with the Castillo and the Osario. Charlot (1931:272) and Klein (2019) identify this figure as Queztalcoatl, while Schele and Mathews (1998:215) see this as the legged fire serpent, or Xiuhcoatl in the Nahuatl language of the Aztecs, with a warrior emerging from its mouth. In framing these figures, Itza artists follow a long history of placing human ritual participants within a cosmological context. At sites like Formative period Cival, rulers stood on temples festooned with deity masks, effectively placing their physical bodies among the gods (Estrada-Belli 2011:84–116). Likewise, stelae at Formative Izapa recorded performances by the ruling elite and repeatedly sandwiched these events between celestial and basal bands (Guernsey 2006:77–79). As emphasized by Schele and Freidel (1990:364), the stelae at Chichen Itza differ from those of Classic Maya sites where the primary actor is the ruler. Instead, columns of the Temple of the Warriors depict many other actors, most notably the numerous warriors.

The most obvious elements that identify these figures as warriors are the atlatl and darts that many of them carry. On Column 40, each figure carries an atlatl in his right hand, which mirrors the common handedness of most people. The left hand grasps a cluster of at least two atlatl darts, and this arm sometimes has a shield (north) or puffy wrap (east, west, south) for protection. Circular back mirrors, or *tezcacuitlapilli* in Nahuatl, are another frequent element of military costume, a tradition that stems from the costume of warriors at Classic period Teotihuacan. The figure on the western face of Column 40 wears such a mirror on the small of his back. On Column 17 (Figure 11.3) from the inside of the

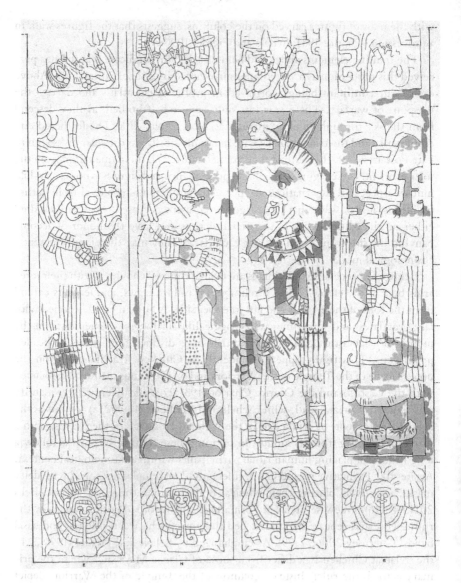

FIGURE 11.3 Column 17, Temple of the Warriors, Chichen Itza.

Source: After Morris et al. 1931:Plate 59.

Temple of the Warriors proper, two other elements surviving from the Teoti-huacan iconography of war appear. Two figures (east, north) have the circular Tlaloc "goggles" associated with the central Mexican rain god and agricultur-ally associated warfare (Schele and Freidel 1990). One of them (east) wears a full Tlaloc mask, replete with the fanged upper jaw of this deity. A third figure on this column (south) sports a distinctive year sign headdress, another military symbol adopted from central Mexico.[12] Elsewhere within the colonnade some

FIGURE 11.4 Column 37, Northwest Colonnade, Temple of the Warriors, Chichen Itza.

Source: After Morris et al. 1931:Plate 103.

warriors carry war clubs embedded with sharp stone blades, but by far, the atlatl is the most common military weapon.

The numerous figures dressed as warriors convey a sense of overwhelming force and military domination, and the few captives surrounded by the armed warriors and clustered near the stairs to the temple only heighten this effect. In all, 30 captives, likely the unfortunate victims of military activities, also process within the hypostyle hall (Figure 11.4). Each captive is richly costumed, some as richly as their captors, but their weapons, if they once had them, have been confiscated.[13] Invariably, each of these figures holds his hands before him, and rope binds the hands together in a clear sign of subjugation.

Even though members of the military and their captives dominate the surfaces of the columns, it would be disingenuous to suggest that every figure sculpted on the columns of the Temple of the Warriors fought as a warrior; a number of figures hold other social positions. Among them, Charlot (1931) identified priests, dignitaries, and what he called sorcerers. Whether these labels precisely capture their roles, those designated as priests do wear long skirts and have heavy collars around their necks. Some carry bowls filled with offerings, revealing that these individuals are part of ritual activities (Charlot 1931:Plate 52). On Column 16 within the temple (Figure 11.5), an aged woman with a sagging, wrinkled stomach wears a shorter skirt than the male priests and probably has a spindle whorl inserted into her hair (Charlot 1931:Plate 58). The elderly woman leans on a staff and carries what might be a water jar. Although these individuals likely hold a higher status than the warriors and may conduct the pivotal ceremonies, they are still enveloped in the overall military symbolism of the structure. For example, on Column 16, where the elderly woman brings her offering, three warriors with back mirrors, atlatls, and atlatl darts accompany her on the other sides of the column. The priests and ritual officials are in what seems to be considered the house of the military, and their activities are meant to celebrate those warriors and their deeds.

The temple and its hypostyle hall, therefore, were a place to memorialize the warriors through the permanence of stone sculpture. The decoration of the columns suggests that a primary function of the hall was for the assembly and procession of the very people depicted on the columns. The hieroglyphic names accompanying certain figures indicate that at least some of the sculptures record the participation of particular, historical individuals or specific representatives of lineages in the rituals (Charlot 1931:311; Coggins 1984a:162–163; Kristan-Graham 1989:197–200, 2001:345–350; Lincoln 1986:154; Tozzer 1930:151). As time passed, other human actors may have taken on the roles of the original individuals, but nevertheless, the decoration offers a precise document of the actual events that took place in the columned hall.

Before the roof collapsed, wooden beams sat upon the columns, and three stone corbel vaults, running north to south, sprang from these wooden beams (E. Morris 1931:15). Considering the nature of Maya architecture before this time, very few people had the opportunity to enter interior spaces during ritual events. Due to the physical limitations of the corbel vault, Maya interior spaces were relatively small, leading to speculation that only a select few elites actually entered the interior spaces during ritual, while the vast majority of the population watched these events in the large plazas below. One of the most revolutionary aspects of the Temple of the Warriors is that the hypostyle hall affords an intermediate space, which is not quite in the temple proper above, but not open and undifferentiated like the plaza outside. Under the expansive roof of the hypostyle hall, the priests, dignitaries, and, most importantly, the militantly dressed warriors were invited inside an architectural space in numbers that are fairly unprecedented in Maya history. Both open to the plaza where the majority

FIGURE 11.5 Column 16, Temple of the Warriors, Chichen Itza.

Source: After Morris et al. 1931:Plate 58.

of the population stood and physically connected to the upper temple where perhaps important leaders met, the covered, interior space of the hall afforded a sense of status and differentiation to those inside and recognized what was likely a growing middle-elite at Chichen Itza. Because of the figurative decoration on the columns, warriors were always present through their images on sculpture, a medium that was usually reserved for royal elites in the Classic Maya past. In sum, the larger interior space and its decoration form one of the clearest articulations of a new social organization in the Maya area where individuals who played a military role rose in status and, therefore, had greater prominence in the architecture and visual art of the city.

The costume of these sculpted warriors serves as additional evidence of their elevated social standing. The processing warriors on the column surfaces are richly dressed. Diverse headdresses grace their heads and signal not only their identity and status but also that they had the economic means to acquire such finery. Sprays of feathers abound, flying over the heads of the warriors from their headgear and dropping from their waists. Some figures have lavish cloaks that appear to be made of feathers, while others have short cloaks over their shoulders or wear a triangular garment resembling the Aztec *quechquemitl*. Quite frequently the warriors have soft, furry pads that wrap around their ankles, below their knees, and on their left arm, the latter presumably for protection in place of a shield. On other occasions dangling elements that probably are copper bells, a material imported to the northern lowlands of Yucatan, encircle their legs below the knee. Numerous figures wear a variety of elaborate breastplates, many of which appear repeatedly, indicating that they designate different group affiliations. Jeweled necklaces, large earflares, and pierced nose ornaments round out these elaborate costumes. The message conveyed by these sumptuously attired warriors is one of remarkable wealth, a statement of status heightened by the fact that they flaunt this affluence in a very public place.

That Maya warriors clad themselves in sumptuous costume is not a new observation, for many exquisitely dressed military figures appear on Late Classic Maya polychrome vessels.[14] Polychrome ceramic vessels were high-status and likely coveted items. If owned by a member of the military, such a vessel and its imagery would have conveyed the elevated status of its owner. The small scale of cylinder vessels limits their efficacy in transmitting status and restricts their visual reading to a small audience in more direct contact with such personal objects. During this period a few warriors increasingly appear on sculpture, but rulers generally accompany them (Martin and Grube 2000:130–131; Schele and Freidel 1990:262–305). For example, on Lintel 8 from Yaxchilan, K'an Tok Wayib' shares the stage with Bird Jaguar and two captives, but the costuming of the king and his vassal makes clear that the king is the more important figure. That this lintel could be seen only when entering a private space is a critical point; such sculptures rarely were public. The Bonampak murals include numerous warriors in the lavish three-room sequence decorating a public structure. That said, the corbel vaulting and doorways limit the viewership of these murals, making them more restrictive than the open colonnade at Chichen Itza, and only a few people can stand in each room at once. As Victoria Lyall (2011) has argued, several Terminal Classic sites in the northern Yucatan continued the southern Maya tradition of mural painting seen at sites like Bonampak. Murals found at Ichmac, Mulchic, and Chacmultun date to AD 750–880 and depict complex battle scenes with a remarkable graphic quality. But again, these appear in small chambers. Thus, Late and Terminal Classic art consistently celebrated the societal role of warriors but in restricted spaces and on small objects seen only by a few. The distinct difference at Early Postclassic Chichen Itza is that the portrayals of individual warriors and their extravagant costumes appear in public sculptural art and in comparatively vast quantities. That artists carved, plastered, and painted these hundreds of images cannot be undervalued, because the extra labor of sculptural programs conveys the increased social value of these warriors to the city.

The lavish wealth displayed on the bodies of the warriors reveals that the role of the military was not solely ideological or protective, but that the military of Chichen Itza focused on the acquisition of that wealth. Their costumes convey prosperity, and presumably, like many warriors in human history, the individuals who fought in the battles shared in the spoils of war. Yet looking closer to home for Mesoamerican parallels, a more accurate model would be that of the *pochteca*. The Aztec *pochteca* were essentially merchant-warriors who moved throughout Mesoamerica engaging in trade with an armed contingent. In the Aztec case, these *pochteca* sometimes functioned as spies, acquiring information about particular locales and their peoples. This intelligence later allowed the military to move into a territory, defeat it, and impose a less balanced, tribute relationship (Sahagún 1950–1982:Book 9). This Aztec model has been profitably applied to cultures that preceded the Late Postclassic. For example, Clara Millon tentatively suggested that figures from Teotihuacan wearing a tassel headdress functioned similarly to the *pochteca*.[15] Various analyses of a vessel found in Problematic Deposit 50 from Tikal offer convincing evidence that she was correct (Coggins 1975, 1979b; Schele and Freidel 1990:161–162; Stuart 2000). That vessel shows tassel headdress-wearing figures carrying Teotihuacan-style vessels who are accompanied by militarily clad figures. As they reach an arguably Maya elite, most likely at Tikal, one figure seems to proffer long quetzal feathers in exchange. This convincing application of a Postclassic warrior-trader model to the Early Classic period supports the contention that Itza warriors not only might have served as military figures, but also engaged in trade-related activities. Such a precedent as well as their rich costuming indicates that at Chichen Itza, military activities were profoundly entangled with the strategies of trade and resource acquisition.

The murals: coastal interactions and resources

Moving from the sculpted art of the Temple of the Warriors to mural art, there is ample evidence that Itza soldiers, like the Aztec *pochteca*, were deployed to distant realms in search of ever more exotic goods. In particular, the mural art from the inner sanctuary of the Temple of the Warriors had a significant portion dedicated to documenting military exploits. Interestingly, large portions of these murals record that the military of Chichen Itza had an important naval role; several include coastal scenes.

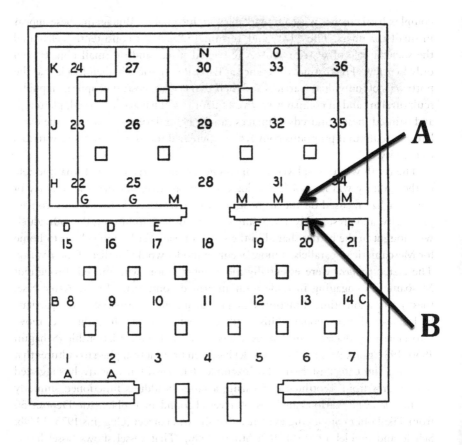

FIGURE 11.6 Plan of the upper Temple of the Warriors indicating the location of the mural fragments: coast scene (A), water battles, and sacrifice scene (B).

Source: B; adapted from Morris et al. 1931:Volume I:Figure 272.

One of the best-known of these murals came from an inner wall that divided the temple proper into two sections (Figure 11.6). Found on the southern wall in the innermost chamber (Area 31), facing to the east, the mural includes certain elements that reveal the strategies that Itza artists employed to develop different identities in their subjects. The original murals no longer exist because they were damaged before they could be properly preserved. They are known today through the color reproductions made by Ann Axtell Morris (Figure 11.7).[16]

To set the location, a variety of fish and shellfish move through the water in the lower section. These as well as the stingrays and crabs are clear markers that the scene depicts a coastal town rather than navigation along a freshwater passage (Ardren and Lowry 2011; Aztzin Martinez 2005:79; A. Morris 1931:423–424). Extensive archaeological work corroborates this identification. Excavations have securely identified an Itza presence along the coast of Yucatan. Documented

FIGURE 11.7 Mural with coastal scene, Temple of the Warriors, Chichen Itza.

Source: After Morris et al. 1931:Plate 159.

ports like Isa Cerritos provide clear evidence that the Itza maintained a coastal presence for economic and military purposes.[17]

Of particular note in this mural is the manner in which the artist has distinguished the individuals by using two different pigments for the skin tones of the figures. The skin of most of the figures appears a warm beige, however, others have a darker umber complexion. It is interesting to note that the figures with the lighter skin appear to be engaged in work or performing routine tasks. For example, two of the male figures on shore use tumplines to carry heavy burdens. A female near the center of the image oversees a cooking pot, and even though a fragment near the top has suffered damage, a light-skinned woman grinds what was most likely corn on a *metate*. Out on the water in the front of the canoes, lighter-skinned individuals have the sole task of paddling through the coastal waters. Furthermore, their simple loincloths, compared to the full garments of their passengers, reflect the lower status of the lighter-skinned oarsmen (A. Morris 1931:423).

In contrast, the darker-skinned individuals seem to hold positions of higher authority. Pairs of dark warriors holding shields, atlatls, and darts stand in the canoes acting like entitled passengers, perfectly content to let their light-skinned companions perform the work of propelling the canoes. Above, two dark-skinned figures inhabit the largest structure in the village, whose importance is further articulated by the feathered serpent iconography of its walls and the large serpent wending its way through the building to the air above (A. Morris 1931:425). The sole frontal figure in the image sits inside this building with another figure facing him to denote his prestige. Frontality was a common trope in Maya art to indicate the primary figure in a scene and, coupled with the elaborate feathered serpent imagery of the building, indicates that this individual is probably the one with the most authority (Spinden 1975).

This mural provides tangible evidence that the Itza military had a mercantile as well as naval aspect.[18] Taken as a whole we see military figures in canoes, clearly demonstrating that the military of Chichen Itza traveled not only by foot but also by ocean-worthy sea craft. There is evidence on the shore that the purpose of their travel was to obtain goods from distant lands. Although they are somewhat indistinct and therefore difficult to identify, bundles with straps to secure their contents rest above two seated women in the upper left section of the mural and along the shoreline. Not surprisingly, a pile of fish sits near the coastline on the right, and another basketful of fish appears inside one of the houses at the center (A. Morris 1931:425). The individuals with the tumplines could be carrying local goods, or they might be participating in the distribution of the trade items from far-flung locales. The walking staff of the man in the upper left is a common feature of Mesoamerican merchants and God L, the patron of merchants, thus their association with long-distance trade is very likely.

The military played a critical role in coastal trade and acquisition of goods. Much like the model of the *pochteca*, the Itza probably employed an armed merchant class to move valuable goods through hostile territories. The fact that this mural appears within the Temple of the Warriors, where images of the military figure prominently, is further testament to the argument that trade was a central responsibility of an Itza warrior. At Chichen Itza, many of the armed men pictured on the carved columns most likely were hardened seamen who traveled to distant lands as they endeavored to bring ever more exotic materials into the city.

Before proceeding to other associated murals, the discussion of skin tone in the murals of Chichen Itza requires some degree of delicacy and a note of caution. We do not in any way imply that Western notions of skin color or ethnicity can be applied to murals painted a thousand years ago. Furthermore, we do not subscribe to the notion that early Europeans or Lost Tribes traveled to the Americas before the time of the conquest. Rather, we emphasize that the artists of this and other murals intentionally marked different identities; these conventions express something like the notion of "us" and "them," or "elites" and "commoners."[19] The need for such a cautionary statement becomes clear with the next set of murals that came from the area on the opposite side of the wall depicting the coastal town.

To their right and in the anteroom, visitors entering the upper Temple of the Warriors would have seen a mural sequence depicting a naval battle and its aftermath. Morris (A. Morris 1931:398–404) largely described and identified the sequence of events in these fragmented murals, but their implications warrant revisiting. Beginning on the southern section of the wall (Figure 11.6, Areas 20 and 21), a large fragment shows a narrative scene taking place in the water (Figure 11.8). At the bottom is a white band punctuated by small black loops, which Morris identified as foam on water. To the right of the scene are portions of two

FIGURE 11.8   Mural with water battle and canoes, Temple of the Warriors, Chichen Itza.

Source: After Morris et al. 1931:Plate 146.

canoes with their typical curled prows.[20] One of these canoes is more intact and dives down in the center of the mural, while only the prow of the other canoe juts into the scene on the right. Clearly visible in the larger canoe are portions of three round shields. These are reminiscent of the shields held by the passengers in the canoes cruising by the coastal town (Figure 11.7), which indicate that the voyagers were warriors. In this mural, however, the artist included the target of these sailors. In the left portion is an unfortunate-looking male who seems to have been thrown from whatever vehicle once conveyed him. Positioned spread-eagled in the water, he is fully naked and suffers the humiliation of having his genitals exposed. His face conveys a slight caricature with a large, prominent nose, and his whole being seems menaced not only by the warriors in the advancing canoe, but also by the large, open-mouthed fish that threatens to bite his arm. Quite curiously, a long cascade of golden hair falls from his head. The incredible length and the careful manner in which the artist punctuated the hair with green beads suggests that this unusual coiffure was of particular interest to the artist and the audience of the mural.

Although broken and fragmented when the Carnegie archaeologists encountered the mural, additional portions emerged from the debris within the structure (Figure 11.9). In each of these artists explicitly depicted figures in the water, rather than riding in a vessel. Feet and arms appear with a watery background, and although complete bodies are no longer preserved, the more complete mural fragment suggests that these figures also fell into the sea. The nakedness of the unfortunate figures also continues, as accentuated by a bare arm grasped by a hand attached to a clothed or painted arm above it. The appearance of additional fair-haired figures indicates that these mural fragments are part of the same epic battle (A. Morris 1931:398; Shatto 1998:221–222). Two of the blond figures have the same green

FIGURE 11.9 Mural fragments of capture in the water, Temple of the Warriors, Chichen Itza.

Source: After Morris et al. 1931:Plate 147b–d.

beads in their hair, and one of these suffers the ignominious fate of having that hair grasped by another. This well-known Mesoamerican symbol of capture, along with another figure who has his hands bound behind his back, definitively relates that the light-haired individuals are defeated by the warriors in the canoes. Here again, the extant faces exhibit large or elongated noses that are not particularly flattering, and their open mouths might even express their cries of dismay.

Just to the north of these naval scenes (Figure 11.6, Area 19), archaeologists found what is arguably the final scene in this sequence of events (A. Morris 1931:398–402). In this image (Figure 11.10) the artist explicitly portrays the sacrifice of a fair-haired victim. The unfortunate man lies on his back with his chest arched to tighten the abdominal muscles and facilitate a more efficient heart extraction. His long golden hair, studded with green beads, sweeps back off his head to cascade down under his body. Two figures restrain the sacrificial victim, one at his feet and one securing his arms. These have darkened skin, like Postclassic Mixtec involved in priestly activities, including sacrifice (Herrera y Tordesillas 1945:165–173). Tozzer (1941:152; Note 378) explained that Itza warriors, priests, and fasting individuals would paint their bodies black. In addition, a third figure, only partially visible, hovers over the victim and has a blackened arm. The remains of his headdress include a circular device and three white feathers with black tips and green stripes that might depict beads. Part of his ensemble includes a trail of feathers down his back, which further conveys his elevated status. His position is clearly explained through the actions of his raised left hand that holds a large, somewhat indeterminate weapon. This individual is the chief executioner who, as Landa recorded, "struck him with a great skill and cruelty a blow between the ribs of his left side under the nipple, and he at

FIGURE 11.10 Mural with sacrifice scene, Temple of the Warriors, Chichen Itza.

Source: After Morris et al. 1931:Plate 145.

once plunged his hand in there and, like a raging jaguar, seized the heart and snatched it out alive."[21] Although Landa's tone is judgmental and sensationalist, it seems reasonable that such events were designed to evoke a sense of horror and fascination, and the actor who conducted the sacrifice surely used some theatrical elements to heighten the impact on the viewers.[22] In Landa's account, the individuals holding the captive are called "*Chacs*," and while the scene only shows two figures involved in the restraint, both Landa (Tozzer 1941:112) and

Sahagún documented that the Maya and Aztec employed four people to hold a victim of heart sacrifice, one for each extremity.[23] Thus it is likely that in the mural of Chichen Itza, the artist simplified the scene in consideration of the two-dimensional nature of painting, and the original viewers mentally included the missing two *Chacs*. A scene on one of the gold disks from the Great Cenote is further testament that four priests restrained the victim. On Disk H (Lothrop 1952:Figure 1; Pillsbury et al. 2017:Cat. 171), four men prominently wearing back mirrors hold each limb of the sacrificial victim who arches over a stone as a bird-clad priest removes his heart. As we will show, events depicted in the murals of the Temple of the Warriors are closely related to the gold disks, so the sacrificial victim shown on Disk H could be the same individual arched over the stone in the mural painting.

An emerald-green feathered serpent that rises above the sacrificial priest, across his body, and under the victim activates the space and gives it a supernatural air and a sense of sacredness. The feathered serpent decorates many of the public buildings in Early Postclassic Chichen Itza and seems to have been a patron deity or the focus of a cult during this period (Ringle et al. 1998). Underneath the serpent and the victim is the first clue that the setting is no longer in coastal waters. The victim arches his back over the well-known stone used to perform heart sacrifice, and this stone is most certainly the very one found in the hallway of the Temple of the Warriors (Figure 11.11). Morris first suggested that this stone and the other architectural references in the scene indicate that this victim lost his life at Chichen Itza, if not at this very temple (A. Morris 1931:400). Near the top of the mural fragment

FIGURE 11.11 Sacrificial stone, Temple of the Warriors, Chichen Itza.

Source: Photo by Annabeth Headrick.

is a decorative band not unlike the Puuc architectural elements seen at the top of many structures in the city. Below this is a red doorway that may represent the door to the temple proper that people accessed via a set of stairs rising above the hypostyle hall. The sacrificial stone, found *in situ* before an altar to the right of these stairs, sits on a lower level than the door, just as it does in the painted image (E. Morris 1931:56). Although the sacrificial stone was not directly below the door, as it is in the mural, the artist may have taken liberties and given an approximation more than a completely faithful representation of the space.

The implications of the Temple of the Warriors as the place of sacrifice are quite profound. The murals indicate that after the naval battle, the victorious Itza brought at least one of their light-haired captives back to Chichen Itza for sacrifice. The detailed and consistent depiction of the golden and often beaded hair suggests that they had a fascination with these individuals, and the transport of at least one individual back to the city allowed the greater populace to witness the exotic prisoner and his death. Such a sacrifice within the city would convey the far reach of the Itza military and its ability to subdue and dominate peoples from distant and exotic locales. That an artist recorded the battle and the execution of at least one figure on the wall of the upper temple indicates that this was an epic event in Itza history worthy of historic documentation. Moreover, the location of the mural in the temple above the stone where the actual event took place chronicles the history and function of the building, signaling that this encounter with these light-haired people was of sufficient import to warrant singling it out among other sacrificial events that doubtlessly took place there. The mural is in dialogue with the other decoration of the building, offering a greater narrative about the function of the military at Chichen Itza. Because the columns below in the hallway record a procession of figures who were predominantly warriors, the pillars include portraits of captives surrounded by warriors, and the murals above picture warriors attacking figures in the water who are subsequently sacrificed at Chichen, we see a structure that celebrates militant deeds in faraway places, the acquisition of foreign sacrificial prisoners, and the warriors who conducted the battles and facilitated the captures. Perhaps the ever-exotic nature of the captives they brought home and the more distant regions they engaged would explain the new prominence that warriors received at the city. The Temple of the Warriors and its hypostyle hall created a space where warriors could publicly conduct ritual, and their accomplishments and portraits recorded in the building were given a visible prominence not seen to this degree before in the Maya area.

The Temple of the Chacmool

A foreign captive in stone

The Temple of the Chacmool, an earlier manifestation of the Temple of the Warriors, serves as testament to the fact that this practice of acquiring prisoners from distant lands preceded the later temple. As the Carnegie archaeologists

FIGURE 11.12 Two views of the chacmool from the Temple of the Chacmool, Chichen Itza.

Source: Gift of the Carnegie Institution of Washington, 1958. © President and Fellows of Harvard College, Peabody Museum of Archaeology and Ethnology, Harvard University, PM 58-34-20/31614 (left), courtesy of Jeremy Coltman (right).

excavated in the earlier temple, they found a sculpted chacmool (Figure 11.12), which the Itza had dragged into the inner sanctum and tipped on its side before burying the earlier temple (E. Morris 1931:160). Conceived in the typical form, this chacmool lies on its back with its knees propped up as he gazes over his right shoulder, his hands rising up to hold a disk on his stomach. Mary Miller (1985) cogently argued that such figures likely depict captured warriors whose humble position conveys their captive state and ultimate sacrifice. This chacmool has trophy heads dangling down each of his thighs, as a suggestion of his previous military victories and identity as a warrior. Interestingly, he wears a nose bar through his septum. In central Mexico and the Mixteca regions persons holding the title of *tecuhtli*, or lineage head, wore such nose ornaments. Thus, the chacmool may record an individual of high status (Byland and Pohl 1994:147; Carrasco 1966:134–135, 1971; Muñoz Camargo 1892:104; Pohl 1994:89–93).[24] Such indications of the wealth and military prowess of the figure indicate that this was a high-value captive with considerable prestige and further explain why he warranted documentation in the permanence of stone.

The most striking feature of this otherwise rather conventional depiction is the headdress worn by the chacmool. It consists of a round disk with an edge punctuated by small squares. Over the nose of the reclining figure, the brim of this hat rises to a V to meet an emanation falling from the mouth of an animal atop the headdress. In striking fashion, the animal lies on the headdress in a splayed manner with its arms and legs jutting out to the sides of its body. While animal headdresses are commonplace in Maya art, the splayed nature of its legs seems anomalous and more closely resembles depictions of caimans in the art of precolumbian Costa Rica and Panama. In addition, animals with similarly splayed bodies appear in imagery such as a gold disk from the collection of the Denver Art Museum, reported to be from Costa Rica (Figure 11.13a), and also on a gold helmet reportedly from Darién, Panama (Figure 11.13b). Similarly, a standing stone figure from Costa Rica in the collections of the American Museum of Natural History depicts an additional example of an elite wearing a headdress festooned with a reptile (Figure 11.14). In the case of the sculpture, the male figure wears earspools, and on his head a coiled serpent with the diamond pattern of a tropical rattlesnake forms the wide band of the headdress. The menacing teeth of the serpent, in even rows more typical in representations of crocodiles than of snakes, are visibly depicted, although the tail is not clearly indicated. Crowning the broad serpent band is an animal that could be construed either as a crocodile or as an iguana. Rather than fully splayed like the one on the head of the figure from the Temple of the Chacmool, this reptile braces itself on its front legs, and its long tail hangs down the back of the figure. A series of striations carved on the upper portion of the body could be construed as the spines of an iguana rather than the scutes of a crocodile. The bared teeth on the head of the creature, nevertheless, indicate that the artist intended to convey the fierce nature of the reptile. We argue, then, that the chacmool from the earlier temple depicts an individual considered foreign, perhaps a person from Costa Rica, where saurians and especially crocodilians are more frequent in the iconography – and much more commonly represented than elsewhere at Chichen Itza. His origin in an exotic and distant land further explains his memorialization in stone and serves as evidence that the merchant-warriors of Chichen Itza pushed beyond the boundaries of the traditional Maya realm in their quest for captives and most likely resources.

The gold disks

Sacrifice the foreigner

The Temple of the Chacmool and the Temple of the Warriors, then, may have been the locus of activities associated with the military and the sacrifice of their captives. Furthermore, the murals and the earlier chacmool reveal a penchant to celebrate exotic captives with features considered foreign to the Itza, and they may also indicate that Itza warriors brought some of these unusual captives back

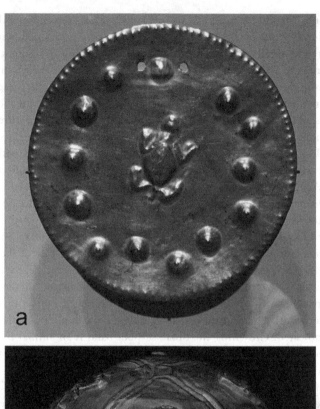

FIGURE 11.13 Gold disk pendant (a) with bossed splayed animal design, Greater Chiriqui, Costa Rica or Panama, AD 800–1522; gold helmet (b), possibly from Coclé, Darién, Panama, AD 700–1000.

Source: Denver Art Museum, Gift of the Collection of Frederick and Jan Mayer, 1995.631; Anonymous Gift and Gift of Thomas Barbour, 1933, photo © President and Fellows of Harvard College, Peabody Museum of Archaeology and Ethnology, Harvard University, PM 33-1-20/209.

FIGURE 11.14   Stone standing figure with reptile and serpent headdress (left), and detail of head (right), Costa Rica, ca. AD 1000–1500.

Source: Photos by John W. Hoopes.

to their city to document their distant victories and impress upon the population the far reach of the Itza military. In the case of the captives with beaded hair, their story continues on the famous gold disks found in the Sacred Cenote. The gold disks came from the dredging and limited diving conducted by Edward Thompson from 1904 to 1909.[25] As part of the actions associated with their deposition

FIGURE 11.15 Disk D, Sacred Cenote, Chichen Itza. Drawing of repoussé-decorated sheet gold disk.

Source: After Lothrop 1952:Figure 32.

in the cenote, the thin disks were crumpled and burned, perhaps as a way of destroying them or transforming their power or meaning as they became offerings to the watery underworld (Coggins 1984a:28–29). Through painstaking drawings made by Helen Gleason and Tatiana Proskouriakoff, the imagery of the disks appears, and they show scenes that are arguably made by Itza artists (Figure 11.15).[26] This is important to note because we have no evidence of metallurgy at Chichen Itza, thus they probably acquired the gold disks already made and decorated them in their own style through a repoussé technique, possibly under the instruction or supervision of foreign artisans familiar with this method.[27]

Chief among the Maya stylistic elements is the frequent appearance of a celestial serpent above and an earth monster below the central scene (Lothrop 1952:32–37). Some of the disks have hieroglyphs, but they may not fully function as literate texts and fall into the category of pseudoglyphs (Proskouriakoff 1952).

The figures in the central sections of the disks nicely mirror individuals seen in the relief carvings of the Temple of the Warriors. For instance, on Disk D, the main, largest figure, just to the left of center, wears a stepped headdress with a descending bird on the front that frequently appears on the warrior costumes of the hypostyle hall. This figure has a smaller attendant behind him, and a serpent glides alongside to further impress the audience with his importance. He holds three lances that he uses to threaten the figure in front of him. The latter wears a large deer headdress with feathers spouting from its mouth, and he turns his rather ugly, misshapen head toward his tormentor. Further accentuating his large, oafish face is some stippling that may represent tattooing or body paint. Apart from his distorted head, nothing stands out as unusual or foreign about his costume, except the hair falling down the back of his head. Round beads stud this hair, and on his left hand, there is an additional hank of beaded hair. We posit that this beaded hair along with the caricatured face indicates that this fellow bears some association with the beaded-hair individuals depicted in the murals of the Temple of the Warriors. Moreover, the manner in which the larger figure threatens him might suggest that the Itza cut his exotic hair as some form of humiliation and forced him to carry it in this procession. The figure to the far right confirms that the military has a role in these activities, because the captive is led forward at spearpoint.

A sacrificial scene with another beaded-hair figure appears on Disk M (Figure 11.16). As on Disk D, the hair is decidedly shorter than in the painted versions, perhaps indicating that this figure too has had his locks shorn. Although the extant imagery does not include the sacrificial stone, we can still assume that the individual was ultimately the victim of heart sacrifice. A human, whose face peeks out of the beak of his bird costume, extends his claw toward the man's beaded chest in an extraordinarily threatening manner.[28] Ruth Krochock (1988) identified this bird as the Knife-Wing Bird and demonstrated its frequency in the art of Chichen Itza. Rex Koontz (2009:96–104) later wrote of these bird impersonators in the contemporary art of El Tajin in Veracruz, arguing that they are featured actors in a narrative of courtly rites of accession and sacrifice. More recently, Jesper Nielsen and Christophe Helmke (2015) composed a compelling essay in which they pulled together the tradition of the Principal Bird Deity of Formative and Classic times with the threatening sacrificial birds of the Terminal to Early Postclassic.[29] They suggest that living peoples may have sought to access the powers of the Great Bird. Thus, in this scene on the gold disk, the priest wearing the costume of the deity also manifested the predatory and sacrificial powers of the bird. Nielsen and Helmke (2015) have further argued that variations of the myth appear not only in Mesoamerica, but also in Amerindian cultures of North and South America. In light of the potential Isthmo-Colombian identification of the chacmool headdress, it is interesting to note that anthropomorphic bird imagery has a similarly long history in Costa Rica, beginning with jadeite celtiform pendants in the Preclassic and the Early Classic and continuing in the form of cast gold-alloy avian pendants contemporary with

FIGURE 11.16 Disk M, Sacred Cenote, Chichen Itza. Drawing of repoussé-decorated sheet gold disk.

Source: After Lothrop 1952:Figure 42.

the Early and Late Postclassic periods (Hoopes 2017). The latter also were used in northern Colombia, so also may relate to Chibchan or South American traditions. Altogether, the appearance of the predatory bird sacrificer indicates that Chichen Itza likely participated in a mythical tradition with a vast geographical range. On Disk M, it is clear that the beaded-hair figure met his fate at the hands of a figure wearing the costume of the Great Bird, thereby positioning this death in a mythical narrative with ancient and widespread roots.

A canoe, rafts, and a battle at sea

Disk G (Figure 11.17) provides critical information because the narrative scene on its surface is more elaborate and comparable to the murals in the Temple of the

FIGURE 11.17 Disk G, Sacred Cenote, Chichen Itza. Drawing of repoussé-decorated sheet gold disk.

Source: After Lothrop 1952:Figure 35.

Warriors. At the top of the disk is a winding feathered serpent and a flying figure dressed as the Great Bird, armed with atlatl and darts. Below this is another naval battle with two distinct types of vessels. To the right is a familiar Maya dugout canoe conveying five people within its hull. Two figures in the back propel the canoe with their long paddles as a third stands in the middle with his atlatl and darts. Two more individuals sit in the bow of the boat holding shields, although the front figure risks falling out as he bends over the prow in pursuit of his prey. Just outside of his reach crouches a man on a floating platform or paddleboard novel to the Maya area. This vessel consists of what appears to be a flat surface buoyed by two semi-circular forms that may be cross-sections of halved balsa logs, looking more like a raft than a canoe. The pursued man desperately tries to fend off his attackers with a long paddle, and his other hand holds a round device that either functions as a fan or a short paddle.

Two other examples of similar watercraft appear on the gold disk. At the bottom left, two figures – largely reconstructed, along with the watercraft itself – crouch while a spear flies past on their right side. The figure in the back holds a circular paddle-like object in his right hand that is similar to that held by the lone figure. The figure in the front may also hold a similar object. At the bottom right, two figures ride on a similar watercraft; the individual in the rear holds a circular paddle-like object in his left hand, possibly dipping it in the water to paddle or to steer. The circular shapes of these objects are odd for paddles, so their identification is unclear. Although they may be for propelling or steering the watercraft (Shatto 1998:119–220), the fact that two individuals hold their objects in the air rather than in the water is puzzling. If these are not paddles, the mechanism for propelling these unusual watercraft is not depicted. It is possible that the artist who made the repoussé composition on Disk G was so unfamiliar with these unusual craft that he was unable to portray them accurately. An alternative interpretation of these paddle-like objects is that they represent "merchant's fans" such as those identified by Mark Miller Graham (1996:241, Figure 11.17) in iconography from the Maya lowlands as well as from northern Colombia. These appear to have been circular, paddle-like objects that were plaited, like basketry, or covered in hide. In a fashion similar to the paddles used for bidding in modern auctions, they may have served as non-linguistic methods of signaling a willingness to undertake a transaction. If this latter interpretation is correct, Disk G may depict the consequences of a trading relationship gone sour.

The eventual fate of these figures is made clear by the figure in the center of the rippling water. Only one arm and the rear portion of this kicking figure survive, but an atlatl dart near his body indicates that he has been struck and fell into the water. The Itza artist undoubtedly wanted to show the tension of battle by illustrating the moment before capture, but there is little doubt that the warriors in the canoe captured or struck down some of these figures.

Even though the rafts are simply rendered, they clearly illustrate the critical aspects of the watercraft. The platform is profoundly flat, and the supporting base suggests logs, perhaps split in half down their length. The presence of these rafts in the imagery is curious because the Maya seemingly used canoes exclusively to ply the waters. According to Spanish accounts, some of these canoes could be quite large, holding upwards of 25 people, and their sighting on the coast is testament that ocean-going canoes existed.[30] As emphasized by Rahilla Shatto (1998:219) in a thesis about maritime trade, this disk includes the only known image of a vessel in Maya art that is not a canoe. The distinct juxtaposition of the two watercrafts in this image denotes that the artist wanted to record a specific encounter with a people considered different from the Itza, that is, the exotic nature of the vessels required their careful documentation in pictorial form. Indeed, rafts did exist in the precolumbian Americas, but the Spanish recorded their presence much farther south off the coast of Ecuador. Francisco de Xeréz, who accompanied Pizarro on his second Peruvian voyage, reported on the sighting and capture of a raft near Punto Galera in AD 1526. He describes the raft as a merchant vessel that was quite large and loaded with a vast cargo of fish, birds, shells, and silver and gold objects. His description of the raft is quite detailed:

> Made with crosspieces and underbody of some poles as thick as pillars, lashed together with line made of henequen, which is like hemp. The upper works were of other thinner poles, also lashed with line, on which the people and merchandise rode so as not to get wet, since the lower part was awash.
>
> *(Sámano-Xérez 1937:67)*

Another account by Miguel de Estete, also on the ship, describes:

> these balsas are of some very thick and long wooden logs, which are as soft and light on the water as cork. They lash them very tightly together with a kind of hemp rope, and above they place a high framework so that the merchandise and things they carry do not get wet. They set a mast in the largest log in the middle, hoist a sail, and navigate all along this coast. They are very safe vessels because they cannot sink or capsize, since the water washes through them everywhere.
>
> *(Estete 1968:66–68)*

Unfortunately, only one possible example of a balsa raft has been found in the archaeological record – at Chan Chan in Peru (Uceda et al. 1980) – probably due to the fact that balsa does not last long in a maritime environment. This is demonstrated by the experiences of John Haslett, who was successful in building and navigating two different reconstructions of these watercraft between the coast of Ecuador and points north in Panama and Costa Rica (Haslett 2006). These accounts have some remarkably similar as well as dissimilar elements to the rafts depicted on the gold disk from Chichen Itza.[31] The most important congruence between the text and images is the large balsa logs used to form the base of the rafts, effectively elevating the main platform and its passengers above the water. One could easily see how a Maya might translate the platform supported by logs into a straight line and two circular crosspieces, especially if they were unfamiliar with the details of the watercraft.

Other than this element, the discrepancies between the accounts and the images must certainly be acknowledged. The imagery on the gold disks does not include the mast or the sail. As noted above, the function of the circular paddle-like objects is unclear, especially given the representation of a clear obvious paddle, possibly being used for steering, in the hands of one of these individuals. Furthermore, balsa rafts have only been reported by the Spaniards for the Pacific coast, not the Caribbean or Gulf coast, which would be the more likely candidates for Itza maritime activities. But rafts were not limited to the Pacific coast. They are well-documented among the Muisca of highland Colombia.

The famous gold raft displayed at the Museo del Oro in Bogotá offers material evidence that peoples in northern Colombia used rafts, at least for freshwater navigation (Lleras-Pérez 2000:121). The raft depicts what might be a chief surrounded by masked individuals and figures who probably served as oarsmen. The golden raft indicates that this type of vessel was more widespread and might have characterized some travel on the Caribbean.

On Disk G, the figure on the raft in front of the canoe wears a round pectoral that may shed light on just why the Itza were so interested in these individuals. This circular object is likely an ornament similar to the one upon which the image appears, a cold-hammered gold disk pectoral. The manufacture of the gold disks of Chichen Itza is a topic of interest to a number of scholars (Cockrell 2014). It is not yet clear whether these were manufactured elsewhere or at the city under the supervision of foreign artisans, although it is likely that the gold itself was acquired from Central America. Columbus, on his fourth voyage in 1502, presents an eyewitness account of a seagoing canoe encountered off the Bay Islands. It was reported to have been loaded with merchandise "almost certainly from the land of Yucatan." Among the items it carried were copper bells and axes, as well as crucibles for smelting metals (Las Casas 1877; Thompson 1949). Many examples of thin gold disks are known from Costa Rica, Panama, and Colombia (cf. Snarskis 1981; Bray 1978; Jones 1985; Falchetti 1995), and when we consider Sámano-Xérez's account of the Ecuadorian raft laden with trade goods, including gold and silver, and the ocean-going canoe off Honduras carrying metal objects and metallurgical technology, we can imagine that the seafaring merchants of Chichen Itza may have encountered gold carried by various forms of watercraft as they plied the Caribbean, even though the documentation of seagoing rafts for this area remains sparse. The wealth of exotic goods on merchant rafts would have made a desirable target for Itza warrior-merchants, and recording successful plunder on the very gold they captured would have been a fitting way to commemorate the event. By way of comparison, on the Arch of Titus the Romans sculpted for eternity an image of the triumph held along the Via Sacra where Roman soldiers paraded through the city displaying the treasures they had sacked from Jerusalem and brought home to Rome. Most prominent in the images is the menorah from the temple, which would have been similarly unfamiliar and precious in its golden beauty to the Roman populace.[32] The murals in the Temple of the Warriors as well as the gold disk depicting the naval battle serve a comparable function, documenting some of the most exotic and profitable excursions – possibly as far east as the Bay Islands of Honduras – conducted by the Itza warriors. It is reasonable to suspect that the Itza also paraded their plundered goods upon their return, and the reflective brilliance of gold must have made for a spectacular display at Chichen Itza. The Itza likely also associated the gold with their pre-existing solar cult. A figure ringed by a solar disk, commonly referred to as "Captain Sun Disk," frequently appears in the art of Chichen Itza, most notably in the murals and lintel of the Upper Temple of the Jaguars (Aztzin Martinez 2005; Coggins 1984b; Miller 1977; Schele and Freidel

1990:371–373, 393–395). Likewise, the back mirrors worn by warriors signaled the burden of the sun carried by these warriors and the promise of a celestial solar afterlife should they die in their military pursuits (Headrick 2007:142; Taube 2000). To a culture where solar sacrifice infused their military practices, the color and reflectiveness of gold was probably equated with the sun.

The warriors of Chichen Itza flaunted their acquisitions when they participated in processions like that shown on the columns of the hypostyle hall of the Temple of the Warriors. There are similar round disks on the chests of several warriors, and the traces of paint captured by Morris reveal that at least some of these were painted yellow.[33] If these disks are images of gold pectorals, then there is good evidence that some of the materials taken in skirmishes like those seen on the disks and murals found their way onto the bodies of those responsible for bringing the exotic goods to the city. The merchant-warriors shared in the economic gains of Chichen Itza, the processions in which they participated gave them public acclaim, and the columns permanently memorialized their deeds.

The final resting place of some disks indicates that not all of the gold stayed in the material world of humans. The disks that have survived to the present day came from the waters of the cenote, and their crumpled state indicates that part of the ritual included partial destruction before deposition. The glimmering substance was worthy of the gods, and the cenote was a place to send such things directly to the Underworld. In an interesting parallel, myths of the fabled El Dorado include accounts of chiefly installation rituals where the new chief covered his body in gold dust and rode a raft to the center of the decidedly round Lake Guatavita, Colombia, to deposit golden offerings in the lake (Enslow 1990:134; Reichel-Dolmatoff 1965:167–168). It has been suggested that the miniature gold Muisca raft may reference such a ritual, so these practices may have inspired similar offerings at the circular Sacred Cenote. As so often happens in evolving trade relations, ideas frequently accompany the material objects and transform cultural symbols and rituals. Gold disks were utilized in a broad region of Chibchan speakers that extended from Costa Rica to Santa Marta, Colombia, an area in which simulation models have demonstrated the feasibility of indigenous maritime contact (Callaghan and Bray 2007). As Mary Helms (1993) has argued, distance confers value and significance, thus to the Itza, the fact that the gold disks came from afar meant that they represented distant people, places, and esoteric traditions that all gave special meaning and added value.

The imagery of the rafts, the gold pectoral on one individual on a raft, and the appearance of this iconography on gold disks lead us to argue that Chichen Itza had direct contact with the areas that produced the gold. Our proposition is that rather than rely on a down-the-line supply chain that moved through all of Central America, on some occasions the seafarers of Chichen Itza may themselves have gone much farther abroad and engaged with peoples who used foreign forms of transportation, had novel costuming, and made exotic prestige items new to the Maya region. To support our hypothesis, we turn to additional markers of otherness included in the narrative scenes of Chichen Itza.

The identity of the foreigners: a few reflections

First among additional markers of a foreign identity is the headdress worn by two of the fleeing raft figures on Disk G (Figure 11.17). The individual immediately in front of the canoe and the squatting man at the very bottom of the disk wear a headdress comprised of two essential parts: a helmet and a feather fan. The domed cap or helmet in the shape of a semi-circle has stipple marks suggesting a textured surface. Attached to the helmet is a fan of feathers that projects from one end of the cap to the other, making a full semi-circle. A similar headdress appears on the victim about to be sacrificed on Disk M (Figure 11.16) – possibly a representation of the same individual. Here the texture of the helmet has a series of diamonds punctuated with circles and might convey a plaited, basketry-like construction, while the upper portion appears to be a fan-like display of layered feathers. Given that the wearers of this headdress on Disk G ride on rafts that may have their origins in northern South America, it would be logical to suggest that this headdress comes from that region. Indeed, Matthew Looper (2003:Figure 3e; personal communication 2015) remarks that the headdress resembles the feathered headdresses seen in Tairona art. These were worn by individuals of high status shown in elaborate costumes with large earflares and seated upon benches or thrones with double-crocodilian designs, signaling a close affiliation with a crocodile or caiman (Figure 11.18). Even today, woven headdresses with feather panaches characterize the costume of Amazonian peoples, so this could be a reference to their precolumbian predecessors. Specific examples are known to be used by the Cofán people of southeast Colombia and northwest Ecuador, a group that may have ancestral relationships with Chibchan-speaking peoples.[34] It also is possible that this is a representation of a headdress similar to the hemispherical gold helmet excavated from Grave 5 at the Coclé site of Sitio Conte in central Panama by Samuel Lothrop (1926:25; Hoopes 2017:Figure 70; Pillsbury et al. 2017:Cat. 96.1).[35] A domed helmet was the heaviest gold object recovered from the Sacred Cenote (Lothrop 1952:67–69; Coggins and Shane 1984:57, Cat. 36; Pillsbury et al. 2017:Cat. 165). Its closest analogues are the gold helmets from central Panama and the Treasure of the Quimbayas in Colombia (Perea et al. 2016). The presence of numerous objects from the Isthmo-Colombian Area in the Sacred Cenote confirms acquisition and disposal of these at Chichen Itza (Lothrop 1952; Coggins and Shane 1984; Pillsbury et al. 2017).

This is an intriguing possibility, but the headdress may have a more local origin. Both Tatiana Proskouriakoff (1950:57) and Victoria Lyall (2011) wrote about a feathered fan headdress that is quite like the one seen in the gold disks. A series of squares arranged in a diamond pattern covers the surface of the cap portion of the headdress worn by the sacrificial victim on Disk M (Figure 11.16). The brim of the cap curls up at each end, and the term "bowler hat" has been applied by Lyall to this particular headdress. A quite similar headdress appears on the middle register of Stela 21 from Oxkintok (Figure 11.19), a Terminal Classic Yucatecan site approximately 148 km from Chichen Itza in the Puuc region. The

FIGURE 11.18 Fine brown-ware Ocarina of figure with an elaborate headdress, seated on a double-crocodilian bench, Tairona culture, AD 800–1600.

Source: Los Angeles County Museum of Art, M.2007.146.448, photo © Museum Associates/ LACMA; photo © Sergei Starosielski.

figure on the Oxkintok stela is a warrior holding a lance and a square shield, and he wears a hat whose cap has the same diamond decoration and curled brim. Just like the one worn by the Disk M victim, the headdress appears to have a row of short feathers directly above the cap, and rising over this is a second row of longer feathers (the Disk M headdress has two additional rows of long feathers). The only major difference between these headdresses is that the one on the gold disk seems to have feathers fanning from the forehead to the back of the head, while the stela version has feathers protruding only from the crown of the cap. Lyall

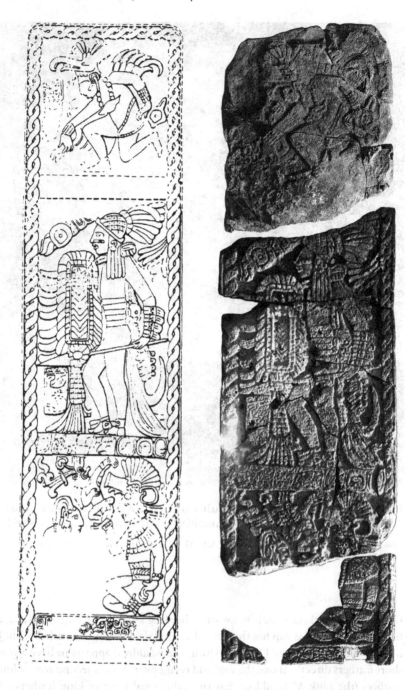

FIGURE 11.19 Stela 21, Oxkintok.

Source: Reprinted by permission from H.E.D. Pollock, *The Puuc: An Architectural Survey of the Hill Country of Yucatan and Northern Campeche, Mexico.* Memoirs of the Peabody Museum of Archaeology and Ethnology, Harvard University, (Cambridge, MA, 1980), Figure 547.

also identified this cap among a procession of warriors in a mural sequence from Ichmac, another Puuc site dating to the Terminal Classic, and this bowler hat similarly has a more restricted panache. Arguably, the reduced feather panache on the stela may result from artistic, spatial considerations. Late Classic Stela 2 of El Caribe in central Peten, Guatemala, depicts a figure holding a shield and lance who stands above a captive (Figure 11.20).[36] That victorious individual wears a version of the bowler hat displaying a full panache from front to back and an additional spray of long feathers from the top.[37]

As Lyall (2011) has argued, Terminal Classic Puuc sites including Oxkintok and Ichmac carried on southern lowland artistic traditions after the earlier sites had collapsed and northern Yucatan became the center of Maya art and architecture. She demonstrates that there are many stylistic and iconographic affinities between art of the Puuc and southern lowlands, and the bowler hat is just one example of a Yucatecan continuance of southern Maya traditions. Ek' Balam is another Yucatecan city that exhibits southern artistic influences, even as the northern Maya evolved and adapted the iconography and its stylistic characteristics into a unique Terminal Classic tradition. Lyall, like Miller and Martin (2004), suggests that Ek' Balam, Uxmal, and the Puuc sites may have been rivals of Chichen Itza, and the defeat of these sites likely led to the ultimate hegemony of Chichen Itza during the Early Postclassic period. Consequently, it is certainly tenable that the individuals wearing the bowler hats on the gold disks could be rivals in the region, that is, Maya who carried on southern traditions as they moved to the north. Memorializing these captives in art would have documented the epic wars that the Itza conducted with their neighbors on the path to regional supremacy.

The iconographic congruencies between these headdresses indicates that a Puuc identity cannot be ruled out for the individuals wearing the bowler hats on the disks from the Sacred Cenote. But this does not explain the rafts on Disk G. To date, there is no evidence that the Maya used rafts; the canoe is the only watercraft recorded for the Maya. The juxtaposition of the Maya canoe with the rafts, as well as the precise manner in which the artist depicted the vessels, reveals an Itza fascination with this foreign craft. We also point out that the feathered headdresses on the raft figures do not have the curled brims, but it is possible that the artist omitted this feature because of the small size. Disk G could depict a different foreigner entirely from the bowler hat figures, and the rafts lead us to argue that Disk G refers to an encounter at sea with individuals from the Isthmo-Colombian area who had made their way up the Caribbean coast as they engaged in trading activities.[38]

What then was the origin of the individuals with the light-colored, beaded hair? In the murals, no evidence of the watercraft used by these figures has survived, and on Disk M the beaded hair appears just below a bowler hat. Further affirming a local origin for the bowler hat is the stippled markings on the face of the captive on Disk M. Lyall's (2011:39–40) careful analysis of the Ichmac murals identified black dots on the face of a bowler hat-wearing figure, indicating that

FIGURE 11.20 Stela 2, El Caribé.

Source: After Morley et al. 1983:Figure 42.

the facial stippling on Disk M could refer to the same people who wore the bowler hats in the Ichmac mural. Additional evidence that the men with the beaded hair could be from Yucatan is on Disk D (Figure 11.15). The beaded-hair figure on Disk D wears a deer headdress that is similar to headdresses seen on Late Classic Maya ceramics.[39] Another interesting feature of Disk D is that the figure with the lance in front of the captive wears a version of the bowler hat. Apparently, some of the people who wore this hat joined with the Itza and became part of their collective identity.[40]

If the bowler hat, facial markings, and deer headdress are markers of Puuc peoples, then the imagery of the murals and the disks have two significant implications. First, the watery skirmishes from the Temple of the Warriors could document the struggle of the Itza to wrangle control of the coast from their Puuc neighbors. The Itza port at Isla Cerritos and the maritime trade it afforded them were key factors in the success of the city, as they looked ever farther afield for exotic goods. As suggested by David Atekpatzin Young (personal communication 2017), the lighter hair could be attributed to a life on the coast and working in the ocean.[41] Perhaps the Itza, as they moved to control the coast, encountered sun-bleached people and engaged in warfare with them to conquer their coastal territory. Second, because beaded hair is an anomaly in Puuc and southern Maya traditions, the beads may have been added to the hair by the Itza themselves to associate these figures with the Maize God (Geoffrey Braswell, personal communication 2015). Mary Miller and Marcos Samayoa (1998) have theorized that the Itza dressed their sacrificial victims richly with jade beads to mark them as the Maize God before depositing them in the Sacred Cenote. Just as Classic period Maya replaced the earflares of captives with paper drawn through their pierced ears, so too the Itza could have arrayed the golden hair of their coastal captives with jade beads. The lighter locks might have resembled the tassels on ears of maize, so dressing them in the jade costume of this deity would have been a logical ritual approach.

Unless we are to presume that the Itza reenacted sea battles in the Sacred Cenote, something for which we have no evidence, the murals with people with fair hair festooned with beads do not depict ritual, but the actual capture of people in a watery battle. If the murals do not collapse time, doubly portraying capture and sacrifice simultaneously, then they suggest that the light-haired people already had beads in their hair, and the Maya artist was quick to document this novel form of dress. Because of the gold medium upon which two of the beaded-hair figures appear, we argue that a more southerly or Caribbean identification is a possibility for these captives.

Thus far, we have not identified the source of this hairstyle, although a few potential candidates have emerged. Laura Wingfield (personal communication 2016) suggests a figure seated on a burial urn from Colombia with stylistic characteristics from both Chimila and the Lower Magdalena (Figure 11.21). This individual does have cylindrical beads in what may be his hair, but the beaded elements form two loops rather than hanging straight as in the Chichen Itza

FIGURE 11.21   Brownish-orange terracotta burial urn with a seated figure on the lid, Chimila and Lower Magdalena stylistic traits.

Source: Los Angeles County Museum of Art, M.2007.146.486. Photo © Sergei Starosielski.

murals and repoussé sculpture. Among the art of the Muisca, who clearly used both gold and rafts, are ceramic figures with rows of circular elements decorating the head (Figure 11.22). The circles have punctuations at their center and could depict beads; however, on one ceramic figure (Labbé 1998:Figure 33), the beads may be part of a rounded headdress, while on the other the beads appear to decorate a folded cloth that serves as a headdress. Each of these examples are tantalizing because they resemble to some degree the Itza imagery and because the gold medium of some images may have referred to the precious material captured along with these exotic people. That said, none of the Colombian images offers enough congruent iconography to firmly establish the identity of the captives depicted at Chichen Itza.

Not until the latter half of the history of Chichen Itza did gold figure prominently in Maya elite accouterments and the objects that the Maya deposited in offerings. It is precisely because the Itza military of the Early Postclassic period

FIGURE 11.22 Variegated gray slip ceramic fragment from an object depicting an anthropomorphic figure, Muisca culture, AD 1000–1540.

Source: Los Angeles County Museum of Art, M.2007.146.682. Photo © Sergei Starosielski.

was engaged in distant maritime encounters and trade that this resource became available. The Tairona of Colombia are one of the better-known manufacturers of gold objects in the precolumbian Americas, but the Muisca and Sinú, also from northern Colombia, are other likely candidates. It seems a small stretch to imagine that the Itza, who had outposts along the Caribbean coast perhaps as far as the Bay Islands of the Gulf of Honduras, encountered individuals with gold and that they engaged them militarily to bring home this new exotic material.

To test this speculation, the gold disks need further investigation of their metallurgical properties. The Itza appetite for exotic goods was not limited to objects obtained from the coast. Turquoise from the American southwest and gold from Oaxaca and the Pacific Coast also serve as testaments to the breadth of the vast trade network of Chichen Itza (Cockrell et al. 2014), as does obsidian from throughout west and central Mexico.[42] When investigating precolumbian sheet gold, Bryan Cockrell (2014) identified the sources as the Coclé culture in central Panama and also peoples of West Mexico. Testing the composition of the gold disks from Chichen Itza would assist in more firmly identifying the source of the metal.

Conclusion

The imagery of Disk G (Figure 11.17), where the opponents in the battle appear on rafts, is especially compelling. The headdress style of the individuals on the rafts, like the bowler headdress, could be that of a Chibchan group. The individual on the left who is chased by the Maya canoe wears a circular element on his chest. This pectoral, we contend, was made of the same substance as the disk itself – gold. To our minds the image records an important event in the history of the Itza when they encountered people who traveled on strangely constructed foreign rafts. The result of the encounter was perhaps the capture of the men, but, more importantly, the Itza likely took the gold as their plunder. Then, as today, the malleable, sun-colored, highly reflective substance proved irresistible.

Evidence that the military profited from such events rests on the chests of the warriors who may have conducted these battles. A number of the figures carved on the columns of the Temple of the Warriors have round disks as pectorals, and because some of these still bore traces of yellow paint when Morris recorded color illustrations just after excavation, the yellow pectorals likely represent gold disks such as the ones found in the Sacred Cenote. But some of the captured golden disks stayed in the human realm where warriors, rewarded for the hazards they faced in foreign regions, kept their booty and displayed it on their bodies.

The splendid costumes worn by the Itza military in their sculpted versions in the colonnade convey a system where warriors shared in the wealth they brought back to the city. The lavish feather cloaks, copper and gold alloy bells, greenstone, and gold show a military with considerable economic power. The ability of warriors to profit from the plunder was likely an incentive to participate in the military and spend periods of time away from their home city in their efforts to acquire ever more exotic goods. The economic as well as the political power of the military explains the emergence over time of depictions of merchant-warriors from the surface of ceramic vessels in the Late Classic to the sculpted columns in the public space of the central plaza of Chichen Itza. At Postclassic Chichen Itza, the economically powerful merchant-warriors were a middle-elite class of people who demanded and required public recognition on a scale unprecedented in Mesoamerica. Trade and the military were key to the success of the Itza, and it was through the expansion of trade that their social structure transformed, making the merchant-warriors visible to the public for all time.

Notes

1 The earliest connection made between Chichen Itza and Tula appears in Charnay (1885, 1887), but he based his observations on scant evidence. Tozzer (1957) presented a more systematic comparison of the two cities primarily using visual analysis. Schele and Freidel (1990:346–376), in contrast, attempt to portray Chichen Itza as a profoundly Maya phenomenon. For additional thoughts on the Tula-Chichen connection, see Kristan-Graham (1989, 2001).

2 Discussions of Maya long-distance trade appear in Ardren and Lowry (2011), Aztzin Martinez (2005), Masson and Freidel (2002), and McKillop (2005). In Aztzin's discussion she notes, "Warfare was probably not the dominant factor in the transition from Classic to Postclassic, but rather increasingly intense trade activity" (Aztzin Martinez 2005:9). We recognize the growth of trade in Postclassic Mesoamerica but argue that it was profoundly entwined with and inseparable from military behaviors and structures.

3 We use the term "Itza" to refer to peoples who lived at Chichen Itza and identified as being from the city. Most likely, there were many identities within its population, and we employ Itza to refer to the collective identity of all the residents of the city.

4 The term "international" is a problematic one, because the notion of nations is a recent fabrication in human development. We use the word more generally to denote interactions among people who considered themselves different from one another, but we do not imply that precolumbian peoples shared the modern concepts of nations or national identity.

5 The term "temple" applied to this structure is the most inaccurate part of the name. The large benches and "altar" inside the temple proper indicate a place for assembly. Furthermore, the painted bench of the Temple of the Chacmool illustrates an assembly of priests and warriors seated on thrones either covered with jaguar skin or decorated with a feline head (A. Morris 1931:367–381). Thus, the structure was more likely a council house following in the tradition of Str. 10-L22A at Copan which Fash and Sharer (1991:171) and Stomper (1996) have identified as a *popol nah*. See also Bey and May (2014).

6 The two volumes of *The Temple of the Warriors at Chichen Itzá* (1931) present the most extensive account of the excavation and decoration of both the Temple of the Chacmool and the Temple of the Warriors. In particular, this text has thorough discussions of the pigments applied to the temple and incredibly valuable color renditions of the murals and reliefs found in these temples.

7 In the temple proper, Charlot (1931:266) identified an additional 60 warriors on its carved, interior columns, which further underscore the militant nature of the structure.

8 The identity of these figures as warriors was credibly established by the Carnegie scholars involved in the excavations of the temples (Morris et al. 1931).

9 For a thorough history of research on solar disks through the lens of the Aztec Calendar Stone, see Villela and Miller (2010). They discuss the seminal publications concerning this monument.

10 Charlot (1931:273) identifies these figures as the Sun God, and although he does note a variety of facial features and headdresses, he does not resolve the problems they pose. Schele and Freidel (1990:503) argue that the solar disk functioned like a cartouche in Classic Maya iconography, thereby indicating that the individual in the solar disk is an ancestor. The presence of wrinkles on the faces of some of these solar warriors (Charlot 1931:273) supports Schele and Freidel's assertion. See also Headrick (1999) for a discussion of partially bodied humans as deceased ancestors.

11 Sahagún (1950–1982:Book 3:49, Book 6:162) recorded these beliefs for the Aztec. For an argument that they preceded the Aztec and existed at Teotihuacan, see Headrick (2003, 2007:124–145).

12 Important explorations of Maya adoption of Teotihuacan imagery (including the year sign) as well as accounts of their interactions appear in Coggins (1975, 1979a, 1979b, 1983), Proskouriakoff (1993), Schele and Freidel (1990), and Stuart (2000).

13 Schele and Freidel (1990:366–369) note how the elaborate costuming of captives at Chichen Itza contrasts with the stripped-to-almost-naked depiction of Classic period southern lowland Maya captives. While acknowledging that the Itza sacrificed many of their captives, they also view the lavish costumes as evidence that some captives were absorbed into the Itza state.

14 See for example Kerr vases 638, 2342, 3478, and 5124 in the *Maya Vase Database*.

15 See also Joyce Marcus (1983) and Janet Berlo (1983) for similar arguments about the Teotihuacan tassel headdress and foreign locations.

16 Ann Axtell Morris (1931:352) held that the artists used a *secco* technique in which pigments mixed with a sticky binding medium were applied to a dry plaster wall. See also Aztzin Martinez (2005:30), Finamore and Houston (2010), and Tokovinine and Beliaev (2013:184).

17 See Andrews et al. (1988), Masson and Freidel (2002), and McKillop (2005). For more on the trade corridor between Chichen Itza and Isla Cerritos, see Ardren and Lowry (2011).

18 See Aztzin Martinez (2005:116, 120) for another commentary on the relationship of the military and merchants at Chichen Itza. In addition, these seafaring merchants in the murals may reflect what J. Eric S. Thompson (1970) characterized as the "Mexicanized" Putun Maya who engaged in trade and warfare (Morley et al.1983:256–257; Schele and Freidel 1990:350).

19 Ann Axtell Morris (1931:402) also commented on the attempt of the artist to distinguish the presence of two differing peoples.

20 See Shatto (1998) for an analysis of Maya watercraft, including canoes with prows such as this one, which Shatto (1998:224) suggests may have typified coastal canoes.

21 Tozzer (1941:119). Ann Axtell Morris first, and quite accurately, applied this passage to this sacrificial scene (Morris et al. 1931: Vol. 2: Plate 145).

22 Hansen (2017) offers an interesting analysis of the potential physiological and psychological effects of violence on audience members witnessing sacrificial events.

23 Sahagún (1950–1982:Book 2:3) indicates that the Aztecs added a fifth person to restrain the head of the victim.

24 In Tozzer's (1957:Volume XI:153–152) vision of Chichen Itza as a hybrid Maya-Toltec site, he identifies the nosebar as appearing on Maya peoples.

25 Clemency Coggins (1984a:24–26) provides an overview of Thompson's work and publications by others, owing to Thompson's failure to publish his findings. See also Lothrop (1952).

26 Lothrop (1952:v) recounts the restoration and documentation of the gold disks. Of the disks in this discussion, Gleason drew Disks D and M, while Proskouriakoff drew Disk G.

27 In her comments on each of the gold disks, Coggins (1984a) elaborates upon the possible techniques used in the decoration.

28 To emphasize the importance of this costume, we note that prominent individuals in bird costumes also appear on Gold Disk G and Gold Disk H.

29 Oswaldo Chinchilla Mazariegos (2017:139–157) also comments on this predatory bird.

30 See Las Casas (1877:Book 2:Chapter 20); Shatto (1998); Thompson (1949, 1970:127).

31 For a more detailed analysis of the precise design of balsa rafts and their seafaring abilities, see Dewan and Hosler (2008).

32 Evidence that the menorah taken from the temple by Emperor Titus in AD 70 was made of gold comes from the first-hand account of Josephus, who served as a priest in the Jerusalem temple and viewed the triumphal parade in Rome (Fine 2016:18–19).

33 Yellow painted disks appear in Morris et al. (1931:Volume II: Plates 76, 77, 81). When discussing the Upper Temple of the Jaguars, Aztzin Martinez (2005:56–57) identifies a yellow painted disk as made of gold.

34 See, for example, Furst (1991:Figure 8.4).

35 Labbé (1998:46) provides an image of a gold cap with feathers, although the feathers only extend up vertically, not in a fan, as in the images from Chichen Itza.

36 El Caribe Stela 2 dates to 9.17.10.0.0 (AD 780; Morley et al. 1983:597).

37 Proskouriakoff (1950:51) first identified this headdress and connected the El Caribe version to Puuc sites and Chichen Itza.

38 In a recent study of strontium isotope ratios of forty human molars from the Sacred Cenote, Price et al. (2019) note that a number of these individuals had strontium ratios lower than the range for Chichen Itza and its immediate environs. Of these, some are similar to ratios recorded for Copan in western Honduras and for Los Naranjos and Yarumela in central Honduras, suggesting that some sacrificial victims came from far to the southeast. The authors included new data from El Salvador. Nonetheless, the database used for comparison did not include samples from farther east in Honduras or Central America. It also did not include ratios for the Antilles. Until more strontium isotope ratios for other regions of Central America are used for comparisons, the ability to more precisely identify foreigners from outside of the Mesoamerican core is limited.

39 See, for example, Kerr vases 1224, 1921, and 6685 (Maya Vase Database n.d.).

40 Schele and Freidel (1990) suggested that the Itza might have had an ideology of incorporation rather than conquest with many of their enemies. This may also explain the priest who sports a possible bowler hat on the south side of Column 59 in the Northwest Colonnade.

41 In a recent post, Stephen Houston (2019) simultaneously suggests that the golden hair was a Maya convention for associating the figures with the Sun God and an unknown ethnic marker.

42 Early attempts to source some Mesoamerican turquoise such as Weigand et al. (1977) and Harbottle and Weigand (1992) suggested the Cerrillos area of New Mexico as a precolumbian source of turquoise. More recent work by Hull et al. (2008) notes that previous sourcing techniques were neither particularly reliable nor reproducible. They offer a refined sourcing method that demonstrates that hydrogen and copper isotopic values are useful in identifying mine sources, and the application of this technique could better pinpoint the original source of the turquoise found at Chichen Itza.

References cited

Andrews, Anthony P., Tomás Gallareta Gallareta Negrón, J. Fernando Robles Castellanos, Rafael Cobos Palma, and Pura Cervera Rivero 1988 Isla Cerritos: An Itza Trading Port on the North Coast of Yucatan, Mexico. *National Geographic Research* 4:196–207.

Ardren, Traci, and Justin Lowry 2011 The Travels of Maya Merchants in the Ninth and Tenth Centuries AD, Investigations at Xuenkal and the Greater Cupul Province, Yucatan, Mexico. *World Archaeology* 43:428–443.

Aztzin Martinez, De Luna Lucha 2005 *Murals and the Development of Merchant Activity at Chichen Itza*. Unpublished M.A. thesis, Department of Anthropology, Brigham Young University, Provo.

Berlo, Janet 1983 The Warrior and the Butterfly: Central Mexican Ideologies of Sacred Warfare and Teotihuacan Iconography. In *Text and Image in Pre-Columbian Art*, edited by Janet Berlo, pp. 79–117. BAR, Oxford.

Bey, George J. III, and Rossana May Ciau 2014 The Role and Realities of *Popol Nahs* in Northern Maya Archaeology. In *The Maya and Their Central American Neighbors: Settlement Patterns, Architecture, Hieroglyphic Texts and Ceramics*, edited by Geoffrey Braswell, pp. 335–355. Routledge, London and New York.

Bray, Warwick 1978 *The Gold of El Dorado*. Times Newspapers Limited, London.

Byland, Bruce E., and John M. D. Pohl 1994 *In the Realm of 8 Deer*. University of Oklahoma Press, Norman and London.

Callaghan, Richard T., and Warwick Bray 2007 Simulating Prehistoric Sea Contacts between Costa Rica and Colombia. *The Journal of Island and Coastal Archaeology* 2:4–23.

Carrasco, Pedro 1966 Rango de Tecuhtli entre los Nahuas tramontanos. *Tlalocan* 5:133–160.

———— 1971 Social Organization of Ancient Mexico. In *Handbook of Middle American Indians, Vol. 10: Archaeology of Northern Mesoamerica*, edited by Gordon Ekholm and Ignacio Bernal, Part I:349–375. University of Texas Press, Austin.

Charlot, Jean 1931 Bas-Reliefs from the Temple of the Warriors Cluster. *The Temple of the Warriors at Chichén Itzá, Yucatán, Mexico*, Vol. 1, pp. 230–346. Carnegie Institution of Washington Publication 406. Carnegie Institution, Washington, DC.

Charnay, Desire 1885 Les anciennes villes du Nouveau Monde. Paris.

———— 1887 *The Ancient Cities of the New World*. Chapman and Hall, London.

Chinchilla Mazariegos, Oswaldo 2017 *Art and Myth of the Ancient Maya*. Yale University Press, New Haven.

Cockrell, Bryan R. 2014 *The Metals from the Cenote Sagrado, Chichén Itzá as Windows on Technological and Depositional Communities*. Ph.D. dissertation, Department of Anthropology, University of California-Berkeley. ProQuest Dissertations Publishing.

Cockrell, Bryan R., Jose Luis Ruvalcaba Sil, and Edith Ortiz Díaz 2014 For Whom the Bells Fall: Metals from the Cenote Sagrado, Chichen Itza. *Archaeometry* 57(6):977–995.

Coggins, Clemency C. 1975 *Painting and Drawing Styles at Tikal: An Historical and Iconographic Reconstruction, Part 1*. Ph.D. dissertation, Department of Fine Arts, Harvard University, Cambridge. University Microfilms, Ann Arbor.

———— 1979a A New Order and the Role of the Calendar: Some Characteristics of the Middle Classic Period at Tikal. In *Maya Archaeology and Ethnohistory*, edited by Norman Hammond and Gordon R. Willey, pp. 38–50. University of Texas Press, Austin and London.

———— 1979b Teotihuacan and Tikal in the Early Classic Period. In *Actes du XLIIe Congrès International des Américanistes, Congrès du Centenaire, Paris 2–9 septembre 1976*, Vol. 8, pp. 251–269. Société des Americanistes, Paris.

———— 1983 An Instrument of Expansion: Monte Alban, Teotihuacan, and Tikal. *In Highland- Lowland Interaction in Mesoamerica: Interdisciplinary Approaches*, edited by Arthur G. Miller, pp. 49–68. Dumbarton Oaks Research Library and Collection, Washington, DC.

———— 1984a The Cenote of Sacrifice: Catalogue. In *Cenote of Sacrifice: Maya Treasures from the Sacred Well at Chichen Itza*, edited by Clemency Chase Coggins and Orrin C. Shane III, pp. 22–155. University of Texas Press, Austin.

———— 1984b Murals in the Upper Temple of the Jaguars, Chichén Itzá. In *Cenote of Sacrifice: Maya Treasures from the Sacred Well at Chichen Itza*, edited by Clemency Chase Coggins and Orrin C. Shane III, pp. 157–165. University of Texas Press, Austin.

Coggins, Clemency, and Orrin C. Shane III (editors) 1984 *Cenote of Sacrifice: Maya Treasures from the Sacred Well at Chichen Itza*. University of Texas Press, Austin.

Dewan, Leslie, and Dorothy Hosler 2008 Ancient Maritime Trade on Balsa Rafts: An Engineering Analysis. *Journal of Anthropological Research* 64:19–40.

Enslow, Sam 1990 *The Art of Prehispanic Colombia: An Illustrated Cultural and Historical Survey*. McFarland & Company, Inc., Jefferson, NC and London.

Estete, Miguel de 1968 [1535] *Noticia del Perú*. Editores técnicos asociados, Lima.

Estrada-Belli, Francisco 2011 *The First Maya Civilization: Ritual and Power before the Classic Period*. Routledge, London and New York.

Falchetti, Ana María 1995 *El oro del Gran Zenú: Metalurgia prehispánica en las llanuras del Caribe colombiano*. Museo del Oro, Banco de la República, Bogotá.

Fash, William L., and Robert J. Sharer 1991 Sociopolitical Developments and Methodological Issues at Copan, Honduras: A Conjunctive Perspective. *Latin American Antiquity* 2:166–187.

Finamore, Daniel, and Stephen D. Houston (editors) 2010 *Fiery Pool: The Maya and the Mythic Sea*. Peabody Essex Museum and Yale University Press, Salem and New Haven.

Fine, Steven 2016 *The Menorah: From the Bible to Modern Israel*. Harvard University Press, Cambridge.

Furst, Peter T. 1991 Crowns of Power: Bird and Feather Symbolism in Amazonian Shamanism. In *The Gift of Birds: Featherwork of Native South American Peoples*, edited by Kenneth Kensinger and Ruben Reina, pp. 92–109. University Museum of Archaeology and Anthropology, University of Pennsylvania, Philadelphia.

Graham, Mark Miller 1996 Merchants and Metalwork in Middle America. In *Paths to Central American Prehistory*, edited by Frederick W. Lange, pp. 237–252. University Press of Colorado, Boulder.

Guernsey, Julia 2006 *Ritual and Power in Stone: The Performance of Rulership in Mesoamerican Izapan Style Art*. University of Texas Press, Austin.

Hansen, Linda Jane 2017 *Aztec Human Sacrifice as Entertainment? The Physio-Psycho-Social Rewards of Aztec Sacrificial Celebrations*. Ph.D. dissertation, Religious and Theological Studies, University of Denver, Denver, CO.

Harbottle, Garman, and Phil C. Weigand 1992 Turquoise in Pre-Columbian America. *Scientific American* 266(2):78–85.

Haslett, John 2006 *Voyage of the Manteno: The Education of a Modern-Day Expeditioner*. St. Martin's Press, New York.

Headrick, Annabeth 1999 The Street of the Dead . . . It Really Was: Mortuary Bundles at Teotihuacan. *Ancient Mesoamerica* 10:69–85.

———— 2003 Butterfly War at Teotihuacan. In *Ancient Mesoamerican Warfare*, edited by M. Katheryn Brown and Travis Stanton, pp. 149–170. AltaMira Press, Walnut Creek, CA.

———— 2007 *The Teotihuacan Trinity: The Sociopolitical Structure of an Ancient Mesoamerican City*. University of Texas Press, Austin.

Helmke, Christophe, and Jesper Nielsen 2015 The Defeat of the Great Bird in Myth and Royal Pageantry: A Mesoamerican Myth in a Comparative Perspective. *Comparative Mythology* 1:23–60.

Helms, Mary 1993 *Craft and the Kingly Ideal: Art, Trade, and Power*. University of Texas Press, Austin.

Herrera y Tordesillas, Antonio de 1945 [160-1-15] *Historia general de los hechos de los castellanos en las islas y tierra firme de Mar Océano*, Vol. 4. Editorial Guarania, Buenos Aires.

Hoopes, John W. 2017 Magical Substances in the Land between the Seas. In *Golden Kingdoms: Luxury Arts in the Ancient Americas*, edited by Joanne Pillsbury, Timothy Potts, and Kim N. Richter, pp. 55–65. J. Paul Getty Museum and the Getty Research Institute, Los Angeles.

Houston, Stephen 2019 Watery War. *Maya Decipherment* June 17. https://mayadecipherment.com/2019/06/17/watery-war/.

Hull, Sharon, Mostafa Fayek, Frances Joan Mathien, Phillip Shelley, and Kathy Roler Durand 2008 A New Approach to Determining the Geological Provenance of Turquoise Artifacts Using Hydrogen and Copper Isotopes. *Journal of Archaeological Science* 35:1355–1369.

Jones, Julie (editor) 1985 *The Art of Precolumbian Gold: The Jan Mitchell Collection*. Wiedenfeld and Nicolson, London.

Klein, Cecelia 2019 The Gift of Life: Rethinking the Composite Creature on the Venus Platform at Chichen Itza. 84th Annual Meeting of the Society for American Archaeology, Albuquerque.

Koontz, Rex 2009 *Lightning Gods and Feathered Serpents: The Public Sculpture of El Tajín*. University of Texas Press, Austin.

Kristan-Graham, Cynthia 1989 *Art, Rulership, and the Mesoamerican Body Politic at Tula and Chichen Itza*. Ph.D. dissertation, Department of Art History, University of California, Los Angeles. University Microfilms, Ann Arbor.

——— 2001 A Sense of Place at Chichén Itzá. In *Landscape and Power in Ancient Mesoamerica*, edited by Rex Koontz, Kathryn Reese-Taylor, and Annabeth Headrick, pp. 317–369. Westview Press, Boulder.

Krochock, Ruth 1988 *The Hieroglyphic Inscriptions and Iconography of the Temple of the Four Lintels and Related Monuments, Chichén Itzá, Mexico*. Unpublished M.A. thesis, Department of Art History, University of Texas, Austin.

Labbé, Armand 1998 *Shamans, Gods, and Mythic Beasts: Columbian Gold and Ceramics in Antiquity*. The American Federation of Arts and University of Washington Press, New York and Seattle.

Las Casas, Bartoleme de 1877 *Historia de las Indias*, 2 vols. Mexico.

Lincoln, Charles 1986 The Chronology of Chichén Itzá. In *Late Lowland Maya Civilization*, edited by Jeremy Sabloff and E. Wyllys Andrews V, pp. 141–196. University of New Mexico Press, Albuquerque.

Lleras-Pérez, Roberto 2000 The Iconography and Symbolism of Metallic Votive Offerings in the Eastern Cordillera, Colombia. In *Precolumbian Gold: Technology, Style, and Iconography*, edited by Colin McEwan, pp. 112–131. Fitzroy Dearborn Publishers, Chicago and London.

Looper, Mathew 2003 From Inscribed Bodies to Distributed Persons: Contextualizing Tairona Figural Images in Performance. *Cambridge Archaeological Journal* 13:25–40.

Lothrop, Samuel Kirkland 1926 *Pottery from Costa Rica and Nicaragua*, 2 vols. Museum of the American Indian and Heye Foundation, New York.

——— 1952 Metals from the Cenote of Sacrifice, Chichen Itza, Yucatan. In *Memoirs of the Peabody Museum of Archaeology and Ethnology, Harvard University*, Vol. 10, No. 2. Peabody Museum of Archaeology and Ethnology, Cambridge.

Lyall, Victoria Isabel 2011 *Between Two Worlds: Northern Maya Mural Painting and the Development of Regional Identity*. Unpublished Ph.D. dissertation, Department of Art History, University of California, Los Angeles.

Marcus, Joyce 1983 Topic 53: Teotihuacan Visitation on Monte Alban Monuments and Murals. In *The Cloud People: Divergent Evolution of the Zapotec and Mixtec Civilizations*, edited by Kent Flannery and Joyce Marcus, pp. 175-181. Harcourt Brace, San Diego.

Martin, Simon, and Nikolai Grube 2000 *Chronicle of the Maya Kings and Queens: Deciphering the Dynasties of the Ancient Maya*. Thames and Hudson, London.

Masson, Marilyn, and David Freidel (editors) 2002 *Ancient Maya Political Economies*. AltaMira Press, Walnut Creek, CA.

Maya Vase Database n.d. http://research.mayavase.com/kerrmaya.html, accessed December 7, 2017.

McKillop, Heather 2005 *In Search of Maya Sea Traders*. Texas A & M University Press, College Station.

Miller, Arthur 1977 Captains of the Itzá: Unpublished Mural Evidence from Chichén Itzá. In *Social Process in Maya Prehistory: Studies in Honor of Sir Eric Thompson*, edited by Norman Hammond, pp. 197–225. Academic Press, London.

Miller, Mary Ellen 1985 A Re-Examination of the Mesoamerican Chacmool. *Art Bulletin* 67:7–17.

Miller, Mary Ellen, and Simon Martin 2004 *Courtly Art of the Ancient Maya*. Thames and Hudson, London.

Miller, Mary Ellen, and Marcos Samayoa 1998 Where Maize May Grow: Jade, Chacmools, and the Maize God. *RES* 33:54–72.

Morley, Sylvanus G. Morley, George W. Brainerd, and Robert J. Sharer 1983 *The Ancient Maya*, 4th edition. Stanford University Press, Stanford.

Morris, Ann Axtell 1931 Murals from the Temple of the Warriors and Adjacent Structures. In *The Temple of the Warriors at Chichen Itzá, Yucatan*, Vol. 1, pp. 347–485. Publication 406. Carnegie Institution of Washington, Washington, DC.

Morris, Earl H. 1931 Description of the Temple of the Warriors and Edifices Related Thereto. In *The Temple of the Warriors at Chichen Itzá, Yucatan*, by Earl H. Morris, Jean Charlot, and Ann Axtell Morris, Vol. 1, pp. 11–227. Publication, No. 406. Carnegie Institution of Washington, Washington, DC.

Morris, Earl H., Jean Charlot, and Ann Axtell Morris 1931 *The Temple of the Warriors at Chichen Itzá, Yucatan*, 2 vols. Publication 406. Carnegie Institution of Washington, Washington, DC.

Muñoz Camargo, Diego 1892 *Historia de Tlaxcala, publicada y anotada por Alfredo Chavero*. Oficina Tipográfica de la Secretaríade Fomento, México.

Nielsen, Jesper, and Christophe Helmke 2015 *The Fall of the Great Celestial Bird: A Master Myth in Early Classic Central Mexico*. Ancient America No. 13. Mesoamerica Center, University of Texas, Austin.

Perea, Alicia, Ana Verde Casanova, and Andrés Guitiérrez Usillos (editors) 2016 *El Tesoro Quimbaya*. Ministerio de Educación, Cultura y Deporte, Seville.

Pillsbury, Joanne, Timothy Potts, and Kim N. Richter 2017 *Golden Kingdoms: Luxury Arts in the Ancient Americas*. J. Paul Getty Museum and the Getty Research Institute, Los Angeles.

Pohl, John M. D. 1994 *The Politics of Symbolism in the Mixtec Codices*. Vanderbilt University Publications in Anthropology, Nashville.

Price, Douglas T., Vera Tiesler, and Carolyn Freiwald 2019 Place of Origin of the Sacrificial Victims in the Sacred Cenote, Chichen Itza, Mexico. *American Journal of Physical Anthropology* 170(1):98-115.

Proskouriakoff, Tatiana 1950 *A Study of Classic Maya Sculpture*. Publication No. 593. Carnegie Institution of Washington, Washington, DC.

———— 1952 Glyphs. In *Metals from the Cenote of Sacrifice, Chichen Itza, Yucatan*, edited by Samuel Lothrop, pp. 33–35. Memoirs of the Peabody Museum of Archaeology and Ethnology, Harvard University, Vol. 10, No. 2. Peabody Museum of Archaeology and Ethnology, Cambridge.

———— 1993 *Maya History*. University of Texas Press, Austin.

Reichel-Dolmatoff, Gerardo 1965 *Colombia*. Praeger, New York.

Ringle, William M., Tomás Gallareta Negrón, and George Bey 1998 The Return of Quetzalcoatl: Evidence for the Spread of a World Religion during the Epiclassic Period. *Ancient Mesoamerica* 9:183–232.

Sahagún, Fray Bernadino de 1950–1982 [1575–1580]. *Florentine Codex: General History of the Things of New Spain*, translated by Arthur J. O. Anderson and Charles E. Dibble. Monographs of the School of American Research and the Museum of New Mexico. School of American Research and the University of Utah, Santa Fe.

Sámano-Xérez, Francisco de 1937 [1534] Relación. *Cuadernos de historia del Perú*, Vol. 2, edited by R. Porras Barrenechea. Imprimeries Les Presses Modernes.

Schele, Linda, and David Freidel 1990 *A Forest of Kings: The Untold Story of the Ancient Maya*. William Morrow, New York.

Schele, Linda, and Peter Mathews 1998 *The Code of Kings: The Language of Seven Sacred Maya Temples and Tombs*. Scribner, New York.

Shatto, Rahilla Corinne Abbas 1998 *Maritime Trade and Seafaring of the Precolumbian Maya*. Unpublished M.A. thesis, Department of Anthropology, Texas A & M University, College Station.

Snarskis, Michael J. 1981 Catalogue. In *Between Continents/Between Seas: Precolumbian Art of Costa Rica*, Harry N. Abrams in association with Detroit Institute of Arts, New York.

Spinden, Herbert J. 1975 *A Study of Maya Art: Its Subject Matter and Historical Development*. Dover, New York.

Stomper, Jeffrey A. 1996 *The Popol Na: A Model for Ancient Maya Community Structure ay Copan, Honduras*. Ph.D. dissertation, Department of Anthropology, Yale University. University Microfilms, Ann Arbor.

Stuart, David 2000 The Arrival of Strangers: Teotihuacan and Tollan in Classic Maya History. In *Mesoamerica's Classic Heritage: From Teotihuacan to the Aztecs*, edited by Davíd Carrasco, Lindsay Jones, and Scott Sessions, pp. 465–513. University Press of Colorado, Boulder.

Taube, Karl A. 2000 The Turquoise Hearth: Fire, Sacrifice, and the Central Mexican Cult of War. In *Mesoamerica's Classic Heritage: From Teotihuacan to the Aztecs*, edited by Davíd Carrasco, Lindsay Jones, and Scott Sessions, pp. 269–340. University Press of Colorado, Boulder.

Thompson, J. Eric S. 1949 Canoes and Navigation of the Maya and Their Neighbors. *Journal of the Royal Anthropological Institute of Great Britain and Ireland* 79:69–78.

———— 1970 *Maya History and Religion*. University of Oklahoma Press, Norman.

Tokovinine, Alexandre, and Demitri Beliaev 2013 People of the Road: Traders and Travelers in Ancient Maya Words and Images. In *Merchants, Markets, and Exchange in the Pre-Columbian World*, edited by Kenneth Hirth and Joanne Pillsbury, pp. 169–200. Dumbarton Oaks Research Library and Collection, Washington, DC.

Tozzer, Alfred M. 1930 Maya and Toltec Figures at Chichén Itzá. *Proceedings of the 23rd International Congress of Americanists*, pp. 155–164. Science Press Printing, New York.

———— 1941 Landa's Relación de las Cosas de Yucatan: A Translation. *Papers of the Peabody Museum of American Archaeology and Ethnology, Harvard University*, Vol. 18.

Reprinted with permission of the original publishers by Kraus Reprint Corporation, New York, 1966.

———— 1957 *Chichen Itza and Its Cenote of Sacrifice: A Comparative Study of Contemporaneous Maya and Toltec*, 2 vols. Memoirs of the Peabody Museum of Archaeology and Ethnology, Vols. 11 and 12, Harvard University, Cambridge.

Uceda, S., M. Cornejo García, and A. M. Hoyle 1980 *Informes de trabajos de excavación llevados a cabo por el Centro de Investigación y Restauración de Bienes Muebles, La Libertad, en la zona: sur 1, sector de Chayhuac, Chan Chan. Trazo de la carretera de evitamiento.* Report to the Instituto Regional de Cultura de La Libertad, Trujillo.

Villela, Khristaan, and Mary Ellen Miller 2010 *The Aztec Calendar Stone.* GettyResearch Institute, Los Angeles.

Weigand, Phil C., Garman Harbottle, and Edward V. Sayr 1977 Turquoise Sources and Source Analysis: Mesoamerica and the Southwestern U.S.A. In *Exchange Systems in Prehistory*, edited by Timothy K. Earle and Jonathon E. Ericson, pp. 15–34. Academic Press, New York, San Francisco, and London.

12

THE SUSTENANCE PROVIDERS

War, sacrifice, and the origin of people in ancient Mesoamerica

Oswaldo Chinchilla Mazariegos

> Then the Blade Stone is birthed by Raxa Xib'alb'ay [and] Q'ana Xib'alb'ay. Then people were created by Tz'aqöl B'itöl; [they were] the sustenance providers for the Blade Stone.
>
> *Xajil Chronicle*[1]

Terse phrases near the beginning of the *Xajil Chronicle* (also known as *Memorial de Sololá* or *Annals of the Kaqchikels*) explain why people were created: they were destined to be "the sustenance providers for the Blade Stone." That is, people were created in order to provide victims to "feed" the sacrificial knife. This view, espoused by a mid-sixteenth-century Kaqchikel writer in the Guatemalan highlands, was widespread in ancient Mesoamerica. Mythical narratives from highland Mexico and the Maya highlands describe how people were created to provide nourishment for the gods and explain that the means to obtain the necessary food was through war and human sacrifice. The myths described how the first victims were procured in primeval conflicts, which, in turn, offered paradigms for earthly warfare and explained the rationale behind the sacrifice of war captives. War was thus conceived as an act of piety and abidance with the will of the gods that ensured the continued rise of the sun and the fertility of the earth. It provided a purpose for the life of those who would take charge of providing sustenance for the gods.

Scholars have long recognized the religious connotations of ancient Mesoamerican warfare. Political and economic motivations were inextricably entwined with ritual and religious explanations that cast war as a sacred duty, performed in the service of the gods (Webster 2000:104–106). In this chapter, I compare sixteenth-century Nahua beliefs from central Mexico with those of the K'iche' and Kaqchikel from the Guatemalan highlands and show that in both regions, the origin of people was closely linked with the

DOI: 10.4324/9781351268004-12

origin of war, to the point that one cannot be understood without the other. These comparisons build on Michel Graulich's insightful studies of Nahua and highland Maya myths (1974, 1987). I also discuss Classic Maya myths related to primeval wars, known from iconographic and epigraphic sources, and argue that they reflect themes that are present in Postclassic highland Maya and Nahua narratives. While the evidence is fragmentary, it suggests that the Classic Maya shared core beliefs with Postclassic peoples about the primeval encounters that explained the origin of war and provided religious justifications for warfare.

The Nahua origin of war

In sixteenth-century Nahua myths, the origin of war was intimately tied to the origin of the sun. The gods created war as a means of providing human victims to feed the sun and created people to serve as food for the sun. The connection was plainly stated in the *Historia de los Mexicanos por sus Pinturas* (hereafter abbreviated as *Historia*):

> The four gods got together and said that, because the earth had no clarity and was dark, and they had nothing to light it, except for the fires that they made, that they would make a sun to illuminate the earth, and that he [the sun] would eat hearts and drink blood, and for that they would make war, in which could be obtained hearts and blood. . . . And at this time, Tezcatlipoca made four hundred men and five women, so that there would be people for the sun to eat.
>
> *(Tena 2002:36–39)*[2]

War began, and the first four hundred men died after four years, while the women stayed alive. One of them, Xochiquetzal, died in the tenth year and was praised as the bravest of all and the first woman who died in war.

In a detailed study, Graulich (1974) compared the extant versions of this episode from different sources. Each source contains several iterations of incidents that are recognizably similar, although the names of the participants and the circumstances vary. They generally refer to a hero or a small group of heroes who vanquished four hundred adversaries, but they can also refer to a hero or heroes who avenged the death of four hundred characters or fought together with the four hundred against a formidable adversary. The blood and hearts of the victims who died in these conflicts served as the first food and drink for the sun and the earth.

Graulich highlighted the parallels between (a) the wars that took place after the creation of the fourth sun, which generally refer to the victories of Mixcoatl over Itzpapalotl and the four hundred Mimixcoa or the four hundred Chichimec, and (b) the birth of the Mexica patron god Huitzilopochtli and his fight against his older sister or his own mother and the four hundred Huitznahua.

Huitzilopochtli's birth was comparable to the advent of a new sun, and Graulich concluded that the Late Postclassic Mexica modeled his triumph after earlier versions of Mixcoatl's myths (1974:313). The following paragraphs trace the core themes of the Mixcoatl and Huitzilopochtli myths.

The Mixcoatl cycle

In the *Historia*, Camaxtle – also known as Mixcoatl – created four men and one woman who fell to the water and did not wage war. Then he created four hundred Chichimec, who got drunk with pulque that the god himself had invented. Camaxtle mustered the five children that he had created first, who fought the four hundred Chichimec and killed most of them. Camaxtle himself became a Chichimec and kept waging war, "with which he fed the sun" (Tena 2002:40–43).

The Legend of the Suns version of the myth began when the goddess Iztac-chalchiuhtlicue gave birth to four hundred Mixcoa (plural: Mimixcoa). She then entered a cave and gave birth to five more Mimixcoa (one female and four males), including Mixcoatl himself. The sun gave arrows to the four hundred, telling them, "with this you will give me food and drink, and also with the shields," and adding that they would also feed Tlalteuctli, the earth goddess (Bierhorst 1992:150). The arrows that he gave them were made with precious feathers from colorful birds. The Mimixcoa disobeyed; they hunted birds for fun, and when they killed a jaguar, they did not offer it to the sun. They slept with women, and, like the four hundred Chichimec in the *Historia*, they got drunk with pulque. The sun called the five Mimixcoa who were born last and gave them arrows made with maguey spines. They defeated the four hundred and thus gave the sun food and drink (Bierhorst 1992:150–151).

The four hundred usually take the role of antagonists who opposed the victorious heroes, but some versions cast them as victims who were killed by a formidable opponent. In the *Annals of Cuauhtitlan*, the opponent was Itzpapalotl, "obsidian butterfly," who killed and devoured the four hundred Mimixcoa. Only Mixcoatl himself escaped and came shooting arrows against Itzpapalotl. He invoked his dead brothers, who reappeared and shot the monster to death. They burned her body and painted their faces with the ashes (Bierhorst 1992:23). Graulich (1974:319–320) compared this passage with a parallel version in the Legend of the Suns, in which two *tzitzimitl* women enticed the brothers Xiuhnel and Mimich to eat and drink with them. Xiuhnel acquiesced and slept with one of the women, who then turned on him and devoured his chest. This terrible woman was Itzpapalotl. After a difficult chase, Mimich (who is named Mixcoatl later in the text) finally defeated her with the help of the gods of fire (*xiuhteteuc-tin*). The fire gods are not numbered in the text, but their role parallels that of the four hundred Mimixcoa who helped the hero in the *Annals of Cuauhtitlan* (Bierhorst 1992:23).

The Huitzilopochtli cycle

The accounts of Huitzilopochtli's victory share key features with the Mixcoatl cycle. A common theme is the participation of a powerful female as the god's main antagonist: Huitzilopochtli's own sister or mother, who opposed the hero like Itzpapalotl did in the Mixcoatl cycle.

Nahua narratives made no clear-cut distinctions between the mythical events that transpired at the time when the sun was born and their iterations situated at Coatepec during the Mexica migration. In fact, the two are merged in the *Historia*, which identified the participants in the Coatepec episode as the same who waged the first war before the sun came out. The Mexica were carrying the mantles of the five women created by Tezcatlipoca at the time of the first war (see earlier quote). At Coatepec, the women came back to life from their mantles and were doing penance in the mountain when one of them, Coatlicue, placed a few white feathers in her breast and became pregnant. The four hundred men who had died before the birth of the sun also came back to life and, realizing that Coatlicue was pregnant, tried to burn her. But her son Huitzilopochtli was born fully armed and killed the four hundred men (Tena 2002:48–51). Coatlicue's prodigious pregnancy is also present in the detailed version recorded by Sahagún's informants, in which the newborn Huitzilopochtli killed the four hundred Huitznahua and dismembered their leader, his older sister Coyolxauhqui, whose broken body rolled down the hill (Sahagún 1978:1–5).

The *Crónica Mexicayotl* offers another version, in which Huitzilopochtli was the leader of the migrating Mexica. Realizing that the *Centzonhuitznahua* (four hundred southerners, also termed Huitzilopochtli's uncles) wanted to become established at Coatepec rather than keep moving, the god became enraged. He killed them all and also killed his own mother, the older sister of the Centzonhuitznahua who took the name Coyolxauhcihuatl in this version. The killing happened at the sacred ball court, and the narrative pays special attention to the fact that Huitzilopochtli extracted the hearts of his opponents and ate them. This happened at midnight, and the Mexica were frightened when they saw the massacre and the terrible visage of Huitzilopchtli at dawn – a clear reference to the sunrise (Alvarado Tezozomoc 2001:58–60; Anderson and Schroeder 1997:83).

Common themes

These accounts subsume themes that are critical to explain Mesoamerican warfare beliefs. The origin of war is closely connected with the origin of the sun, and the explanation for warfare was the need for victims to provide the sun and the earth with food and drink. Seler (1996:49) noted that four hundred, the number that is normally associated with the vanquished, is a trope for a multitude. Considering that they were created to feed the sun, their death was perhaps inevitable, and yet the texts take pains to justify their defeat as resulting from their misconduct and immorality. Some versions portray them as drunkards who failed to fulfill their duties. Graulich (1974:334) and Taube (1993) highlighted their connection with the gods of pulque, also referred to as the *centzontotochtin*, "four hundred rabbits." Ultimately, their behavior amounted to a failure to recognize their creators. In the Legend of the Suns, the sun referred to them as "the ones who fail to say, 'Mother! Father!'" (Bierhorst 1992:150). In contrast, their vanquishers behaved in exemplary ways, did not drink, and responded readily to the call of the sun. The failure to recognize their mother and father cast the Mimixcoa as akin to deer and other animals of the first creation in the Popol Vuh, who were unable to say the names of their creators and therefore were condemned to be hunted and eaten (Graulich 1997a:435; Olivier 2015:101). Hunting and warfare were frequently likened to each other in ancient Mesoamerica (Faugère 2008; Houston et al. 2013:219–220; Olivier 2010).

The precious weapons that the sun gave to the four hundred Mimixcoa in the Legend of the Suns were a sign of their doom. They paralleled the costly implements made of quetzal feathers, gold, coral, and incense that the lunar hero used to perform sacrifice in Sahagún's version of the origin of the sun and the moon. In contrast, the solar hero used only maguey spines, fir branches, green water rushes, and grass balls (Sahagún 1953:4). When the time came, the lunar hero hesitated, while the solar hero threw himself at once into the blazing pyre from which he emerged as the sun. The humble arrows made of maguey spines that the sun gave to the five Mimixcoa were akin to the solar hero's sacrificial instruments and marked them as true warriors, capable of overcoming their wealthier but dissolute foes (Graulich 1997b:162).

The role of Itzpapalotl and other female goddesses in the myths is intriguing. One of the five Mimixcoa in the Legend of the Suns was a woman named Cuitlachcihuatl, "wolf woman" (Tena 2002:184–187). While her four brothers killed the four hundred, the text does not mention Cuitlachcihuatl as actively engaging in battle. When females take active roles, they are normally antagonists. In the Mixcoatl cycle, Itzpapalotl was the most formidable opponent of the hero, and the same is true for Coyolxauhqui – whether sister or mother – in the Huitzilopochtli cycle. Another goddess who was somehow involved in the first wars was Xochiquetzal, evoked in a terse statement of the *Historia* as "the first who died in the war, and the bravest of all who died in it" (Tena 2002:38–39). While there are no further details, the very fact that Xochiquetzal died makes it likely that she was an opponent of the hero or heroes who won the first war in this version.

Seler (1963:196, 1996:53) identified the Mimixcoa as stellar beings, based on the study of representations of war captives destined for sacrifice who shared the black facial paint of Tlahuizcalpanteuctli, the warlike god of the morning star. The black facial paint also corresponded to the description of the Mimixcoa, who painted their faces with the ashes of Itzpapalotl in the *Annals of Cuauhtitlan* (Bierhorst 1992:23). While the astral interpretation of Huitzilopochtli's ordeal is sometimes questioned (Gonzáles de Lesur 1968), the iconographic identification of the Mimixcoa as stellar beings is well-established (Graulich 1987; López Austin and López Luján 2009:365–366; Taube 1993:3).

The *Cronica Mexicayotl* placed the key events of Huitzilopochtli's ordeal at midnight and at dawn, thus linking them with the solar cycle. Seler (1996:96) realized that Huitzilopochtli fought against nocturnal beings, and his terrible appearance at dawn alluded to the rise of the sun. Although Huitzilopochtli was not identified explicitly with the sun, his cult had a significant solar component, and his birth was likened to the advent of the sun of a new era (Graulich 1987:224–231; Nicholson 1971:425). This may explain the recurrent accounts of the origin of war in the *Historia*; for Graulich, each corresponded to a different era, culminating with the birth of Huitzilopochtli and Mexica warfare in the fifth era. The reiteration of similar events, time and again from mythical to historical times, is commonplace in Mesoamerican narratives.

After recounting the birth of Huitzilopochtli and his victory over the four hundred Chichimec, the author of the *Historia* added, "and each year they celebrated this feast of his birth, and death of these four hundred men, as will be recounted in the chapter on the feasts that they had" (Tena 2002:50–51). The myth was thus merged with the reenactments that took place every year in the ritual cycle of the sixteenth-century Nahua. Graulich recognized that it was a paradigm for the rituals that took place during the monthly feast of Panquetzaliztli, which celebrated the birth of the sun and the origin of war and captive sacrifice that allowed men to provide sustenance to the sun (1974:323–325).

The K'iche' origin of war

In the *Popol Vuh*, the creation of people from maize was the outcome of a long series of trials and errors. In the rhetoric of the K'iche' text, the gods were not initially cognizant of the proper way to populate the world, but they had a very clear concept of the purpose, which they stated in the form of questions: "How should the sowing be, and the dawning? Who is to be the provider, nurturer?" (Tedlock 1996:65). Tedlock showed that these questions referred to the interrelated creational processes that explained the daily rise of the sun, the growth of plants – especially maize – and the origin of people. Implicit in the last question was the intention of the gods to create creatures who would take charge of nourishing them. Tedlock noted, "the providers or nurturers ultimately intended here are human beings, who will one day sustain the gods through prayer and sacrifice" (1996:226). Later passages of the *Popol Vuh* made it clear that the means to sustain the gods included taking animal and human victims, in addition to prayer and self-sacrifice.

The *Popol Vuh* contains no explicit statements about the creation of war. Yet there are two passages that relate with the origin of war and human sacrifice: (a) the death of the four hundred boys and (b) the first wars of the K'iche' forebears. In parallel with highland Mexican sources, the former was linked with the mythical origins of the sun, while the latter occurred during the legendary migration of the K'iche' forebears to the Guatemalan highlands.

The death of the four hundred boys

Graulich (1974:321–322) compared Nahua myths with the story of Zipacna and the four hundred boys in the *Popol Vuh*. The sequence of events in the K'iche' narrative corresponds with the *Annals of Cuauhtitlan*, in which Itzpapalotl initially killed the four hundred Mimixcoa but was subsequently defeated by Mixcoatl (Bierhorst 1992:23). In the *Popol Vuh*, Zipacna initially killed the four hundred boys and was later defeated by the Hero Twins. Learning that the four hundred boys plotted to kill him, Zipacna outwitted them and misled them to think that he was dead. The boys prepared pulque and got drunk – paralleling the inclinations of the Mimixcoa in the Legend of the Suns. Zipacna threw down their house over the senseless boys, killing all of them. Distressed by the power of the monster, the brothers Hunahpu and Xbalanque devised a stratagem and threw a mountain over Zipacna, who finally turned to stone. At the end of their ordeal, Hunahpu and Xbalanque rose to the sky as the sun and the moon, and the four hundred boys joined them as stars (Tedlock 1996:81–85).

Zipacna's defeat was part of a series of encounters in which Hunahpu and Xbalanque overcame the monstrous beings that prevailed in a previous era, namely Seven Macaw, the proud avian monster who pretended to be the sun; his wife Chimalmat; and their sons, Zipacna and Cabracan. The Hero Twins realized that these mighty beings had to be tamed before people could thrive: "Good shall never come of this. People will never be able to live here on the face of the earth" (Christenson 2003:95). The *Popol Vuh* described them separately, but these monsters overlap with each other, and they also overlap in complex ways with their counterparts in Nahua myths. But in contrast with the warlike violence employed by the Nahua heroes, the heroes of the Popol Vuh employed their wits and their magical prowess to confront their foes. They deceived Seven Macaw and killed him by plucking out the resplendent eyes and teeth that were the source of his glory, and his wife Chimalmat died together with him.

Chimalmat is an intriguing member of this fearful family. Her name relates with that of Chimalman, the aggressive woman who confronted Mixcoatl in the Legend of the Suns. The hero had to subdue her with arrows, and only then was he able to impregnate her. Graulich (1974:331–336) noted Chimalman's correspondences with Itzpapalotl, Coatlicue, Coyolxauhqui, and Xochiquetzal, the warlike women who opposed the heroes in Nahua myths. In previous work, I argued that Chimalmat embodied the female aspect of Seven Macaw and that the couple can be understood as a dual gendered pair who opposed the rise of the sun (Chinchilla Mazariegos 2011a, 2017:137–138). Mentions of Chimalmat in the *Popol Vuh* are reminiscent of the women who participated in the primeval wars of the Mexica, sometimes in passive roles, sometimes as members of the triumphant group, and sometimes as forbidding adversaries of the heroes.

The K'iche' forebears at war

In the *Popol Vuh*, there is no indication that the death of the four hundred boys was intended to feed the sun, which had not yet risen. The demands of the gods for sustenance began after the first sunrise, when they made requests to the first four men, the forebears of the K'iche' noble houses, whose names were B'alam K'itz'e, B'alam Aqab', Majucutaj, and Ik'i B'alam. Throughout the Popol Vuh, these men are referred to as "penitents, sacrificers," in reference to their acts of self-sacrifice and their role as providers of sacrificial victims for the gods (Tedlock 1996:291; Christenson 2003:203–203).

The gods initially begged the K'iche' forebears to bring them the blood of animals. "And the bloody drink was drunk by the gods" (Tedlock 1996:164). Then the gods commanded them to abduct the people of the *amaq'*, a term that referred to peoples who, according to the *Popol Vuh*, were already established in the Guatemalan highlands when the K'iche' arrived. In a previous episode, the *amaq'* had requested fire from the K'iche' and, in exchange, they had promised to allow themselves to "be suckled on their sides, under their arms" (Tedlock 1996:155–156). The metaphor referred to breastfeeding a baby, but it amounted to offering themselves as sacrificial victims (Tedlock 1996:299; Christenson 2003:216). Graulich and Olivier (2004) cited sources that compared Mesoamerican deities with babies who had to be nurtured from the breasts of their mothers. People were abducted and, the *Título de Totonicapán* added, "the blood [of the victims] went before the idols" (Carmack and Mondloch 1983:178).

The abductions triggered the first wars between the K'iche' and the *amaq'*. But rather than describing warlike victories, the authors of the *Popol Vuh* highlighted the magical skills of the K'iche' forebears. First, they avoided the trap of falling in the embrace of the daughters of the lords of the *amaq'*, which would have brought their downfall. In this attempt, the daughters of the lords are comparable to the deer women who enticed Xiuhnel and Mimich in the Legend of the Suns. Accepting their sexual offers was tantamount to defeat and death – a trope that is also present in ancient Maya art (Chinchilla Mazariegos 2011b:67, 2017:199–201).

Then the lords of the *amaq'* armed their warriors with arrows, shields, and precious metals: "Their metal ornaments were countless, they looked beautiful, all the lords, the men." But the warriors fell asleep, and the K'iche' forebears stripped them of all their finery and plucked out their eyebrows and whiskers (Tedlock 1996:170–171). The *Popol Vuh* does not explain why the warriors fell asleep, but their slumbering is reminiscent of the fate of the four hundred boys, who were defeated while sleeping in drunkenness. Their beautiful metal armor parallels the gold and greenstone that Seven Macaw boasted. The K'iche' forebears plucking out the warriors' facial hair and stripping them of their finery parallels the way in which the Hero Twins took Seven Macaw's wealth and plucked off his shining eyes and teeth made of precious stones and metals. Admirable, beautiful, and costly weapons are normally held by those who will suffer defeat in Mesoamerican myths, like the beautiful arrows that the sun gave to the four hundred Mimixcoa in the Legend of the Suns, which proved no match for the maguey spine arrows of Mixcoatl and his companions (Bierhorst 1992:150).

In the description of the next attack, the authors of the *Popol Vuh* highlighted the multitude of warriors of the *amaq'*, which counted no less than sixteen thousand or twenty-four thousand (Tedlock 1996:172). In contrast, the K'iche' forebears were alone, joined only by their wives – an important fact to which we shall return. The disparity is indeed familiar from the primeval myths that involved four hundred against one or only a handful of champions, who nevertheless emerged victorious. Once again, the K'iche' forebears employed cunning and magic. They deceived their foes by dressing up manikins as warriors, and they filled four jars with wasps and hornets. When the warriors approached the citadel, they opened the jars and the insects swarmed over the assailants, biting them until they were senseless. The K'iche' forebears finished them off, and their wives participated in the killing (Tedlock 1996:173).

War and sexuality in the Título de Totonicapán

The warlike stance of the K'iche' forebears' wives evokes other passages in Mesoamerican narratives that involve women partaking in war. Women are sometimes described as capable of engaging in violent physical attacks, but their participation often involves sexual aggression and magic (Chinchilla Mazariegos 2011c; Klein 1994). This is indeed the case in the *Título de Totonicapán*, which contains parallel versions of the two encounters described in the *Popol Vuh*. In the first encounter with the *amaq'*, rather than the facial hair, the K'iche' forebears cut off the little finger and the little toe of the warriors (Carmack and Mondloch 1983:178). In Mesoamerica, mutilations of body members are comparable to castration. From this perspective, plucking off the facial hair and severing the fingers and toes of the *amaq'* warriors are metaphorical expressions of sexual aggression (Chinchilla Mazariegos 2011a; Galinier 1984; Klein 1994:234–235).

The *Título de Totonicapán* accorded the wives of the K'iche' forebears a crucial role in the second encounter, with sexual aggression implicit. In this version, they were the ones who opened the jars to let the biting insects out against the assaulting warriors (Carmack and Mondloch 1983:179). This is consistent with widespread metaphors that relate jars and other containers with women's wombs. For the sixteenth-century Nahua authors of the *Codex Carolino*, broken or perforated vessels in a wedding indicated that the bride was not virgin, and pregnant women should not eat tamales that stuck to a pot while cooking, lest the fetus adhere to the womb and die (Burkhart 1997:44; Garibay 1967:27; Sahagún 1989:299). The modern Otomí and Mixtec liken pregnancy to the cooking processes that take place inside jars (Galinier 1997:63; Monaghan 2001:293). In addition, stinging and poisonous creatures are closely associated with feminine sexuality. In Q'eqchi' myths, they originated from the spilled blood of the moon – sometimes identified as menstrual blood – recovered and incubated by the sun in womb-like jars or boxes (Braakhuis 2005; Chinchilla Mazariegos

2017:95–99; De la Cruz Torres 40–43; Thompson 1930:128–129). Narratives from several regions describe how those creatures originated as a result of sexual transgressions, and in some versions, they were born from the body of goddesses who engaged in sexual encounters (Chinchilla Mazariegos 2021; Montoliú Villar 1990).

The wives of the K'iche' forebears opening the jars to let the biting insects out evoked metaphors related to sexual magic and sexual aggression, casting the victories of the K'iche' forebears as tantamount to sexual assault against the *amaq'* warriors. While the *Popol Vuh* described the wives of the K'iche' forbears as participants in the fight, in the *Título de Totonicapan* they acted as purveyors of powerful sexual magic that brought about the defeat of their opponents.[3] The subtle allusions to sexual aggression in these passages are not strange. The *Popol Vuh* is rich in sexual metaphors and double entendres that imply sexual meanings, and the victories of the K'iche' forebears against the *amaq'* paralleled the feats of the Hero Twins, earlier in the *Popol Vuh*, who repeatedly employed sexual magic and sexual aggression against their foes (Chinchilla Mazariegos 2018).

Warfare and the Kaqchikel

The *Xajil Chronicle* contains no parallel for the defeat of the four hundred boys in the *Popol Vuh* or the four hundred Mimixcoa in Nahua myths. But the Kaqchikel text offers some of the clearest statements about the purpose of the creation of people and its relationship with war. The passage (see epigraph) seems to involve two complementary acts: first, "the Blade Stone is birthed by Raxa Xib'alb'ay [and] Q'ana Xib'alb'ay" (Maxwell and Hill 2006:8). In highland Guatemalan texts, Xib'alb'ay normally refers to an underworld location, but in this sentence, it seemingly designates a pair of deities – perhaps a male-female pair – or two aspects of one deity that probably had connotations of fear and death. In response, people were created by Tz'aqöl B'itöl, "the framer, the shaper" (Christenson 2003:60). They were destined to be "the sustenance providers for the Blade Stone [*Chay Ab'äj*]" (modified from Maxwell and Hill 2006:8).

Following Brinton (1885:69), editors of the *Xajil Chronicle* translated *Chay Ab'äj* as "obsidian stone" (Recinos 1950:49; Otzoy 1999:155; Maxwell and Hill 2006:8). Van Akkeren (2000:182) suggested that it was an alternative name for Jun Tijax, one of the patron gods that the Kaqchikel received at Tulan, whose name can be translated as "One Flint Knife" (Maxwell and Hill 2006:28). Literally, the word *chay* designates obsidian (called *pedernal* or *pedernal negro* in colonial Spanish sources). But colonial Kaqchikel and K'iche' dictionaries gloss *chay* as referring not simply to the material but to obsidian blades, particularly those that were used for human sacrifice. The relevant glosses include:

Chay. la nabaxa (Vico n.d., folio 58v).

Nauajón de pedernal a modo de machete, con [que] mataban y desquartiçaban a la gente delante de los ídolos: *Chay puzbal vinak, pehal, o qhaibal vinak cumal he oher vinak* (Coto 1983:367).

Nauaja de pedernal con que mataban hombres ante sus ídolos: *chay* (Basseta 2005:232)

Caxquillo de saeta: *cha* (Basseta 2005:89).

Piedra que ponen en la flecha: *cha*; idem "la lanzeta con que sangran" (Basseta 2005:255).

Chai: Navaja de pedernal (Ximénez 1985:177).

Chaa. la piedra que le llaman cuchillo del diablo (Dürr and Sachse 2017:101).

In attention to these glosses, I prefer to translate *Chay Ab'äj* as "Blade Stone," a phrasing that refers more accurately to a sacrificial knife. The semantic connotations are important. Rather than creating obsidian, the gods created the Blade Stone, which would require sustenance in the form of sacrificial victims. People were created to provide it.

The idea of "feeding" the sacrificial blades is attested in the Classic Maya inscriptions. Lacadena García-Gallo (2009:43) translated the war-related phrase *wi'aj utook' upakal* on Naranjo Stela 23 as "the flint and shield were fed" and noted the same literary image in the sixteenth-century Yucatec *Diccionario de San Francisco*, which offered the gloss "matanza grande haber en la guerra y hacerse" for the phrases *wi'il jalal* and *wi'il tok'*, which literally mean "the food of the arrow" and "the food of the flint" (Barrera Vásquez 1980:923).[4]

Presumably, providing sustenance for the gods was the duty of all peoples. But in the rhetoric of the Kaqchikel text, this duty was particularly entrusted to the Kaqchikel. When all peoples arrived at the fabled city of Tulan, they were divided into two groups: the "warriors," who were the Kaqchikel forebears, were lined to the right. Other peoples, known as the seven *amaq'*, were lined to the left of Tulan. Their placement is significant in terms of Mesoamerican notions about the solar cycle. According to Gossen (1979), the Tzotzil of Chamula, Chiapas, associate the right hand with the day, sunlight, the counterclockwise movement of the sun, and, by extension, with masculinity and righteousness. The left hand is associated with the night, the moon, femininity, and the underworld. After taking their positions, each group received a different burden:

> First, he bestowed the burden of the seven *amaq'*. Immediately, then, he bestowed the burden of the warriors. Just jade, precious metal, quetzal feathers, trogon feathers [and] scarlet feathers along with writings, carvings, weavings; flutes, songs, 260-day calendars; cacao in ears, cacao as beans; just riches were carried forth from Tulan [by the seven *amaq'*]. As for the warriors, [they received] just arrows [and] shields; just rounded wood, just straight cane was their burden when they came from Pa Tulan.
>
> *(modified from Maxwell and Hill 2006:15–16)*

The purpose of the warriors' burden was clearly stated in the next sentence: "This is your burden; this you must nourish, you must sustain. It is called the Blade Stone" (modified from Maxwell and Hill 2006:17).

The contrasting qualities of the burdens given to the seven *amaq'* and the warriors are familiar. The elaborate objects of precious materials given to the former are like the precious arrows of the four hundred Mimixcoa and the shining armor of the *amaq'* in the Popol Vuh. Like them, the seven *amaq'* of the Xajil narrative were destined to fall prey to the warriors, who would eventually gain lordship and take their wealth from them (Maxwell and Hill 2006:20–22). Indeed, the *Xajil Chronicle* recounts how the Kaqchikel warriors carried their burden to the Guatemalan highlands, fighting their way to establish supremacy.

At a later stage, the chronicle describes the feeding of the Blade Stone, also referred to as K'axtok'. Colonial dictionaries usually gloss this deity name as "devil" or "deceiver" (Basseta 2005:368; Ximénez 1985:169). A passage from the *Xajil Chronicle* suggests that K'axtok' was an alternative name for the blade stone:

> Then the feeding of K'axtok' began. Each seven days, each thirteen days, it was fed with: only green sap, green fruit, green scrapings, green bark; and only young animals, cats, the signs of the night, would be burned before it. As for the tree-mushroom caps, they would finish their ears. The fruits with which the Blade Stone was fed long ago were not great, they say. But then the measure of the feedings of this K'axtok' grew larger; so, too, grew the measure of his glory.
>
> *(Maxwell and Hill 2006:126–127)*

The description seems to parallel the progression of foods that were offered to the gods by the K'iche' forebears in the *Popol Vuh*, which began with animals and then progressed to human victims. The Kaqchikel account refers to forest plants followed by animals and does not mention human sacrifice. But this passage is immediately followed by the account of a battle in which the enemies surrounded the Kaqchikel on top of a hill. The Kaqchikel threw rolling logs downhill, until their enemies "were dissolved into death" (Maxwell and Hill 2006:129). The incidents are different, but the encounter is reminiscent of the battles fought by the K'iche' forebears when they were surrounded by numerous enemies on top of a hill and outdid them by performing magical feats. The death of the seven *amaq'* in this battle is tantamount to the encounters that provided the first human victims for the gods in K'iche' and Nahua myths.

Classic Maya War myths

Representations on Classic Maya vases and brief but significant hieroglyphic passages refer to primeval struggles among the gods. The ceramic vases discussed in the following sections refer to (a) a primeval encounter that involved stellar beings and deities; and (b) a quasi-historical encounter between a group of courtiers who carried items of wealth and a group of warriors who carried weapons, led by the forebear of a major ruling dynasty. Despite their fragmentary character, these accounts shared important themes with the primeval wars described in sixteenth-century highland Mexican and Guatemalan sources.

The war of the stars

The notion of a primeval conflict that involved stellar warriors is relevant to explain the warlike connotations of the stars in Classic Maya beliefs. Scholars have long debated the role of astronomical phenomena in Maya warfare beliefs (Aldana 2005; Aveni and Hotaling 1994; Carlson 1993; Freidel and Schele 1990:444–446; Justeson 1989; Lounsbury 1981; Martin 2020:220–222; Nahm 1994). Most studies have focused on the planet Venus, which was regarded as bringer of war and death in sixteenth-century Mesoamerica (Seler 1904). But there is evidence that other stellar beings were equally significant for the Classic Maya. Examples include the four constellations – a flock of peccaries, two human-bodied characters, and a turtle – that preside over the presentation of captives on the north vault of Room 2 at Bonampak (Figure 12.1). Their nature is indicated by *ek'*, "star" signs that mark a variety of celestial beings in Maya art, including stars, planets, and constellations (Bricker and Bricker 1992; Chinchilla Mazariegos 2006; Milbrath 1999:249–293; V. Miller 1989; Spinden 1916).

Lounsbury (1981) interpreted the constellations at Bonampak as portraying the night sky on the date of the battle, although this is hard to test due to the poor conservation of the date in the associated inscription (Miller and Houston 1998). An important and often overlooked fact is that the constellations occupy

FIGURE 12.1 Detail from reconstruction of the mural paintings of Bonampak, Room 2, upper register (AD 791). Above: South side, showing probable royal ancestors portrayed in solar cartouches. Below: North side, showing four constellations.

Source: Yale University Art Gallery, Gift of Bonampak Documentation Project (illustrated by Heather Hurst and Leonard Ashby).

only one side of the celestial tableau that extends to both sides of the upper vault of Room 2. The opposite side shows three characters portrayed inside solar cartouches and two captives that flank the central cartouche. Comparisons with ancestor portraits at Palenque, Yaxchilan, and other sites suggests that these are ancestors of the Bonampak royal lineage, elevated to a solar destiny in the afterlife (Chinchilla Mazariegos 2006; Miller and Brittenham 2013:102; Taube 2004).

The representation of stars as the companions of solar ancestors is not limited to Bonampak. On the legs and the lid of the Palenque Sarcophagus, deceased noblemen who were prominent members of K'inich Janahb' Pakal's royal court were portrayed as stellar companions of the king, whose transit to death was likened to the dawn of a new sun (Chinchilla Mazariegos 2006; Stuart and Stuart 2008:176). Another example is the ancestral royal couple seated within solar and lunar cartouches above a sky band in the upper register of Yaxchilan Stela 4. They are joined by two portraits of the Jaguar War God that hang down from *ek'*, "star" signs below the sky band, as if witnessing the performance of dynastic ritual by the current king. A major deity associated with the night and fire, the Jaguar War God was also a patron of war in Classic Maya religion, and his visage appears frequently on warriors' shields. While commonly labeled as "Jaguar God of the Underworld," his portraits point to heavenly and stellar, rather than underworld connotations (Chinchilla Mazariegos 2006; Milbrath 1999:124–126). A glaring example is a monumental portrait in the Jaguar Stairway at Copan, where his face is flanked by two enormous *ek'* signs, in an architectural setting that was likely associated with the display and sacrifice of war captives (M. Miller 1988). The Jaguar War God is one of the warlike Venus patrons in the Dresden Codex, although his name glyph suggests a Postclassic merge with God L (Figure 12.4).

In sixteenth-century Nahua beliefs, the souls of the warriors who died on the battlefield or were captured and sacrificed found their afterlife destiny in the eastern sky, where they greeted the sunrise with warlike cries and skirmishes (Sahagún 1969:162). As noted above, Seler (1996:41–45) identified these stellar beings with the Mimixcoa, the stellar warriors who died in primeval wars and thus provided food for the sun. In addition, the Nahua associated the stars with the souls of deceased lords. Sahagún reported "that the lords when they died became gods . . . and that some turned into the sun, others into the moon, and others into other planets" (1989, vol. 2:673). Representations of deceased kings in solar cartouches and deceased warriors and courtiers as stars hint that the Classic Maya conceived of similar destinies for the souls of deceased kings and noblemen. But the question is whether Maya beliefs about the afterlife destinies of warriors and lords found explanations in primeval myths that involved warfare among the stars.

A positive answer to this question is suggested by representations on Late Classic ceramic vases. The Vase of the Stars (Figure 12.2) shows a contingent of stellar beings: gods, animals, and human-bodied characters with bizarre facial features that depart from Classic Maya standards of beauty. The majority can

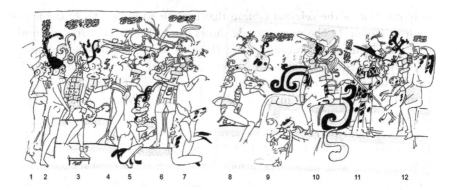

FIGURE 12.2 Rollout drawing of the Vase of the Stars (drawing by Oswaldo Chinchilla). The Jaguar War God (character 6) leads a group of stellar beings (Characters 1–7), presenting two captives (characters 8 and 9) to an enthroned lord accompanied by a stellar God S and the Maize God in his lunar aspect (characters 10–12).

be identified as personified stars or constellations because of the *ek'* signs that appear on their back or behind their armpits – like perspiration oozing out of their bodies. Two of them take the stance of humiliated captives presented before an enthroned lord, and one of the captives has a crocodilian body, evoking the reptilian or piscine qualities suggested by the name of Zipacna in the *Popol Vuh* (Chinchilla Mazariegos 2005, 2011b:199–203). The victorious lord is badly eroded but appears to be an aspect of the Maize God, joined on the throne by a stellar manifestation of God S and by the Maize God in his lunar aspect. Chief among a crowded group of seven characters who witness the presentation of captives from another room is the Jaguar War God (Figure 12.3: Character 6 in Figure 12.2). His frontal pose denotes a leading role, possibly as the main warrior in the celestial confrontation that led to the capture and presentation of the stellar crocodile and his companion.

Further hints appear in the Star War Vase (Zender 2020). The Jaguar War God and his frequent partner, the Pax God, occupy the rings of a large star sign, seemingly bringing about cosmic destruction signaled by a falling building and by the deathly transit of the Maize God. A short textual caption suggests that this mythical catastrophe was like-in-kind with some of the most important historic battles that were commemorated using the "earth-star" verb in Classic Maya inscriptions (Martin 2020:208–209). The fragmentary data – compounded by overpainting on the Star War Vase – hamper the possibilities of reconstructing coherent narratives, but the presence of some of the same characters suggests that the episodes depicted in both vases were not unrelated. The distinctions between them may correspond to different versions of myths that explained the origin of war, perhaps comparable in their range of variation to the sixteenth-century Nahua variants of the Mixcoatl myths.

FIGURE 12.3 Detail from the Vase of the Stars, showing Character 6. The jaguar ear and white cruller under the spiral eye correspond to the Jaguar War God. The star sign is attached to his right arm.

Source: Photograph by Nicholas Hellmuth, courtesy of Museo Popol Vuh, Universidad Francisco Marroquín.

The participation of stellar characters in representations related with war and human sacrifice, and their association with deceased kings elevated to solar status, suggest that the Classic Maya shared elements of Postclassic Nahua and highland Maya beliefs about the origin of war and the religious explanations of warfare. They conceived of primeval encounters in which the participants included multitudes of stellar beings. While the specific incidents are missing, those encounters

FIGURE 12.4 Detail from Dresden Codex, page 46b, showing the Jaguar War God as a Venus God. The crenellated beard and jaguar ear are distinctive, although the associated name glyph corresponds to the name normally used by God L in the codices.

Source: SLUB Dresden Mscr. Dresden.R.310.

were likely the paradigms for the conduct of warfare and the ritual sacrifice of war captives by earthly lords. The ancient Maya myth of the war of the stars has correspondences with the primeval narratives of Mixcoatl in Nahua mythology and with the death of the four hundred boys in the Popol Vuh.

The confrontation in codex-style vessels

"The confrontation" was an appropriate label coined by Robicsek and Hales (1981:80–82) to designate a group of Late Classic codex-style ceramic vessels that show two groups of males facing each other (Figure 12.5). The members of one group are warriors wearing facial paint and wild animal headdresses, holding spears, and displaying shields. Those in the other group have no facial paint, and most wear simple cloth headdresses. Instead of weapons, they carry bundles of cloth, mat ornaments, shells, and tufts of feathers. Their loads are entirely similar to the wealth items that are commonly presented to lords as tribute or gifts in courtly scenes (McAnany 2010:273–278; Stuart 1998). In contrast with the warriors, the members of this group are carriers of wealth and finery. The two groups are immersed in water, which, Robicsek and Hales (1981:137) noted, may indicate either a mythical location or the fact that the participants are crossing a body of water.

FIGURE 12.5 Two examples of the confrontation scene on codex-style vessels. (a) Vase K4117; (b) Vase K1248.

Source: Rollout photographs by Justin Kerr.

The Calendar Round dates on some of these vessels are contrived and cannot be fixed securely in the Long Count – a frequent characteristic of Classic Maya mythical dates. Grube (2004:124–127) identified the hieroglyphic name of the founder of the Kaanul dynasty of Calakmul, nicknamed "Skybearer," on vessel K4117. This raised the question of whether the vessels may be partly historical, especially considering that Martin (2017) tentatively dated the Kaanul dynastic founder in the second or early third century AD. The vessels show no signs of fighting between the two groups, but the presence of warriors suggests warlike connotations. The brief captions on vessels K1338 and K4117 describe an "axing" (*ch'ahkaj*) event, while other vessels describe the event as *och'[u]cheen*, "enters the domain/settlement of," a phrase that Martin (2004:107; 2020:213–214) interpreted as denoting a military invasion. On vase K4117, the *ch'ahkaj* verb is followed by the name of Skybearer, leaving some ambiguity as to whether the dynastic founder was the object of the verb or the actor – whether he was axed or he axed someone else.

Several authors have offered interpretations of the mythical and quasi-historical contents of confrontation scenes. Taube (2004:74) suggested that they showed the capture of the Wind God – the leader of the carriers of wealth – by the leader of the warriors, named Chahk Xib' in the associated captions. Helmke and Kupprat (2016, 2017) argued that the vessels portrayed a mythical confrontation that led to the defeat and decapitation of the Maize God, rather than the Wind God, at the hands of Chahk Xib' and his warriors. Grube (2004:126) recognized an opposition between ferocious warriors associated with the wilderness, and cultured and refined members of civilized communities; for García Barrios (2006) the scenes involved negotiation among two differentiated social groups, one related to warfare and the other to knowledge and courtly life, culminating with the victory of Chahk Xib', who adopted the name of Skybearer and became the founder of the Kaanul dynasty.

The Maize God – or an impersonator that resembles him – is fitting as the leader of the wealthy and sophisticated group. More than just maize, the Maize God relates with abundance and riches represented by valuables such as cacao and jade (Chinchilla Mazariegos 2017:194; Martin 2006). The overlap of the saga of a dynastic founder with mythical events enacted by gods is not strange in Mesoamerica. Notwithstanding the prevailing uncertainties, the confrontation scenes seem to portray incidents from a mythical narrative related to the legendary establishment of the Kaanul dynasty, and in this sense they are reminiscent of the Mexica, K'iche', and Kaqchikel migration narratives. The opposing groups portrayed in the confrontation vessels are reminiscent of the contrast between the "warriors" and the "seven *amaq'*" in the *Xajil Chronicle* and the burdens that each group received at Tulan. Arrows and shields were the burden of the warriors, while the seven *amaq'* were given items of wealth, jewelry, feathers, songs, calendars, and writing – an almost perfect correspondence with the items that each of the opposing groups carry in the confrontation vessels.

Similar contrasts prevail in narratives of origin across Mesoamerica. Nahua narratives contraposed the uncultured and destitute Chichimec with the wealthy and civilized Toltec (Graulich 1987:300–302, 1997a:126–129), while those of the Purhépecha described the struggles of the Uacúsecha Chichimec against the well-established "Islanders" (Arnauld and Michelet 1991; Haskell 2018:198–205; Martínez González 2010). These accounts oppose an ingroup of destitute and uncultured but severe and pious warriors, to an outgroup of civilized, wealthy peoples who possessed knowledge and riches. The former people – always the writers' forebears – are invariably destined to overcome the latter in the earliest wars, not only because of their martial prowess, but also because of their piety and their abidance with the gods' request to provide victims to nourish them. Subsequent passages usually describe intermarriage between both groups, which allowed the members of the ingroup to acquire the trappings of civilization.

The aquatic setting of confrontation scenes is significant. Considering the analogy with sixteenth-century accounts of the origin of highland Maya dynasties, it is worth considering whether it may relate to the crossing of the sea during a primordial migration. In the detailed account of the Xajil Chronicle, the seven *amaq'* were waiting hopelessly at the edge of the water. Despite their precious burdens, they could not find a way to proceed. The Kaqchikel forebears magically opened the waters using a red tree that they brought from Tulan, allowing all peoples to cross (Maxwell and Hill 2006:35–41). The crossing of the sea involved no confrontation, but it reaffirmed the superiority of the warriors over the seven *amaq'*. It appears that the painters of the codex-style confrontation scenes explained the origins of the Kaanul ruling dynasty in terms of a primeval migration that included the crossing of the sea or another body of water, much like the origin stories of the sixteenth-century K'iche' and Kaqchikel.

The confrontation scenes convey the familiar contrast of warriors versus civilized peoples that prevails in Postclassic origin myths. Although admirable, the items of wealth and the refined culture of civilized peoples carry with them the seeds of their downfall (Graulich 1997b:127–128). The vessels do not portray outright warfare, but the wealth items likely imply the eventual defeat of their carriers and the triumph of the warriors that led to the establishment of the Kaanul dynasty.

Final comments

Sixteenth-century Nahua and highland Guatemalan myths about the origin of war share basic themes that include: (a) statements about the intention of the gods to create people who would provide for them, and of the origins of war as the means by which people would procure sustenance for the gods, in the form of human victims; (b) primeval confrontations that involved a multitude of characters with significant moral shortcomings, who fought against one or a small group of stark and pious heroes, who inevitably emerged victorious and provided nourishment for the gods; (c) the frequent involvement of stellar beings as warriors in primeval confrontations; (d) iterations of similar encounters that took place at different times, beginning with the first wars that happened after the sun was created, and continuing with accounts of quasi-historical wars that took place during the legendary migrations; while enacted by different partici-pants, the latter encounters reiterate themes and episodes from the former; (e) the participation of female goddesses or women who were sometimes passive but in many versions were formidable warriors, and whose role often involved sexual aggression; and (f) the opposition between a wealthy, civilized group and a group of rough and unsophisticated warriors who corresponded to the writers' people and inevitably emerged triumphant.

No single narrative contains all of these themes, but they reappear in coher-ent ways in the variants that were discussed in this chapter. The records that are extant in Classic Maya art and writing are generally shorter and less detailed, with a smaller subset of themes that are nonetheless consistent with those of Late Postclassic myths. Classic Maya iconographic sources are not explicit about the relationship between the creation of people and the creation of war or the role of people as providers for the sun and the earth, but they allude to primeval encoun-ters that involved a multitude of stellar characters and to the role of stellar beings as companions of the sun, all of which is consistent with the beliefs of Postclassic peoples. Codex-style vessels contain quasi-historical depictions of encounters between a wealthy and cultivated group and a group of wild, well-armed war-riors, who were linked to the origin of the Kaanul dynasty that ruled Calakmul during the Late Classic period. The actors are different, but the oppositions are like-in-kind to those that were recounted by sixteenth-century writers in Gua-temala and Mexico. These narratives explained why the gods created people: to provide and nurture them with their words in prayer, their performance in ritual, and the victims that they procured in war.

Acknowledgments

I thank Stephen D. Houston for his comments to an earlier version of this article, and Guilhem Olivier for his stimulating ideas transmitted in correspondence, conversations, and publications. The interpretations presented in this chapter are the sole responsibility of the author.

Notes

1 Modified from Maxwell and Hill 2006:8. The translation is further discussed later in this chapter.
2 All translations from Spanish to English were made by the author. The four gods listed at the beginning of this account were the sons of the primeval couple formed by Tona-cateuctli and Tonacacihuatl (or Xochiquetzal): Tlatlauhqui Tezcatlipoca (also known as Camaxtle), Yayauhqui Tezcatlipoca, Quetzalcoatl (also known as Yohualli Ehecatl), and Omiteotl (also known as Maquizcoatl or Huitzilopochtli; Tena 2002:24–25).
3 A parallel passage in the Título Yax also mentions the participation of the women (Car-mack and Mondloch 1989:76–77). In the Título K'oyoi, the women take the names Xur, Xpuch, and Xtax. The last two correspond to the names of the daughters of the lords who tried to seduce the K'iche' gods at their bath in the Popol Vuh and the Título de

Totonicapán. While the passage is obscure, it also mentions how the wasps and bees killed the enemies of the K'iche' (Carmack and Mondloch 2009:23).
4 The poor conservation of glyph block D13 in Naranjo Stela 23 opens uncertainties about the correct reading of the verb that Lacadena read as *wi'aj* (Stephen Houston, personal communication 2019).

References cited

Aldana, Gerardo 2005 Agency and the "Star War" Glyph: A Historical Reassessment of Classic Maya Astrology and Warfare. *Ancient Mesoamerica* 16:305–320.

Alvarado Tezozomoc, Hernando de 2001 *Crónica Mexicana*, edited by Gonzalo Díaz Migoyo and Germán Vázquez Chamorro. Dastin S. L., Madrid.

Anderson, Arthur J. O., and Susan Schroeder 1997 *Codex Chimalpahin*, Vol. 1. University of Oklahoma Press, Norman and London.

Arnauld, Marie-Charlotte, and Dominique Michelet 1991 Les migrations postclassiques au Michoacán et au Guatemala, problèmes et perspectives. In *Vingt années d'études sur le Mexique et le Guatemala à la mémoire de Nicole Percheron*, edited by A. Breton, J. P. Berthe, and S. Lecoin, pp. 67–92. Presses Univérsitaires de Mirail, Toulouse.

Aveni, Anthony F., and Lorren D. Hotaling 1994 Monumental Inscriptions and the Observational Basis of Maya Planetary Astronomy. *Archaeoastronomy (Supplement to Journal for the History of Astronomy)* 19: S21–S54.

Barrera Vásquez, Alfredo (editor) 1980 *Diccionario Maya. Maya-Español, Español-Maya*. Ediciones Cordemex, Mexico City.

Basseta, Domingo de 2005 *Vocabulario de Lengua Quiché*, edited by René Acuña. Universidad Nacional Autónoma de México, Mexico City.

Bierhorst, John (editor) 1992 *History and Mythology of the Aztecs: The Codex Chimalpopoca*. The University of Arizona Press, Tucson.

Braakhuis, H. E. M. 2005 Xbalanque's Canoe: The Origin of Poison in Q'eqchi'-Mayan Hummingbird Myth. *Anthropos* 100:173–191.

Bricker, Harvey M., and Victoria R. Bricker 1992 Zodiacal References in the Maya Codices. In *The Sky and Mayan Literature*, edited by Anthony F. Aveni, pp. 148–183. Oxford University Press, Oxford.

Brinton, Daniel G. (editor) 1885 *The Annals of the Cakchiquels: The Original Text, with a Translation, Notes, and Introduction*. Brinton's Library of Aboriginal American Literature, Vol. 6. PA.

Burkhart, Louise M. 1997 Mexica Women on the Home Front: Housework and Religion in Early Mexico. In *Indian Women in Early Mexico*, edited by Susan Schroeder, Stephanie Wood, and Robert Haskett, pp. 25–54. University of Oklahoma Press, Norman.

Carlson, John 1993 Venus-Regulated Warfare and Ritual Sacrifice in Mesoamerica. In *Astronomies and Cultures*, edited by Clive L. N. Ruggles and Nicholas J. Saunders, pp. 202–252. University Press of Colorado, Boulder.

Carmack, Robert M., and James L. Mondloch (editors) 1983 *El Título de Totonicapán*. Universidad Nacional Autónoma de México, Mexico City.

——— 1989 *El Título de Yax y otros documentos quichés de Totonicapán, Guatemala*. Universidad Nacional Autónoma de México, Mexico City.

——— 2009 Título K'oyoi. In *Crónicas Mesoamericanas*, edited by Horacio Cabezas Carcache, Vol. 2, pp. 15–67. Universidad Mesoamericana, Guatemala City.

Chinchilla Mazariegos, Oswaldo 2005 Cosmos and Warfare on a Classic Maya Vase. *Res: Anthropology and Aesthetics* 47:107–134.

———— 2006 The Stars of the Palenque Sarcophagus. *Res: Anthropology and Aesthetics* 49/50:40–58.

———— 2011a La vagina dentada: Una interpretación de la estela 25 de Izapa y las guacamayas del juego de pelota de Copán. *Estudios de Cultura Maya* 36:117–144.

———— 2011b *Imágenes de la mitología Maya*. Museo Popol Vuh, Universidad Francisco Marroquín, Guatemala.

———— 2011c La muerte de Moquihuix: Los mitos cosmogónicos mesoamericanos y la historia azteca. *Estudios de Cultura Nahuatl* 42:77–108.

———— 2017 *Art and Myth of the Ancient Maya*. Yale University Press, New Haven.

———— 2018 Imágenes sexuales en el Popol Vuh. *Anales de Antropología* 52:153–164.

———— 2021 Where Children Are Born: Centipedes and Feminine Sexuality in Ancient Maya Art. In *Sorcery in Mesoamerica*, edited by Jeremy D. Coltman and John M. D. Pohl, pp. 206–235. University Press of Colorado, Boulder.

Christenson, Allen J. (editor) 2003 *Popol Vuh: The Sacred Book of the Maya*. O Books, Winchester and New York.

Coto, Thomás de 1983 *[Thesavrvs verborṽ] Vocabvlario de la lengua Cakchiquel v[el] Guatemalteca, nueuamente hecho y recopilado con summo estudio, trauajo y erudición*, edited by René Acuña. Universidad Nacional Autónoma de México, Mexico City.

De la Cruz Torres, Mario 1978 *Rubelpec. Cuentos y leyendas de Senahú, Alta Verapaz*. Editorial del Ejército, Guatemala City.

Dürr, Michael, and Frauke Sachse (editors) 2017 *Diccionario K'iche' de Berlin. El vocabulario en lengua 4iche otlatecas: Edición crítica*. Estudios Indiana 10. Ibero-Amerikanisches Institut, Preußischer Kulturbesitz/Gebr. Mann Verlag, Berlin.

Faugère, Brigitte 2008 Le cerf chez les anciens P'urhépecha du Michoacan (Mexique): guerre, chasse et sacrifice. *Journal de la Societé des Américanistes* 94:109–142.

Freidel, David, and Linda Schele 1990 *A Forest of Kings: The Untold Story of the Ancient Maya*. William Morrow & Co., Inc., New York.

Galinier, Jacques 1984 L'homme sans pied: Métaphores de la castration et imaginaire en Mésoamérique. *L'Homme* 24(2):41–58.

———— 1997 *The World Below: Body and Cosmos in Otomí Indian Ritual*. University Press of Colorado, Boulder.

García Barrios, Ana 2006 Confrontation Scenes on Codex-Style Pottery: An Iconographic Review. *Latin American Indian Literatures Journal* 22:129–152.

Garibay, Ángel María 1967 Códice Carolino: Manuscrito náhuatl del siglo XVI en forma de adiciones a la primera edición del vocabulario de Molina. *Estudios de Cultura Náhuatl* 7:11–58.

Gonzáles de Lesur, Yolotl 1968 El dios Huitzilopochtli en la peregrinación mexica de Aztlán a Tula. *Anales del Instituto Nacional de Antropología e Historia* 19:175–190.

Gossen, Gary H. 1979 Temporal and Spatial Equivalents in Chamula Ritual Symbolism. In *Reader in Comparative Religion: An Anthropological Approach*, edited by William A. Lessa and Evon Z. Vogt, pp. 126–129. Harper & Row, New York.

Graulich, Michel 1974 Las peregrinaciones aztecas y el ciclo de Mixcoatl. *Estudios de Cultura Nahuatl* 11:311–354.

———— 1987 Los mitos mexicanos y mayas-quichés de la creación del sol. *Anales de Antropología* 24:289–325.

———— 1997a Chasse et sacrifice humain chez les Aztèques. *Bulletin des Séances de l'Academie Royale des Sciences d'Outre-mer* 43(4):433–446.

———— 1997b *Myths of Ancient Mexico*. University of Oklahoma Press, Norman.

Graulich, Michel, and Guilhem Olivier 2004 ¿Deidades insaciables? La comida de los dioses en el México antiguo. *Estudios de Cultura Nahuatl* 35:121–155.

Grube, Nikolai 2004 El origen de la dinastía Kaan. In *Los cautivos de Dzibanché*, edited by Enrique Nalda, pp. 117–131. Instituto Nacional de Antropología e Historia, Mexico City.

Haskell, David L. 2018 *The Two Taríacuris and the Early Colonial and Prehispanic Past of Michoacán*. University Press of Colorado, Louisville.

Helmke, Christophe, and Felix A. Kupprat 2016 Where Snakes Abound: Supernatural Places of Origin and Founding Myths in the Titles of Classic Maya Kings. In *Places of Power and Memory in Mesoamerica's Past and Present: How Sites, Toponyms and Landscapes Shape History and Remembrance*, edited by Daniel Graña Behrens, pp. 33–83. Estudios Indiana 9. Ibero-Amerikanisches Institut, Berlin.

——— 2017 Los glifos emblema y los lugares sobrenaturales: El caso de Kanu'l y sus implicaciones. *Estudios de Cultura Maya* 50:95–135.

Houston, Stephen, David Stuart, and Karl Taube 2013 *The Memory of Bones: Body, Being, and Experience among the Classic Maya*. University of Texas Press, Austin.

Justeson, John S. 1989 Ancient Maya Ethnoastronomy. In *World Archaeoastronomy*, edited by Anthony F. Aveni, pp. 76–129. Cambridge University Press, Cambridge.

Klein, Cecelia F. 1994 Fighting with Femininity: Gender and War in Aztec Mexico. *Estudios de Cultura Nahuatl* 24:219–253.

Lacadena García-Gallo, Alfonso 2009 Apuntes para un estudio sobre literatura maya antigua. In *Text and Context: Yucatec Maya Literature in Diachronic Perspective*, edited by Antje Gunsenheimer, Tsubasa Okoshi Harada, and John F. Chuchiak, pp. 31–52. Shaker Verlag, Aachen.

López Austin, Alfredo, and Leonardo López Luján 2009 *Monte Sagrado, Templo Mayor*. Universidad Nacional Autónoma de México, Mexico City.

Lounsbury, Floyd G. 1981 Astronomical Knowledge and Its Uses at Bonampak, Mexico. In *Archaeoastronomy in the New World*, edited by Anthony F. Aveni, pp. 143–168. Cambridge University Press, Cambridge.

Martin, Simon 2004 Preguntas epigráficas acerca de los escalones de Dzibanché. In *Los cautivos de Dzibanché*, edited by Enrique Nalda, pp. 105–115. Instituto Nacional de Antropología e Historia, Mexico City.

——— 2006 Cacao in Ancient Maya Religion: First Fruit from the Maize Tree and Other Tales from the Underworld. In *Chocolate in Mesoamerica: A Cultural History of Cacao*, edited by Cameron L. McNeil, pp. 154–183. University of Florida Press, Gainesville.

——— 2017 *Secrets of the Painted King List: Recovering the Early History of the Snake Dynasty*. Blog post in "Maya Decipherment: Ideas on Ancient Maya Writing and Iconography." Consulted on May 8, 2017. https://decipherment.wordpress.com/2017/05/05/secrets-of-the-painted-king-list-recovering-the-early-history-of-the-snake-dynasty/

——— 2020 *Ancient Maya Politics: A Political Anthropology of the Classic Period 150–900 CE*. Cambridge University Press, New York.

Martínez González, Roberto 2010 La dimensión mítica de la peregrinación tarasca. *Journal de la Societé des Américanistes* 96:39–73.

Maxwell, Judith M., and Robert M. Hill II (editors) 2006 *Kaqchikel Chronicles: The Definitive Edition*. University of Texas Press, Austin.

McAnany, Patricia 2010 *Ancient Maya Economies in Archaeological Perspective*. Cambridge University Press, Cambridge.

Milbrath, Susan 1999 *Star Gods of the Ancient Maya: Astronomy in Art, Folklore, and Calendars*. University of Texas Press, Austin.

Miller, Mary 1988 The Meaning and Function of the Main Acropolis, Copan. In *The Southeast Classic Maya Zone*, edited by Elizabeth Hill Boone and Gordon R. Willey, pp. 149–194. Dumbarton Oaks, Washington, DC.

Miller, Mary, and Claudia Brittenham 2013 *The Spectacle of the Maya Court: Reflections on the Murals of Bonampak*. University of Texas Press, Austin.

Miller, Mary, and Stephen D. Houston 1998 Algunos comentarios sobre las inscripciones jeroglíficas en las pinturas de la estructura 1 de Bonampak. In *La pintura mural prehispánica en México: Área maya*, edited by Leticia Staines Cicero, Vol. 2, pp. 245–254. Universidad Nacional Autónoma de México, Mexico City.

Miller, Virginia E. 1989 Star Warriors at Chichen Itza. In *Word and Image in Maya Culture*, edited by William F. Hanks and Don S. Rice, pp. 287–305. University of Utah Press, Salt Lake City.

Monaghan, John D. 2001 Physiology, Production, and Gender Difference: The Evidence from Mixtec and Other Mesoamerican Societies. In *Gender in Pre-Hispanic America*, edited by Cecelia F. Klein, pp. 285–304. Dumbarton Oaks, Washington, DC.

Montoliú Villar, María 1990 Un mito del origen de las enfermedades en Izamal, Yucatán (análisis social de sus símbolos y contenido social). In *Historia de la religión en Mesoamérica y áreas afines: II coloquio*, edited by Barbro Dahlgren de Jordán, pp. 81–88. Universidad Nacional Autónoma de México, Mexico City.

Nahm, Werner 1994 Maya Warfare and the Venus Year. *Mexicon* 16:6–10.

Nicholson, Henry B. 1971 Religion in Pre-Hispanic Mexico. In *Handbook of Middle American Indians, Vol. 10: The Archaeology of Northern Mesoamerica, Part I*, edited by Gordon F. Ekholm and Ignacio Bernal, pp. 395–446. University of Texas Press, Austin.

Olivier, Guilhem 2010 El simbolismo sacrificial de los mimixcoa: Cacería, guerra, sacrificio e identidad entre los Mexicas. In *El sacrificio humano en la tradición religiosa mesoamericana*, edited by Leonardo López Luján and Guilhem Olivier, pp. 453–482. Instituto Nacional de Antropología e Historia/Universidad Nacional Autónoma de México, Mexico City.

———— 2015 *Cacería, sacrificio y poder en Mesoamérica: Tras las huellas de Mixcóatl, "serpiente de nube."* Fondo de Cultura Económica, Mexico City.

Otzoy C., Simón (editor) 1999 *Memorial de Sololá*. Comisión Interuniversitaria Guatemalteca de Conmemoración del Quinto Centenario del Descubrimiento de América, Guatemala City.

Recinos, Adrián (editor) 1950 *Memorial de Sololá (Memorial de Tecpán Atitlán). Anales de los Cakchiqueles. Título de los Señores de Totonicapán*. Fondo de Cultura Económica, Mexico City.

Robicsek, Francis, and Donald M. Hales 1981 *The Maya Book of the Dead: The Ceramic Codex: The Corpus of Codex Style Ceramics of the Late Classic Period*. University of Virginia Art Museum, Charlottesville, VA.

Sahagún, Bernardino de 1953 *Florentine Codex: Book 7: The Sun, Moon, and Stars, and the Binding of the Years*, edited by Arthur J. O. Anderson and Charles E. Dibble. School of American Research, Santa Fe, New Mexico.

———— 1969 *Florentine Codex: Book 6: Rhetoric and Moral Philosophy*, edited by Arthur J. O. Anderson and Charles E. Dibble. School of American Research, Santa Fe, New Mexico.

———— 1978 *Florentine Codex: Book 3: The Origin of the Gods*, edited by Arthur J. O. Anderson and Charles E. Dibble. School of American Research, Santa Fe, New Mexico.

———— 1989 *Historia general de las cosas de Nueva España*, 2 vols., edited by Josefina García Quintana and Alfredo López Austin, 2nd edition. Consejo Nacional para la Cultura y las Artes, Mexico City.

Seler, Eduard 1904 Venus Period in the Picture Writings of the Borgian Codex Group. In *Mexican and Central American Antiquities, Calendar Systems, and History*, edited by Charles P. Bowditch, pp. 355–391. Bureau of American Ethnology Bulletin 28. Smithsonian Institution, Washington, DC.

———— 1963 *Comentarios al Códice Borgia*, 3 vols. Fondo de Cultura Económica, Mexico City.

———— 1996 Myths and Religion of the Ancient Mexicans. In *Collected Works in Meso-american Linguistics and Archaeology*, edited by Frank Comparato, Vol. 5, pp. 1–99. Labyrinthos, Lancaster, California.

Spinden, Herbert 1916 The Question of the Zodiac in America. *American Anthropologist* 18:53–80.

Stuart, David 1998 "The Fire Enters His House": Architecture and Ritual in Classic Maya Texts." In *Function and Meaning in Classic Maya Architecture*, edited by Stephen D. Houston, pp. 373–425. Dumbarton Oaks, Washington, DC.

Stuart, David, and George Stuart 2008 *Palenque: Eternal City of the Maya*. Thames & Hudson, New York.

Taube, Karl 1993 The Bilimek Pulque Vessel: Starlore, Calendrics, and Cosmology of Late Postclassic Central Mexico. *Ancient Mesoamerica* 4:1–15.

———— 2004 Flower Mountain: Concepts of Life, Beauty, and Paradise among the Classic Maya. *Res: Anthropology and Aesthetics* 45:69–98.

Tedlock, Dennis (editor) 1996 *Popol Vuh: The Mayan Book of the Dawn of Life*. Touchstone Books, New York.

Tena, Rafael (editor) 2002 *Mitos e historias de los antiguos Nahuas*. Consejo Nacional para la Cultura y las Artes, Mexico City.

Thompson, J. Eric S. 1930 *Ethnology of the Mayas of Southern and Central British Honduras*. Anthropological Series 17(2). Field Museum of Natural History, Chicago.

van Akkeren, Ruud 2000 *Place of the Lord's Daughter: Rab'inal, Its History, Its Dance-Drama*. CNWS Publications, Leiden.

Vico, Domingo de n.d. Vocabulario de la lengua Cakchiquel con advertencia de los vocablos de las lenguas quiché y tzutuhil, se trasladó de la obra compuesta por el Ilmo Padre, el venerable Fr. Domingo de Vico. Manuscript in the Bibliothèque Nationale de France, Fonds Américains, No. 46. Photocopy in Dumbarton Oaks, Washington, DC.

Webster, David 2000 The Not So Peaceful Civilization: A Review of Maya War. *Journal of World Prehistory* 14:65–119.

Ximénez, Francisco 1985 *Primera parte del tesoro de las tres lenguas cakchiquel, quiché y zutuhil, en que las dichas lenguas se traducen a la nuestra, española*, edited by Carmelo Sáenz de Santa María. Academia de Geografía e Historia, Guatemala City.

Zender, Marc 2020 Disaster, Deluge, and Destruction on the Star War Vase. *The Mayanist* 2(1):57–76.

13

POWER AND POLITICS ON THE LATE COLONIAL FRONTIER OF BRITISH HONDURAS

Brooke Bonorden and Brett A. Houk

Along the western bank of the Rio Bravo in the jungles of northwestern Belize (formerly British Honduras), a scatter of glass bottles, broken dishes, and rusting industrial equipment lies near Cedar Crossing. Approximately 20 km to the southwest, a separate scatter of glass bottles, cooking implements, and curious rock clusters surrounds a lush *aguada* choked with water lettuce. These materials are the vestiges of settlements inhabited by two distinct groups of people: Creole loggers and San Pedro Maya. Although an initial observation of the two sites implies that they are two entirely separate entities with distinct histories, inhabitants, and archaeological assemblages, an exploration of the larger historical context surrounding both sites reveals their intricate relationship within a broader historical framework and how the colonial system in British Honduras intentionally marginalized both groups.

Qualm Hill camp, located on the right bank of the Rio Bravo, served as the seasonal headquarters of British Honduras Company (BHC) throughout the mid-to-late-1800s (Figure 13.1). Kaxil Uinic village, located 2 km from the western Belize-Guatemala border, was settled sometime after 1868 by a group of San Pedro Maya seeking refuge from the Caste War in Yucatan (1847–1901; Jones 1977). The village was included in the land holdings of BHC, later renamed Belize Estate and Produce Company (BEC), and the inhabitants paid rent to the company to use the land for their *milpa* farms (Bonorden and Kilgore 2015). The logging camp at Qualm Hill and the San Pedro Maya village at Kaxil Uinic are thus bound by their associations with BHC/BEC, which ultimately became the largest logging firm in British Honduras (Ng 2007).

The logging labor force in British Honduras largely comprised formerly enslaved Africans, who were prohibited from owning land after their emancipation in 1833 (Ng 2007). As a result, many former slaves ultimately returned to the logging industry, where a system of advanced wages combined with the high

DOI: 10.4324/9781351268004-13

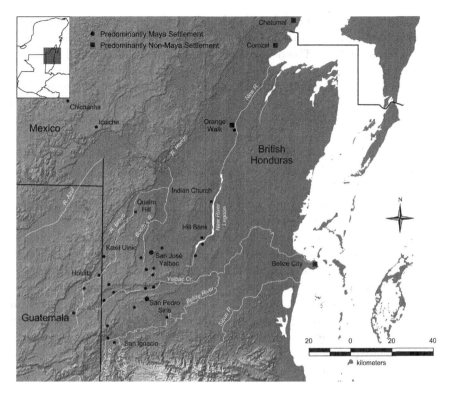

FIGURE 13.1 Map of colonial period sites in northern British Honduras. Base map courtesy NASA/JPL-Caltech, SRTM Mission. Site locations after Church et al. (2011:Figure 9.1) and Jones (1977:Map 5-1).

price of imported goods forced many of these laborers into a perpetual state of debt servitude to the logging companies that employed them (Cal 1991). Following the Battle of San Pedro between British and Maya forces in 1867, the Lieutenant Governor of British Honduras issued a decree to delegitimize San Pedro Maya claims to land in northwestern British Honduras, undermining their subsistence economy and forcing them to seek similar positions as wage laborers in the *chicle* industry to obtain cash for paying rent to landowning logging companies (Church et al. 2011).

Both the residents of Qualm Hill camp and Kaxil Uinic village were therefore involved with a company that managed to keep the general population of British Honduras dependent upon it for access to resources and jobs (Bolland 1977), offering these disenfranchised groups limited opportunities for socioeconomic advancement (Ng 2007). Despite these circumstances, archival and archaeological data from both Qualm Hill camp and Kaxil Uinic village suggest that these two groups combated institutionalized marginalization within the colonial system through their own political and economic devices. The San

Pedro Maya at Kaxil Uinic, for example, selectively participated in the colonial cash economy in ways that allowed them to maintain their autonomy despite being tenants of BEC. This deliberation is evident from data collected at the site, where items purchased from colonial merchants were used in the perpetuation of local practices (Bonorden 2016; Bonorden and Houk 2019). At Qualm Hill, the loggers adopted Maya construction techniques for their buildings and Maya foodways to offset the debts they accrued in the "advance system" implemented by logging companies to create a continuously indentured workforce. It appears, therefore, that these two groups actively negotiated alliances with one another, manipulating the politics and power dynamics of the region in the face of restrictive colonial policies (see also Harrison-Buck et al. 2019).

We synthesize recently collected archival and archaeological data from the two late colonial period (ca. AD 1800–1900) sites to elucidate this interplay between politics, social relations, and materiality. Bonorden directed one season of testing at Qualm Hill camp in 2015 and two seasons of more intensive work at Kaxil Uinic village in 2015 and 2016 under the auspices of the Belize Estates Archaeological Survey Team, directed by Houk. The inhabitants of these two sites cleverly traversed the complex contours of the cultural landscape in British Honduras to determine their places within the colonial system, sometimes in ways inconsistent with corporate group beliefs and alliances or legislative mandates. Evidence of this continuous negotiation is manifested in the archaeological record at both Qualm Hill camp and Kaxil Uinic village.

A history of power and politics in British Honduras

Archaeological studies of power and politics tend to focus on the establishment and maintenance of formal, large-scale structures (i.e., institutions of "the state"), often overlooking the "practices and social relations that are constituent of these structures and crucial for understanding change and continuity" within the context in which it occurs (Johansen and Bauer 2011:3). Studies of the late colonial period in Belize, for example, generate narratives of the establishment and perpetuation of British colonial supremacy over Maya and Creole groups within the region. Such narratives detail how the "forestocracy" of mahogany industry leaders, together with an oligarchy that controlled the local law-making legislature (the Public Meeting), concentrated lands in western British Honduras into the hands of a few mercantile houses based in England (Cal 1991). Leveraging power over the colonial administration through their advantageous economic position as both the largest employers and tax base in the colony, logging companies were able to influence both the colonial government and its legislative policies (Kray et al. 2017), pushing the political boundaries of the colony to the northwest to take advantage of the poorly defined borders with Mexico and Guatemala (Cal 1991; Houk and Bonorden 2020), ultimately inciting military action against Caste War Maya refugees inhabiting those profitable mahogany forests.

Conflicts inevitably arose between the Maya and logging companies as a result of differing uses of the landscape by the two groups. British mercantile capitalists and colonial administrators lobbied against Maya agricultural pursuits in the region because the traditional *milpa* farming techniques (slash and burn agriculture) destroyed valuable timber resources in the region (Ng 2007). The Maya, meanwhile, perceived British expansion into the previously uninhabited forests of northern British Honduras as a threat to their territory and independence in the midst of the Caste War (Bolland 2003).

A series of contentious treaties between the Maya and the Mexican government, seemingly endorsed by the British colonial administration in British Honduras (Cal 1991), led the Maya to reason that loggers should set up rental agreements with them for use of land in the disputed zone, but larger logging firms had little intention of honoring the terms of such agreements (Ng 2007). Continuous defaults on land rent by logging firms prompted the Maya to forcibly coerce payment from the logging companies, resulting in numerous raids on mahogany works in northwestern British Honduras. One such raid actually took place at Qualm Hill camp in 1866, serving as a catalyst for the Battle of San Pedro (1867), a punitive expedition led by Lieutenant Colonel Robert William Harley into San Pedro territory with orders to drive off any hostile "Indians" his troops encountered (Jones 1977). Although tensions between the Maya and the logging companies diminished to a smolder after the Battle of San Pedro, Maya leader Marcus Canul's attack on a military barracks in Orange Walk in 1872 reignited hostilities (Eltringham 2010). The Battle of Orange Walk, which resulted in Canul's death and a Maya retreat, caused relations between the Maya and the British colonial administration to change (Ng 2007).

According to the traditional narrative of events, the formalization of the Anglo-Mexican border with the ratification of the Spenser-Mariscal Treaty in 1893 allowed British troops to occupy the San Pedro Maya settlement area without fear of reprisals from Mexico (Ng 2007). Almost simultaneously, a series of epidemics and drought severely reduced the populations of San Pedro Maya villages, considerably diminishing their autonomy (Church et al. 2011). As the sizes of San Pedro settlements dramatically decreased, the remaining inhabitants of many of the smaller villages and hamlets coalesced into larger settlements, and timber firms displaced or relocated the remaining villages during the 1920s and 1930s (Jones 1977). BEC forcibly relocated the inhabitants of Kaxil Uinic village to San José Yalbac in 1931 (Thompson 1963), possibly due to an estimated loss of $300,000 in mahogany stands from *milpa* farming activities at Xaxe Venic (Kaxil Uinic) as cited by the company manager, C. S. Brown, in 1935 (Kray et al. 2017). This shift in British-Maya relations (ca. 1872–1900) is typically characterized as a period during which the British colonialists consolidated their jurisdiction over the Maya, and the Maya were ultimately "incorporated into the colonial social structure of British Honduras as a defeated, dispossessed, and dependent people" (Bolland 2003:125). The loss of *milpa* farmland, which had sustained Maya self-sufficiency in colonial British Honduras, forced the Maya to participate in the colonial cash economy. As a result, practically all of those resources previously acquired from *milpas* had to be imported (Church et al. 2011), and the pressure to obtain cash for paying rent to logging companies drove larger numbers of San Pedro men into the logging or *chicle* industries as wage laborers (Kray et al. 2017).

A similar narrative generally describes experience of Creole loggers in British Honduras. Although the first logging ventures in British Honduras were undertaken by former British buccaneers (known as Baymen) who were seeking new opportunities, the extremely uncomfortable and unhealthy nature of logging meant that only a generation or so of white Baymen extracted wood from British Honduras (Cal 1991). Between 1700 and 1833, slaves of African descent provided most of the logging labor force (Cal 1991). Slaves were brought to British Honduras from Africa via Jamaican markets to cut logwood (Bolland 2003). Along with their descendants, they formed the largest demographic in British Honduras in the early 1800s, although the colony was ruled by an elite Anglo minority (Yaeger et al. 2004).

Since mahogany stands are rather diffuse and sparsely distributed, logging gangs camped in remote areas, which complicated logistics, such as provisioning crews from Belize Town (Cal 1991). The "truck system" was subsequently developed, in which supplies were brought to the logging camps from larger towns in the colony via company trucks. When slavery was abolished in 1833, former slave masters were able to manipulate the truck system to ensure a continued labor supply for their logging enterprises. Known as the "advance system," this amounted to a state of semi-slavery or debt servitude (Bolland 2003). Many former slaves, who were prohibited from acquiring farmland (Ng 2007), returned to the timber industry as wage laborers after emancipation. These workers were based in Belize Town and given an advance of three month's wages when hired right before the Christmas season, which they would inevitably spend celebrating with family (Cal 1991). Bound by contract to take half of their wages in goods from their employer (who sold them at exorbitant prices), the workers fell into debt as the logging season progressed and were obligated to continue working until their debts were repaid (Bristowe and Wright 1888). Goods, which often consisted of inferior quality items that British merchants were unable to sell in Belize Town, were trucked in to the company commissary by the employers at marked-up prices and made available on a credit system (Cal 1991), so that the laborers virtually became enslaved for life as they accrued debt at a faster rate than they were able to compensate with labor (Britsowe and Wright 1888). In addition to this economic exploitation and social isolation, improvements in transportation in the 1920s further marginalized the loggers economically, as the increased efficiency that accompanied mechanization of the logging process condensed the traditional nine-month field season to six, severely reducing the income of laborers (Ng 2007).

Although these descriptions of power dynamics during the late colonial period – which are reconstructed from archival data – accurately but superficially reflect the historical narrative of colonialism in British Honduras, they fail to acknowledge the agency of the Maya and the loggers with whom they interacted in determining or bettering their places within the colonial system despite their de facto marginalization by the colonial government. As noted by Ng (2007), "the incorporation of European goods does not simply equate with an embrace of European values" or "incorporation" into the capitalist colonialist social structure of British Honduras. The Maya and their logger counterparts, for example, selectively participated in the colonial economy and strategically interacted with elements of the colonial administration and the "forestocracy" as it suited their needs, making decisions both individually and communally. Sometimes these decisions were inconsistent with the beliefs of their larger groups but allowed them as individuals to survive. Following the theoretical framework laid out by Johansen and Bauer (2011), we view politics as a series of fluid and dynamic social interactions where power relations are continually mediated, challenged, sustained, and reinvented by the actions of people or groups. Through this theoretical lens, even the most commonplace objects can be viewed as indicators of meaningful social struggles, alliances, or transformations (Mullins 2007).

Reinterpreting the "incorporation" of subaltern groups into the British social structure

In the remainder of this chapter, we aim to reevaluate the metanarrative of power and politics in British Honduras during the late colonial period, beginning with the perpetually indentured status of Creole loggers and then turning to the San Pedro Maya. Without undermining the harsh reality of the situation, we present the ways in which both disenfranchised groups combated their systematic marginalization, employing their own agency to actively negotiate their place within the colonial system as opposed to being passively absorbed into it. The following sections examine everyday life at Qualm Hill camp and Kaxil Uinic as revealed by archival and archaeological data. We discuss these data within the historical framework of the late colonial period to provide a more complex understanding of the dynamic nature of power relations under British colonial rule.

Qualm Hill camp

Re-located by archaeologists with the Programme for Belize Archaeological Project in 2006 (Cackler et al. 2007), Qualm Hill camp was initially surveyed and mapped by members of the Belize Estates Archaeological Survey Team in 2014 (Sandrock and Willis 2014). Bonorden (2016) spent one additional field season surveying, mapping, and excavating the site. Qualm Hill camp is located roughly 5 km west of a group of prehistoric ruins sharing the same name, in a wooded area approximately 100 m east of Cedar Crossing on the right bank of the Rio Bravo (Sandrock and Willis 2014). Bonorden's crews identified 60 surface finds, which consisted of several scatters of glass, ceramics, and industrial logging equipment (Bonorden and Smith 2015). Over the course of one field season, crews opened 19 excavation units and analyzed 1,602 artifacts from the site, including 699 pieces of glass, 336 ceramic sherds, 477 metal artifacts, 24 pieces of chipped stone including tools and debitage, 62 shell artifacts, and two pieces of animal bone.

Although it is unknown precisely when Qualm Hill was established, the logging camp was present as early as 1852. Major Luke Smythe O'Connor (1852) of the First West India Regiment mentioned it in his travelogue written that same year. Although it is unclear from archival data when the camp officially closed, it was obviously sometime before 1970, when BEC went bankrupt (Cal 1991). The manufacture dates of artifacts recovered from Qualm Hill camp indicate that the site was occupied from approximately 1830 to 1920 (Bonorden 2016).

During his expedition, O'Connor (1852) observed that "Betsin's Bank" served as a depot to supply provisions to Qualm Hill camp. Aside from O'Connor's (1852) brief mention of Qualm Hill in his travelogue, accessible historical documentation regarding the logging camp is relatively scarce, save for the numerous accounts of a raid on the camp by the Maya in the 1860s. According to Cal (1991), the raid on Qualm Hill took place on April 27, 1866, shortly before breakfast, when a force of 125 Icaiche Maya troops led by Marcus Canul marched on the camp via Betson's Bank. The company storekeeper at Betson's Bank fired on the Icaiche, and two individuals were killed and another wounded in the skirmish (Cal 1983).

At Qualm Hill, Canul and his troops rounded up all of the women and children before setting two houses on fire and scattering the loggers' provisions (Cal 1983). A Garifuna man nicknamed "Black Devil" was then killed in the fighting, and the Icaiche took 79 to 85 prisoners and 175 head of cattle hostage upon the workers' return from the forest, marching the prisoners to Santa Clara de Icaiche in Mexico (Cal 1983). According to Cal (1983), 53 men, 15 women, and 11 children were among the captives. Sir John Alder Burdon (1935) asserts that the abducted individuals included an English foreman (Mr. Robateau) and a Canadian. Reports of the raid on Qualm Hill mention the presence of a company store, implying that the advance system was in place at the camp by 1866. We recovered no concrete archaeological evidence of the raid on the sawmill, however, as very few weapons were identified in the artifact assemblage, and those present seem to pre- or post-date the raid by several decades (Bonorden 2016). Furthermore, the discovery of numerous burned ceramic sherds at the site is also circumstantial. It is possible that the sawmill was moved after its original location was burned during the raid, and this later location was the one subjected to archaeological investigation. Mahogany camps typically only enjoyed a lifespan of one to three years, so this possibility is reasonable (Kray et al. 2017).

Following the raid, Lieutenant Governor Austin (1866) wrote to Captain Delamere that he should attempt to capture any Maya who participated in it, because Mr. Hodge (the owner of BHC) could only get two laborers to return to the camp unless the government provided military protection. Apart from the various accounts of what occurred during the raid on Qualm Hill camp, virtually nothing is known of the logging enterprise there or of the nature of the relationship between the mostly Creole labor force and its managers.

Mahogany extraction generally required an organized labor force of 10 to 50 men assigned to specialized activities (Cal 1991; Finamore 1994), often subdivided into smaller groups of 10 to 12 (Bolland 2003). The mahogany industry was thus limited to those individuals with enough resources to garner a large labor force, such as the London merchants who formed the BHC enterprise. Field managers and overseers (mostly British) were appointed to coordinate and supervise these larger endeavors, although the nature of mahogany extraction made direct supervision rather difficult (Cal 1991).

If a given location was likely to yield mahogany for several seasons, small, semi-permanent hamlets were sometimes created, with entire families settling in them (Bolland 2003). The managers did not live side-by-side with the rest of the loggers, however, but usually resided with their families at a considerable distance from the rest of the gang (Ng 2007). The establishment of more permanent camps by wealthier entrepreneurs, although not necessarily the most effective strategy for mahogany activities, allowed these businessmen to manage the structure of social relations among the loggers by controlling the central locus of social intercourse (Finamore 1994). Archival data (Cal 1983) suggests that at least two houses were present at Qualm Hill prior to the 1866 raid, and two areas of the camp subjected to archaeological investigation appear residential in nature (Bonorden 2016). These two areas are located relatively far apart from one another, as well as from the industrial center of the camp (Figure 13.2). The residential area associated with SubOp QHC-02-C is presumed to be within the vicinity of the foreman's residence based on the density and variety of cultural material observed in that location (Bonorden 2016). Because Burdon (1935) refers to both a manager and a Canadian foreman at Qualm Hill, it is possible that the second residential area, where a cooking feature and decorative lamp chimney were recovered at SubOp QHC-02-F, was the second administrator's home (Bonorden 2016). Additionally, the only porcelain fragments recovered from the site were found in the vicinity of the proposed foreman's residence, pointing to class distinctions between the general laborers at the site and the foreman or manager (Bonorden 2016; Ng 2007).

The lack of semi-permanent structures at Qualm Hill indicates that the transient nature of logging compelled the workers to live in huts, likely adopting Maya construction techniques (Finamore 1994). The relatively scant number of nails recovered from Qualm Hill, considering that archival data suggests anywhere from 50 to 85 individuals lived in the camp, supports this assertion (Bonorden 2016). Ng (2007) theorizes that these structures were probably wooden, built on raised blocks or stilts with thatched or wood roofs, and therefore perishable. Alternatively, they were prefabricated structures that were disassembled and moved once the camp closed (Ng 2007).

According to Cal (1991), slaves – and by extension the indentured workers who followed them – exercised a reasonable amount of control over their free

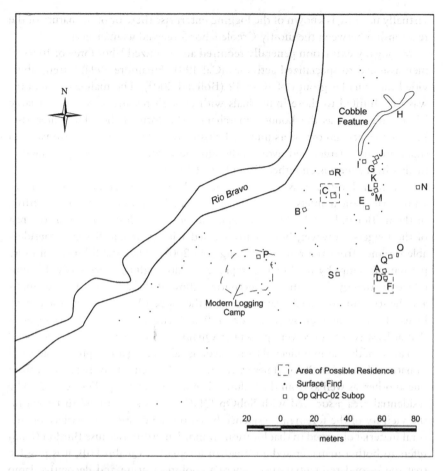

FIGURE 13.2 Map of Qualm Hill camp showing the locations of 2015 surface finds and excavation units.

time upon completing their assigned tasks. In 1857, mahogany subcontractors reportedly paid their laborers $7.50 per month, half in goods and half in cash (Cal 1991). This rate did not change until 1888, when it was increased to $12 per month, including rations. With such low wages, loggers would labor five days a week, hunt wild cattle and hogs on the weekends to supplement the items sold to them at exorbitant prices by logging firms, or "make plantation" by cultivating a small plot of land near the camp to supplement their pork and dough diet, even selling excess produce in Belize Town at the end of the season (Cal 1991). Alternately, some loggers may have plundered food from nearby Maya villages. Luciano Tzuc (*comandante general* of the Chichanha Maya) attacked a mahogany works operated by Young, Toledo, & Company along the east bank of Blue Creek, claiming that the loggers "[took] everything they set eyes on." This suggests that loggers occasionally stole food from Maya *milpas* to avoid purchasing from company stores (Zuc 1856). Such accounts point to the ways in which slaves actively determined their own lives within the limited circumstances permitted, and it appears wage laborers utilized the same opportunities under the advance system (which remained in effect until the 1930s) after emancipation (Cal 1991).

It may thus be assumed that the seasonal inhabitants of Qualm Hill spent their personal time in a similar fashion. At Qualm Hill, we recovered a single mammalian premolar and a fragment of a turtle carapace, providing the only hints about the consumption of wild animals by the loggers (Bonorden 2016). It is possible that loggers dumped their refuse into the nearby Rio Bravo, which could explain the lack of faunal material observed at the site (Finamore 1994). Alternatively, the lack of faunal material at Qualm Hill could indicate an increased reliance on imported foodstuffs via the truck system. Numerous rectangular cans, winding keys, and barrel hoops were found at the site, but only two shotgun shells indicative of hunting were recovered (Bonorden 2016). The dominance of patent pharmaceutical medicine bottles in the Qualm Hill glass assemblage may be interpreted as evidence of the aches and pains of physical labor associated with logging activities (Ng 2007) or the desire of loggers to purge their digestive systems from the monotonous high-starch, high-fat diet they were allotted in the field (Franzen 1995).

Additionally, it appears that loggers consumed *jute* from the nearby Rio Bravo. Most of the specimens of *jute* from the site are spire-lopped, indicating that the shells were boiled so that the meat could be removed and eaten in a thick, spicy soup commonly consumed by the Maya (Bonorden 2016; Healy et al. 1990), or roasted and eaten with pepper sauce (Ng 2007). One pepper sauce-style bottle was recovered from the site. Unlike cultivation, which would not be a feasible subsistence strategy for a gang of highly mobile loggers, aquatic resources were attractive because specialized skills were not necessary to acquire them and it was not a labor- or time-intensive task (Finamore 1994).

Identifiable maker's marks on plates found at Qualm Hill indicate that most of these items were produced in England. Inhabitants of the colony had a narrow range of occupations, and ceramic production was not common. The lack of craftspeople facilitated a reliance on imports for even the most basic household items (Finamore 1994). Restrictions on the availability of manufactured goods and participation in the cash economy of British Honduras also altered consumption habits in isolated logger camps (Miller and Hurry 1983). Ceramics were thus likely acquired as they were available through the truck system, with few options in style and decoration. Furthermore, loggers probably kept their most valuable china at home in Belize City, choosing to bring items with less personal investment to camp where they might be easily broken (Ng 2007). Either of these factors may have shaped the ceramic assemblage at Qualm Hill, where an age disparity is evident between ceramic and glass artifacts observed at the site (Figure 13.3), and no consistent pattern is present among the ceramic vessels identified in the assemblage (Bonorden and Smith 2015).

With the exception of ceramic vessels, there is very little variety in the material culture recovered from Qualm Hill, which reflects the consumption of

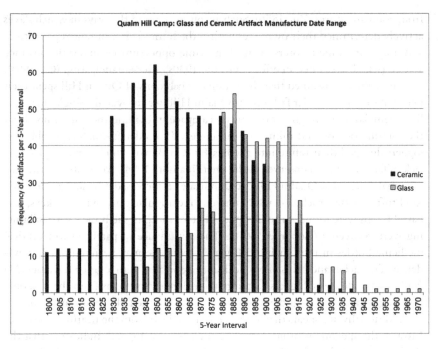

FIGURE 13.3 Comparison of age ranges for ceramic and glass artifacts from Qualm Hill camp.

mass-produced, commercial commodities available in limited varieties through the truck system (Finamore 1994). The lack of faunal material from the site in comparison to the abundance of tin cans and barrel hoops is also indicative of a subsistence strategy that relied heavily on prepackaged goods, although this may be biased by trash disposal methods at the site. Despite their negligible purchasing power under the advance system, though, it appears that the loggers at Qualm Hill camp sought economic independence by supplementing the foodstuffs acquired at the camp store with local aquatic resources. Since the loggers that inhabited the camp considered Belize City their permanent residence (Cal 1991), it should also be considered that field conditions in remote logging camps likely engendered different consumption patterns among these individuals at work versus at home (as evidenced by the relatively low density of artifacts at Qualm Hill, which is likely due to the transient nature of occupation of the site), and so interpretations of logger participation in the colonial economy might be better studied outside of the working realm. As noted by Hulse (1989), logging camps were managed, constructed, and supplied under company direction and control, and so these sites should be viewed as economic satellites of corporate philosophy rather than reflecting the free behavior of individuals. Therefore, the material culture of Qualm Hill camp must be viewed within an appropriate cultural-historical context when considering the participation of its inhabitants within the colonial economy of British Honduras.

Kaxil Uinic Village

Bonorden (2016) spent two seasons surveying, mapping, and excavating Kaxil Uinic village (Figure 13.4), initially re-located by Houk (2012),. The site surrounds a small *aguada* in the jungle, approximately 1.8 km east of Guatemala. Bonorden's crews identified 10 three-stone hearths and 66 surface finds, which included several large artifact scatters covering over 100 m² (Bonorden and Kilgore 2016). Over two seasons, crews opened 30 excavation units and analyzed 5,320 artifacts from the site, including 1,070 pieces of glass, 1,370 ceramic sherds, 993 metal artifacts, 1,527 pieces of chipped stone (including tools and debitage), 14 shell artifacts, and 343 pieces of animal bone.

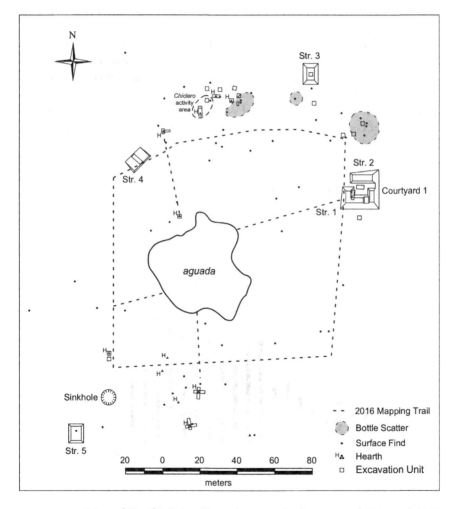

FIGURE 13.4 Map of Kaxil Uinic village showing the locations of 2015 and 2016 surface finds, excavation units, and cultural features.

Grant Jones (1977) speculated that Kaxil Uinic was settled in the 1880s by migrants from Holuitz, a San Pedro Maya village to the southwest on the Guatemalan side of the border. Thompson (1963) reported the village was abandoned before Easter in 1931, meaning it was occupied for approximately 40 to 50 years. The manufacture date ranges of artifacts (Figure 13.5) recovered from Kaxil Uinic village reaffirm historic accounts that the village was occupied from approximately 1880 to 1930 (Bonorden 2016; Bonorden and Kilgore 2016). The village was connected by a series of footpaths to Icaiche in the north, San José Yalbac in the southeast (Jones 1977), Yaloch in Guatemala to the southwest, and the Peten region to the west (Miller 1887). Considering its strategically inconspicuous location, Kaxil Uinic village was perhaps intentionally hidden in the forests to isolate the Maya population from colonial contact, conflict, and disease and to prevent nearby loggers or *chicleros* from stealing crops grown by the Maya (Bonorden 2016).

The village appears infrequently in the archival record, but a handful of sources provide a general sketch of its place in the San Pedro Maya political and social structure. The earliest mention of Kaxil Uinic comes from a statement to the Police Inspector of British Honduras in January 1885 (paraphrased in Jones 1977), which mentions that several Mexicans escaped through the village to Icaiche after committing murders at a mahogany bank near San José Yalbac.

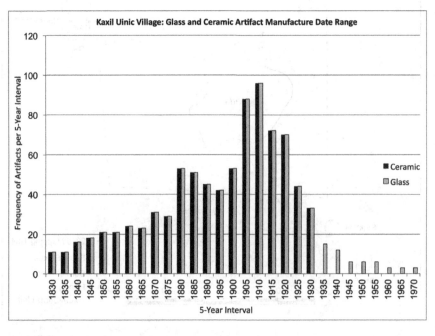

FIGURE 13.5 Comparison of age ranges for ceramic and glass artifacts from Kaxil Uinic village.

On August 18, 1886, J.P.H. Gastrell (1886) noted in a letter to the Earl of Rosebery that an enclosed copy of the "Gavarrete Map" was annotated with the locations of "Ycaiché" Indians, who "[kept] their power or jurisdiction to nearly as far south as Garbutt's Falls and control . . . Xaxa Venic which [was then] supposed to be within [the] Belize frontier." This reference to "Xaxa Venic" (Kaxil Uinic) is consistent with observations that the local *alcalde*, Antonio Baños, considered his village to be in Mexican territory (Bolland 2003) and displayed strong Icaiche sympathies the same year (Jones 1977). The village is later illustrated on an 1887 map published by William Miller for his official survey of the British Honduras-Guatemala border in the late 1880s. At the time of the survey (January 17, 1887), however, a regent of Governor Goldsworthy wrote that General Tamay (chief of the Icaiche) referred to the surveyed boundary line as a "tentative" one, emphasizing the strained relations between the British and the Maya concerning the frontier zone (Author Unknown 1887).

Miller (1887) notes that the inhabitants of the villages included on his map "are not savages," as they "cultivate the soil and grow maize, rice, and beans, and raise pigs and fowls." They likely sold surplus crops from their *milpas* to nearby loggers or at markets in Orange Walk (Cal 1991). There is little archaeological evidence of *milpa* farming at Kaxil Uinic, but we expect that the archaeological traces of such activity would be faint. Several machetes recovered from Kaxil Uinic could have been used for this endeavor, but only one axe was found at the site. Alternatively, stone tools may have been used for this traditional form of agriculture, and there is ample evidence of lithic tool production at Kaxil Uinic village in the form of debitage, cores, and bifaces. It is possible that the continued use of such tools, as opposed to metal implements, may reflect either cultural continuity in farming techniques – as Duval (1881) states that the Maya did not use plows, hoes, or spades to farm – or the fact that stone tools were cheaper and granted the San Pedro Maya more economic autonomy.

Miller (1887) additionally states that the Maya were considered somewhat dangerous, referencing the 1872 Battle of Orange Walk that took place between Maya forces and the West India Regiments. In contrast to San Pedro Sirís, the principal San Pedro Maya settlement in northwestern British Honduras where numerous crimped or bent gun barrels were recovered in association with the aftermath of the Battle of San Pedro (Yaeger et al. 2005), few weapons or munitions were found at Kaxil Uinic. Over two seasons, Bonorden's crews recovered only one shotgun stock, six shotgun shells, and one .44–40 bullet casing dating to the historic occupation of the village. The lack of arms or ammunition recovered from Kaxil Uinic may reflect the decreasing ability of the San Pedro Maya to acquire firearms from the British after the Battle of San Pedro (Houk and Bonorden 2015).

From 1891 to 1892, a serious smallpox epidemic spread through the northern and western districts of British Honduras, and according to *The Angelus* (cited by Bolland 2003), at least 30 deaths were reported at Kaxil Uinic by March 1892. When the acting Commissioner of the Cayo District later visited Kaxil Uinic in 1895, he described the settlement as "a very dirty Indian village . . . claimed by Ycaiche Indians" (quoted in Bolland 2003:149). He also noted that the *alcalde* of Kaxil Uinic still maintained close ties with General Gabriel Tamay of the Icaiche, although the central village of the settlement cluster of Kaxil Uinic (San José Yalbac) appeared somewhat wary of that group (Bolland 2003). As noted by C. H. Eyles (the surgeon of the colony) on May 7, 1897, for the first time since records were kept by the colonial administration, "the number of deaths among the Indian population in the Colony [did] not exceed the births." That same year, a letter from Icaiche general Gabriel Tamay indicates that he adopted a more cooperative attitude towards the British (Tamay 1897; Wilson 1897).

As previously mentioned, dramatic decreases in the populations of San Pedro Maya settlements rife with diseases led the remaining inhabitants of many smaller villages to coalesce into larger settlements. A letter to the Colonial Secretary from Cayo District Commissioner Rob H. Franklin (1913), for example, mentions that Franklin recently received a report from the *alcalde* of San José stating that "strangers from Xaxe Tenic and elsewhere" wished to settle in San José Yalbac. The following month, Manuel Perez (1913), the *alcalde* of San José, wrote to Franklin that settlers from "Churchquitam" arrived at "Cashiwinik" (Kaxil Uinic), applying for a place to live. According to Perez (1913), when asked if they planned to obey the laws and regulations of "the company" (BEC), the settlers said that they were willing. This interaction marks a contrast in the level of cooperation exhibited by the inhabitants of Kaxil Uinic during Miller's survey of the frontier in the 1880s.

Despite the development of a tenuous alliance with colonial authorities, it appears that the attitude of the government in British Honduras towards the Maya remained unsympathetic. In a report from the General Registry of Belize to the Colonial Secretary dated April 7, 1920, "the high death rate among the Indians [was] partly . . . explained by the fact that they [comprised] the most backward section of the population, and [evinced] little desire to effect recovery from disease" (General Registry of Belize April 7, 1920).

The archaeological data help to paint a picture of life at the village. At Kaxil Uinic, alcohol and patent medicine bottles dominate the glass artifact assemblage. These data potentially corroborate colonial accounts (Cal 1991; Rugeley 2001) that alcoholism was endemic among Maya groups in British Honduras and Yucatan. Rum was often paid to planters in lieu of wages. Alternatively, Church et al. (2011) note that interviews with locals provided a consensus that San Pedro Maya villages were "dry." The large number of alcohol and patent medicine bottles recovered could therefore be explained by ethnohistorical accounts of the importance of alcohol in Maya religious ceremonies, including feasts and funeral wakes, or that empty bottles were obtained from nearby logging camps to be reused as containers for local products (such as honey; Church et al. 2011). Considering that a serious smallpox epidemic spread through the northern and western districts of British Honduras from 1891 to 1892, killing 30 individuals at Kaxil Uinic, funeral wakes associated with this epidemic alone could have generated numerous alcohol bottles as refuse. It is important to note that a peak in the manufacture date range of glass (see Figure 13.4) collected from the site corresponds to this time frame (Bonorden 2016). Alcohol consumption among the San Pedro Maya, therefore, may have been ritual in nature.

The only physical description of the village comes from Thompson (1963), who described it shortly after its abandonment in 1931 as a "score of huts scattered around a dirty water hole" that presented a "melancholy" appearance. Thompson (1963) also noted that the *aguada* was the only source of drinking water for the villagers and that he did not find the village attractive because there were too many fleas and the hogs wallowed in the drinking water. Twenty or so huts suggest that perhaps the population of the village was around 100 to 120 people prior to relocation of the villagers to San José Yalbac. We know from correspondence between Thompson and government officials earlier in 1931 that the village had a *cabildo*, or court house, and was still governed by an *alcalde* (Colonial Secretary 1931). Bolland (2003) notes that the *alcalde* system, which was a modified, traditional Maya political system stretching back to the Postclassic period in the northern lowlands, was sanctioned by colonial legislation in 1858. Colonial administrators found that this system was a relatively cheap and easy way to govern the Maya because indigenous leaders were essentially unpaid officers who served as a buffer between the Maya and the colonial government. Although no clear evidence of the "court house" was identified during archaeological investigations at Kaxil Uinic, the structure was likely perishable and would not have had a three-stone hearth, the feature type that made identifying structure locations possible at the site (Bonorden 2016).

The Crown Lands Ordinance of 1872 prohibited the Maya from owning land within the colony (Bolland 2003), and Kaxil Uinic was situated on land that belonged to the BEC despite the assertions of residents in 1886 that their village was in Mexican territory. Inhabitants thus probably turned to wage labor as loggers or *chicleros* to acquire cash to pay rent to BEC (see Thompson 1963). *Chiclero* work is reflected archaeologically at Kaxil Uinic by the presence of numerous *chicle* pots, machete fragments, files, and *chiclero* spurs.

Nonetheless, it appears that the Maya may have abandoned their wage-labor positions once they acquired enough cash for their immediate needs, as noted by Gann (1918). We interpret this as a further effort to maintain autonomy in the face of external pressures. Even temporary employment as loggers or *chicleros*, however, impacted the villagers' ability to continue their traditional *milpa* farming way of life. We discovered several food cans at Kaxil Uinic. These artifacts, combined with the lack of farming implements found at the site, support observations (Bolland 2003; Church et al. 2011) that the loss of *milpa* farmland caused by colonial legislation impelled the San Pedro Maya to import food that they once grew for themselves. Moreover, most of the produce still grown was sold to loggers or in Belize Town in order to acquire cash.

Engagement with the colonial economy also may have impacted other traditional activities to varying degrees. In Gann's (1918:17) report of Caste War Maya settlements, he states that, among other activities, the women would make pottery each day but that "the old customs [were] rapidly dying out . . . [and] pottery making [was] rendered unnecessary by the introduction of cheap iron cooking pots." At Kaxil Uinic, locally produced ceramic forms included bowls, jars, and basin-shaped vessels. Imported vessel types included plates, saucers, and cups/mugs. Like San Pedro Sirís, no complete table settings were recovered from Kaxil Uinic village. Although the absence of flatware, tableware, and imported bowls at Kaxil Uinic does not necessarily equate to evidence, it is possible that the villagers were selective about what types of imported food service items they used. At San Pedro Sirís, such data are interpreted as a reflection of self-sufficiency, with the San Pedro Maya using only those imported vessels that still allowed them to pursue traditional food ways (Church et al. 2011; Leventhal et al. 2001). These Maya groups may have also chosen to continue using hollowed gourds as plates, cups, and storage containers as described in ethnohistoric accounts (Rugeley 2001). Similarly, Yaeger et al. (2004) point to the lack of metal utensils at San Pedro Sirís as evidence that the residents may have instead used tortillas to scoop food. It appears, then, that utensils that could be substituted by items acquired freely were not purchased by the San Pedro Maya.

The artifact assemblage at Kaxil Uinic reflects traditional food preparation techniques and the use of imported tools to perform the same tasks. *Manos* and *metates* were found alongside American-made corn grinders. The Maya may have become increasingly reliant on imported goods following the smallpox epidemics of the 1890s. As the population of Kaxil Uinic dwindled and the residents turned to wage labor as loggers or *chicleros*, they probably had less time to produce locally made ceramics but enough disposable income to buy cheaper metal vessels (as opposed to more expensive imported ceramics). Several of the "cheap iron cooking pots" noted by Gann (1918) were found at Kaxil Uinic. The predominance of cheaper tin vessels at the site in comparison to the large number of imported ceramic vessels at San Pedro Sirís indicates that the ability to purchase the latter may have diminished in the later years of the late colonial period. Tin and enamel wares were relatively inexpensive, durable, easy to clean, light-weight, and readily available, which may explain their popularity in the later years of the Caste War (Rohe 1996).

Yaeger et al. (2005) assert that such vessels were likely used to cook food *pibil*-style, with the pots used as Dutch ovens for pit-roasted meals. According to Dornan (2004), the use of imported cooking vessels reflects the desire of the San Pedro Maya to selectively utilize more efficient, imported technologies while maintaining traditional foodways. The same can likely be said for Kaxil Uinic, where it appears that villagers used cast iron pots and locally produced earthenware vessels to cook traditional meals and both American hand mills and *metates* to grind corn. The material record at Kaxil Uinic ultimately creates an archaeological paradox, then, as most of the items purchased from colonial merchants were used in the perpetuation of local practices – namely foodways – which were markedly different from the customs of other groups in the colony (Church et al. 2011).

Remote as it was within the geography of the colony, Kaxil Uinic was connected to other San Pedro Maya villages in British Honduras, Mexico, and Guatemala (Houk and Bonorden 2020), and it is likely that the residents had direct contact with loggers from Qualm Hill either through formal visits between the village and the camp or through informal contact in the forest (Harrison-Buck et al. 2019). The sources, then, of the imported artifacts at Kaxil Uinic are potentially many because goods could have been acquired from other Maya or from Creole loggers. The presence of six European clay pipe fragments at Kaxil Uinic is perhaps circumstantial evidence for direct contact with Creole loggers, as the Maya preferred to smoke cigars (Cook 1989) and the Creole smoked pipes as evidenced by the large number (n=49) of pipe fragments found at Qualm Hill camp. Complicating things further are O'Connor's (1852:516) rumors that the Maya would make away with "axes, machettes [sic], iron pots, and sundry other articles 'too numerous to mention'" as soon as the logging gangs vacated the camps for the season. It is possible that the Maya acquired some objects from empty logging camps; such activity might in part explain the comparatively lower artifact frequencies at Qualm Hill.

Conclusions

To accurately study late colonial relations and power dynamics in British Honduras, it is necessary to create more contextually detailed illustrations of the political and economic interactions that possibly occurred between the Creole loggers at Qualm Hill and their San Pedro Maya counterparts of Kaxil Uinic (see also Harrison-Buck et al. 2019). Although conflicts arose between the Maya and logging companies as a result of differing uses of the landscape by the two groups, an exploration of the larger historical context surrounding Kaxil Uinic and Qualm Hill highlights their intricate relationship within a broader historical framework and illuminates how both groups were marginalized by the colonial system in British Honduras. The logging labor force, comprised largely of formerly enslaved Africans and their descendants, was prohibited from acquiring farmland following their emancipation in 1833. Similarly, although the Maya were never formally enslaved in British Honduras, they repeatedly faced colonial military action and were prohibited by colonial legislation from owning land.

At Qualm Hill, it appears that despite the Maya raid on the camp, the loggers interacted somewhat peaceably with their Maya neighbors in the following years, adopting Maya construction techniques for their buildings and Maya foodways that offset the debts they accrued in the advance system. At Kaxil Uinic, it is possible that the San Pedro Maya traded locally produced goods with neighboring loggers to acquire imported items, because both groups had limited purchasing power in the colonial cash economy. Although Maya and Creole loggers are commonly perceived as at odds over their differing uses of the forest, we argue that they actively negotiated alliances with one another in the face of restrictive colonial political and economic policies to better navigate the colonial landscape of British Honduras and improve their positions within this system.

Acknowledgments

We thank Dr. John Morris and the staff of the Institute of Archaeology, National Institute of Culture and History, in Belize for issuing a permit to work at Qualm Hill camp and Kaxil Uinic village. Mr. Jeff Roberson and Mr. Alex Finkral kindly granted us permission to excavate on Yalbac Ranch and Laguna Seca Ranch. We also extend our sincere thanks to Mr. Alan Jeal of Gallon Jug Ranch and the staff at Chan Chich Lodge for hosting our field crew. The staff and students on the Belize Estates Archaeological Survey Team were responsible for much of the hard work that made this chapter possible. Finally, we extend our deepest gratitude to Alphawood Foundation for supporting the 2016 fieldwork at Kaxil Uinic village and our archival research in Jamaica and England.

References cited

Austin, John Gardiner 1866 Letter to Captain Delamere. September 24, 1866. 1B5/56/33. Jamaica Archives, Spanish Town.

Author Unknown 1887 Letter from Regent of Governor Goldsworthy. January 17, 1887. CO 123/181. Public Records Office, Kew.

Bolland, O. Nigel 1977 *The Formation of a Colonial Society: Belize, from Conquest to Crown Colony.* Johns Hopkins University Press, Baltimore.

———— 2003 *Colonialism and Resistance in Belize: Essays in Historical Sociology.* University of the West Indies Press, Trinidad and Tobago.

Bonorden, Alyssa Brooke 2016 *Comparing Colonial Experiences in Northwestern Belize: Archaeological Evidence from Qualm Hill Camp and Kaxil Uinic Village.* Texas Tech University Electronic Theses and Dissertation Collection. Unpublished M.A. thesis, Department of Sociology, Anthropology, and Social Work, Texas Tech University, Lubbock.

Bonorden, Brook, and Brett A. Houk 2019 Kaxil Uinic: Archaeology at a San Pedro Maya Village in Belize. In *Archaeologies of the British Empire in Latin America*, edited by Charles Orser, Jr., pp. 13–35. Springer International Publishing, Cham, Switzerland.

Bonorden, Brooke, and Gertrude Kilgore 2015 Results of the 2015 Excavations at Kaxil Uinic Village. In *The 2015 Season of the Chan Chich Archaeological Project*, edited by Brett A. Houk, pp. 105–144. Papers of the Chan Chich Archaeological Project, Number 9. Department of Sociology, Anthropology, and Social Work, Texas Tech University, Lubbock.

———— 2016 Results of the 2016 Excavations at Kaxil Uinic Village. In *The 2016 Season of the Chan Chich Archaeological Project*, edited by Brett A. Houk, pp. 81–134. Papers of the Chan Chich Archaeological Project, Number 10. Department of Sociology, Anthropology, and Social Work, Texas Tech University, Lubbock.

Bonorden, Brooke, and Briana N. Smith 2015 Results of the 2015 Excavations at Qualm Hill Camp. In *The 2015 Season of the Chan Chich Archaeological Project*, edited by Brett A. Houk, pp. 67–104. Papers of the Chan Chich Archaeological Project, Number 9. Department of Sociology, Anthropology, and Social Work, Texas Tech University, Lubbock.

Bristowe, L. W., and R. B. Wright 1889 *The Handbook of British Honduras for 1888–89.* William Blackwood and Sons, London.

Burdon, Sir John Alder 1935 *Archives of British Honduras*, Vol. 3. Sifton Praed, London.

Cackler, Paul R., Stanley L. Walling, David M. Hyde, and Fred Valdez, Jr. 2007 Qualm Hill: Reconnaissance, Rediscovery, and Mapping. In *Research Reports from the Programme for Belize Archaeological Project*, edited by Fred Valdez, Jr., pp. 177–125. Occasional Papers Number 8. Mesoamerican Archaeological Research Laboratory, The University of Texas, Austin.

Cal, Angel Eduardo 1983 *Anglo Maya Contact in Northern Belize: A Study of British Policy Toward the Maya during the Caste War of Yucatán, 1847–1872*. M.A. thesis, Department of History, University of Calgary, Calgary.

———— 1991 *Rural Society and Economic Development: British Mercantile Capital in Nineteenth-Century Belize*. Ph.D. dissertation, Department of History, University of Arizona, Tucson. University Microfilms, Ann Arbor.

Church, Minette C., Jason Yaeger, and Jennifer L. Dornan 2011 The San Pedro Maya and the British Colonial Enterprise in British Honduras. In *Enduring Conquests: Rethinking the Archaeology of Resistance to Spanish Colonialism in the Americas*, edited by Matthew Liebmann and Melissa S. Murphy, pp. 173–197. School for Advanced Research Press, Santa Fe.

Colonial Secretary 1931 Letter to Alcalde, Xaxe Venic. March 5, 1931. Field Museum Archives, Chicago.

Dornan, Jennifer L. 2004 *"Even by Night We Only Become Aware They Are Killing Us"*: *Agency, Identity, and Intentionality at San Pedro Belize (1857–1930)*. Ph.D. dissertation, University of California, Los Angeles. University Microfilms, Ann Arbor.

Duval, B. R. 1881 *A Narrative of Life and Travels in Mexico and British Honduras*. W.F. Brown & Co. Printers, Boston.

Eltringham, Peter 2010 *The Rough Guide to Belize*, 5th edition. Rough Guides, London.

Eyles, C. H. 1897 Medical Reports from 1896. May 7, 1897. CO 123/223. Public Records Office, Kew.

Finamore, Daniel 1994 *Sailors and Slaves on the Wood-Cutting Frontier: Archaeology of the British Bay Settlement, Belize*. Unpublished Ph.D. dissertation, Department of Archaeology, Boston University, Boston.

Franklin, Rob H. 1913 Letter to the Colonial Secretary. March 2, 1913. CO 123/275. Public Records Office, Kew.

Franzen, John G. 1995 Comfort for Man or Beast: Alcohol and Medicine Use in Northern Michigan Logging Camps, Ca. 1880–1940. *The Wisconsin Archaeologist* 76:294–337.

Gann, Thomas W. 1918 *The Maya Indians of Southern Yucatan and Northern British Honduras*. Bureau of American Ethnology, Bulletin 64. Smithsonian Institution, Washington, DC.

Gastrell, J. P. H. 1886 Letter to the Earl of Rosebery. August 18, 1886. CO 123/181. Public Records Office, Kew.

General Registry of Belize 1920 Report of 1919 Vital Statistics to the Colonial Secretary. April 7, 1920. CO 123/300. Public Records Office, Kew.

Harrison-Buck, Eleanor, Brett A. Houk, Adam R. Kaeding, and Brooke Bonorden 2019 The Strange Bedfellows of Northern Belize: British Colonialists, Confederate Dreamers, Creole Loggers, and the Caste War Maya Refugees of the Late Nineteenth Century. *International Journal of Historical Archaeology* 23(1):172–203.

Healy, Paul F., Kitty Emery, and Lori E. Wright 1990 Ancient and Modern Maya Exploitation of the *Jute* Snail (*Pachychilus*). *Latin American Antiquity* 1:170–183.

Houk, Brett A. 2012 Kaxil Uinic: A Report on Archival Investigations and Reconnaissance of the Historic Maya Village. In *The 2012 Season of the Chan Chich Archaeological Project*, edited by Brett A. Houk, pp. 31–43. Papers of the Chan Chich Archaeological Project, Number 6. Department of Sociology, Anthropology, and Social Work, Texas Tech University, Lubbock.

Houk, Brett A., and Brooke Bonorden 2015 The Frontier Colonial Experience of the Maya at Kaxil Uinic, Belize. *Paper presented at the 114th American Anthropological Association Annual Meeting*, Denver, CO.

———2020 The "Borders" of British Honduras and the San Pedro Maya of Kaxil Uinic Village. *Ancient Mesoamerica* 31:554–565.

Hulse, Charles A. 1989 *Archaeological Investigations at Spruce, WV: A Company-Owned Railroad and Mill Community of the Late Industrial Revolution*. Shepherd College Cultural Resource Management Series, Number 7. Shepherd College, Shepherdstown, WV.

Johansen, Peter G., and Andrew M. Bauer 2011 Reconfiguring the "Political" in the Reconstruction of Past Political Production. In *The Archaeology of Politics: The Materiality of Political Practice and Action in the Past*, edited by Peter G. Johansen and Andrew M. Bauer, pp. 1–28. Cambridge Scholars Publishing, Newcastle upon Tyne.

Jones, Grant D. 1977 Levels of Settlement Alliance among the San Pedro Maya of Western Belize and Eastern Petén, 1857–1936. In *Anthropology and History of the Yucatán*, edited by Grant D. Jones, pp. 139–190. University of Texas Press, Austin.

Kray, Christine A., Minette Church, and Jason Yaeger 2017 Designs on/of the Land: Competing Visions, Displacement, and Landscape Memory in Colonial British Honduras. In *Legacies of Space and Intangible Heritage: Archaeology, Ethnohistory, and the Politics of Cultural Continuity in the Americas*, edited by Fernando Armstrong-Fumero and Julio Holi Gutiérrez, pp. 53–77. University Press of Colorado, Boulder.

Leventhal, Richard M., Jason Yaeger, and Minette C. Church 2001 *San Pedro Maya Project: Preliminary Report of the 2000 Field Season*. Report submitted to the Belize Department of Archaeology, Belmopan.

Miller, George L., and Silas D. Hurry 1983 Ceramic Supply in an Economically Isolated Frontier Community: Portage County of the Ohio Western Reserve, 1800–1825. *Historical Archaeology* 17(2):80–92.

Miller, William 1887 Notes on a Part of the Western Frontier of British Honduras. *Proceedings of the Royal Geographic Society and Monthly Record of Geography, New Monthly Series* 9(7):420–423.

Mullins, Paul R. 2007 Ideology, Power, and Capitalism: The Historical Archaeology of Consumption. In *A Companion to Social Archaeology*, edited by Lynn Meskell and Robert W. Preucel, pp. 195–212. Blackwell Publishing, Malden.

Ng, Olivia 2007 *View from the Periphery: A Hermeneutic Approach to the Archaeology of Holotunich (1865–1930), British Honduras*. Ph.D. dissertation, University of Pennsylvania, PA. University Microfilms, Ann Arbor.

O'Connor, Luke Smythe 1852 An Exploring Ramble among the Indios Bravos, in British Honduras. *Littell's Living Age* 34(434):513–517.

Perez, Manuel 1913 Letter to the Cayo District Commissioner. February 26, 1913. CO 123/275. Public Records Office, Kew.

Rohe, Randall 1996 The Material Culture of an 1870s Logging Camp: The Sherry and Gerry Sites, Wisconsin. *Material Culture* 28(1):1–68.

Rugeley, Terry 2001 *Maya Wars: Ethnographic Accounts from Nineteenth-Century Yucatan*. University of Oklahoma Press, Norman.

Sandrock, David, and Mark D. Willis 2014 Results of the 2014 Field Season of the Belize Estates Archaeological Survey Team. In *The 2014 Season of the Chan Chich Archaeological Project*, edited by Brett A. Houk, pp. 111–129. Papers of the Chan Chich Archaeological Project, Number 8. Department of Sociology, Anthropology, and Social Work, Texas Tech University, Lubbock.

Tamay, Gabriel 1897 Letter to Frederic Keyt, District Commissioner of Orange Walk. November 11, 1897. CO 123/226. Public Records Office, Kew.

Thompson, J. Eric S. 1963 *Maya Archaeologist.* University of Oklahoma Press, Norman.

Wilson, D. 1897 Letter to J. Chamberlain. October 21, 1897. CO 123/255. Public Records Office, Kew.

Yaeger, Jason, Minette C. Church, Jennifer Dornan, and Richard M. Leventhal 2004 *San Pedro Maya Project: Preliminary Report of the 2003 Field Season.* Report submitted to the Belize Institute of Archaeology, Belmopan.

——— 2005 Investigating Historic Households: The 2003 Season of the San Pedro Maya Project. *Research Reports in Belizean Archaeology* 2:257–268.

Yaeger, Jason, Minette C. Church, Richard M. Leventhal, and Jennifer Dornan 2004 Maya Caste War Immigrants in Colonial British Honduras: The San Pedro Maya Project, 2000–2003. *Research Reports in Belizean Archaeology* 1:103–114.

Zuc, Luciano 1856 Letter from Indian Chief Luciano Zuc to Young Toledo of Belize. August 20, 1856. CS 704/16. Jamaica Archives, Spanish Town.

INDEX

abandonment 203, 209; of Dzehkabtun
250; of Kaxil Uinic 345; of Nimlipunit
125; peri-abandonment contexts
212–13, 216, *217*, 218, 220, 227, 232;
of Pusilha 143–4; of Uxbenka 132
acropolis 189, 203; of Cahal Pech 56–57,
63, 66; of Cancuen 191–203; Central
Acropolis of Tikal 187, 194; of
Lubaantun 83, 146; of Nakum 26–9; of
Nim li Punit 104, 113–14; of Pusilha
11, 138, 142–3, 154; triadic acropolises
188; of Yaxha 31–42
Actuncan 21, 31, 104, 213, 220, **225**
advance system 17, 330, 332, 334, 336,
339–40, 347
Ah Pam phase 21, *23*, 31
ajaw title 8, 13, 17, 43, 140, 142, 156, 178,
184–5, 189, 201–202, 209; *ek' xukpi
ajaw* title 117
alcalde 5, 343–5
Altun Ha 11, 119, 155; as "Water Scroll"
site 118, 125, 140, 142
AMS dating 14, 91–92, 211, 213, 222,
224, 228, **230**, 232–3
Archaic period 2, 10, 20, 41, 48, 218; in
southern Belize 89–93, 96, 99, 153
architecture 54, 79, 211, 241, 257, 262,
289; analysis of Cancuen palace
199–201; of Cahal Pech 63–7, 69–70,
72; of Lubaantun 145–6, 152; of
Nakum *25*, *27*, 41–2; pre-Mamom 7,
21, 24, 48; and social structure 186; of
southern Belize 12, 82–6, 94–5, 99,

153; study of 6, 184–5; and termination
rituals 52, 71; of Uxbenka 126, 131; of
Waka' 162, *169*; of Yaxha 8, 19, *40*, 41
armor 311, 315
assassination 5
astronomical commemorative groups
see E-groups
Austin, Lieutenant Governor 336
Ayim phase *23*

Baking Pot 14, 70, 210–18, 220–33
ball game 30; ballcourt 8, 19, 24, 41, 66,
86, 126, 137, 144, 146–7, 152, 155, 307;
ball players 194, 198
Barton Ramie 14, 48–9, 56–7, 210–11,
220, 221, 223–4, 226–33
Battle of San Pedro 17, 331, 333, 343
Baymen 334
Belikin, consumption of 100
Belize Estates Archaeological Survey
Team 332, 348
Belize Town 334, 338, 345
Betsin/Betson's Bank 336
"Black Devil" 336
Blackman Eddy 8, 9, 21, 49–50, 57, 67,
70, 211, 214, **225**
boats/watercraft 16, 281–4, 289, 296n20
Bonampak 223, 264, 316–17
British Honduras 330–5, 339–40, 342–4,
347
Brown, C. S. 333
Buenavista (del Cayo) 26, 211, 220
Burial traditions 52, 70, 224–8, 230–2

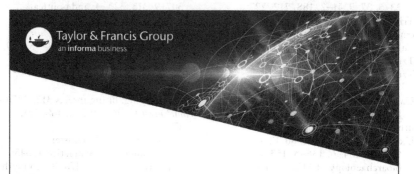

Taylor & Francis eBooks

www.taylorfrancis.com

A single destination for eBooks from Taylor & Francis
with increased functionality and an improved user
experience to meet the needs of our customers.

90,000+ eBooks of award-winning academic content in
Humanities, Social Science, Science, Technology, Engineering,
and Medical written by a global network of editors and authors.

TAYLOR & FRANCIS EBOOKS OFFERS:

A streamlined
experience for
our library
customers

A single point
of discovery
for all of our
eBook content

Improved
search and
discovery of
content at both
book and
chapter level

REQUEST A FREE TRIAL
support@taylorfrancis.com

 Routledge
Taylor & Francis Group

 CRC Press
Taylor & Francis Group

9781138577053